# IFIP Advances in Information and Communication Technology

**461**

## Editor-in-Chief

*Kai Rannenberg, Goethe University Frankfurt, Germany*

## Editorial Board

# IFIP – The International Federation for Information Processing

IFIP was founded in 1960 under the auspices of UNESCO, following the First World Computer Congress held in Paris the previous year. An umbrella organization for societies working in information processing, IFIP's aim is two-fold: to support information processing within its member countries and to encourage technology transfer to developing nations. As its mission statement clearly states,

> *IFIP's mission is to be the leading, truly international, apolitical organization which encourages and assists in the development, exploitation and application of information technology for the benefit of all people.*

IFIP is a non-profitmaking organization, run almost solely by 2500 volunteers. It operates through a number of technical committees, which organize events and publications. IFIP's events range from an international congress to local seminars, but the most important are:

- The IFIP World Computer Congress, held every second year;
- Open conferences;
- Working conferences.

The flagship event is the IFIP World Computer Congress, at which both invited and contributed papers are presented. Contributed papers are rigorously refereed and the rejection rate is high.

As with the Congress, participation in the open conferences is open to all and papers may be invited or submitted. Again, submitted papers are stringently refereed.

The working conferences are structured differently. They are usually run by a working group and attendance is small and by invitation only. Their purpose is to create an atmosphere conducive to innovation and development. Refereeing is also rigorous and papers are subjected to extensive group discussion.

Publications arising from IFIP events vary. The papers presented at the IFIP World Computer Congress and at open conferences are published as conference proceedings, while the results of the working conferences are often published as collections of selected and edited papers.

Any national society whose primary activity is about information processing may apply to become a full member of IFIP, although full membership is restricted to one society per country. Full members are entitled to vote at the annual General Assembly, National societies preferring a less committed involvement may apply for associate or corresponding membership. Associate members enjoy the same benefits as full members, but without voting rights. Corresponding members are not represented in IFIP bodies. Affiliated membership is open to non-national societies, and individual and honorary membership schemes are also offered.

More information about this series at http://www.springer.com/series/6102

Alex Orailoglu · H. Fatih Ugurdag
Luís Miguel Silveira · Martin Margala
Ricardo Reis (Eds.)

# VLSI-SoC:
# At the Crossroads
# of Emerging Trends

21st IFIP WG 10.5/IEEE International Conference
on Very Large Scale Integration, VLSI-SoC 2013
Istanbul, Turkey, October 6–9, 2013
Revised and Extended Selected Papers

 Springer

*Editors*
Alex Orailoglu
University of California at San Diego
La Jolla, CA
USA

H. Fatih Ugurdag
Ozyegin University
Istanbul
Turkey

Luís Miguel Silveira
University of Lisbon
Lisbon
Portugal

Martin Margala
University of Massachusetts
Lowell, MA
USA

Ricardo Reis
Universidade Federal do Rio Grande do Sul
Porto Alegre
Brazil

ISSN 1868-4238 ISSN 1868-422X (electronic)
IFIP Advances in Information and Communication Technology
ISBN 978-3-319-37093-4 ISBN 978-3-319-23799-2 (eBook)
DOI 10.1007/978-3-319-23799-2

Printed on acid-free paper

Springer International Publishing AG Switzerland is part of Springer Science+Business Media
(www.springer.com)

# Preface

This book contains extended and revised versions of the highest-quality papers that were presented during the 21$^{st}$ edition of the IFIP/IEEE WG10.5 International Conference on Very Large Scale Integration (VLSI-SoC), a global system-on-chip design and CAD conference. This edition of the conference was held at Novotel Hotel in Istanbul, Turkey (October 6–9, 2013). Previous conferences have taken place in Edinburgh, Trondheim, Vancouver, Munich, Grenoble, Tokyo, Gramado, Lisbon, Montpellier, Darmstadt, Perth, Nice, Atlanta, Rhodes, Florianopolis, Madrid, Hong Kong, and Santa Cruz.

The purpose of this conference, which was sponsored by IFIP TC 10 Working Group 10.5, the IEEE Council on Electronic Design Automation (CEDA), and the IEEE Circuits and Systems Society, and In-Cooperation of ACM SIGDA, was to provide a forum for the exchange of ideas and presentation of industrial and academic research results in the field of microelectronics design. The current trend toward increasing chip integration and technology process advancements have brought new challenges both at the physical and system design levels as well as in the test of these systems. The VLSI-SoC conference aims to address these exciting new issues.

The quality of submissions (244 papers from 48 countries, excluding PhD Forum and embedded tutorials) made the selection process a very difficult one. Finally, 49 were accepted as full papers (6 pages in the proceedings), 19 as short papers (4 pages), and 14 as extended abstracts (2 pages). Out of the 48 full papers presented at the conference, 11 papers were chosen by a selection committee to have an extended and revised version included in this book. An extended version of a previously unpublished high-quality paper from VLSI-SoC 2012 is also included. The selection process of these papers considered the evaluation scores during the review process as well as the review forms provided by members of the technical program committee and session chairs as a result of the presentations. The Technical Program Committee comprised 97 members.

The chapters of this book have authors from Algeria, France, Germany, Greece, Italy, Japan, Sweden, Switzerland, United Arab Emirates, and USA.

VLSI-SoC 2013 was the culmination of the work of many dedicated volunteers: paper authors, reviewers, session chairs, invited speakers, and various committee chairs and members, especially the local organizers. We thank them all for their contributions. We also thank Aydin Dirican, Cagatay Ozmen, and Nurettin Tan (University of Massachusets Lowell) for their critical help in the revision of the book chapters.

This book is intended for the VLSI community, mainly those who did not have the chance to attend the conference. We hope you will enjoy reading this book and that you will find it useful in your professional life and for the development of the VLSI community as a whole.

July 2015

Alex Orailoglu
H. Fatih Ugurdag
Luís Miguel Silveira
Martin Margala
Ricardo Reis

# Organization

The IFIP/IEEE International Conference on Very Large Scale Integration-System-on-Chip (VLSI-SoC) 2013 took place during October 6–9, 2013, in Novotel, Istanbul, Turkey. VLSI-SoC 2013 was the 21$^{st}$ in a series of international conferences, sponsored by IFIP TC 10 Working Group 10.5 (VLSI), IEEE CEDA, and ACM SIGDA.

## General Chairs

| | |
|---|---|
| H. Fatih Ugurdag | Ozyegin University, Turkey |
| Luís Miguel Silveira | INESC ID/IST - University of Lisbon, Portugal |

## Program Chairs

| | |
|---|---|
| Alex Orailoglu | UC San Diego, USA |
| Luigi Carro | UFRGS, Brazil |

## Special Sessions Chair

| | |
|---|---|
| Yankin Tanurhan | Synopsys, USA |

## Local Arrangement Chair

| | |
|---|---|
| Nizamettin Aydin | Yildiz Technical University, Turkey |

## Publication Chairs

| | |
|---|---|
| Martin Margala | University of Massachusetts, Lowell, USA |
| Ricardo Reis | UFRGS, Brazil |

## Publicity Chair

| | |
|---|---|
| Ricardo Reis | UFRGS, Brazil |

## Registration Chair

| | |
|---|---|
| Sezer Goren | Yeditepe University, Turkey |

## Finance Chair

| | |
|---|---|
| Sule Ozev | Arizona State University, USA |

## PhD Forum Chair

Mahmut Kandemir             Penn State University, USA

## VLSI-SoC Steering Committee

| | |
|---|---|
| Manfred Glesner | TU Darmstadt, Germany |
| Matthew Guthaus | UC Santa Cruz, USA |
| Salvador Mir | TIMA, France |
| Ricardo Reis | UFRGS, Brazil |
| Michel Robert | University of Montpellier, France |
| Luís Miguel Silveira | INESC ID/IST - University of Lisbon, Portugal |
| Chi-Ying Tsui | HKUST, Hong Kong, SAR China |

## Program Committee

### Track 1 - Analog and Mixed-signal IC Design

| | |
|---|---|
| Günhan Dündar | Boğaziçi University, Turkey (chair) |
| Jose M. de La Rosa | CNM, Spain (chair) |
| Abhijit Chatterjee | Gatech, USA |
| Dongsheng Ma | UT Dallas, USA |
| Haralambos Stratigopoulos | IMAG, France |
| Jerzy Dobrowski | Linköping University, Sweden |
| Piero Malcovati | University of Pavia, Italy |
| Pui-In Mac | University of Macau, China |
| Sergio Bampi | UFRGS, Brazil |

### Track 2 - Circuits for Applications
### (DSP, Image processing, Communications, Medical)

| | |
|---|---|
| Tobias Noll | RWTH-Aachen, Germany (chair) |
| Urs Frey | Riken, Japan (chair) |
| Andreas Demosthenous | University College London, UK |
| Andrew Mason | Michigan State University, USA |
| George Jie Yuan | UST, Hong Kong – China |
| Goksenin Yaralıoğlu | Özyeğin University, Turkey |
| Jun Ohta | Nara Institute of Science and Technology, Japan |
| Vijaykrishnan Narayanan | Pennsylvania State University, USA |

### Track 3 - Application Systems
### (DSP, Image Processing, Communications, Medical)

| | |
|---|---|
| Luc Claesen | University of Hasselt, Belgium (chair) |
| İlker Hamzaoğlu | Sabancı University, Turkey (chair) |
| Berna Ors | Istanbul Technical University, Turkey |
| Chun-Jen Tsai | National Chiao Tung University, Taiwan |

| Hassan Ghasemzadeh | UCLA, USA |
| Pai Chou | UC Irvine, USA |
| Yun Pan | Zhejiang University, China |

## Track 4 - VLSI Test, Diagnosis and Silicon Debug

| Matteo Sonza Reorda | Politecnico di Torino, Italy (chair) |
| Zain Navabi | University of Tehran, Iran (chair) |
| Erik Larsson | Lund University, Sweden |
| Hans-Joachim Wunderlich | University of Stuttgart, Germany |
| Fernanda Kastensmidt | UFRGS, Brazil |
| Michiko Inoue | Nara Institute of Science and Technology, Japan |
| Xiaoqing Wen | Kyutech, Japan |

## Track 5 - Variability, Security, Reliability

| Srinivas Devadas | MIT, USA (chair) |
| Özgür Sinanoğlu | NYU, UAE (chair) |
| Bruno Rouzeyre | LIRMM, France |
| Maria Michael | University of Cyprus, Cyprus |
| Mehdi Tahoori | Karlsruhe Institute of Technology, Germany |
| Paolo Prinetto | Politecnico di Torino, Italy |
| Ramesh Karri | NYU, USA |
| Swaroop Ghosh | USF, USA |

## Track 6 - Devices, Circuits and Systems for Emerging Technologies

| Wenjing Rao | University of Illinois Chicago, USA (chair) |
| Swarup Bhunia | Case Western Reserve University, USA (chair) |
| Andras Moritz | UMass Amherst, USA |
| Dmitry Strukov | UC Santa Barbara, USA |
| Fabien Clermidy | CEA LETI, France |
| Ian O'Connor | Ecole Centrale de Lyon, France |
| Sorin Cotofana | TU Delft, Netherlands |
| Valeriu Beiu | United Arab Emirates University, UAE |

## Track 7 - Prototyping, Verification, and Validation

| Masahiro Fujita | University of Tokyo, Japan (chair) |
| Franco Fummi | University of Verona, Italy (chair) |
| Alper Şen | Boğaziçi University, Turkey |
| Andreas Veneris | University of Toronto, Canada |
| Graziano Pravadelli | University of Verona, Italy |
| Ian Harris | UC Irvine, USA |
| Laurence Pierre | IMAG, France |

### Track 8 - Embedded Systems, HW-SW Codesign, Logic and High-Level Synthesis

| | |
|---|---|
| Andreas Gerstlauer | UT Austin, USA (chair) |
| Jason Xue | City University of Hong Kong, Hong Kong – China (chair) |
| Fadi Kurdahi | UC Irvine, USA |
| Frederic Rousseau | IMAG, France |
| Jarmo Takala | Tampere University of Technology, Finland |
| Joerg Henkel | Karlsruhe Institute of Technology, Germany |
| Petru Eles | Linköping University, Sweden |
| Sri Parameswaran | UNSW, Australia |

### Track 9 - Reconfigurable, Adaptive, FPGA

| | |
|---|---|
| Koen Bertels | TU Delft, Netherlands (chair) |
| Juergen Becker | Karlsruhe Institute of Technology, Germany (chair) |
| Apostolos Dollas | Technical University of Crete, Greece |
| Joao Cardoso | University of Porto, Portugal |
| Michael Huebner | Karlsruhe Institute of Technology, Germany |
| Pascal Benoit | LIRMM, France |
| Philip Brisk | UC Riverside, USA |
| Rainer Hartenstein | Kaiserslautern University of Technology, Germany |

### Track 10 - SOC Design and Interconnect

| | |
|---|---|
| Cristina Silvano | Poltecnico di Milano, Italy (chair) |
| Jose Ayala | Complutense University of Madrid, Spain (chair) |
| Jiang Xu | Hong Kong University of Science & Technology, China |
| Gilles Sassatelli | LIRMM, France |
| Leandro Soares Indrusiak | The University of York, UK |
| Luca Carloni | Columbia University, USA |
| Smail Niar | LAMIH/University of Valenciennes, France |
| Xiaoxia Wu | Qualcomm, USA |

### Track 11 - Processor Architecture, Embedded Processors, Multicores

| | |
|---|---|
| Onur Mutlu | CMU, USA (chair) |
| Stephan Wong | TU Delft, Netherlands (chair) |
| Ayse K. Coskun | Boston University, USA |
| Chengmo Yang | University of Delaware, USA |
| Gang Qu | University of Maryland, USA |
| Mirko Loghi | University of Udine, Italy |
| Soontae Kim | KAIST, Korea |
| Tulika Mitra | National University of Singapore, Singapore |

## Track 12 - Transistor Level Digital VLSI Circuits and Memory

| | |
|---|---|
| Massimo Alioto | University of Siena, Italy (chair) |
| Saibal Mukhopadhay | Gatech, USA (chair) |
| Alexander Fish | Bar-Ilan University, Israel |
| Ali Afzali-Kusha | University of Tehran, Iran |
| Alper Demir | Koç University, Turkey |
| Armin Tajalli | EPFL, Switzerland |
| Joachim Rodrigues | Lund University, Sweden |
| Yajun Ha | National University of Singapore, Singapore |

# Contents

Debugging Methods Through Identification of Appropriate Functions
for Internal Gates .................................................. 1
   *Kosuke Oshima, Takeshi Matsumoto, and Masahiro Fujita*

Gate Sizing Under Uncertainty ...................................... 23
   *Nathaniel A. Conos, Saro Meguerdichian, and Miodrag Potkonjak*

New Scan-Based Attack Using Only the Test Mode and an Input
Corruption Countermeasure ......................................... 48
   *Sk Subidh Ali, Samah Mohamed Saeed, Ozgur Sinanoglu,*
   *and Ramesh Karri*

Quantitative Optimization and Early Cost Estimation of Low-Power
Hierarchical-Architecture SRAMs Based on Accurate Cost Models ........ 69
   *Yuan Ren and Tobias Noll*

Low-Power Low-Voltage $\Delta\Sigma$ Modulator Using Switched-Capacitor
Passive Filters....................................................... 94
   *Ali Fazli Yeknami and Atila Alvandpour*

Fine Grain Precision Scaling for Datapath Approximations in Digital
Signal Processing Systems ........................................... 119
   *Seogoo Lee and Andreas Gerstlauer*

A Complete Real-Time Feature Extraction and Matching System Based on
Semantic Kernels Binarized ......................................... 144
   *Michael Schaffner, P.A. Hager, L. Cavigelli, Z. Fang, P. Greisen,*
   *F.K. Gürkaynak, A. Smolic, H. Kaeslin, and L. Benini*

An FPGA-Based Real-Time System for 3D Stereo Matching, Combining
Absolute Differences and Census with Aggregation and Belief Propagation ... 168
   *Kyprianos Papadimitriou, Sotiris Thomas, and Apostolos Dollas*

Minimizing Test Frequencies for Linear Analog Circuits: New Models
and Efficient Solution Methods....................................... 188
   *Mohand Bentobache, Ahcène Bounceur, Reinhardt Euler,*
   *Salvador Mir, and Yann Kieffer*

Partition-Based Faults Diagnosis of a VLIW Processor ................ 208
   *Davide Sabena, Matteo Sonza Reorda, and Luca Sterpone*

Enhanced Compressed Look-up-Table Based Real-Time
Rectification Hardware. . . . . . . . . . . . . . . . . . . . . . . . . . . . . . . . . . . . . .   227
Abdulkadir Akin, Luis Manuel Gaemperle, Halima Najibi,
Alexandre Schmid, and Yusuf Leblebici

A Flexible ASIC for Time-Domain Decision-Directed Channel Estimation
in MIMO-OFDM Systems . . . . . . . . . . . . . . . . . . . . . . . . . . . . . . . . . . .   249
Andreas Minwegen, Dominik Auras, and Gerd Ascheid

**Author Index** . . . . . . . . . . . . . . . . . . . . . . . . . . . . . . . . . . . . . . . . . .   267

# Debugging Methods Through Identification of Appropriate Functions for Internal Gates

Kosuke Oshima[1], Takeshi Matsumoto[2], and Masahiro Fujita[3]([✉])

[1] Department of Electrical Engineering and Information Systems,
The University of Tokyo, Tokyo, Japan
oshima@cad.t.u-tokyo.ac.jp
[2] Department of Electronics and Information Engineering,
Ishikawa National College of Technology, Sapporo, Japan
matsumoto@ishikawa-nct.ac.jp
[3] VLSI Design and Education Center, The University of Tokyo, Tokyo, Japan
fujita@ee.t.u-tokyo.ac.jp

**Abstract.** In this chapter, we propose methods for correcting gate-level designs by identifying appropriate logic functions for internal gates. We introduce programmable circuits, such as look up table (LUT) and multiplexer (MUX) to the circuits under debugging, in order to formulate the correction processes mathematically. There are two steps in the proposed methods. The first one is to identify sets of gates and their appropriate inputs whose functions are to be modified. The second one is to actually identify logic functions for the correction by solving QBF (Quantified Boolean Formula) problems with repeated application of SAT solvers. There are a number of bugs which cannot be corrected unless the inputs of the gates to be modified are changed from the original ones, and the selection of such additional inputs is a key for effective debugging. We show a couple of methods by which appropriate inputs to the gates can be efficiently identified. Experimental results for each such a method as well as their combinations targeting benchmark circuits as well as industrial ones are shown.

**Keywords:** Gate-level circuit · Design debugging · Programmable circuit

## 1 Introduction

Thanks to the advancement of semiconductor technology, VLSI designs keep becoming larger and more complicated continuously. Now verifying such huge VLSI chips is a big challenge and needs lots of human efforts and time, which can approach to 80 % or more of the total design time. Moreover, some bugs may not be detected in the verification processes before fabrication and are only recognized by running an actual chip after fabrication. In such cases, re-spin of the whole design processes, including very time-consuming physical and timing design processes, must be performed again. Re-spins often happen due to the

© IFIP International Federation for Information Processing 2015
A. Orailoglu et al. (Eds.): VLSI-SoC 2013, IFIP AICT 461, pp. 1–22, 2015.
DOI: 10.1007/978-3-319-23799-2_1

insufficient time for verification and debugging in pre-silicon design phases. Due to the design schedule, sometimes the verification and debugging efforts must be terminated before the design is fully examined. If the verification and debugging processes become more efficient and effective, significantly more bugs could be detected and corrected before fabrication. Usually, more than a half of the verification time is spent for correcting the buggy portions of the designs rather than identifying them, since debugging is much less automated than checking correctness of the designs. Thus, automating and shortening the debugging processes is now one of the most important issues in VLSI designs. The efficiency of verification is very important to find more bugs or most bugs in a shorter time, and debugging is equally or more important since same or longer time is now spent for correcting the buggy portions of the design after recognizing that the design is not correct.

In this chapter, we focus on debugging gate-level designs. We assume existence of a specification in terms of golden models in RTL or in gate level. Our method tries to let a given circuit under debugging behave equivalently to the specification through modifications inside the circuit. To this end, our method tries to identify the appropriate new functions for some of the internal gates in the circuit, so that the circuit as a whole can have an equivalent logic function to the specification. For the purpose of formulating the debugging process mathematically, we introduce some amount of programmability in the circuit under debugging and find a way to appropriately program it for correction. Note that, after identifying such appropriate functions for internal gates, those gates are assumed to be completely replaced with new gates corresponding to the those functions. In other words, programmability is introduced only for mathematical modeling and is nothing to do with actual implementations.

In [1], Yamashita et al. proposed Partially-Programmable Circuit (PPC) where programmable circuits such as look-up tables (LUTs) and multiplexers (MUXs) are added to the original circuit in order to correct bugs and/or defects in fabricated chips. While their purpose of introducing programmability is to make chips re-programmable or correctable in post-silicon (*patching* in their words), our purpose in this work is to find correct logic functions for internal gates by which the entire designs can be rectified in pre-silicon design phases. Therefore, in principle, we can freely add programmable circuits in the target circuit under debugging without considering physical implementation. Once a circuit is corrected, its logical and physical design can be performed again in such a way that the programmable circuits that are introduced for debugging are replaced with appropriate standard logic gates. If it is better to keep physical structures of the circuit similar as much as possible in order to avoid performing complicated physical design processes again, the corrected logic may be implemented utilizing various Engineering Change Order (ECO) techniques.

Debugging consists of two processes: locating the suspicious portions in the designs and correcting them through replacements with appropriate sets of gates. In the locating process, designers try to find locations of bugs (or candidate locations) which should be the root cause of the bugs. Then, they modify logic functions at those possibly buggy locations in the correcting process. There exist researches for locating bugs in gate-level circuits such as path tracing and SAT-based diagnosis [8]. Note that the methods such as [8] examine the designs only with given counterexamples and do not refer to specifications. This makes the analysis much simplified, but appropriate locations for all the bugs in the designs may not be found, as counterexamples may be related only to the specific bugs in the designs. Moreover, it is very difficult to identify a small set of logic gates that need to be modified for correction, especially when there are multiple bugs in a design. In addition, some methods such as [8] require designers to come up with a new logic function that can correct the current buggy one, which may take a long time if that is a manual process. Since the methods such as [8] assume that any primary input can be used when creating the functions for correction, in the worst case, the circuit size can become almost doubled. Based on the above discussion, there is a large demand for methods which generate logic functions for the set of logic gates identified in the bug locating processes, by which the entire designs become correct.

The basic idea of our proposed debugging methods is to correct a circuit under debugging by finding another logic function for a set of gates that is identified as a bug location, in such a way that the entire circuit becomes equivalent to its specification [9]. In the methods, the logic function for each gate for correction has the same set of inputs as the original gate. In other words, our method tries to replace each of the original (possibly) buggy gates with a different logic gate having the same input variables. So, the new gate to be used for replacement may have to realize a complicated logic function with the same inputs and can only be implemented with a set of simple gates, such as, NAND, NOR, etc. As described in the following sections, we utilize an existing method proposed in [2,7] to efficiently generate logic functions for programmable circuits. There are, however, bugs which cannot be corrected if the input variables of the gates remain the same. In such cases, we need to add an additional input variable to LUTs or MUXs. When the number of variables in a circuit is very large, it is not practical to check all the variables one by one. To quickly find variables which cannot improve the chance of getting a correct logic when they are connected to LUTs or MUXs, we introduce a necessary condition that should be satisfied by each variable in order to improve the chance of correction. We also propose an efficient selection method based on that condition.

The contributions of this chapter are summarized as follows.

- We propose a method to find a correction by introducing programmability in a circuit under debugging based on LUTs or MUXs and mathematically formulating the debugging problem.
- To deal with cases where a correction is impossible due to a lack of certain input variables to LUTs or MUXs, we propose a method to filter out variables which cannot contribute to improving the possibility of correction.
- Through the experiments with various designs and bugs including industrial ones, we show that our proposed method can provide a correction in a short time in many cases.

The remainder of this chapter is organized as follows. In Sect. 2, we introduce an existing method to efficiently find a logic function of each programmable circuit for correction. In Sect. 3, our proposed method is described in detail. In Sect. 4, we show experimental results with bugs in an industrial on-chip network circuit and ARM Cortex microprocessor designs as well as benchmark circuits. Section 5 gives ideas for extensions of the proposed debugging methods with preliminary experimental results. Finally, in Sect. 6, concluding remarks and future directions are discussed.

## 2    Related Work: Finding a Configuration of LUTs Using Boolean SAT Solvers

For easiness of explanation, in this chapter, we assume the number of output for the target buggy circuit is one. That is, one logic function in terms of primary inputs can represent the logic function for the entire circuit. This makes the notations much simpler, and also extension for multiple outputs is straightforward. Also, variables in this chapter are mostly vectors of individual ones.

As there is only one output in the design, a specification can be written as one logic function with the set of primary inputs as inputs to the function. For a given specification $SPEC(x)$ and an implementation with programmable circuits $IMPL(x, v)$, where $x$ denotes the set of primary input variables and $v$ denotes the set of variables to configure programmable circuits inside, the problem is to find a set of appropriate values for $v$ satisfying that $SPEC$ and $IMPL$ are logically equivalent. This problem can be described as QBF (Quantified Boolean Formula) problem as follows:

$$\exists v. \forall x. SPEC(x) = IMPL(x, v).$$

That is, with appropriate values for $v$, regardless of input values (values of $x$), the circuits must be equivalent to the specification (i.e., the output values are the same), which can be formulated as the equivalence of the two logic functions for the specification and the implementation. There are two nested quantifiers in the formula above, that is, existential quantifiers are followed by universal quantifiers, which are called QBF in general. Normal SAT formulae have only existential quantifiers and no universal ones.

In [2], CEGAR (Counter-Example Guided Abstraction Refinement) based QBF solving method is applied to the circuit rectification problem. Here, we explain the method using 2-input LUT for simplicity, although LUT having any numbers of inputs can be processed in a similar way.

Logic functions of a 2-input LUT can be represented by introducing four variables, $v_{00}, v_{01}, v_{10}, v_{11}$, each of which corresponds to the value of one row of the truth table. Those four variables are multiplexed with the two inputs of the original gate as control variables, as shown in Fig. 1. In the figure a two-input AND gate is replaced with a two-input LUT. The inputs, $t_1$, $t_2$, of the AND gate becomes the control inputs to the multiplexer. With these control inputs,

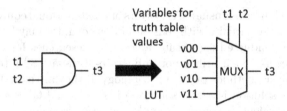

**Fig. 1.** LUT is represented with multiplexed four variables as truth table values.

the output is selected from the four values, $v_{00}, v_{01}, v_{10}, v_{11}$. If we introduce $M$ of 2-input LUTs, the circuit has $4 \times M$ more variables than the variables that exist in the original circuit. We represent those variables as $v_{ij}$ or simply $v$ which represents a vector of $v_{ij}$. $v$ variables are treated as pseudo primary inputs as they are programmed (assigned appropriate values) before utilizing the circuit. $t$ variables in the figure correspond to intermediate variables in the circuit. They appear in the CNF of the circuits for SAT/QBF solvers.

If the logic function at the output of the circuit is represented as $f_I(v, x)$ where $x$ is an input variable vector and $v$ is a program variable vector, after replacements with LUTs, the QBF formula to be solved becomes:

$$\exists v. \forall x. f_I(v, x) = f_S(x),$$

where $f_S$ is the logic function that represents the specification to be implemented. Under appropriate programming of LUTs (assigning appropriate values to $v$), the circuit behaves exactly the same as specification for all input value combinations.

Although this can simply be solved by any QBF solvers theoretically, only small circuits or small numbers of LUTs can be successfully processed [2]. Instead of doing that way, we here like to solve given QBF problems by repeatedly applying normal SAT solvers using the ideas shown in [3,4].

Basically, we solve the QBF problem only with normal SAT solvers in the following way. Instead of checking all value combinations on the universally quantified variables, we just pick up some small numbers of value combinations and assign them to the universally quantified variables. This would generate SAT formulae which are just necessary conditions for the original QBF formulae. Note that here we are dealing with only two-level QBF, and so if universally quantified variables get assigned actual values (0 or 1), the resulting formulae simply become SAT formulae. The overall flow of the proposed method is shown in Fig. 2. For example, if we assign two combinations of values for $x$ variables, say $a1$ and $a2$, the resulting SAT formula to be solved becomes like: $\exists v. (f_I(v, a1) = f_S(a1)) \wedge (f_I(v, a2) = f_S(a2))$. Then we can just apply any SAT solvers to them. If there is no solution, we can conclude that the original QBF formulae do not have solution neither. If there is a solution found, we need to make sure that it is a real solution for the original QBF formula. Because we have a solution candidate $v_{assigns}$ (these are the solution found by SAT solvers) for $v$, we simply make sure the following:

$$\forall x. f_I(v_{assigns}, x) = f_S(x).$$

This can be solved by either usual SAT solvers or combinational equivalence checkers. In the latter case, circuits with tens of millions of gates may be processed, as
there have been conducted significant amount of researches for combinational
equivalence checkers which utilize not only state-of-the-art SAT techniques but
also various analysis methods on circuit topology. If they are actually equivalent,
then the current solution is a real solution of the original QBF formula. But if
they are not equivalent, a counterexample, say $x_{sol}$, is generated and is added
to the conditions for the next iteration:

$$\exists v.(f_I(v, a1) = f_S(a1)) \wedge (f_I(v, a2) = f_S(a2)) \wedge (f_I(v, x_{sol}) = f_S(x_{sol})).$$

This solving process is repeated until we have a real solution or we prove the non-
existence of solution. In the left side of Fig. 2, as an example, the conjunction of
the two cases where inputs/output values are $(0, 1, 0)/1$ and $(1, 1, 0)/0$ is checked
if satisfiable. If satisfiable, this gives possible solutions for LUTs. Then using those
solutions for LUTs, the circuit is programmed and is checked to be equivalent with
the specification. As we are using SAT solvers, usually non-equivalence can be
made sure by checking if the formula for non-equivalence is unsatisfiable.

Satisfiability problem for QBF in general belongs to P-Space complete. In
general QBF satisfiability can be solved by repeatedly applying SAT solvers,

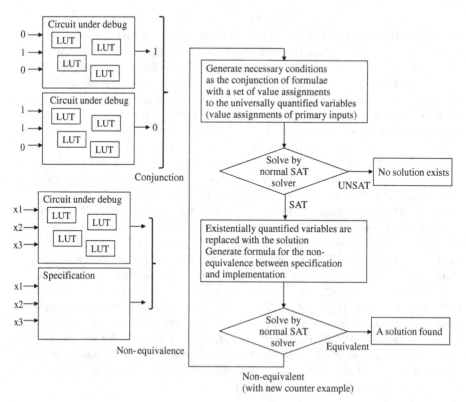

**Fig. 2.** Overall flow of the rectification method in [2]

which was first discussed under FPGA synthesis in [5] and in program synthesis in [6]. The techniques shown in [3,4] give a general framework on how to deal with QBF only with SAT solvers. These ideas have also been applied to so called partial logic synthesis in [7].

# 3   Our Proposed Method to Correct Gate-Level Circuits

## 3.1   Overall Flow

Figure 3 shows an overall flow of our proposed correction method. Given

- a specification,
- an implementation circuit that has bugs, and
- a set of candidate locations of the bugs,

the method starts with replacing each logic gate corresponding to a candidate bug location with an LUT. Each inserted LUT has the same set of input variables as its original gate. Then, by applying the method in [2,7], we try to find a configuration of the set of LUTs so that the specification and the implementation become logically equivalent. Once such a configuration is found, it immediately means we get a logic function for correction. Then, another implementation will be created based on the corrected logic function, which may require re-synthesis or synthesis for ECO. Although the method to compute a configuration of LUTs for correction in [2,7] is relatively more efficient than most of the other methods, it can solve up to hundreds of LUTs within a practical runtime. Therefore, it is

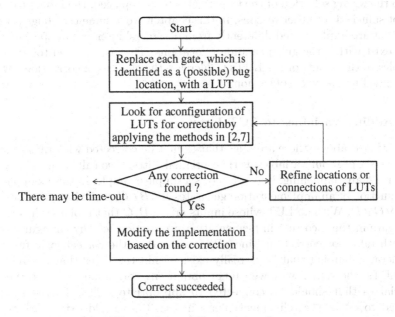

**Fig. 3.** An overall correction flow

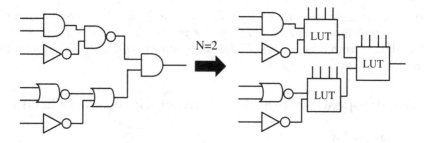

**Fig. 4.** An example of LUT insertions

not practical to replace all of the gates in the given circuit with LUTs, and the number of LUTs inserted into the implementation influence a lot on the runtime. In order to obtain candidate locations of bugs, existing methods such as [8] can be utilized. In this work, we employ a simple heuristic, which is something similar to the path tracing method that all gates in logic cones of erroneous primary outputs are replaced with LUTs when they are within a depth of $N$ levels from the primary outputs. Figure 4 shows an example of such introduction of LUTs. In this figure $N = 2$. In the experiments described in Sect. 4, $N$ is set to Sect. 5. This number is determined through experiments. If the number is larger, there are more chances for the success of corrections. On the other hand, if the number is smaller, we can expect faster processing time.

There can be cases where any correction cannot be found for a given implementation with LUTs. There can be varieties of reasons on the failure. It may be due to the wrong selection of the target gates to be replaced, the inputs to LUTs are not sufficient, or other reasons. In this chapter, we assume that bugs (or portions that are implemented differently from designers' intention or specification) really exist within the given candidate locations. That is, we need to add more variables to the inputs of the LUTs to increase the chances of corrections, which is discussed in the next subsection.

### 3.2   Adding Variables to LUT Inputs

As mentioned above, there are bugs that cannot be corrected with LUTs having the same set of input variables as their original gates, if so called "missing wire" bugs in [12] are happening. Figure 5 shows a simple example. In this example, the logic function of an implementation generates $A \wedge B \wedge C$, while its specification is $A \vee B \vee C \vee D$. With an LUT whose inputs are $A, B, C$ that replaces the original AND gate in the incorrect implementation, we cannot get any configuration of its truth table for correction, since $D$ is essential to the correct logic function. In general, assuming that bugs really exist within the gates that are replaced with LUTs, the reason why we cannot obtain any correction is due to the lack of variables that should be connected to appropriate LUTs. Therefore, what we need to do in the refinement phase in Fig. 3 is to add extra variables to LUT inputs and try to find a correction again. If we inappropriately add a set

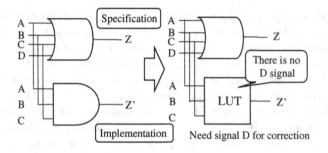

**Fig. 5.** An example bug that cannot be corrected with LUTs having the same inputs

of variables to inputs of some LUTs, however, it simply results in no solution in the next iteration of the loop in Fig. 3. The numbers of ways to add extra variables to input of LUTs are large, and we cannot check one by one. In our method, we try to correct the implementation by adding as small numbers of variables as possible. First, all possible ways to add one variable to LUTs are tried. If no correction can be found, then the method looks for correction with two additional variables to one or two LUTs. Basically, we continue this process until we find corrections.

## 3.3   Using MUXs to Examine Multiple Additional Variables

As discussed above, the method looks for any correction by adding variables to the inputs of LUTs. Even if only one variable is added to the inputs of some LUT, we need to iterate the loop in Fig. 3 many times until a correction is found or a proof of no solution is obtained. For a large circuit, the number of iterations may be too large even for the case of adding one variable to an LUT. To make this process more efficient, we introduce a multiplexer and connect multiple variables, which are candidates to be added to an LUT, to its inputs. The output of the MUX and the additional input of the LUT are connected as shown in Fig. 6. Then, we can select a variable to be added to the LUT by appropriately assigning values to the control variables of the MUX.

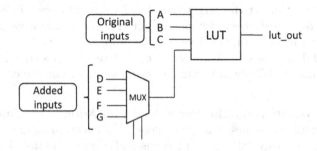

**Fig. 6.** Additional input variables to an LUT

Figure 6 shows how multiplexers work for examining candidate variables that may need to be added to the inputs of the LUT in order to get a correction. The LUT in the example originally has three inputs, $A, B$, and $C$, which means this LUT is supposed to be replaced with some 3-input logic gate for corrections. Suppose that we want to examine multiple variables to be added as an input of the LUT at the same time, instead of examining one by one. Using the MUX in the example, we can examine four additional candidate variables $D, E, F$, and $G$ at one iteration. Here, we need to treat the control variables as program variables, same as the ones in the LUTs. If any correction is found, the corresponding values of the control variables identify a variable for addition. That is, if it becomes an input of the LUT connected to the MUX, the implementation can be equivalent to its specification. Otherwise, all variables connected to inputs of the LUT cannot make the incorrect implementation equivalent to its specification. A straightforward way to realize something similar is to introduce LUTs having larger numbers of inputs rather than using MUX. This is definitely more powerful in terms of the numbers of function which can be realized at the output of the LUTs. In the example shown in Fig. 6, instead of using a MUX, an LUT having seven inputs may be used, and that LUT can provide many more distinct functions for possible corrections. The problem, however, is the number of required program variables. If we use a MUX in the example, we need $2^4 + 2 = 18$ variables. If we use a seven-input LUT, however, we need $2^7 = 128$ variables, which may not be practical with our methods if we deal with multiple of such cases simultaneously.

Even when MUXs are used to examine multiple variables at the same time, we should be aware of the increase of the number of program variables. As can be seen in [2,7], larger numbers of program variables increase runtime for finding a correction, which corresponds to the runtime spent for each iteration of the loop in Fig. 3. Note that one iteration in Fig. 3 may include many iterations in Fig. 2. In the experiments, we show a case study with varieties of numbers of inputs to MUX.

### 3.4 Filtering Out Variables Based on Necessary Condition

When a variable is added to an input of an LUT, it may or may not be an appropriate variable to correct the target bug. Even with the more efficient method using MUXs described above, we should not try to examine a variable which cannot correct the bug. In this subsection, we propose a method for filtering out such non-useful variables from the set of candidate variables that can be connected to inputs of LUTs by utilizing necessary conditions on the correctability.

**Necessary Condition for the Variables to be Added.** For simplicity, the following discussion assumes that there is one LUT added to an implementation circuit. It can be easily extended to the cases of a set of multiple LUTs where each LUT does not have any other LUTs in its fan-in cone (i.e. an LUT depends on other LUTs). However, we here omit such cases.

When no correction is found, which corresponds to taking "NO" branch in Fig. 3, we cannot correct an implementation under debugging with the current LUT, which is the only LUT added, with its current input variables. The reason why there is no correction (i.e. no configuration of LUTs works correctly) is that the LUT outputs the same value for different two input values to the LUT. This happens when "No solution" is reached in Fig. 2. Figure 7 explains the situation. In the figure, $x_i$ is an input pattern added in one of the previous iterations of the process shown in Fig. 2, and $x_j$ is the pattern that is added as a result of the last iteration. Then, there can be situations where the following two conditions are satisfied.

1. For a pair of primary input patterns $x_i$ and $x_j$, the input values to the LUT $l_{in}(x_i)$ and $l_{in}(x_j)$ are the same, where $l_{in}$ represents a logic function that determines an input value to the LUT for a given primary input pattern. Therefore, the output values from the LUT are also the same, that is, $l_{out}(x_i) = l_{out}(x_j)$.
2. In order to make the implementation equivalent to the specification for both $x_i$ and $x_j$, that is, $f_I(x_i) = f_S(x_i) \wedge f_I(x_j) = f_S(x_j)$, $l_{out}(x_i)$ and $l_{out}(x_j)$ must be different, where $f_S$ and $f_I$ denote logic functions of the primary outputs of the specification and the implementation, respectively.

Note that $f_S(x_i)$ can be a different value from that of $f_S(x_j)$. With the conditions, there is no way to have an LUT configuration that satisfies the specification for both $x_i$ and $x_j$ at the same time. In this case, it cannot make an LUT configuration for both $x_i$ and $x_j$ even if we add a variable $v$ to the LUT that has the same value for $x_i$ and $x_j$ ($v(x_i) = v(x_j)$), since $l_{out}(x_i)$ and $l_{out}(x_j)$ are still the same. This is because the output of the LUT can be represented as $l_{out}(l_{in}(x), v(x))$ for a primary input pattern $x$ and $l_{in}(x_i) = l_{in}(x_j) \wedge v(x_i) = v(x_j)$ implies $l_{out}$ are equivalent for $x_i$ and $x_j$ for any configuration of the LUT.

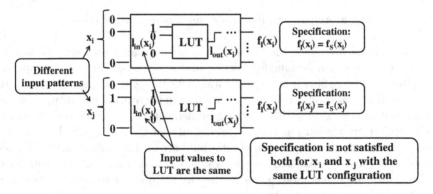

**Fig. 7.** Reason of no correction

The observation above suggests that we must not add a variable to the LUT inputs if it has the same value for $x_i$ and $x_j$. It gives us a necessary condition that the added variable to an LUT must have different values for $x_i$ and $x_j$. If this necessary condition is satisfied, there is an LUT configuration where $l_{out}(x_i) \neq l_{out}(x_j)$ is satisfied, which is a requirement to make $f_S = f_I$ for both $x_i$ and $x_j$. Note that $f_S = f_I$ may not be satisfied even $l_{out}$ is different for the two input patterns.

Figure 8 shows how to make the output of the LUT different by adding a variable that satisfies the necessary condition. Here, we denote the added variable to the LUT as $A(x)$, where $x$ is the primary input variables. An LUT configuration with its input $l_{in}(x)$ and $A(x)$ is represented by $l'_{out}(x)$, which is rewritten as $l'_{out}(x) = P_{\bar{A}}(l_{in}) * \bar{A} + P_A(l_{in}) * A$, where $P_{\bar{A}}(l_{in})$ and $P_A(l_{in})$ represents truth table values for $l_{in}$ when $A = 0$ and $A = 1$, respectively. This is nothing but Shannon's expansion of $l'_{out}$. If the added variable $A(x)$ that satisfies the necessary condition takes 1 for $x_i$ and 0 for $x_j$, we can make an LUT configuration satisfying $l'_{out}(x_i) \neq l'_{out}(x_j)$ by setting the two truth tables $P_{\bar{A}}$ and $P_A$ appropriately. For the case of $x_i = 0$ and $x_j = 1$, an LUT configuration can be obtained in a similar way.

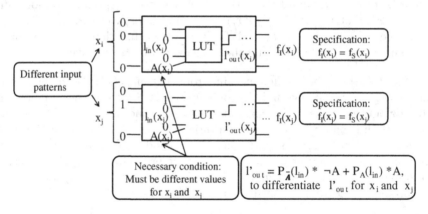

Fig. 8. Adding a variable satisfying a necessary condition

Based on the discussion above, we can filter out variables from candidates when they have the same value for both $x_i$ and $x_j$. Now we show an example of such filtering. Figure 9(a) is the specification which is $Z = A \vee B \vee C \vee D$. Here we assume that this is one of the specifications and there are other outputs in the target circuit. Now assume that a wrong implementation is generated as shown in Fig. 9(b). Here the output only depends only on $C$ and $D$, which is clearly wrong. For the input values where all of inputs are 0, this implementation looks correct as it generates the same output value, 0, as the specification. Note that the implementation has more gates in the circuit in order to realize the other outputs which are not shown in the figure.

Then we find a counterexample, which is $A = 0, B = 1, C = 0, D = 0$ as shown in Fig. 10(a). For these values, the correct output value is 1, but the value of the output in the implementation is 0 as seen from Fig. 10(b). Our debugging method first replaces the suspicious gate, the OR gate, with an LUT

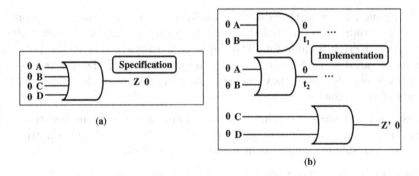

**Fig. 9.** An example specification and its buggy implementation

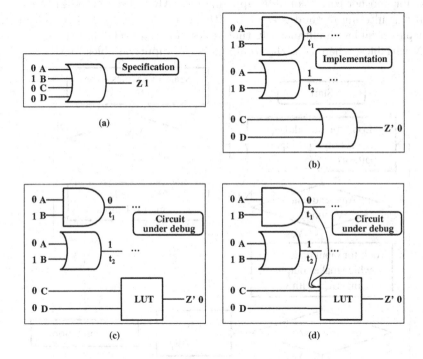

**Fig. 10.** A debugging process for the design in Fig. 9 with a necessary condition

as shown in Fig. 10(c). Unfortunately, there is no configuration for the LUT which makes the implementation correct, and so we need to add an variable to the LUT. Now we have two candidates, $t_1$ and $t_2$ as shown in Fig. 10(d). The necessary condition discussed in the above requires that the value of the variable must be different between the two cases, $A = 0, B = 0, C = 0, D = 0$ and $A = 0, B = 1, C = 0, D = 0$. From this condition, the variable $t_1$ is eliminated and the variable $t_2$ is selected.

**An Improved Flow with Filtering Variables.** Figure 11 shows an improved flow with variable filtering based on the necessary condition discussed above. When no correction is found for all the input patterns so far, the method searches for a set of variables that can be added to inputs of an LUT. During this search, variables which do not satisfy the necessary condition are filtered out. This consists of the following two steps:

1. Find an input pattern $x_i$ that is added in one of the previous iterations and has the same input values of an LUT as those of the lastly added pattern $x_j$.
2. Find a variable having different values for $x_i$ and $x_j$.

As a result, the method tries to add a variable satisfying the necessary condition to inputs of some LUT. Then, with the added LUT input, the method looks for another correction $v$ by applying CEGAR based method in [2,7].

If this filtering method is applied with the method using MUXs to examine multiple variables simultaneously that is described in Sect. 3.3, it needs to pick up $N$ variables, where $N$ is the total number of input variables to MUXs.

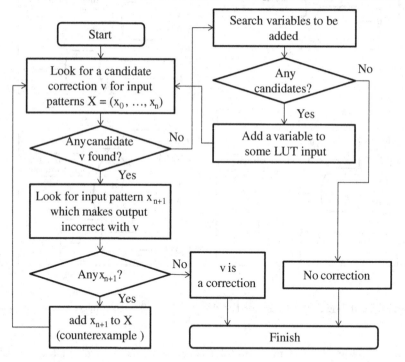

**Fig. 11.** An bypass flow including filtering out variables

## 4    Experimental Results

### 4.1    Experimental Setup

Four sets of experiments are conducted in order to evaluate our debugging methods proposed in this chapter. We use the following circuits for the experiments:

ISCAS85 benchmark circuits, an industrial on-chip network circuit ("Industrial"), and an ARM Cortex microprocessor ("ARM processor"). While ISCAS85 circuits are combinational ones, the last two circuits are sequential ones. All are in gate level designs except for the last experiment which deals with bugs in RTL designs. Table 1 shows the characteristics of these circuits. In order to apply our method, sequential circuits needs to be time-frame expanded. The number of expanded time-frames (i.e. clock cycles for examinations) are shown in the second column for Industrial and ARM processor.

We use PicoSAT [10] as a SAT solver. In order to convert the netlists written in Verilog into SAT formulae, we use ABC [11] and AIGER [13]. All experiments reported in this section are run on a machine with Intel Core 2 Duo 3.33GHz CPU and 4GB Memory.

Table 1. Characteristics of circuits

| | # of expansion | Inputs | Outputs | Gates |
|---|---|---|---|---|
| ISCAS85 benchmarks | | | | |
| c499 | | 202 | 41 | 32 |
| c880 | | 383 | 60 | 26 |
| c1355 | | 546 | 41 | 32 |
| c1908 | | 880 | 33 | 25 |
| c2670 | | 1193 | 233 | 140 |
| c3540 | | 1669 | 50 | 22 |
| c5315 | | 2307 | 178 | 123 |
| c7552 | | 3512 | 207 | 108 |
| Others | | | | |
| Industrial | 3 | 1201 | 1216 | 8289 |
| ARM processor | 1 | 895 | 923 | 4666 |

## 4.2 Simultaneous Examination on Multiple Variables Using Multiplexers

First, we perform an experiment with our method that introduces multiplexers (MUXs) into a circuit under debugging so that multiple extra variables are connected to LUTs through MUXs. In this experiment, we identify the erroneous primary outputs through simulation, and replace all gates in their logic cones within the depth of 5 levels from the erroneous primary outputs with LUTs. Then, we insert a $N$-input MUX to the circuit, and its output is connected to all LUTs. We randomly choose sets of variables out of all primary inputs of the circuit to be debugged, and they are connected to the inputs of MUXs.

If no solution for correction can be found, we replace all the input variables to MUXs with another set of variables that are not examined yet, and execute the method again. In this experiment, the runtime is limited up to 5 h.

The results are shown in Table 2. $N$, the number of inputs to MUX, varies from 1 to 256. $N = 1$ means no MUX, in other words, a variable is directly added to inputs of all LUTs. "Change inputs" represents the number of variable sets that are examined for correction. If this number is $M$, $N \times M$ variables are examined in total. As can be seen in the table, we need to run the method in [2,7] only a few times when the number of MUX inputs is 64 or 256. "Time" shows the total runtime. We can see the runtime for 256-input MUX is the shortest in both circuits. Also, it is notable that we cannot find a correction within 5 h without MUX, since a lot of iterations are required in order to check many variables one by one.

**Table 2.** Experimental results of simultaneous examination of candidate variables using MUXs

|  | Inputs of MUX | Change inputs | Time (sec) |
|---|---|---|---|
| Industrial | 1(no MUXs) | - | Timeout (-) |
|  | 16 | 15 | 5281 |
|  | 64 | 4 | 12794 |
|  | 256 | 1 | 211 |
| ARM processor | 1(no MUXs) | - | Timeout (-) |
|  | 16 | 8 | 11204 |
|  | 64 | 2 | 8857 |
|  | 256 | 1 | 5909 |

### 4.3   Candidate Variable Filtering Using the Necessary Condition

Next, we conduct another experiment to evaluate our method in terms of how well the necessary conditions works. In this experiment, only an incorrect gate is replaced with an LUT. The candidates of variables are all variables in the circuit under debugging. For this experiment, we need to record the values of internal variables for all input patterns. For this purpose, we use Icarus Verilog simulator [14].

The results are shown in Table 3. In this experiments, there is no MUX inserted for the simultaneous examination of multiple variables. Instead, each variable is examined one by one. From the table, we can see only small numbers of iterations are required. Comparing to the results in Table 2 with $N = 1$, where any correction is not obtained within 5 h, the proposed filtering method based on the necessary condition makes the execution time much shorter. It implies that a large number of variables examined in the results shown in Table 2 do not satisfy the necessary condition. The necessary condition works pretty well as filtering.

### 4.4   Applying Both Multiple Variable Examination and Candidate Filtering

In the previous experiments, we evaluate our proposed methods for finding variables which can correct circuits when added to inputs of LUTs. That is, simultaneous examination of multiple candidate variables using MUXs and filtering

**Table 3.** Experimental results of filtering candidate variables based on the necessary condition

|  | Changed inputs | Time (sec) |
|---|---|---|
| Industrial | 29 | 524 |
| ARM processor | 24 | 293 |

candidate variables based on necessary condition are examined. In this section, we see the effects of applying both of the methods at the same time. For this experiment, we use ISCAS85 circuits and an industrial circuit.

In order to generate buggy designs, one gate in each ISCAS circuit is replaced with an LUT, and one of its inputs is removed from the LUT. As a result, we realize cases where a potentially buggy gate is replaced with an LUT, but it lacks one input for correction because we intentionally remove it. The gate replaced with an LUT and a variable to be removed are randomly chosen, and we make five instances for each ISCAS circuit. For Industrial circuit, we replace one of the buggy gates with an LUT. The replaced LUT needs one more input for correction (without intentionally removing one of its original input) as the original circuit is buggy.

We apply the following three methods for each instance.

- **(PI).** Examining all primary input variables one by one until one can correct the circuit.
- **(Filtering).** Examining only primary input and internal variables one by one which satisfy the necessary condition discussed in Sect. 3.4.
- **(Filtering + MUX).** Examining multiple variables which satisfy the necessary condition using MUX.

The results are shown in Table 4. In the table, # of var, Corrected, and # of examined represent the total number of candidate variables, (the number of successfully corrected)/(the total number of instances), and the average number of examined variables in successfully corrected cases, respectively. When # of examined is N/A, it means that none of the experimented instances can be corrected by the corresponding method. Ratio means the ratio of the number of examined variables with filtering to the total number of variables. Runtime in the table is the average runtime of the experimented instances.

From the table, we can see the following.

- When we want to correct circuits utilizing programmability of LUT and one additional input to LUT, we need to add some internal variables (not primary input variables) to the LUT.
- When applying the filtering method to filter out variables not satisfying the necessary condition, we can reduce the numbers of examined candidates to 10 %–30 % of all variables.
- Examining multiple candidates simultaneously using MUXs reduces the runtime significantly.

**Table 4.** Experimental results of applying both of our proposed method

| Circuit | # of var | Method | Corrected | # of examined(ratio) | Runtime(sec) |
|---|---|---|---|---|---|
| c499 | 243 | PI | 0/5 | N/A | 46.4 |
| | | Filtering | 5/5 | 88.6 (36%) | 48.3 |
| | | Filtering + MUX | 5/5 | 88.6 (36%) | 2.3 |
| c880 | 443 | PI | 1/5 | 61.0 (14%) | 80.8 |
| | | Filtering | 5/5 | 54.2 (12%) | 57.0 |
| | | Filtering + MUX | 5/5 | 54.2 (12%) | 2.6 |
| c1355 | 587 | PI | 0/5 | N/A | 60.6 |
| | | Filtering | 5/5 | 155.8 (27%) | 227.7 |
| | | Filtering + MUX | 5/5 | 155.8 (27%) | 3.3 |
| c1908 | 911 | PI | 2/5 | 34.0 (4.0%) | 69.2 |
| | | Filtering | 5/5 | 194.2 (21%) | 284.5 |
| | | Filtering + MUX | 5/5 | 194.2 (21%) | 3.9 |
| c2670 | 1194 | PI | 0/5 | N/A | 708.1 |
| | | Filtering | 5/5 | 142.2 (12%) | 83.2 |
| | | Filtering + MUX | 5/5 | 142.2 (12%) | 4.7 |
| c3540 | 1670 | PI | 0/5 | N/A | 154.9 |
| | | Filtering | 5/5 | 503.8 (30%) | 915.9 |
| | | Filtering + MUX | 5/5 | 503.8 (30%) | 7.8 |
| c5315 | 2476 | PI | 0/5 | N/A | 915.5 |
| | | Filtering | 5/5 | 324.6 (13%) | 268.1 |
| | | Filtering + MUX | 5/5 | 324.6 (13%) | 8.8 |
| c7552 | 3604 | PI | 0/5 | N/A | 1484.3 |
| | | Filtering | 5/5 | 1016.0 (28%) | 3990.1 |
| | | Filtering + MUX | 5/5 | 1016.0 (28%) | 15.9 |
| Industrial | 3209 | PI | 0/1 | N/A | Time out |
| | | Filtering | 1/1 | 100 (3.1%) | 972.3 |
| | | Filtering + MUX | 1/1 | 100 (3.1%) | 172.5 |

## 4.5   Debugging Bugs in RTL Designs

As a final experiment, the proposed debugging method is applied to the bugs in RTL designs, i.e., incorrect statements in RTL design descriptions, in order to understand how much portions of bugs in RTL designs can be corrected. In general, it is much harder to debug bugs in RTL designs, as multiple portions of the synthesized gate level circuits may have to be corrected even when one statement in RTL is wrong.

We insert one wrong RTL statement into the RTL design descriptions. There are four types of wrong statements we introduce as shown in Table 5. Please note that "Incorrect variable" and "Missing variable" most likely need extra inputs to LUTs, and so they are relatively difficult cases. Also "Incorrect logic" can be difficult cases as the incorrect logic function may make it possible for logic synthesis tools to minimize the circuits incorrectly too much, which results in similar situations as "Missing variable".

The results are shown in Table 6. From the results, we can observe the following.

- Bugs in RTL statements are in general more difficult than the ones in gate level designs. Mostly 30–40 % cases can be corrected.
- The bugs as "Extra variable" are relatively easy as expected. This is mostly because we do not need extra variables to be added to LUTs.
- The bugs as "Incorrect logic" are relatively difficult as they mostly need multiple gates to be corrected.

These observations are important as they suggest for future directions targeting bugs in RTL designs.

**Table 5.** Examples of bugs inserted into ARM processor

| Type of bugs | Correct statement | Buggy statement |
|---|---|---|
| Incorrect logic | assign Z = A & B; | assign Z = A \| B; |
| Extra variable | assign Z = A & B; | assign Z = A & B & C; |
| Incorrect variable | assign Z = A & B; | assign Z = A & C; |
| Missing variable | assign Z = A & B; | assign Z = A; |

**Table 6.** Results on RTL debugging

| Type of bugs | Success ratio | #Added variables | #Candidates | #Iterations | Time (sec) Success | Fail |
|---|---|---|---|---|---|---|
| Incorrect logic | 3/10 | 0 | N/A | 10.4 | 29563.0 | 213.8 |
| Extra variable | 9/10 | 0 | N/A | 16.9 | 38141.4 | 1550.2 |
| Incorrect variable | 3/10 | 3 | 4282.7 | 13.0 | 39192.1 | 173.2 |
| Missing variable | 4/10 | 4 | 5333.8 | 39.0 | 38016.6 | 480.3 |

## 5   Discussions for Extensions

One thing we can observe from the experimental results is that we need sometimes many iterations especially when we need to add additional variables to LUTs. Also, if we can utilize LUTs which have larger numbers of inputs may make the proposed methods more efficient and more effective. For that direction, one way is, on behalf of LUTs having large numbers of inputs, to introduce fixed topology circuits consisting of a set of LUTs having smaller numbers of inputs, such as the one shown in Fig. 12. Here a 12-input circuit is defined with a set of LUTs: two of 4-input/3-output LUTs, three of 4-input/2-output LUTs, and one 4-input/1-output LUT. If we implement 12-input LUT directly, we need $2^{12} = 4$K bits. On the other hand, the circuit shown in Fig. 12 needs only $2^4 \times (2 \times 3 + 3 \times 2 + 1) = 832$ bits, although the number of logic functions that can be realized is much less. The fact that the circuit shown in Fig. 12 can only realize very small subset of all possible logic functions with 12-inputs may not be a critical problem if it can represent many or most of the logic functions with 12-inputs actually appearing in real designs.

As a first step of experiments, we apply the proposed debugging methods to synthesize the configuration of the LUTs in the circuit shown in Fig. 12 from given specifications. Hence, this corresponds to the identification of logic functions for the LUTs of the 12-inputs circuit, which as a whole can be used in larger circuits. That is, this is an effort to try to accommodate gates with larger number of inputs as candidates of modification when debugging circuits.

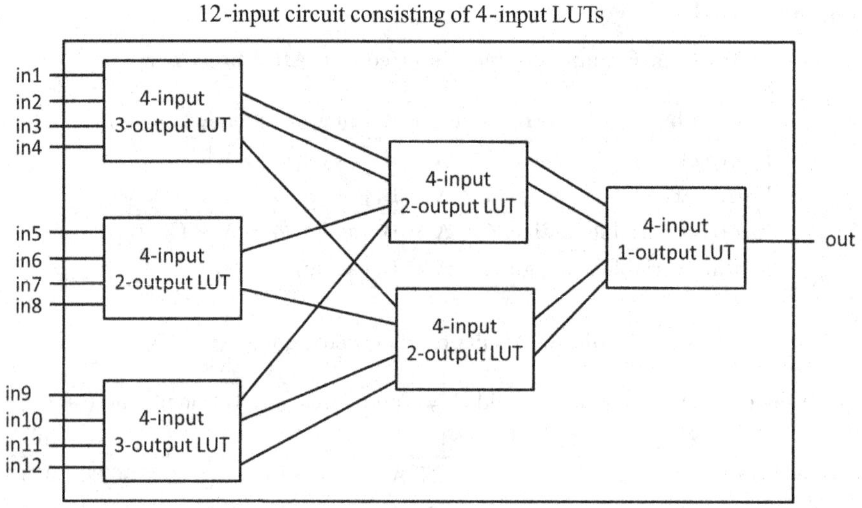

**Fig. 12.** Small LUT-based circuit having 12 inputs

There is a research on enumerating all logic functions appearing in various benchmark circuits [15]. As seen from the chapter, there are not so many logic functions with 12-inputs actually appearing under NPN-equivalence. The chapter also shows the most frequently appearing twenty functions. We have successfully obtained appropriate configurations for the LUTs of the circuit shown in Fig. 12 targeting those twenty logic functions. The processing time for one logic function is rather quick, varying from seconds to hundreds of seconds. Although these results are just for the most frequent twenty logic functions, it is suggesting that the circuit shown in Fig. 12 has good flexibility to accommodate various frequently used logic functions and that the proposed debugging methods can really work for the circuits replacing the buggs gates.

# 6   Conclusions and Future Work

In this chapter, we have proposed debugging methods for gate-level circuits applying partial synthesis techniques shown in [2,7]. In the methods, possible bug locations, which may be given from bug locating methods, are replaced with LUTs, and a configuration of LUTs that makes an implementation under debugging equivalent to its specifications is searched. To deal with the missing input variables to LUTs, we have also proposed methods to examine variables for LUT inputs in trial-and-error manner. Using MUXs, multiple variables are examined simultaneously, which largely reduces the number of iterations of the processes. In addition, we have introduced a necessary condition that variables added to LUT inputs must be satisfied, so that variables not satisfying the condition can be removed quickly from the candidates. Through the experiments with ARM processor design, on-chip network controller taken from industry, and benchmark circuits, we have shown that both of our proposals can significantly speed-up the process to get a correction (i.e. an appropriate configuration of LUTs to make an incorrect implementation correct). We have also shown preliminary experimental results for bugs in RTL designs.

We have also discussed possible extensions of our proposed method, introducing sub-circuits having relatively larger numbers of inputs, such as 12 inputs to the buggy locations of the design under debugging. For such large numbers of inputs, it is not practical to represent the entire sub-circuit with a single 12-input LUT. Instead we have discussed about introduction of decomposition of such sub-circuits with a sets of LUTs having much smaller numbers of inputs.

As a future work, we plan to develop a method to reduce the candidate variables based on the necessary condition discussed in this chapter for the cases where LUTs are dependent with each other. In such cases, the necessary condition may need to be refined to deal with dependency.

# References

1. Yamashita, S., Yoshida, H., Fujita, M.: Increasing yield using partially-programmable circuits. In: Proceedings of Workshop on Synthesis And System Integration of Mixed Information technologies, pp. 237–242 (2010)
2. Jo, S., Matsumoto, T., Fujita, M.: SAT-based automatic rectification and debugging of combinational circuits with LUT insertions. In: 2012 IEEE 21st Asian Test Symposium (ATS), pp. 19–24. IEEE Press, New York (2012)
3. Janota, M., Marques-Silva, J.: Abstraction-based algorithm for 2QBF. In: Sakallah, K.A., Simon, L. (eds.) SAT 2011. LNCS, vol. 6695, pp. 230–244. Springer, Heidelberg (2011)
4. Janota, M., Klieber, W., Marques-Silva, J., Clarke, E.: Solving QBF with counterexample guided refinement. In: Cimatti, A., Sebastiani, R. (eds.) SAT 2012. LNCS, vol. 7317, pp. 114–128. Springer, Heidelberg (2012)
5. Ling, A., Singh, D.P., Brown, S.D.: FPGA logic synthesis using quantified boolean satisfiability. In: Bacchus, F., Walsh, T. (eds.) SAT 2005. LNCS, vol. 3569, pp. 444–450. Springer, Heidelberg (2005)

6. Solar-Lezama, A., Tancau, L., Bodik, R., Seshia, S.A., Saraswat, V.A.: Combinatorial sketching for finite programs. In: Proceedings of the 12th International Conference on Architectural Support for Programming Languages and Operating Systems, pp. 404–415. ACM, New York (2006)
7. Fujita, M., Jo, S., Ono, S., Matsumoto, T.: Partial synthesis through sampling with and without specification. In: 2013 IEEE/ACM International Conference on Computer-Aided Design (ICCAD), pp. 787–794. IEEE Press, New York (2013)
8. Fahim Ali, M., Veneris, A., Smith, A., Safarpour, S., Drechsler, R., Abadir, M.: Debugging sequential circuits using Boolean satisfiability. In: IEEE/ACM International Conference on Computer Aided Design 2004, pp. 204–209. IEEE Press, New York (2004)
9. Oshima, K., Matsumoto, T., Fujita, M.: A debugging method for gate level circuit designs by introducing programmability. In: IFIP WG10.5 VLSI-SoC, pp. 78–83, October 2013
10. Biere, A.: PicoSAT essentials. J. Satisfiability Boolean Model. Comput. (JSAT) **4**, 75–97 (2008)
11. Brayton, R., Mishchenko, A.: ABC: an academic industrial-strength verification tool. In: Touili, T., Cook, B., Jackson, P. (eds.) CAV 2010. LNCS, vol. 6174, pp. 24–40. Springer, Heidelberg (2010)
12. Abadir, M.S., Ferguson, J., Kirkland, T.E.: Logic design verification via test generation. IEEE Trans. Comput. Aided Des. Integr. Circ. Syst. **7**(1), 138–148 (1988). IEEE Press, New York
13. AIGER. http://fmv.jku.at/aiger/
14. Icarus Verilog. http://iverilog.icarus.com/
15. Mishchenko, A.: Enumeration of irredundant circuit structures. In: Proceedings of International Workshop on Logic and Synthesis (2014)

# Gate Sizing Under Uncertainty

Nathaniel A. Conos$^{(\boxtimes)}$, Saro Meguerdichian, and Miodrag Potkonjak

University of California, Los Angeles, 4403 Boelter Hall,
Los Angeles, CA 90095, USA
{conos,saro,miodrag}@cs.ucla.edu

**Abstract.** We present a gate sizing approach to efficiently utilize gate switching activity (SA) and gate input vector control leakage (IVC) uncertainty factors in the objective function in order enable more efficient power and speed yield trade-offs. Our algorithm conducts iterative gate freezing and unlocking with cut-based search for the most beneficial gate sizes under delay constraints. In an iterative flow, we interchangeably conduct gate sizing and IVC refinement to adapt to new circuit configurations. We evaluate our approach on benchmarks in 45 nm technology and demonstrate up to 62 % (29 % avg.) energy savings compared to a traditional objective function that does not consider SA and IVC. We further adapt our approach to optimize yield objectives by addressing processing variation (PV). Significant improvements were achieved under identical timing yield targets of up to 84 % max (55 % avg.) and 74 % max (25 % avg.) mean-power savings for selected ISCAS-85 and ITC-99 benchmarks, respectively.

**Keywords:** Gate sizing · Low power · Input vector control · Switching activity · Yield optimization

## 1 Introduction

Gate sizing is a powerful optimization technique used to minimize power and/or area under strict timing constraints by altering the widths of transistors in gates. Gate sizing has been extensively studied over the past three decades [2–5] and several approaches have been proposed. Previous approaches, however, do not consider optimization uncertainty factors, such as switching activity (SA) and the impact of input vector control leakage (IVC), which greatly impact the overall optimization strategy. Additionally, the impact technological uncertainty, i.e., process variation (PV), has increased in the deep-micron regime, and traditional techniques lack the ability to effectively address yield targets. As a result, the modern design flow imposes a number of modeling and optimization challenges, that require new methods in accounting for uncertainty, both technological and optimization.

One major challenge is the simplification of timing and power models, which may lead to suboptimal solutions when mapping out to real designs, thus, increasing optimization uncertainty. Accounting for accurate gate and interconnect delay and its dependencies on capacitive load slew are often ignored [5].

© IFIP International Federation for Information Processing 2015
A. Orailoglu et al. (Eds.): VLSI-SoC 2013, IFIP AICT 461, pp. 23–47, 2015.
DOI: 10.1007/978-3-319-23799-2_2

Additionally, nominal gate switching activity and/or average gate leakage are generally assumed in previous works limiting the potential improvements by accounting for realistic operating conditions. Moreover, previous approaches are either dynamic or leakage power-centric in their optimization flows, which do not address the varying application usage characteristics present in high-performance systems (e.g., data-centers, super-computing) to energy constrained mobile devices (e.g., tablets, smart-phones).

Cell library-based optimization has emerged as the de facto standard for modeling power and delay of a circuit design. Many previous approaches, however, utilize simplified timing models by assuming convex and/or linear delay and power models [4]. Empirical analysis has shown that accurate timing models are non-linear/non-convex. Furthermore, optimizing circuit designs using a discrete cell library, however, leads to solving an NP-Hard problem [6]. As a result, many heuristics have been developed in order to address the huge optimization problem search space. A major drawback of these methods is that they require heavy parameter tuning and are difficult to reproduce, since they are technology dependent and are driven by a set of sensitivity functions. These methods often perform iterative per-gate or per-group improvement and are too compute intensive and are impractical to be applied on modern IC sizes, even with incremental updates. Furthermore, these approaches mainly perform local optimization (i.e., local-moves) and are susceptible to be trapped in local minimas [7]. In this work, we interchangeably use the term gate and cell to represent the granularity in which we size gates, which is at the cell-level.

The usage of modern cell libraries, however, have enabled the support of various supply/threshold voltages, and drive strengths, thus, enabling a rich performance and energy trade-off to address the potentially vastly differing device usage characteristics. However, current tools do not account for realistic conditions into their objective functions (e.g., gate activity, duty cycle, input vector control), with respect to their applications, potentially impacting obtained results.

In this chapter we focus on two main contributions. The first contribution, introduced in [1], improves state-of-the-art sizing methodologies by simultaneously considering gate switching activity ($SA$) and gate input vector control ($IVC$) uncertainty. The key contribution is that significant benefits of incorporating actual gate SA and gate IVC in the objective function over the equivalent approach that only uses averaged values. Additionally, we show how the obtained solution varies when accounting varying duty cycles. The second contribution, introduced in this chapter, is the integration our SA+IVC technique with a pre-characterization step to improve power and yield targets.

The focal point of our approach is a scalable gate sizing algorithm that considers gate $SA$ and $IVC$ leakage. The steps are to: (1) extract the SA of gates based on simulation of real workloads; and (2) conduct IVC to obtain the input vector that induces the lowest total leakage energy across all gates, and (3) an iterative gate sizing approach freezes maximally-constrained gates (ones that are at high-power states as determined by SA and IVC) while searching for a sizing option that best improves the current picture. The objective function in step 3

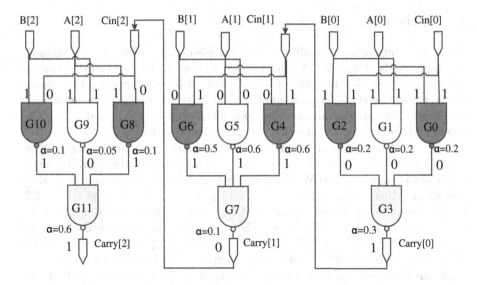

**Fig. 1.** Carry propagation for 3-bit carry-ripple adder

to be considered at the iteration depends on the types of options available and their impacts on both delay and energy. The algorithm prevents the algorithm from reaching a local minima by freezing gates as they are sized until all gates have been frozen, then unfreezes all gates, re-conducts IVC (since new gates may be energy-dominant), and reiterates steps 2 and 3 until the solution converges or the delay constraint cannot be met.

The concept introduced in this chapter is the extension of our gate sizing technique to account for the impact of process variation for maximizing yield targets with respect to specified delay and power targets. Efficient yield optimization is achieved by a pre-characterization step which identifies the most critical cells that are likely to impact delay targets through an efficient Monte Carlo simulation that considers epsilon-paths ($\varepsilon$-paths). The intuition is to simultaneously speed-up critical paths in order to minimize the impact of process variation across generated circuit instances and minimize the power costs by conducted gradual gate sizing.

We evaluate our gate sizing approach on benchmarks included in ISCAS-85/89, ITC99 and arithmetic units first without consideration of PV. Our results indicate over 62 % (29 % avg.) energy improvement over a method that assumes nominal $SA$ and $IVC$, demonstrating that gate $SA$ and $IVC$ play an major role in the guiding sizing decisions over an equivalent sizing algorithm that does not. We then present results using our PV-aware technique, which further imroves our original gate sizing algorithm to address yield objectives. We demonstrate the effectiveness of our process variation-aware (PV-aware) against a non PV-aware technique across ISCAS-85 and ITC99 benchmarks, achieving 64 % and 48 % power savings with respect to identical target delays.

## 2    Motivation

We begin by providing a small realistic example demonstrating the importance of considering both SA and IVC uncertainty factors in the gate sizing optimization process. Consider the carry propagation of a 3-bit carry-ripple adder, shown in Fig. 1. Assume that 2- and 3-input NAND gates have input-dependent leakage power consumption values for two possible sizes, small (X1) and large (X2), shown in Table 1. Also assume that the given input vectors ($A = 101, B = 101$, and $C_{in} = 1$) are realized throughout the entire duration of the application. Figure 1 shows the input vectors to each gate. Therefore, the overall leakage power of the circuit is 288 nW. For simplicity, ignoring load and slew dependencies, assume that all gates have delay of 10 ps at size X1 and 5 ps at size X2. Finally, assume that at the beginning of the optimization process, all gates are nominally sized to size X1. Therefore, there are eight nominal critical paths (colored), $\{G0, G2\} \to G3 \to \{G4, G6\} \to G7 \to \{G8, G10\} \to G11$, with nominal delay 60 ps. Consequently, total leakage energy of the circuit is $1.73 \times 10^{-17}$ J.

As an example, consider a delay constraint of 55 ps. It is clear that one of gates G3, G7, or G11 should be sized up to X2, as all critical paths pass through these bottleneck gates and decrease the delay of each of these gates will decrease the overall delay. A traditional approach to gate sizing would consider these gates equally. In other words, increasing the size of either would decrease delay and increase switching and leakage power by the same amounts. However, from Table 1, we see that the leakage power of a gate, due to transistor stacking, strongly depends on its applied inputs, with up to a 43X difference between the lowest-leakage state (input vector "100": 1.29 nW) and highest-leakage state (input vector "111": 55.8 nW) of a 3-input NAND gate. Furthermore, switching energy of a gate is directly proportional to its activity factor, or the likelihood that the gate will switch. Therefore, because the gates have both different applied input vectors and different activity factors, sizing up each one will have a different effect on overall power and energy consumption, so they should not be weighted equally in the optimization process.

First, consider the case where the duty cycle of the adder is low and therefore leakage energy dominates. We can determine from Table 1 that increasing the size of gates G3, G7, or G11 will increase leakage power by 9.96 nW, 167.42 nW, or 56.35 nW, respectively, while decreasing the overall delay by 5 ps. Therefore, the optimal decision is to increase the size of gate G3, which will have minimal impact on leakage energy, increasing leakage power to 298 nW and *decreasing* leakage energy to $1.64 \times 10^{-17}$ J. Increasing the size of G7 would instead increase leakage power to 455 nW, *increasing* leakage energy to $2.50 \times 10^{-17}$ J. Thus, considering IVC in this example in the optimization algorithm can improve the energy by roughly 60 %.

Now, consider the high duty cycle scenario, where switching energy is the dominant factor. Again, for simplicity, assume that all gates consume 10 nJ and 20 nJ of switching energy at nominal activity factor 1.0 for a given application at sizes X1 and X2, respectively. Figure 1 shows the activity factors ($\alpha$) for each gate. Therefore, overall switching energy consumption at the nominal size is 35.5 nJ. In this case, increasing the size of gate G7 is the optimal decision, since it has the lowest activity factor and consumes less switching energy than when up-sizing either G3 or G11. In fact, this decision results in a switching energy of 36.5 nJ, whereas increasing the size of G11 would result in a switching energy of 41.5 nJ. Therefore, the decision that considers SA performs roughly 14 % better.

Another key component modern design flow that requires attention is the process variation (PV) impact on sizing moves. For example, sizing alterations, such as the ones discussed in this section, are mostly performed in the pre-silicon phase. Therefore, there is uncertainty in how sizing alterations are affected by on-chip variations once the design has been manufactured. Optimizing for yield can be exhaustive and require extensive statistical characterization; however, conducting a pre-characterization step may reveal more suitable circuit alterations that may not be possible to capture in a traditional static flow. For example, designers may leverage spatial and temporal correlations in a design to determine the best cell(s) to size. For example, G3 may belong to a path whose delay is more susceptible by PV; thus, it would be more beneficial for G3 to be up sized eve though G7 was identified to be a more efficient move in terms of power-speed trade-off under a traditional static optimization approach. As a result, the benefits of accounting the impact of PV in a circuit is clear when optimizing for yield.

**Table 1.** NAND gate leakage values ($nW$) for two sizes (X1, X2) based on input vector control (IVC) from a single threshold 45 nm cell library [8], where min and max leakage states are represented by bold and italicized fonts, respectively.

| NAND-3 | | |
|---|---|---|
| IVC | X1 | X2 |
| 000 | 3.32 | 13.28 |
| 001 | 18.18 | 72.73 |
| 010 | 4.21 | 16.84 |
| 011 | 39.49 | 157.97 |
| **100** | **1.29** | **5.15** |
| 101 | 18.78 | 75.13 |
| 110 | 3.76 | 15.04 |
| *111* | *55.8* | *223.22* |

| NAND-2 | | |
|---|---|---|
| IVC | X1 | X2 |
| **00** | **3.48** | **13.93** |
| 01 | 24.8 | 99.2 |
| 10 | 4.09 | 16.34 |
| *11* | *37.21* | *148.83* |

To present these motivations, we have made a number of assumptions that when relaxed make the optimization much more complex in practice. It is reasonable to assume that additional information (gate switching, input vector state, and pre-characterization statistics) can be readily obtained by modern CAD tools and/or by implementing a simple gate-level simulator combined with statistical packages. Such information is beneficial since it enables the simultaneous consideration of low duty cycle and high duty cycle scenarios, as in real use cases at current and pending deep-submicron feature sizes, leakage and switching may both have significant impacts on overall energy. For example, sizing up G7 in the high duty cycle scenario may in reality not be optimal, since its input gates have higher values for $\alpha$ than, the input gates of G3, and thus their switching energies would increase by larger factors. Thus, this IVC depends on how the circuit is sized and its duty-cycle. Therefore, a feedback loop exists between gate sizing and IVC that must be addressed simultaneously during the optimization. The example here demonstrates that both IVC and SA are crucial considerations in gate sizing for energy optimization in the presence of delay deadlines. Furthermore, combining PV-uncertainty can further provide key insight in guiding circuit alterations.

## 3    Related Work

We cover a set of related gate sizing approaches that have considered a variant of $SA$ or $IVC$. Several approaches exist that address continuous and discrete gate sizing. Common methods to solve the gate sizing problem have been convex optimization [4], Lagrangian Relaxation [2,3,17], and gradient and sensitivity-based optimization [9,18].

Gate sizing methods have also been combined with $V_{dd}$ and $V_{th}$ assignment to minimize power under various gate $SA$ ratios [10,11]. These works, however, have only considered average leakage values when accounting for leakage and have not explored real application activity factors when considering gate switching activity. Leakage minimization using $IVC$ is a popular technique for due to its strong dependency on the input vector state [12]. $IVC$ and gate replacement techniques have also been combined [13] by replacing gates at their worse-case leakage state with equivalent gates with lower leakage power.

To the best of our knowledge, we are the first to consider gate sizing in the presence of both $SA, IVC$, and duty cycle. Prior approaches have at most considered one or two terms accurately [16], and/or do not differentiate between the duty cycle with respect to switching and leakage energy weights, leaving many approaches to be either dynamic or leakage power-centric. For example, the state-of-the-art gate sizing contest considers only nominal leakage power [5]. Our technique minimizes total energy, such that both the switching and leakage energy components are accurately accounted for in accordance to their usage or duty cycle.

## 4    Cell Library Energy and Delay

The total energy of a CMOS integrated circuit can be characterized into two main components: (1) dynamic (switching) energy due to charging of input pin/output load capacitance's; and (2) static (leakage) energy, which we model from the dominant sub-threshold leakage and gate leakage currents. Thus, the total energy consumed can be computed as:

$$E_{total} = E_{switch} + E_{leak} \qquad (1)$$

$$E_{switch} = \sum_{i}^{N} es(g_i), \qquad E_{leak} = \sum_{i}^{N} el(g_i) \qquad (2)$$

*es* and *el* represent the switching and leakage energies, respectively, for gate $g_i$. *es* is the product between probability that a gate's input pin $j$ will switch, $\alpha$ (SA), and the estimated full-cycle ($e_{fc}$) power consumed from propagating a signal from input pin $j$ to output pin $k$. *el* is the sum of leakage energies consumed at each possible leakage state of a gate, which is also dependent the ratio of the total time spent at each leakage state for both *active* and *standby* (idle) periods. The total time ($T$) is directly proportional to product of the circuit delay ($D$) and total cycles, where $D$ represents the critical output-pin arrival time (*rise* or *fall*) of a primary output gate $ot^{r,f}(g_i)$:

$$D = max(ot^{r,f}(g_i)) \qquad s.t. \; g_i \in G_{out} \tag{3}$$

$G_{out}$ represents a circuit's set of primary output gates. Therefore, the delay of a circuit can be determined by solving:

$$ot^{r,f}(g_i) = dl^{r,f}(g_i) + max(ot(fin_j^{f,r})) \tag{4}$$
$$s.t. \, fin_i \in FI_i$$

$fin_j^{f,r}$ is the *fall, rise* arrival time of a fan-in gate $j$ in the set $FI_i$ of gate $g_i$. Note that the propagation of delay depends on the unateness assumption. For simplicity, we assume all cells are negative unate, thus, rise ($r$) and fall ($f$) gate delays are propagated as assumed to the next stage.

We use a cell table library look-up as [5] to model gate *rise* and *fall* delay ($dl^{r,f}$) as a function of its input slew (transition time), and driving load. However, we use an alternate 45 nm cell library (Nandgate) [8] to account for switching

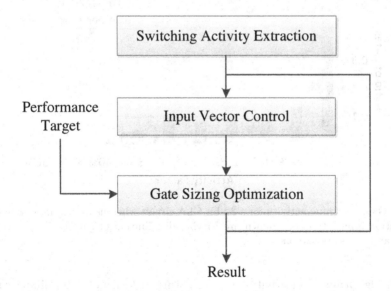

**Fig. 2.** Gate sizing optimization flow

and input vector dependent leakage power, which are obtained in a similar look-up table fashion, provided per-input pin accurate switching, and input vector state probabilities, which can be obtained using gate-level simulation.

# 5    Technical Approach

## 5.1    Gate Sizing

Our gate sizing procedure is composed of three major phases (Fig. 2). The first phase extracts gate switching activity factors ($SA$) for a given circuit by performing event-driven gate simulation from a set of input bit vectors. Figure 3 illustrates an example $SA$ extraction for a carry-look-ahead unit (cla4) from two applications (mpeg2enc/dec). The second step identifies a primary input bit vector that places gates in low leakage states in order to minimize the total energy of the circuit, which accounts for leakage consumption for both active (obtained from SA) and idle periods. IVC techniques range from random simulation to satisfiability (SAT) and model counting-based formulations. The final component is the gate sizing algorithm, where the goal is to minimize total energy consumption under a delay constraint. The approach is iterative; at each iteration, gates are either frozen or unlocked based on their leakage (IVC) and switching (SA) impact, while a search is conducted for the most beneficial current *move*.

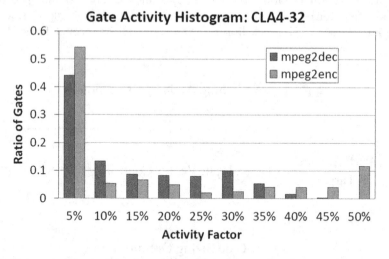

**Fig. 3.** Gate switching activity for a 32-bit CLA circuit when using real mpeg2enc/dec application input stimulus. Shown are varying distribution of gate activity within a circuit and across two applications.

Our algorithm is sensitivity-based in nature in terms of determining which move or set of moves to perform. A gate sizing move can have 1 of 3 effects (increase, decrease, have no effect) on 2 parameters (energy and delay), leading to a total of 9 separate possible classes for a move. The algorithm classifies each move to and enforces a priority scheme in order to select a move that has higher precedence. There are three precedence levels, where level 1 is the highest priority. Moves that improve both parameters are at precedence 1, moves that improve just one parameter and do not affect the other are at precedence 2, and moves that improve one parameter at the expense of degrading another are of precedence 3. Note that moves that degrade both parameters are never selected. Each precedence level has its own objective function for selecting the best move: (1) the product of the respective improvements; (2) the single improvement; and (3) the normalized ratio of improvement and degradation.

The algorithm considers a cut of $M$ gates at a time and restricts one gate to be sized per group visit. Once a size move is committed, the gate is locked and is no longer considered within that phase. The completion of a phase is defined as having locked all gates, or having no more acceptable moves among sizable gates that improve the objective function. The algorithm terminates after the solution converges or if a target delay $(D_{target})$ can not be met after a number of phases. All gates are unlocked before the start of each new sizing phase.

The algorithm initially freezes the top $K$ energy-critical gates by setting them to their minimal sizes at the beginning of the phase. We note that this initial set potentially restricts some delay critical gates, as improving the delay of these gates may be required in meeting a deadline. To relax this constraint (i.e., if a solution cannot be obtained), $K$ is relaxed through a locking threshold ratio $\gamma$, where a new $K$ is computed (e.g., $K = K' \cdot \gamma$), thereby, enabling potentially more delay critical gates to be reduced. It is crucial to identify the top $K$ energy-critical gate, which in turn depends on both SA and IVC; this maximally-constrained gate locking is one of the key innovations of the approach, and prevents being trapped at a local minima by encouraging global circuit optimization.

We utilize an epsilon tree to minimize circuit delay updates $(\varepsilon_{path})$, which consists of gates that were on the critical path during the last accurate delay computation (Fig. 4a). Since the critical path may change during optimization, we also include the immediate fan-out gates of each critical gate (e.g., nodes 1 and 3), fan-in nodes may be added for greater accuracy as their slews may also impact timing propagation. The figure shows bold-outlined nodes (e.g., 7, 8, 9, 5 and 6) are the primary outputs $(G_{out})$, and are transitively connected to at least one node belonging to the critical path (e.g., 0, 2, 4, 8). Thus, the delay cost of sizing a gate on the $\varepsilon_{path}$ can be estimated by the sum of its $\delta_i$ with respect to the target delay $(D_{target})$ is used to estimate the delay impact of each move via a delay cost formula, as shown below:

$$D_{cost} = \sum_i^{|G_{out}|} (\delta_i - D_{target})^2 \tag{5}$$

This formulation enables very efficient delay estimation by only considering the delay impact of a small subset of gates at a time. A drawback of this approach, however, is that a potentially new critical path may emerge. This remains to be a major challenge for existing gate sizing techniques that attempt to maintain delay accuracy during optimization [9,17,18]. To address this issue, the frequency of delay updates can be increased by adjusting $M$ and $\gamma$ to be larger values, as we have done. These parameters can be adjusted, to trade-off accuracy vs run-time.

Our used values of $M$ and $\gamma$ achieved a delay accuracy to be within 5 %, while achieving linear run-time scaling with respect to circuit size (Fig. 4b).

## 5.2    Maximizing Yield

In this section, we extend our gate sizing technique to account for the impact of process variation in order to maximize yield targets with respect to delay and power.

**Cell Characterization.** As a pre-processing step, we characterize each cell's ability to improve the circuit delay when its size is increased by one. The objective is to capture its delay impact on a set of $\varepsilon$-critical paths when its size is increased. We define the $\varepsilon$-critical paths as the set of paths whose cell slack is within an $\varepsilon$-threshold value with respect to the critical slack. The distinguishing factor of our PV gate sizing method against our non-PV method is that we aim to improve a set of $\varepsilon$-critical paths. Doing so improves the circuit's resiliency against the potentially harmful effects of PV by over-optimizing one or few critical paths that do not consider PV.

The major challenge of our cell characterization phase is that it incurs additional run-time overhead of $O(n^2)$, since the delay impact of sizing each cell is required to be computed. The timing overhead, however, can be minimized by considering a smaller $\varepsilon$-critical set and is practical, since this step can be performed only once or a few times. Additionally, the typical distribution of critical cells in the circuit is anywhere from 1 % to 10 % during the initial stages of our gate sizing method when all cells are initially set to their valid minimal size configuration. It is important to note, however, the number of cells that belong within $\varepsilon$-critical paths increases as the circuit becomes more sensitive. At these inflection points, additional characterization phases can be performed in order to improve accuracy.

Figure 5 presents the circuit slack impact (y-axis) when increasing the size of each cell (x-axis) independently. The y-axis represents a normalized slack sum value across a set of 1000 generated circuit instances with process variation using 3-sigma normal threshold-voltage and gate effective length distribution [19]. The x-axis lists cell id's ranked in ascending order from left to right with respect to its *initial* slack value for a circuit without PV. It is important to note that a larger slack for a given cell indicates that it has a greater potential to improve circuit delay (increase overall slack) when it is up sized. Also note that cells are originally listed in ascending order with respect to their original slack computed without PV, thus demonstrating that greedily up sizing the most critical gates (left-most gates) does not yield a result in the most delay improvement when increasing their size. In fact, some cells that are not on the critical path yield better delay improvements than cells with smaller slack, as shown with some cells in between 60 and 160 for circuit $c432$. This behavior can be attributed to cells that may not be initially on the critical path, but are an immediate fan-out of a cell that is, and therefore, increasing their size may cause subsequent up-sizing of their critical transitive fan-in cells, thus improving circuit delay greater

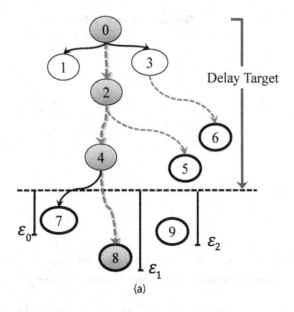

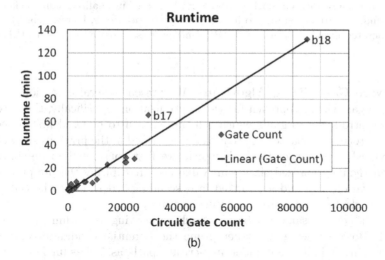

**Fig. 4.** (a) An example of $\varepsilon$ critical path ($\varepsilon_{path}$); the critical path in dashed-red; transitive fan-out output nodes in bold outlines; and $\varepsilon_i$ corresponds to the absolute delay difference w.r.t to the target delay used for estimating delay cost of a move. (b) The linear run-time of the new gate sizing approach

than individually sizing a gate on the critical path. For our approach, we then rank the cells by their normalized slack value when considering which cells are more critical with respect to timing when conducting gate sizing.

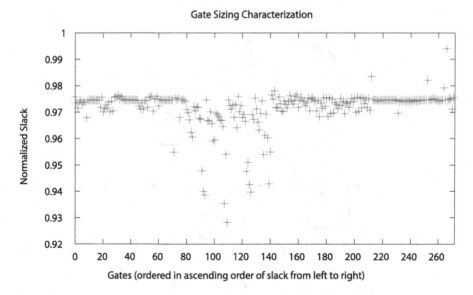

**Fig. 5.** Impact of independent gate sizing. Gates are ordered left to right in ascending order with respect to their slack (without PV). Larger normalized sum slack values (y-axis) indicate greater ability to improve delay (reduce delay, increase slack) across 1000 generated circuit instances with PV when size is increased to the next discrete size.

**PV-Aware Gate Sizing Algorithm.** We present several extensions to our PV-aware gate sizing approach for yield optimization. Specifically, these extensions are introduced to guide which cells are chosen to be sized first based on their pre-processing characterization result described in the previous subsection. As previously mentioned, the cells which are first considered to be sized are based on their normalized slack sum value acquired during the pre-processing characterization step and are ranked in descending order. Thus, the cells with the largest slack-sum are sized or configured first.

We conduct the same cut-based search gate sizing algorithm presented in Sect. 5.1. However, we also further prune the potential candidate cells to be sized by sizing cells that fall under an $\varepsilon$-critical path, as well as further selecting cells which are the least constraining cells (smallest size) to be sized. We define the least constraining cells as the set of cells currently in the sizing phase set that are currently configured as the minimum size among the cells belonging to the $\varepsilon$-critical paths. For example, assume that the current $\varepsilon$-set include cells A, B, C, and D with sizes 1X, 1X, 2X, and 3X, respectively. Then, cells A and B are to be considered to be sized first during this phase. To break ties between cells A and B, their respective cost score (Eq. 5) is multiplied by their respective normalized slack sum value. Increasing the size of these cells enable more balanced $\varepsilon$-critical paths, thus, effectively enabling more efficient delay-power trade-offs to be performed in later sizing iterations that achieve tighter delay constraints; this is achieved since optimizing a set of $\varepsilon$-critical prevents from over optimizing a few paths, which may cause certain paths to converge to a timing wall.

# 6   Experimental Results

We evaluated our gate sizing approach on a set of benchmarks in ISCAS-85/89, ITC-99 suites, as well as integer arithmetic units consisting of adders (carry ripple, carry-look-ahead, Kogge-Stone) and multipliers (array, Dadda). All units were synthesized using a single threshold (HVt) 45 nm open cell library from [8] under the typical cell configuration. An in-house timing/power engine was implemented in C++ and was correlated to an industrial tool, Synopsys Prime-Time, to be within $10^{-3}$ps. All results were optimized using identical rules such as ensuring no slew or load violations exists in the final design, as presented in [5]. The only differences in our framework is the choice in cell library, which was done in order to enable accurate IVC computations, as well as the choice of circuit benchmarks. In handling slew and load violations, we adopt an iterative approach as proposed in [18].

The SA of gates and IVC for each circuit were obtained from simulation of random input vectors. However, real application switching activity factors were obtained from mpeg2enc/dec benchmarks from recorded operand values from each unit type, running ARM7TDMI-ISA mpeg2-enc/dec traces [14,15]. The initial simulation parameters set were, $K = 25\%$, $M =$ twice the length of average critical path, $\gamma = 0.2$, and were fixed across all benchmarks. The delay target for each circuit was set as the median between the achieved delay when all gates were set to their maximal size, and the achieved delay when all gates are at their minimal size. Five duty cycle scenarios (D0 = 10 %, D1 = 20 %, D2 = 33 %, D3 = 50 %, and D4 = 100 %) were considered.

## 6.1   Gate Sizing Under Switching Activity and IVC Uncertainty

We first evaluate our sizing algorithm under two gate sizing assumptions: (1) SA+IVC, which considers gate switching activity factors and input vector control in the objective function; and (2) *Base*, where the objective function uses only nominal gate switching (50 %) and average gate leakage values for total energy computation. Table 2 compares the two methods, where Max (%) savings corresponds to the maximum energy improvement achieved over the *Base* method across the five duty cycle cases (D0 to D4) for each circuit under the same timing constraint. As expected, the maximum improvement observed varies across duty cycles and circuits, motivating the advantage of utilizing accurate power and delay knowledge.

Table 4 provides overall energy improvements across the benchmark suites. The results generated by the new approach achieved a maximum energy improvement of 62 % for circuit c2670 and 29 % average overall for the same delay.

Figure 6 provides a normalized energy and delay plot for c2670, which illustrates the advantage of using more accurate power and delay information. A delay of 0.87 shows that the *Perceived* energy deviates from the trend of the *Actual*

**Table 2.** Energy savings when considering gate $SA$ and $IVC$ during the gate sizing procedure over the *Base* method. The obtained switching and leakage energies are presented for the $SA+IVC$. The maximum energy deltas ($\Delta$ %), corresponds to the max difference in energy profile "perceived" by the *Base* method during optimization.

| Circuit | No. gates | Max energy savings | | | $SA + IVC$ | | | | | |
|---------|-----------|-----------|-----------|-----------|-----------|-----------|-----------|-----------|-----------|-----------|
| | | Total (%) | Sw (%) | Lk (%) | Sw ($\mu$J) | Max ($\Delta$%) | Lk ($\mu$J) | Max ($\Delta$%) | Duty Cycle | Delay (ns) |
| c880 | 383 | 8.14 | 8.16 | 8.05 | 125.11 | 31.22 | 15.75 | 3.01 | D2 | 0.73 |
| c1355 | 554 | 14.35 | 15.01 | 13.26 | 264.13 | 31.12 | 164.79 | 15.19 | D1 | 0.74 |
| c1908 | 932 | 13.41 | 13.72 | 9.41 | 405.7 | 29.57 | 32.06 | 6.75 | D4 | 1.14 |
| c7552 | 3568 | 43.65 | 44.02 | 41.32 | 1685 | 30.27 | 284.6 | 3.21 | D2 | 1.20 |
| c5315 | 2330 | 58.72 | 59.1 | 54.57 | 855.6 | 32.93 | 87.58 | 3.19 | D4 | 1.34 |
| c432 | 272 | 30.15 | 35.24 | 22.35 | 68.54 | 33.15 | 53.55 | 23.67 | D1 | 0.62 |
| c2670 | 1202 | 62.64 | 62.74 | 60.78 | 407.6 | 31.91 | 24.62 | 1.39 | D4 | 0.85 |
| c3540 | 1703 | 28.84 | 29.66 | 24.14 | 799.1 | 31.09 | 152.2 | 2.47 | D2 | 0.79 |
| s1488 | 698 | 46.38 | 46.49 | 44.81 | 182.6 | 35.54 | 14.09 | 12.05 | D2 | 0.42 |
| s1494 | 692 | 35.5 | 36.08 | 33.84 | 283.9 | 36.36 | 103.3 | 12.55 | D1 | 0.42 |
| s15850 | 10547 | 31.34 | 30.76 | 34.48 | 3803 | 33.69 | 662.1 | 4.98 | D3 | 2.22 |
| s838 | 473 | 32.49 | 38.89 | 27.17 | 139.3 | 31.76 | 199.8 | 10.84 | D1 | 1.64 |
| s5378 | 3054 | 16.76 | 30.08 | 15.06 | 826.6 | 36.2 | 7876 | 26.34 | D0 | 0.68 |
| s9234 | 5897 | 50.19 | 50.52 | 47.23 | 2041 | 32.51 | 242.5 | 4.43 | D3 | 1.50 |
| s38417 | 23963 | 53.2 | 53.85 | 46.17 | 6661 | 30.65 | 714.2 | 8.58 | D3 | 1.29 |
| s35932 | 21035 | 22.27 | 22.31 | 21.25 | 8317 | 29.28 | 332.1 | 37.26 | D3 | 0.80 |
| s38584 | 18161 | 29.01 | 31.52 | 28.75 | 5820 | 32.24 | 59720 | 4.77 | D0 | 1.52 |
| b10 | 204 | 44.69 | 45.06 | 32.43 | 40.56 | 34.45 | 1.55 | 54.83 | D2 | 0.36 |
| b11 | 633 | 35.53 | 35.79 | 31.74 | 250.9 | 32.37 | 18.77 | 61.52 | D2 | 1.10 |
| b12 | 1183 | 22.91 | 27.89 | 3.31 | 314.0 | 37.03 | 107.3 | 60.54 | D1 | 0.61 |
| b13 | 375 | 22.05 | 22.78 | 15.01 | 161.23 | 31.85 | 18.4 | 55.33 | D1 | 0.33 |
| b14 | 6498 | 28.42 | 28.65 | 26.21 | 3024 | 33.22 | 320.7 | 54.94 | D2 | 1.31 |
| b15 | 8920 | 27.62 | 27.7 | 26.75 | 1666 | 38.99 | 166.1 | 54.24 | D3 | 1.58 |
| b17 | 28911 | 21.25 | 25.29 | 20.79 | 8.53 | 38.76 | 80.58 | 55.99 | D3 | 1.68 |
| b18 | 85188 | 7.02 | 8.67 | 5.96 | 44.54 | 37.84 | 71.4 | 54.72 | D1 | 2.10 |
| b20 | 14322 | 27.85 | 28.57 | 24.07 | 3.66 | 33.2 | 0.74 | 55.8 | D2 | 2.08 |
| cra32 | 225 | 38.32 | 45.14 | 37.76 | 6.72 | 44.90 | 92.22 | 32.09 | D0 | 2.08 |
| cla432 | 305 | 22.25 | 25.02 | 12.18 | 10.18 | 42.87 | 3.28 | 13.62 | D2 | 0.35 |
| ks32 | 611 | 24.2 | 23.18 | 24.63 | 17.64 | 44.76 | 40.83 | 14.6 | D0 | 0.30 |
| arr8 | 512 | 35.96 | 36.3 | 23.18 | 178.5 | 34.69 | 22.84 | 21.29 | D1 | 0.81 |
| dad8 | 542 | 30.35 | 30.99 | 36.33 | 101.3 | 35.83 | 9.12 | 11.98 | D2 | 0.62 |

energy plot. In performing move-trace analysis, we noted that the *Base* method caused the algorithm to over-size a few selected critical paths and encountered a timing wall much earlier, whereas $SA+IVC$ was able to efficiently trade-off delay for an additional 0.05 delay units, as shown.

**Table 3.** Energy savings of $(SA+IVC)$ over *Base* using extracted gate switching activity and input vector control from mpeg2enc/dec applications assuming a (D2) "33 %" duty cycle. The units represent an single-adder (32b) and multiplier (8b) configuration of an ARM7TDMI core [15].

| mpeg2 | Energy savings | | | cla432 | | | | dad8 | | | |
|---|---|---|---|---|---|---|---|---|---|---|---|
| | Total (%) | Sw (%) | Lk (%) | Sw ($\mu$J) | Sw Imp (%) | Lk ($\mu$J) | Lk Imp (%) | Sw ($\mu$J) | Sw Imp (%) | Lk ($\mu$J) | Lk Imp (%) |
| enc | 15.31 | 17.15 | 8.55 | 742.7 | 4.73 | 628.7 | 1.09 | 2267 | 20.61 | 498.6 | 13.92 |
| dec | 25.10 | 29.89 | 6.21 | 11.02 | 6.42 | 24.30 | 1.20 | 101.4 | 30.99 | 9.24 | 21.58 |

Figure 7 shows a cumulative distribution of gate switching and leakage energies of the max improved result for $SA+IVC$ over *Base* for circuit c2670. Our approach shows that accurate knowledge enabled the algorithm to efficiently guide the circuit to a lower energy state, as shown with higher percentage of gates falling under lower energy profiles for both leakage and switching energy. This is important to note since due to the difficulty of comparing gate sizing algorithms, many existing algorithms are sensitivity-based in nature, thus, the ability to guide an algorithm to determine more promising "moves" greatly impacts the optimization procedure.

Table 3 presents results comparing the minimal configuration found by $SA+IVC$ and the perceived minimal configuration obtained by *Base*. The minimum energy configuration determined was cla432 and dad8, optimized under the same timing constraints determined by the multiplier. For these configurations,

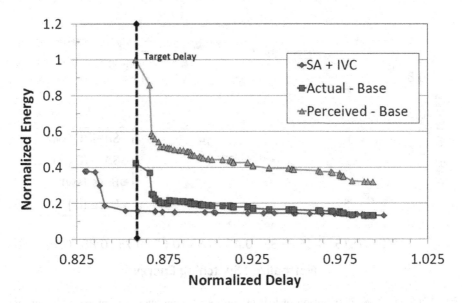

**Fig. 6.** Energy vs delay plot of c2670. The $SA+IVC$ approach consistently outperforms the *Base* method.

**Table 4.** Overall energy savings with respect to benchmark suite

| Benchmark suite | Max tot (%) | Avg. tot (%) | Avg. Sw (%) | Avg. Lk (%) |
|---|---|---|---|---|
| ISCAS-85 | 62.64 | 29.70 | 30.58 | 26.74 |
| ISCAS-89 | 53.20 | 28.33 | 29.99 | 26.96 |
| ITC-99 | 58.83 | 29.23 | 30.90 | 24.15 |
| Arith | 57.19 | 30.48 | 33.23 | 33.15 |

our approach shows additional savings in both leakage and switching categories where the majority of the savings for both cases (15 % mpeg2enc, 25 % mpeg2dec) were achieved by the multiplier circuit.

### 6.2   Yield Optimization

Figure 8(a–b) compares the power reduction (%) of using a PV-aware gate sizing approach against one that does not. Each result compares the highest performance target (smallest delay), where both the PV-aware and non-PV-aware solution are able to satisfy. Average power savings of up to 64 % and 48 % were achieved for ISCAS-85 and ITC-99 benchmarks, respectively. We compare the highest comparable performance delay target since solutions obtained at lower performance delays require few circuit alterations, thus, achieve similar power results.

The complete sizing optimization procedure can be observed in Figs. 9 and 10 for ISCAS-85 and ITC-99 benchmarks, respectively. Two sizing solutions are

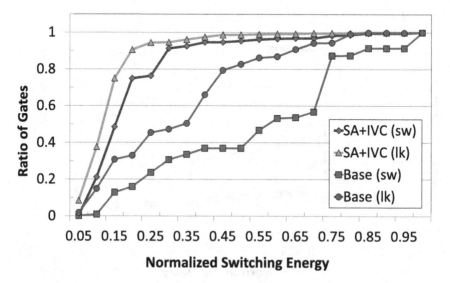

**Fig. 7.** Cumulative distribution of leakage and switching energy after sizing for gates in c2670. The accurate $SA+IVC$ approach results in a higher percentage of gates at lower energy.

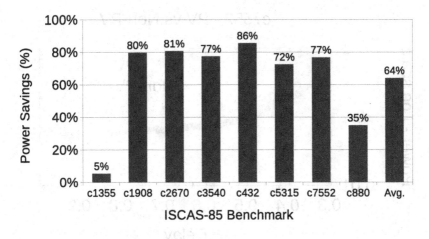

(a)

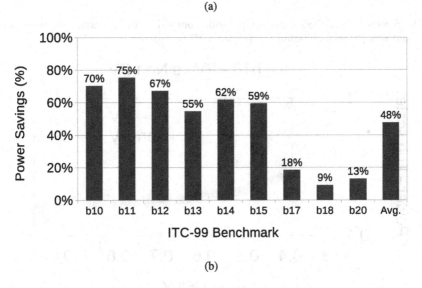

(b)

**Fig. 8.** Power savings (%) achieved when comparing generated sizing solutions using a process variation-aware over a non-process variation-aware gate sizing technique. Reported savings are generated from the minimum delay result achieved with respect to each approach.

compared for each benchmark: (1) PV-aware gate sizing (red circle); and (2) non-PV gate sizing (blue triangle). Each point corresponds to a sizing phase where up to $K$ cells are sized simultaneously. Therefore, for each circuit, the gate sizing procedure begins with all cells set to their minimal power configuration and is represented by the right-most point. The left-most point corresponds to the fastest achieved delay for each sizing procedure.

Significant savings were achieved in six out of the eight ISCAS-85 benchmarks since the enhanced PV-aware algorithm was able to avoid hitting a timing wall.

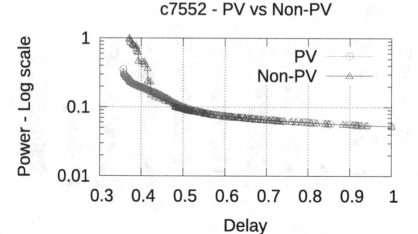

**Fig. 9.** Selected ISCAS-85 gate sizing result comparing the process variation-aware (PV) and non-process variation-aware (non-PV) techniques

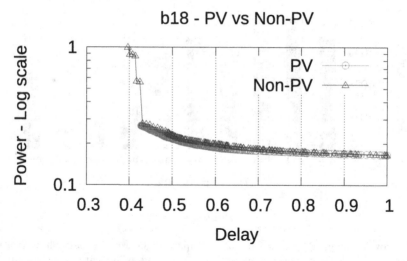

**Fig. 10.** Selected ITC-99 gate sizing result comparing the process variation-aware (PV) and non-process variation-aware (non-PV) techniques

The greatest savings were achieved from solutions where the non-PV sizing approach hit the timing wall earlier than the PV approach; however, this is not always the case as shown by one instance where the PV-aware sizing procedure achieved a lower performance delay target than its corresponding non-PV-aware approach as shown in Fig. 12(h), thus, high lighting the optimization uncertainty and room for potential improvement. It is also important to note that in circuit *c1355*, the target delays between 0.48 and 0.58 show solutions where the non-PV technique obtained superior results, which can be explained by speeding up a larger set of cells that belong in the $\varepsilon$-critical path early in the sizing effort, resulting with potentially more cells sized earlier than needed in order to achieve a lower performance target. However, sizing these $\varepsilon$-paths, enabled more efficient gate sizing, in terms of power-delay trade-offs, to be performed since the circuit was placed at a less-constrained sizing state, where each cell drives a smaller capacitive load, thus reducing the likelihood of getting stuck in a timing wall.

A timing wall scenario can be described where the cells that belong on the $\varepsilon$-critical paths are in such a state that increasing their size no longer improves circuit critical delay. Our experiments show that a gate sizing procedure that focus on the current critical path, result with over-optimizing a small set of critical paths, which in turn increases the convergence rate to an achievable target delay.

Tables 5 and 6 present yield results for selected ISCAS-85 and ITC-99 benchmarks. Yield results are acquired from computing the normalized delay and power values from 1000 PV-generated circuits for each benchmark. Timing and power values are reported for each benchmark from two obtained solutions in the previous gate sizing procedure. For fair comparison, each benchmark was optimized to meet an identical delay target. We report results obtained using two scenario optimization assumptions: (1) process variation-aware (PV), which uses the enhanced gate sizing algorithm presented in this Sect. 5.2; and (2) non-process variation-aware (nPV), which uses the standard gate-sizing algorithm presented in Sect. 5.1. The min, max, mean, standard deviation (std.), and variation values are presented for each benchmark. Variation is computed as $\frac{std.}{mean}$ and represents how much each yield result varies with respect to the mean. To summarize the results: ISCAS-85 benchmarks achieved a mean-power savings of 55 % (9 % min, 84 % max), whereas ITC-99 benchmarks achieved a mean-power savings of 25 % (2 % min, 74 % max).

Figures 11 and 12 present the cumulative distribution graphs for their respective delay (left-graph) and power (right-graph) yield results for selected benchmarks, as presented in Tables 5 and 6. As shown, the circuits optimized using the PV-aware approach achieved significant power yield improvements with respect to target delay yields. Note that although the obtained solutions were originally optimized to satisfy the same target delay under both PV and non-PV gate sizing techniques, their representative yields demonstrate that the PV-aware approach achieved significant yield improvements in both delay and power. For instance, circuit $c432$ achieved a normalized mean delay yield of 0.875 under the PV scenario compared to 0.920 for the non-PV scenario. Additionally, the delay variation factor of the PV scenario is 22 % less compared to the non-PV scenario. Collectively, the PV-aware solutions obtained lower variation factors in 14 out of the 19 studied benchmarks. Significant power reductions are also shown in the respective $c432$ power yield graphs, achieving an 84 % mean-power savings (0.125 PV vs. 0.818 nPV), demonstrating the effectiveness of combining cell characterization and the gradual gate sizing technique over our presented gate sizing technique. Overall, the PV-aware solutions also achieved reduced variation factors in 14 out of the 19 benchmarks.

**Table 5.** ISCAS-85: yield results comparing 1000 generated process variation instances from a base circuit utilizing a: (1) process variation-aware (PV); or (2) non-process variation-aware (nPV) technique

| Benchmark | Scenario | Metric | Min | Max | Mean | Std | Variation |
|-----------|----------|--------|-----|-----|------|-----|-----------|
| c1355 | PV | Delay | 0.853 | 0.983 | 0.900 | 0.022 | 0.956 |
|  | nPV |  | 0.862 | 1.000 | 0.919 | 0.023 | 1.000 |
|  | PV | Power | 0.738 | 0.946 | 0.829 | 0.029 | 1.000 |
|  | nPV |  | 0.827 | 1.000 | 0.913 | 0.027 | 0.850 |
| c1908 | PV | Delay | 0.869 | 0.980 | 0.914 | 0.017 | 0.943 |
|  | nPV |  | 0.887 | 1.000 | 0.939 | 0.018 | 1.000 |
|  | PV | Power | 0.368 | 0.457 | 0.406 | 0.016 | 0.980 |
|  | nPV |  | 0.818 | 1.000 | 0.895 | 0.036 | 1.000 |
| c2670 | PV | Delay | 0.870 | 0.994 | 0.915 | 0.018 | 1.000 |
|  | nPV |  | 0.872 | 1.000 | 0.913 | 0.016 | 0.901 |
|  | PV | Power | 0.195 | 0.233 | 0.211 | 0.007 | 0.830 |
|  | nPV |  | 0.801 | 1.000 | 0.881 | 0.034 | 1.000 |
| c3540 | PV | Delay | 0.877 | 0.966 | 0.921 | 0.014 | 0.974 |
|  | nPV |  | 0.899 | 1.000 | 0.939 | 0.015 | 1.000 |
|  | PV | Power | 0.385 | 0.504 | 0.441 | 0.019 | 1.000 |
|  | nPV |  | 0.825 | 1.000 | 0.916 | 0.033 | 0.869 |
| c432 | PV | Delay | 0.828 | 0.951 | 0.875 | 0.019 | 0.771 |
|  | nPV |  | 0.858 | 1.000 | 0.920 | 0.026 | 1.000 |
|  | PV | Power | 0.107 | 0.157 | 0.125 | 0.008 | 1.000 |
|  | nPV |  | 0.706 | 1.000 | 0.818 | 0.053 | 0.992 |
| c5315 | PV | Delay | 0.872 | 0.959 | 0.906 | 0.015 | 0.729 |
|  | nPV |  | 0.882 | 1.000 | 0.928 | 0.021 | 1.000 |
|  | PV | Power | 0.324 | 0.376 | 0.347 | 0.009 | 0.863 |
|  | nPV |  | 0.861 | 1.000 | 0.930 | 0.028 | 1.000 |
| c6288 | PV | Delay | 0.914 | 1.000 | 0.946 | 0.013 | 1.000 |
|  | nPV |  | 0.890 | 0.968 | 0.926 | 0.012 | 0.940 |
|  | PV | Power | 0.172 | 0.196 | 0.182 | 0.004 | 0.820 |
|  | nPV |  | 0.860 | 1.000 | 0.916 | 0.024 | 1.000 |
| c7552 | PV | Delay | 0.856 | 0.945 | 0.891 | 0.014 | 0.836 |
|  | nPV |  | 0.882 | 1.000 | 0.920 | 0.017 | 1.000 |
|  | PV | Power | 0.309 | 0.346 | 0.328 | 0.007 | 0.967 |
|  | nPV |  | 0.860 | 1.000 | 0.929 | 0.020 | 1.000 |
| c880 | PV | Delay | 0.822 | 0.954 | 0.872 | 0.021 | 0.875 |
|  | nPV |  | 0.833 | 1.000 | 0.891 | 0.025 | 1.000 |
|  | PV | Power | 0.640 | 0.828 | 0.724 | 0.037 | 0.828 |
|  | nPV |  | 0.746 | 1.000 | 0.841 | 0.051 | 1.000 |

**Table 6.** ITC-99: yield results comparing 1000 generated process variation instances from a base circuit utilizing a: (1) process variation-aware (PV); or (2) non-process variation-aware (nPV) technique

| Benchmark | Scenario | Metric | Min | Max | Mean | Std | Variation |
|---|---|---|---|---|---|---|---|
| b10 | PV | Delay | 0.720 | 0.900 | 0.789 | 0.029 | 0.885 |
| | nPV | | 0.727 | 1.000 | 0.809 | 0.034 | 1.000 |
| | PV | Power | 0.486 | 0.866 | 0.608 | 0.057 | 0.961 |
| | nPV | | 0.571 | 1.000 | 0.703 | 0.068 | 1.000 |
| b11 | PV | Delay | 0.748 | 0.912 | 0.806 | 0.024 | 0.620 |
| | nPV | | 0.759 | 1.000 | 0.849 | 0.041 | 1.000 |
| | PV | Power | 0.193 | 0.247 | 0.219 | 0.009 | 0.663 |
| | nPV | | 0.682 | 1.000 | 0.841 | 0.052 | 1.000 |
| b12 | PV | Delay | 0.749 | 0.946 | 0.815 | 0.035 | 1.000 |
| | nPV | | 0.775 | 1.000 | 0.834 | 0.029 | 0.802 |
| | PV | Power | 0.285 | 0.389 | 0.332 | 0.019 | 0.837 |
| | nPV | | 0.673 | 1.000 | 0.815 | 0.056 | 1.000 |
| b13 | PV | Delay | 0.707 | 0.885 | 0.772 | 0.026 | 0.683 |
| | nPV | | 0.760 | 1.000 | 0.846 | 0.042 | 1.000 |
| | PV | Power | 0.579 | 0.874 | 0.698 | 0.046 | 0.849 |
| | nPV | | 0.630 | 1.000 | 0.756 | 0.058 | 1.000 |
| b14 | PV | Delay | 0.816 | 0.925 | 0.847 | 0.016 | 0.974 |
| | nPV | | 0.885 | 1.000 | 0.928 | 0.018 | 1.000 |
| | PV | Power | 0.546 | 0.664 | 0.587 | 0.017 | 1.000 |
| | nPV | | 0.838 | 1.000 | 0.906 | 0.024 | 0.943 |
| b15 | PV | Delay | 0.833 | 0.926 | 0.866 | 0.014 | 0.888 |
| | nPV | | 0.893 | 1.000 | 0.938 | 0.017 | 1.000 |
| | PV | Power | 0.545 | 0.675 | 0.602 | 0.023 | 0.910 |
| | nPV | | 0.789 | 1.000 | 0.867 | 0.037 | 1.000 |
| b17 | PV | Delay | 0.896 | 0.984 | 0.929 | 0.013 | 1.000 |
| | nPV | | 0.912 | 1.000 | 0.943 | 0.013 | 0.993 |
| | PV | Power | 0.864 | 0.978 | 0.903 | 0.016 | 0.995 |
| | nPV | | 0.899 | 1.000 | 0.937 | 0.017 | 1.000 |
| b18 | PV | Delay | 0.873 | 0.946 | 0.897 | 0.010 | 0.841 |
| | nPV | | 0.919 | 1.000 | 0.949 | 0.013 | 1.000 |
| | PV | Power | 0.886 | 0.978 | 0.906 | 0.008 | 0.949 |
| | nPV | | 0.907 | 1.000 | 0.930 | 0.009 | 1.000 |
| b20 | PV | Delay | 0.814 | 0.901 | 0.845 | 0.015 | 0.665 |
| | nPV | | 0.857 | 1.000 | 0.912 | 0.024 | 1.000 |
| | PV | Power | 0.863 | 0.967 | 0.902 | 0.015 | 0.875 |
| | nPV | | 0.881 | 1.000 | 0.928 | 0.018 | 1.000 |

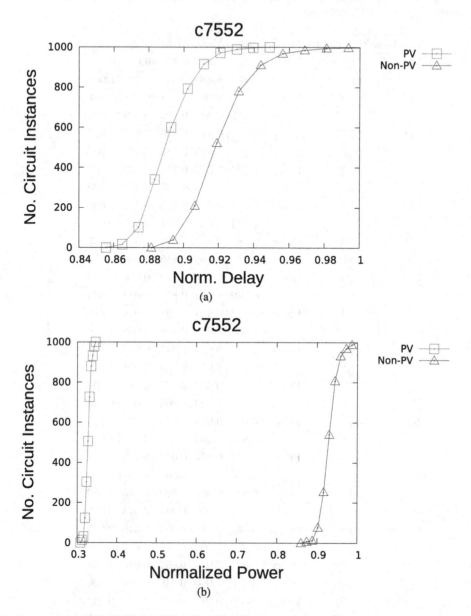

**Fig. 11.** Selected ISCAS-85 yield result comparing generated 1000 process varia-tion instances with respect to identical target delay using generated solution from: (a) process variation-aware (PV); and (2) non-process variation-aware (non-PV)

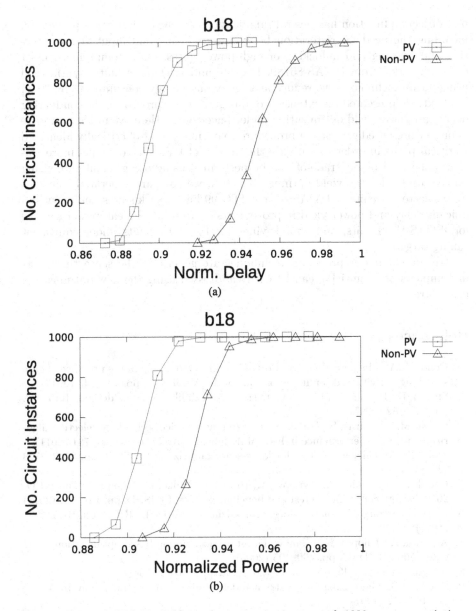

**Fig. 12.** Selected ITC-99 yield result comparing generated 1000 process variation instances with respect to identical target delay using generated solution from: (a) process variation-aware (PV); and (2) non-process variation-aware (non-PV)

## 7    Conclusion

We have presented a new gate sizing approach that includes the switching activity (SA) and input vector control (IVC) to minimize overall energy. First, the new objective function has several ramifications on the optimization procedure, including the need for reiteration between gate sizing and input vector selection and freezing and unlocking of high-power gates. On a comprehensive set of benchmarks, from ISCAS-85/89, ITC-99, and arithmetic units, synthesized using 45 nm technology, we reduce average actual energy consumption by 30 %.

Next, we presented an extension of our gate sizing procedure for conducting delay and power yield optimization under uncertainty. Here, we further improve upon our presented gate sizing procedure to optimize a set of critically identified $\varepsilon$-critical paths in order to mitigate the impact of PV, thus, enabling more efficient delay and power trade-offs to be performed using our gradual gate sizing procedure. Under the yield optimization task, we compare generated solutions from selected circuits in ISCAS-85 and ITC-99 benchmark suites and show significant delay and power yield improvements of up to 55 % mean-power savings for ISCAS-85 circuits, and 25 % savings for ITC-99 circuits under equivalent timing targets.

We note that our presented techniques are generic in the sense that thermal impacts and multi-$V_{th}$ can be easily addressed using the new optimization procedure.

# References

1. Conos, N.A., Meguerdichian, S., Potkonjak, M.: Gate sizing in the presence of gate switching activity and input vector control. In: VLSI-SoC, pp. 138–143 (2013)
2. Shiyan, H., Ketkar, M., Hu, J.: Gate sizing for cell library-based designs. In: DAC, pp. 847–852 (2007)
3. Ozdal, M.M., Burns, S., Hu, J.: Gate sizing and device technology selection algorithms for high-performance industrial designs. In: ICCAD, pp. 724–731 (2011)
4. Joshi, S.: An efficient method for large-scale gate sizing. In: TCSI, pp. 2760–2773 (2008)
5. Ozdal, M.M., Amin, C., Ayupov, A., Burns, S., Wilke, G., Zhuo, C.: The ISPD-2012 discrete cell sizing contest and benchmark suite. In: ISPD, pp. 161–164 (2012)
6. Li, W.N.: Strongly NP-hard discrete gate-sizing problems. In: ICCD, pp. 1045–1051 (1993)
7. Agarwal, A., Chopra, K., Blaauw, D.: Statistical timing based optimization using gate sizing. In: DAC, pp. 400–405 (2005)
8. Nangate FreePDK 45 nm Library (2011). http://www.si2.org/
9. Coudert, O.: Gate sizing for constrained delay/power/area optimization. In: VLSI, pp. 465–472 (1997)
10. Srivastava, A., Sylvester, D., Blaauw, D.: Power minimization using simultaneous gate sizing, dual-Vdd and dual-Vth assignment. In: DAC, pp. 783–787 (2004)
11. Huang, Y.-H., Chen, P.-Y., Hwang, T.: Switching-activity driven gate sizing and Vth assignment for low power design. In: ASPDAC, pp. 24–27 (2006)
12. Abdollahi, A., Fallah, F., Pedram, M.: Leakage current reduction in CMOS VLSI circuits by input vector control. In: VLSI, pp. 140–154 (2004)
13. Yuan, L., Qu, G.: A combined gate replacement and input vector control approach for leakage current reduction. In: VLSI, pp. 173–182 (2006)

14. Lee, C., Potkonjak, M., Mangione-Smith, W.H.: MediaBench: a tool for evaluating and synthesizing multimedia and communicatons systems. In: MICRO, pp. 330–335 (1997)

15. Mudge T.: The SimpleScalar-Arm power modeling project. http://eecs.umich.edu/panalyzer/

16. Tsui, C., Au, R.Y., Choi, R.Y.: Minimizing the dynamic and subthreshold leakage power consumption using least leakage vector assisted technology mapping. In: VLSI Journal, pp. 76–86 (2008)

17. Li, L., Kang, P., Lu, Y., Zhou, H.: An efficient algorithm for library-based cell-type selection in high-performance low-power designs. In: ICCAD, pp. 226–232 (2012)

18. Hu, J., Kahng, A.B., Kang, S.H., Kim, M.-C., Markov, I.L.: Sensitivity-guided metaheuristics for accurate discrete gate sizing. In: ICCAD, pp. 233–239 (2012)

19. Asenov, A.: Random dopant induced threshold voltage lowering and fluctuations in sub-0.1 um MOSFET's: a 3-D atomistic simulation study. In: IEEE T-ED, pp. 2505–2513 (1998)

# New Scan-Based Attack Using Only the Test Mode and an Input Corruption Countermeasure

Sk Subidh Ali[1]([✉]), Samah Mohamed Saeed[2], Ozgur Sinanoglu[1], and Ramesh Karri[2]

[1] New York University Abu Dhabi, New York, USA
{sa112,os22}@nyu.edu
[2] New York University Polytechnic School of Engineering, New York, USA
{sms22,rkarri}@nyu.edu

**Abstract.** Scan-based design-for-testability, which improves access and thus the test quality, is highly vulnerable to scan attack. While in-field test is enabled through the scan design to provide debug capabilities, an attacker can leverage the test mode to leak the secret key of the chip. The scan attack can be thwarted by a simple defense that resets the data upon a switch from the normal mode to the test mode. We proposed a new class of scan attack in [15] using only the test mode of a chip, circumventing this defense. In this book chapter we extend our earlier work by introducing case studies to explain this new attack in greater detail. Furthermore, we study the effectiveness of existing countermeasures to thwart the attack and propose a new input corruption countermeasure that requires a smaller area overhead compared to the existing countermeasures.

**Keywords:** AES · Scan chain · Scan attack · Scan-based dft · Testability · Security

## 1 Introduction

Scan-based design-for-testability (DFT) technique is widely used, which provides internal access to the circuit in order to enhance the testability of manufacturing defects. To provide debug capabilities, in-field test is enabled, by retaining scan capabilities. However, the scan design can be misused by an attacker to leak secret information of a crypto-chip. The intermediate results of a crypto-chip can be shifted out during the test mode through the scan interface. This attack is known as a *scan-based side-channel attack*, and was reported first in [1], which targets Data Encryption Standard (DES) chip. The attacker applies the plaintext in the normal mode after which he/she switches to the test mode to observe the intermediate result of the DES chip. With this information in hand, the attacker can retrieve the secret key by applying differential analysis on the response patterns. Scan-based side-channel attack can also reveal the 128-bit secret key of Advanced Encryption Standard (AES) chip even in the presence of advanced DFT techniques such as partial scan [3], X-masking [4], and

© IFIP International Federation for Information Processing 2015
A. Orailoglu et al. (Eds.): VLSI-SoC 2013, IFIP AICT 461, pp. 48–68, 2015.
DOI: 10.1007/978-3-319-23799-2_3

X-tolerant architecture [5,6]. Other ciphers such as RSA [7,8], ECC [9,10], and stream ciphers [11], are also vulnerable to scan attack.

The existing scan-based attacks switch the chip between the normal mode and the test mode and assume that the content of the scan cells is retained intact. A mode-reset countermeasure [12] thwarts these attacks by resetting the scan cells upon switching from the normal mode to the test mode.

We proposed a new scan-based attack on AES using only the test mode to circumvent the mode-reset countermeasure [15]. The attack showed how to overcome the challenges introduced by the mode-reset countermeasure and to leak the secret key of a AES crypto core. In this book chapter we explain the attack in greater detail with case studies. We also discuss some of the existing countermeasures and their effectiveness against our test-mode-only attack. We also propose a novel cost-effective input corruption countermeasure, crafted to thwart our test-mode-only scan attack.

The remainder of the paper is organized as follows. Section 2 provides background on AES and DfT. Section 3 provides motivations and challenges of the test-mode-only attack. Section 4 describes the proposed test-mode-only attack. Section 5 gives an overview of the existing countermeasures against scan attacks while Sect. 6 provides a new countermeasure to thwart the test-mode-only attacks. Finally, we conclude the paper and elaborate on our future work in Sect. 7.

## 2 Preliminaries

### 2.1 AES

AES is a 128-bit symmetric key block cipher available in three different key lengths: 128, 192 and 256 bits. The entire AES algorithm is divided into several identical round operations. The number of rounds in the three different versions of AES are 10 (128-bit key), 12 (192-bit key) and 14 (256-bit key) respectively. Each round comprises of following four basic transformations,

- SubBytes is a non-linear substitution operation.
- ShiftRows is the byte-wise permutation.
- MixColumns is the four-byte mixing operation.
- AddRoundKeys is the XORing the state with the round key.

We will refer to these operations as $SB$, $SR$, $MC$ and $ARK$ respectively. Figure 1 shows the structure of first round of AES which contains an extra key XORing at the beginning.

Each transformation of AES round has specific properties. We use the following properties in our attack.

### 2.2 Differential Properties of AES

In S-box, for an input $X$ and the input difference $\alpha$, the output difference $\beta$ is represented as

$$\beta = SB(X \oplus \alpha) \oplus SB(X) \tag{1}$$

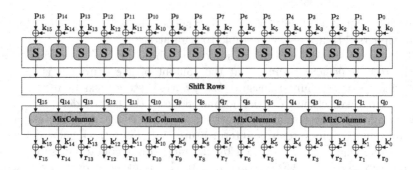

**Fig. 1.** First round of AES: $p_i$ is the plaintext byte, $k_i$ is the initial key byte, $q_i$ is the $SR$ output byte, $k_i'$ is the round key byte, and $r_i$ is the round output byte.

For a given value of $(\alpha, \beta)$, there could be two, four or no solution of $X$ [13]. In case of two solutions, if one solution is $\delta$, the other solution will always be $\delta \oplus \alpha$. On the other hand for four solutions, the solutions will be $\delta$, $\delta \oplus \alpha$, 0 and $\alpha$.

**Lemma 1.** *For a given input $X$ and two one-bit differences $e_i$ and $e_j$ (where $e_i$ and $e_j$ are eight bit strings with a 1 in position $i$ and $j$ respectively where $i \neq j$), the output differences $d_i$ and $d_j$ are generated as*

$$d_i = SB(X) \oplus SB(X \oplus e_i)$$
$$d_j = SB(X \oplus e_j) \oplus SB(X \oplus e_j \oplus e_i) \qquad (2)$$

*For any value $X$, $d_i$ can not be the same as $d_j$.*

*Proof.* We prove this by contradiction. Let as assume that there is a value $x$ of $X$ for which $d_i = d_j$. We also have $y = x \oplus e_j$. Therefore, we have two equations:

$$d_i = SB(x) \oplus SB(x \oplus e_i)$$
$$d_j = SB(y) \oplus SB(y \oplus e_i), \qquad (3)$$

where $d_i = d_j$ implies $x$ and $y$ are the two solutions of (1) where $\beta = d_i = d_j$ and $\alpha = e_i$. If $x$ and $y$ are the two solutions of the equation, then either $y = x \oplus e_i$ or one of these two values must be zero and the other equals $e_i$. If we consider the first case then $y = x \oplus e_i \Rightarrow x \oplus e_j = x \oplus e_i \Rightarrow e_j = e_i$ which contradicts our assumption. Let us consider the second case, $x = 0$ and $y = e_i$ which implies $y = x \oplus e_j = e_i \Rightarrow e_j = e_i$. Again this contradicts our assumption. Therefore, $d_i$ and $d_j$ can not be the same under the given condition.

### 2.3  DFT Structure

Scan design is a well-known DFT technique that provides direct access to flip-flops. Scan design converts each flip-flop into a fully accessible scan cell that can be controlled and observed easily through shift operations. Due to the limited number of tester channels, especially for integrated circuits with a large

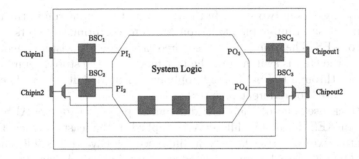

**Fig. 2.** DFT structure for a design with two scan chains; TDI/TDO pins not shown

number of input/output pins, boundary scan design [14] is used, which associates a boundary scan cell to each primary input/output of the circuit (BSC in Fig. 2). Boundary scan design enables a cost-effective few-pin access to the primary inputs/outputs in the test mode. On one hand, in the normal mode, the input pins directly drive the primary inputs (PIs) of the chip, while the primary outputs (POs) drive the output pins. On the other hand, in the test mode, the boundary scan cells break the connection between the chip pins and the primary input/outputs. The test mode consists of shift and capture operations. During shift operations, the test vectors are serially shifted into the scan chains through the chip input pins, while test responses can be observed through the chip output pins. During the capture operation, the scan cells capture the response of the combinational logic, while the boundary scan cells drive the PIs and capture the POs. As a result, there is no direct path from the chip inputs to the primary inputs in the test mode.

## 3    Motivation and Challenges

In this section we review the existing state-of-the-art scan attack on AES and discuss its limitations. Subsequently, we elaborate on how to overcome these limitations and propose a new scan attack on AES: test-mode-only scan attack.

### 3.1    State-of-the-Art Scan Attack

The state-of-the-art scan attack requires switching between the normal and test modes. Figure 3 shows the AES core with a single scan chain which consists of AES round register flip-flops (SC in the figure). In the normal mode, a plaintext is applied to the AES core through the primary input and the results are stored in the round register. The round register content is again applied to the AES in the next round operation. The round operation is highlighted green in Fig. 3. After completion of ten rounds the ciphertext output is generated at the primary outputs. In the test mode, the flip-flops of the round register are connected into a scan chain. During the shift cycle a test vector is shifted to the scan chain, while in the capture cycle the response of the AES core is captured and shifted out through the SO line.

The attack works in two steps. In the first step, the chip is run in the normal mode with a desired input plaintext applied from the primary inputs for only one round of AES. The round output is stored in the round register. Then, in the second step, the chip is switched to the test mode and the stored round output is shifted out through the SO line by applying repeated shift cycles. These two steps are repeated for different plaintexts.

The attack uses one of the basic differential properties of the AES round operation. In AES, if one-bit difference is applied in the least significant bit of any one of the sixteen bytes, the output difference can have 18 possible hamming distances. Out of these hamming distances, only four can be generated by a unique pair of S-box inputs. Therefore, the attacker should follow the above two steps for all possible $2^7$ pairs of plaintexts, in order to get any such hamming distance. Once the hamming distance is observed, the corresponding key byte is retrieved by XORing the plaintext byte with the corresponding unique pair of S-box inputs. Therefore, each unique pair will produce two possible key bytes. The same procedure is repeated for all the sixteen key bytes. Finally, by applying $2^7 \cdot 16 = 2^{11}$ plaintext pairs, the search space of the AES key is reduced to $2^{16}$. These $2^{16}$ key hypotheses can be brute-forced by using the plaintext-ciphertext pairs in negligible time.

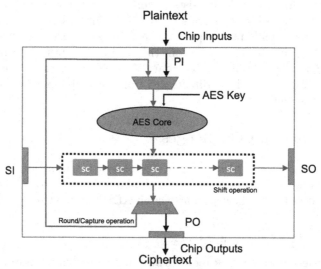

**Fig. 3.** AES Core with a single scan chain; SC represents the flip-flop/scan cell of the round register (Color figure online).

## 3.2   Limitations of the Existing Scan Attacks

One fundamental limitation of this kind of attacks is that they require switching from the normal mode to the test mode under the assumption that the data in the scan cells can be preserved intact during the switch. One simple countermeasure is resetting the device whenever there is a switch from the normal mode to the test mode. In this case, the attacker can perform the first step of the attack and the round output will be stored in the round register. However, whenever the second step of the attack is applied i.e., switching to the test mode, the content of the SCs will reset. Hence, the second step will only produce the zero response of the AES core. Therefore, any scan attack that requires switching between the normal and test modes is bound to fail against this simple countermeasure.

### 3.3 Overcoming the Limitations of Existing Scan Attacks

In order to overcome the limitations of the above attack, the attacker must come up with an attack that will only use the test mode. As there is no switching required from the normal mode to the test mode, the aforementioned mode-reset countermeasure will be circumvented. The attacker is then constrained to use only the operations highlighted in blue and green in Fig. 3.

The major challenge associated with such an attack is to apply the desired input plaintext to AES. As explained in Sect. 2.3, the primary inputs are not directly accessible in the test mode. The inputs should rather be applied by shifting them in as test vectors through SI line. However, the problem is that the attacker does not know which scan cell drives which input of AES. The physical placement tools determine the mapping between scan cells and the AES inputs.

We need to leverage some of the basic differential properties of AES to (1) find out the exact order of the scan cells which correspond to the AES input register, and (2) launch the attack and leak out the secret key.

## 4    Test-Mode-Only Attack on AES

In this section we explain our test-mode-only attack on AES [15]. In this attack, the plaintexts are applied in the form of test vectors. Before going into the detail of the attack we first define the attackers ability in the form of the resources and information he/she has. As in the conventional scan attack, we assume that the attacker knows the AES algorithm running inside the security chip and the in-field debug of the chip is enabled. For the sake of simplicity, we assume that there are only 128 scan cells in the design, which correspond to the 128-bit round register.

Let us first consider one example of AES operation. Figure 4 shows the results corresponding to each step of the AES first round, and finally the corresponding round-output difference. $P$ and $P_{120}$ are the two plaintexts (120 is the bit position of 1 from the right), while $K_0$ and $K_1$ are the first and the second round keys, respectively. It may be noted that $K_0$ is the whitening key, which is also the 128-bit AES key. The goal of the attacker is to retrieve $K_0$. The values in the figure are represented in 32-digit hexadecimal format.

In test-mode-only attack, the major challenge to the attacker is to figure out which scan cell corresponds to which input bit of AES. For $P$, the test vector is same as the plaintext. However, in order to apply $P_{120}$, the attacker should precisely know which scan cell corresponds to the 120-th input bit of

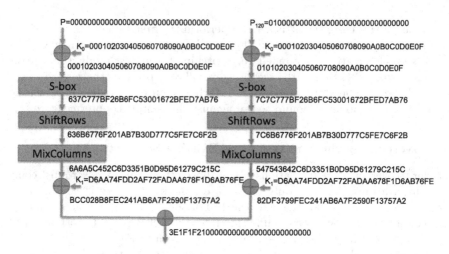

**Fig. 4.** Example input-outputs of each transformation of first round of AES

AES. Therefore, to attack AES using only the test mode the attacker has to determine the mapping between the scan cells and the AES inputs. The mapping is determined by the physical placement tool and it is considered as almost random. We determine the mapping in three steps. In the first step, we determine the scan cells corresponding to the AES words. The second step determines the scan cells corresponding to the AES bytes. In the third step, the order of the bytes in a word is determined. Finally, we determine the order of the scan cells in a byte, and identify the corresponding key. Once we have the key bytes, we combine them as per the assumed order, and deduce the possible key hypotheses. In the next subsection, we explain the first step.

### 4.1 Determining the Mapping Between Scan Cells and AES Input Words

Similar to Fig. 4, we use two types of test vectors. One with all zero bits $(P)$ and the other $(P_i)$ with only one bit set to one ($i$-th bit where $0 \leq i \leq 127$) and the rest of the bits set to zero. At first, the test vector $P$ is shifted in and the response $R$ is captured and shifted out. It may be noted that $R$ is the jumbled up value of the round output $BCC028B8FEC241AB6A7F2590F13757A2$.

Next, in each step a test vector $P_i$ is shifted in and the corresponding response $R_i$ is captured and shifted out. The difference $D_i = R \oplus R_i$ will pinpoint the positions where the bits are flipped. In our example, $P_0$ and $P_{120}$ differ in the 120-th bit. For this input pair, we apply a one-bit difference to the leftmost input byte. The figure shows that the output difference (0x3e1f1f21) confines within only the leftmost four bytes of the same word. The one-bit input difference affects only one output word. Therefore, two such input differences in the same input word will affect the same output word. We use this property of AES to partition the scan cells into AES input words.

Say, $D_i^j$ is the $j$-th bit of $D_i$ and $FD_i = \{j|\ D_i^j = 1\}$. So, $FD_i$ is the set of output bit-flip positions corresponding to input bit-flip at $i$. In 128 iterations, 128 different sets of output bit-flip positions ($FD = \{FD_i|0 \le i \le 128\}$) are generated. These 128 sets are combined into four sets by considering the common bit-flip positions in the sets.

Algorithm 1 describes the detailed procedure, where $Enc()$ is the AES round function. The first loop determines the 128 sets $FD_0 \ldots FD_{127}$. In the second loop, in each iteration, a set $FD_x$ is chosen from $FD$, and compared with the rest of the sets for common output bit-flip positions. If a common bit-flip position is found in any set ($FD_y$), both sets are combined into one set ($FD_x$) and the new set ($FD_y$) is deleted from $FD$. Therefore, at the end of the iteration, $FD_x$ will have all the output bit-flip positions, which correspond to a particular word. These bit-flip positions, which represent the positions of the scan cells, are saved in $W_i$. Hence, four iterations of the second loop will partition the 128 scan cells into four words $W_0 \ldots W_3$, which correspond to four different $MC$ operations of AES.

---

**Algorithm 1.** Determining the bits in the words

---

**Input**: $P$ and $P_i$ where $0 \le i \le 127$
**Output**: $W_0, W_1, W_2, W_3$

$R = Enc(P)$
**for** $i = 0$ *to* 127 **do**
    $R_i = Enc(P_i);\ D_i = R \oplus R_i$
    **for** $j = 0$ *to* 127 **do**
        **if** $D_i^j = 1$ **then**
            $FD_i = FD_i \cup j$
        **end**
    **end**
    $FD = FD \cup FD_i$
**end**
**for** $i = 0$ *to* 3 **do**
    Select any element $FD_x$ from $FD$
    $FD = FD - FD_x$
    **for** *Each element $FD_y$ in $FD$* **do**
        **if** $FD_x \cap FD_y \ne \emptyset$ **then**
            $FD_x = FD_x \cup FD_y;\ FD = FD - FD_y$
        **end**
    **end**
    $W_i = FD_x$
**end**

---

## 4.2 Determining the Mapping Between Scan Cells and AES Input Bytes

In order to determine the mapping between scan sells and AES input bytes we use Lemma 1. Similar to previous step, we create four test vectors: $P$, $P_i$, $P_j$ and $P_{ij}$. We already have the response for the base plaintext $P$. Now we choose any two bit positions, say $i$ and $j$, where $i \neq j$. We then create $P_i$ and $P_j$. Say the byte corresponding to bit $i$ is $B_l$, where $0 \leq l \leq 15$. We get the response $R_i = Enc(P_i)$ corresponding to $P_i$. Therefore, the difference is $D_i = R \oplus R_i$. It may be noted that any non-zero value in $D_i$ is due to the input difference in byte $B_l$ from the plaintext pair $(P, P_i)$. In the rest of the 15 bytes, both plaintexts have the same values.

Next, we create $P_j$ and $P_{ij}$, where $P_{ij}$ is the same as $P_j$ except in the $i$-th bit, which is also 1; $P_{ij}$ has only two ones in positions $i$ and $j$. It may be noted that the $j$-th bit may be in the same byte as the $i$-th bit or in a different byte. We get the response $R_j = Enc(P_j)$ and $R_{ij} = Enc(P_{ij})$ corresponding to plaintexts $P_j$ and $P_{ij}$ respectively. Therefore, we have another difference $D_j = R_j \oplus R_{ij}$. Still, this difference is due to the input difference in byte $B_l$ generated from the plaintext pair $(P_j, P_{ij})$.

Now there are two possibilities: the $j$-th and the $i$-th bits are either in different bytes, or in the same byte $B_l$. Let us consider the first case; the input difference in byte $B_l$ is only due to the flip in the $i$-th bit which is the same for both plaintext pairs $(P, P_i)$ and $(P_j, P_{ij})$. Therefore, the differences $D_i$ and $D_j$ corresponding to the two plaintext pairs will be the same. On the other hand if the $i$-th and $j$-th bits are both in $B_l$, then we have the same input difference corresponding to bit $i$, but in addition to other differences as well. Therefore, as per Lemma 1, this should result in different output differences; the $MC$ operation is linear. Therefore, $D_i$ and $D_j$ will be different in the second case.

For example in Fig. 5, the two plaintext pairs $(P, P_{124})$ and $(P_{120}, P_{124,120})$ have two bit-flips with respect to $P$; one in the 124-th bit and the other one in the 120-th bit. It may be noted that both bit-flips are in the same byte. Therefore, we have two different input pairs with the same input differences (in bit

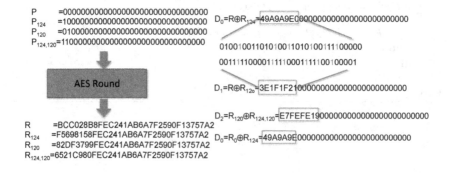

**Fig. 5.** Four inputs and the corresponding one round outputs, and the differences

position 124). Hence, the output difference should always be different. As shown in the figure, the output differences $D_0$ and $D_2$ are unequal. If the second bit-flip (120-th) were in a different byte, say in the 100-th bit, the corresponding output differences would be the same. Therefore, by comparing the output differences we can determine whether the two input bit-flips are in the same byte. This way by flipping bits in input pairs we can partition the bits into the AES bytes.

So one can determine whether two different bits are in the same byte by just observing the output differences $D_i$ and $D_j$, and checking whether they are different. In order to determine the same for all the bytes, we follow Algorithm 2. It takes the set of bits $W$ corresponding to a word, which is generated in the previous step, and partitions the bits into four bytes $B_0 \ldots B_3$. The outer loop selects a bit from $W$ and passes it to the inner loop. The inner loop finds all the bits, which lie in the byte that corresponds to the given bit. The four iterations of the outer loop determine the four bytes $B_0 \ldots B_3$. In order to reduce the number of test vectors, we can use a single pair of test vectors to identify the differences in all the four words in one shot. As the four $MC$ operations of AES in a round are independently calculated, we can apply the above technique to determine the bytes in all the four words simultaneously by flipping bits in four words of the input plaintexts. Therefore, the number of input test vectors will reduce by four.

---

**Algorithm 2.** Determining the bits in the bytes

---

**Input:** $W$
**Output:** $B_0, B_1, B_2, B_3$

for $l = 0$ to $3$ do
    $B_l = \emptyset; W_t = \emptyset$
    Select $i$ where $i \in W$
    $B_l = B_l \cup i$ ; $W = W - i$; $P_i = P \oplus (\texttt{0x1} \ll i)$
    $R_i = Enc(P_i); R = Enc(P); D_i = R \oplus R_i$
    for $Each$ $j \in W$ do
        $W = W - j$
        $P_j = P \oplus (\texttt{0x1} \ll j); P_{ij} = P_j \oplus (\texttt{0x1} \ll i)$
        $R_j = Enc(P_j); R_{ij} = Enc(P_{ij}); D_j = R_j \oplus R_{ij}$
        if $D_i \neq D_j$ then
            $B_i = B_i \cup j$
        end
        else
            $W_t = W_t \cup j$
        end
    end
    $W = W_t; W_t = \emptyset$
end

---

**Note.** It may be noted that there could be more than 128 registers in the AES design. However, these extra registers can be identified by considering their effects on the AES round output. If the registers are not part of the round operation (e.g. AES controller registers), they will not affect the round output. If they are part of the round operation, their effect on the output will reveal their position in the round operation. Once identified, the extra registers can be discarded in the attack.

### 4.3   Determining the Order of Bytes in a Word

In this section, we try to determine the position of each byte in the words. In order to do that, we use the properties of the AES $MC$ operation. Figure 6(a) shows the basic operation of AES $MC$ in terms of a matrix multiplication operation. As illustrated in Fig. 6(b), if there is a non-zero value $a$ in only one of the four input bytes, the output bytes will have values $(a, a, 2a, 3a)$.

We analyze the hamming distance to determine the order of the bytes. As per the AES $MC$ operation, two of the four output bytes will always have the same hamming distance (two output bytes with values $a$).

We apply two plaintexts ($P$ and $P'$) in a way that only one input byte of the $MC$ operation gets a non-zero difference and the rest of the three bytes all get zero differences. Say we have scan cells corresponding to the four bytes $B_0, B_1, B_2, B_3$ of a word. We need to find the actual order of these bytes corresponding to $MC$, i.e., to $a_0 \ldots a_3$ in Fig. 6(a). If the input difference value $a$ is applied in $B_0$, the output difference value $2a$ should be loaded in this byte. We need to determine which two bytes will have the same hamming distance. However, for some value of $a$, the rest of the three bytes (other than the byte $B_0$) may have the same hamming distance.

We experimentally observed that in 52 out of the 255 different values of $a$, more than two bytes will have the same hamming distance. We need to try at least 53 different values of $a$ to exactly know the two bytes that correspond to the output differences $a$ and $a$ respectively. Say, $B_2$ and $B_3$ are the two bytes. Then we also determine that $B_1$ corresponds to the output difference $3a$.

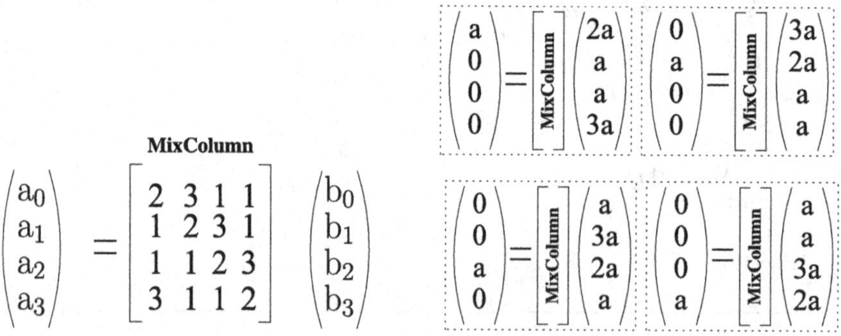

(a) AES MC operation          (b) Byte difference distribution in MC

**Fig. 6.** AES Mixcolumns operation and its differential properties

However, as $B_2$ and $B_3$ have the same value, we can't directly identify the order of these two bytes. In order to determine their order, we next apply the input difference to the byte $B_1$. Then $B_0$ corresponds to output difference $a$, and either $B_2$ corresponds to $a$ and $B_3$ corresponds to $3a$ or vice versa. In the first case, the exact order of the four bytes is identified to be $(B_0, B_2, B_3, B_1)$, which corresponds to the first of the four cases presented in Fig. 6(b). We can have three more possible permutations, which are the circular rotations of this permutation. The procedure is repeated for the rest of the three words. It may be noted that instead of applying difference in one byte at a time, we can apply the byte difference in four words corresponding to four different $MC$ operations, which will help determine the order of the bytes in the four words simultaneously.

So, given the four bytes in a word, we can tell the four possible permutations as per the AES input.

### 4.4   Determining the Order of Bits in a Byte

At this point, we do not know which scan cell corresponds to which bit of a given byte although we know the order of the bytes. If we apply the existing attack [5] by varying the input pairs in order to get a particular hamming weight, we will uniquely determine the key byte. In our case we don't know the exact value of the input plaintext as we do not know the order of the bits in a byte. Therefore, the key byte which we determined is corresponding to the assumed order of the scan cells in the bytes. Eight scan cells corresponding to a byte can be arranged in $\frac{8!}{4! \cdot 4!} = 70$ (consider the average case where half of the bits are one and rest are zero) ways. Therefore, in average each byte can have 70 possible values. If we combine all the sixteen bytes we get $(10)^{16}$ values, which is a large number. Therefore, we must determine the order of the scan cells.

We develop a new technique to determine the key despite the unknown order of the scan cells in the byte. In this scheme, instead of considering the difference in any particular bit, we consider eight different differences, each corresponding to a one-bit difference in one of the eight input bits. As all the bits are considered, the output signature is irrespective of the order of the bits. In order to do that, we choose an input plaintext $P$ with all zero bits. Therefore, the chosen byte will have the value $B = 00000000$. Then we produce eight different plaintexts $P_0$ to $P_7$ by varying the bit-flip position 0 to 7.

Let us consider the chosen byte is the first byte. Then the first bytes of the eight plaintexts are $0 \times 01$, $0 \times 02$, $0 \times 04$, $0 \times 08$, $0 \times 10$, $0 \times 20$, $0 \times 40$, and $0 \times 80$. It may be noted that in these eight values, the bit-flip position varies from the right-most bit to the leftmost bit. Each of these eight plaintexts is paired with $P$. We compute the output difference $D_i$ ( $0 \le i \le 7$) of each pair and get the hamming distance. From $D_i$ we get the hamming distance of the four bytes. Two of these bytes will have the same hamming distance as shown in Fig. 6(b). So, we consider only one of these two.

We maintain a signature table where, for each value of $K$, we have eight the three-byte hamming distances corresponding to eight input differences. The values are shown in Table 1. The data in the table shows that the last eight

**Table 1.** Signature table

| K | $B_0$ | $B_1$ | $B_2$ | $B_3$ | $B_4$ | $B_5$ | $B_6$ | $B_7$ |
|---|---|---|---|---|---|---|---|---|
| 0 | 525 | 224 | 334 | 446 | 334 | 455 | 446 | 455 |
| 1 | 525 | 233 | 444 | 466 | 367 | 233 | 358 | 233 |
| 2 | 222 | 224 | 222 | 112 | 556 | 455 | 556 | 334 |
| 3 | 222 | 233 | 556 | 224 | 222 | 556 | 334 | 345 |
| 4 | 334 | 255 | 334 | 222 | 112 | 345 | 145 | 255 |
| $\vdots$ | $\vdots$ | $\vdots$ | $\vdots$ | $\vdots$ | $\vdots$ | $\vdots$ | $\vdots$ | $\vdots$ |
| 255 | 255 | 224 | 334 | 266 | 134 | 233 | 244 | 345 |

columns uniquely determine the row. Therefore, given eight hamming distances corresponding to eight input differences, one can uniquely determine the value of $K$, which is the key byte itself. It may be noted that we have sixteen tables corresponding to sixteen S-boxes of AES. We need to search the eight hamming distances in all the sixteen tables.

Algorithm 3 shows the detail technique of determining the value of the key byte and the order of the bits in a byte. The attacker get the output differences corresponding to eight pair of plaintexts. She then determines the four output bytes which have got the non-zero output differences. The function $Trim()$ determines four none-zero bytes and reduce them to three after removing the duplicate one. $HD$ will have eight hamming distances correspond to eight input differences. These eight value are searched in the rows of Table 1. When a row matches, the value of $K$ corresponding to that row is the value of the key byte. The position of the bit is determined by the column index of the hamming weight corresponding to the bit. The position of the $i$-th bit is the index of the column of $HD_i$ in the row $K$.

---

**Algorithm 3.** Determining the key byte and the order of the bits in a byte

---

**Input**: $P$ and $P_i$ where $0 \leq i \leq 7$
**Output**: Key and order of the bits

$HD = \emptyset$ $R = Enc(P)$ **for** $i = 0$ *to* 7 **do**
    $R_i = Enc(P_i)$
    $D_i = R \oplus R_i$
    $HD_i = Trim(D_i)$
    /*Getting three bytes*/ $HD = HD \cup HD_i$
**end**
**for** $K = 0$ *to* 255 **do**
    Search $HD$ in row $K$ of Table 1
    **if** *All elements of $HD$ is found in row $K$* **then**
        Key=K
        Order of the bit is the column index of the element of $HD$
    **end**
**end**

---

### 4.5 Determining the AES Key

In the previous section, we determine the order of the scan cells in a byte as well as the key corresponding to the byte. Now we have to determine the order of bytes in a word (Sect. 4.3). We have four possible permutations of the four bytes in a word. Therefore, if we know the position of the four words, then there will be $4^4 = 2^8$ possible values of the key. However, we don't know the order of the four words, which can be arranged in $4! = 24$ ways. The total possible hypotheses of the AES key is $24 \cdot 256 = 6144 = 2^{12.58}$. As we know the plaintext and the ciphertext, we can brute-force the key hypotheses in negligible time.

### 4.6 Attack Complexity Analysis

In the first step of the attack (Sect. 4.1), we need $128 + 1 = 129$ test vectors to partition scan cells into the AES words. In determining the bytes in a word in the second step (Sect. 4.2), we need $(1 + 31 \cdot 2) + (1 + 23 \cdot 2) + (1 + 15 * 2) = 141$ test vectors. For getting the order of the bytes in a word in the third step (Sect. 4.3), we used $52 \cdot 2 = 104$ test vectors. In the fourth step (Sect. 4.4), where we determine the order of the bits in bytes, we don't need any extra test vectors, because the required test vectors are already available from the first step. Therefore, in total we need $129 + 141 + 104 = 375$ test vectors to determine the secret key.

Regarding the time complexity, it can be observed that most of the execution time is spent on partitioning the scan cells corresponding to bytes and in determining the order of bits in a byte. For the first part, the time complexity is $31 + 15 + 7 = 53$. In the second part the time complexity is $256 \cdot 8 = 2^{11}$. However, the final key hypotheses is around $2^{12.58}$, which need to be brute-forced to get the master key. Therefore, the time complexity of the complete attack is $2^{12.58}$.

## 5 Existing Countermeasures

So far we have shown that the mode-reset countermeasure, which provides protection against all the existing attacks, fails against the proposed test-mode-only attack. In this section we discuss some of the other existing countermeasures and their level of effectiveness against our proposed test-mode-only attack. Our goal is to devise a countermeasure for our attack.

### 5.1 Insertion of Inverters in the Scan Path

In this technique the scan chain is divided into multiple subchains in the form of a scan tree [16]. The subchains are placed in a random order so that it will be difficult for the attacker to figure out the exact round output. Some of the scan cell values are flipped by placing inverters selectively on the scan paths (Fig. 7). The location of the inverters is known only to the designer or the tester.

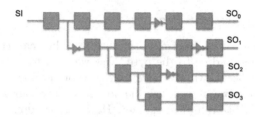

**Fig. 7.** Insertion of inverters in the scan path

Therefore, only the designer or the tester can retrieve the exact response of the chip, while the attacker can only observe the modified response of the chip.

In the differential scan attack, such countermeasures will fail, as the effect of the inverters will be cancelled out in the output difference. Therefore, the proposed test-mode-only attack can easily overcome this countermeasure through the differential analysis it employs. In the same way, our proposed scan attack can thwart the scan scrambling technique proposed in [17].

## 5.2   Masking

There are two masking countermeasures proposed in [6]. The first method masks the 128-bit round register and then unmasks it for the subsequent round operation. The mask value is generated by using an input and a key of size 128-bit (Fig. 8). During the normal operation, the masking remains transparent. In the capture operation during the test mode, the scan chain captures the masked response of the circuit. Only the tester and the designer have the knowledge about the mask value. Therefore, they can unmask the scan output and retrieve the actual response of the circuit. On the other hand, the attacker will be unable to retrieve the actual response, hence failing to apply the differential analysis to reveal the secret key. Thus the attack will fail. The drawback of this countermeasure is not only the area overhead, but also the prolongation of the critical path, and thus the performance degradation.

To overcome the critical path issue, a second masking technique is proposed, which modifies the response compactor output (Fig. 9). This technique is based on an enhanced Linear Feedback Shift Register (eLFSR), which can either operate as a register or an LFSR. In the test mode, the LFSR output is XORed with the response compactor output bit-stream. Therefore, each compacted slice is XORed with a pseudorandom bit. A 128-bit LFSR is used to prevent the attacker from retrieving the initial state of the LFSR. Although the countermeasure has no impact on the critical path delay, the area overhead remains a problem, which is around 5 % of the AES chip.

## 5.3   Noise Injection in the Scan Output

This technique is similar to the previous masking technique. It includes two levels of security: one is the LFSR and the other one is the True Random Number

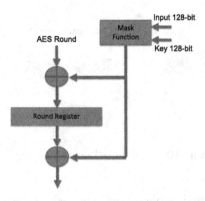

**Fig. 8.** Round register masking

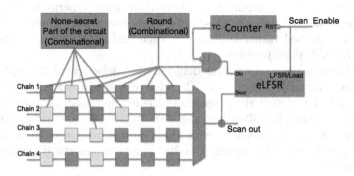

**Fig. 9.** Masking the compactor output

Generator (TRNG) [18]. Figure 10 shows the architecture of the countermeasure. In this case, the masking values are controlled by both the LFSR and the TRNG. Therefore, on average half of the scan output bits are masked and the rest of the bits remain unchanged. As the TRNG hides some of the LFSR outputs, the designer can choose a smaller LFSR, which will drastically reduce the area overhead of this countermeasure. The success rate of the attack in the presence of this countermeasure depends on how frequently the masking is done. It was shown that the attack will fail, only when the masking is done in each clock cycle.

### 5.4 On-chip Comparison of Responses

The countermeasure in [19] provides a scan protection scheme using an on-chip comparison of the circuit response and the expected response that is shifted in. The attacker can only observe a one pass-fail bit per test vector, which is insufficient to leak the secret key of the chip. Similar to the traditional test process, the test vector is shifted into the scan architecture during the shift operations. Then, the response is captured during the capture operation. Instead

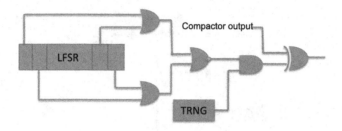

**Fig. 10.** Randomized noise injection

of shifting out the captured response, the expected response is shifted in through another pin that replaces the scan output pin, while shifting in the next test vector by using the scan input pin. This countermeasure performs an on-chip comparison, which produces a pass, only when the whole captured response matches the expected response. The test time and data volume is the same compared to traditional testing.

This countermeasure impacts the diagnosis and debug capabilities of the IC, as the entire information about the IC under test consists of one pass-fail bit per test vector. To support the diagnosis of the IC, an expected faulty response of one fault at a time is shifted into the scan architecture instead of the fault-free response, which is compared with the captured response. However, such procedure is only valid for modeled faults. Furthermore, the diagnostic time becomes unaffordable.

## 6   Proposed Countermeasure

As we have seen in the previous section, there are various proposed countermeasures to provide a certain level of security against scan-based side-channel attack. However, all these countermeasures have been proposed with the existing scan attack model in mind, thus failing to provide protection against a fundamentally different attack model, such as the proposed test-mode-only attack. In this section, we present a countermeasure judiciously crafted for the test-mode-only attack that relies on the access to the scan input pin, which no other existing scan attack requires.

Our proposed test-mode-only attack is based on launching an individual bit-flip from each scan cell in the round register independently of the remaining scan cells. Disabling this capability will prevent the attacker from mapping each scan cell to its corresponding word and byte of the AES. We propose a defense mechanism, which injects random noise by randomly flipping the bits of the test vectors, while they are shifted through the scan input pin, hampering the attack's ability to classify scan cells into words and bytes. The LFSR randomly selects the locations of the bit-flips of each test vector. The LFSR generates a new bit per clock cycle that is XORed with the shifted test vector bit. In other words, the shifted bit is flipped if the output of the LFSR is one. No countermeasure for the existing scan attacks has considered the alteration of the test vector shifted through the scan input pin, mainly because the previously proposed scan attacks assume that the attacker can apply the plaintext through the primary inputs.

Without the capability of controlling the data delivered into the scan cells, the attacker fails to launch the desired bit-flips. The attacker thus needs to circumvent this defense by deciphering the LFSR sequence, which requires the LFSR structural details. The only way the attacker can identify the LFSR configuration is to apply the same test vector for a sufficient number of times by using the scan flush test capabilities, where the test vector can be shifted in and out without any capture operation. If the LFSR consists of $m$ bits, the attacker has to apply the same test vector for $2^m - 1$ times to figure out the structure of the LFSR that can be chosen to implement a primitive polynomial. For an LFSR of medium size, this can be quite costly for the attacker.

To provide a higher level of security, we propose the optional integration of a second defense mechanism to disallow a specific number of continuous shift cycles. Another possible smaller LFSR can be used to inject extra noise on the shifted stimulus, once a specific number of consecutive shift cycles with no capture operation in between is detected. The maximum allowed number of continuous shift cycles should be selected carefully to maintain both security and testability of the chip. If the maximum number of continuous shift cycles is too small, the scan flush test will be affected. On the other hand, permitting a large number of continuous shift cycles may enable the identification of the first LFSR structure, and thus, compromise the security of the chip. An n-bit counter can be used to allow up to $2^n - 1$ consecutive shift operations. Every clock pulse during the test mode increments the counter as long as the scan enable signal is high, indicating a shift operation. When the counter saturates, it signals the second LFSR to kick in and add a second level of bit flipping.

To circumvent the second level of defense, an attacker can employ a dummy capture attack as shown in Fig. 11; in this scheme, the attacker pulls down the scan enable signal (to indicate capture) in between the active clock edges. The goal of the attacker is to reset the counter and be able to extend the number of the consecutive shift cycles without corrupting the scan chain content with a capture operation. To thwart such attacks, the reset structure of the counter is designed carefully. The counter is reset only with a capture during an active clock. Figure 12 provides the implementation details.

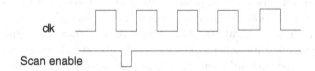

**Fig. 11.** Timing diagram of the clock signal and the scan enable signal in a dummy capture attack

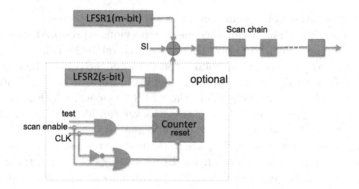

**Fig. 12.** The proposed countermeasure for test-mode-only attack

The area cost is an m-bit LFSR and one XOR gate for the level-1 defense, and an s-bit LFSR, c-bit counter, 3 AND gates, one OR gate, one inverter, and one XOR gate in addition for the optional level-2 defense.

## 7   Conclusion and Ongoing Work

With a simple yet effective chip mode-reset countermeasure in place, none of the existing scan attacks can leak the secret information of a security-critical IC. In this work, we bring a new perspective to scan attack research by introducing a new class of scan attacks, test-mode-only attack, that targets circumventing this commonly used mode-reset countermeasure. The proposed attack misuses the in-field debug capabilities of the IC by leveraging operations, such as shift and capture that the test mode offers. By remaining in the test mode, the proposed attack circumvents the mode-reset countermeasure.

A fundamentally different type of scan attack comes with its own challenges to be tackled. As the boundary scan cells block the access to the primary inputs during the test mode, the proposed attack ends up having to use the scan interface to load the attack patterns, in contrast to all the existing scan attacks that benefit from the available PI access in the normal mode. The prerequisite for applying the proposed test-mode-only attack is therefore to decipher the mapping between the scan cells and the AES inputs, which is dictated by the physical position of the scan cells and the physical placement tools used by the designer.

In this work, we tackle the aforementioned challenges and devise a test-mode-only attack, which we illustrate for AES, while we note that the technique herein can be easily extended for other ciphers as well. The attack analysis shows that only 375 test vectors are sufficient to reveal the 128-bit AES secret key where the 128-bit key is reduced to only 12 bits. Furthermore, we also present a brief overview of existing countermeasures, and devise a cost-effective one that can circumvent the proposed test-mode-only attack. We thus present a two-level defense with an underlying input corruption countermeasure that prevents an attacker from launching the bit-flips required to leak the secret key.

Our future work will focus on contemporary scan architectures where a test stimulus decompressor and a response compactor reside on the scan path. We have already made some progress on attacks using compactor [20] and boundary scan chains [21]. The technique we present in this paper is readily applicable on ICs that enable debug and diagnostics with a bypass of such advanced DFT features. When this bypass capability is not supported, however, the attack should be enhanced by developing techniques to launch bit-flips through the decompressor in the scan cells, and to perform differential analysis on the compacted responses. The ultimate goal of this line of work is to develop techniques that facilitate the design of **testable yet secure ICs**.

# References

1. Yang, B., Wu, K., Karri, R.: Scan based side channel attack on dedicated hardware implementations of data encryption standard. In: ITC, pp. 339–344. IEEE (2004)
2. Yang, B., Wu, K., Karri, R.: Secure scan: a design-for-test architecture for crypto chips. In: Joyner Jr., W.H., Martin, G., Kahng, A.B. (eds.) DAC, pp. 135–140. ACM (2005)
3. Kapur, R.: Security vs. test quality: are they mutually exclusive? In: Proceedings of International Test Conference, ITC 2004, p. 1414, October 2014
4. DaRolt, J., Natale, G.D., Flottes, M.L., Rouzeyre, B.: Are advanced DfT structures sufficient for preventing scan-attacks? In: VTS, pp. 246–251. IEEE (2012)
5. Ege, B., Das, A., Ghosh, S., Verbauwhede, I.: Differential scan attack on AES with X-tolerant and X-masked test response compactor. In: DSD, pp. 545–552. IEEE (2012)
6. DaRolt, J., Natale, G.D., Flottes, M.L., Rouzeyre, B.: Scan attacks and countermeasures in presence of scan response compactors. In: European Test Symposium, pp. 19–24. IEEE Computer Society (2011)
7. Nara, R., Satoh, K., Yanagisawa, M., Ohtsuki, T., Togawa, N.: Scan-based side-channel attack against RSA cryptosystems using scan signatures. IEICE Trans. **93–A**(12), 2481–2489 (2010)
8. Da Rolt, J., Das, A., Di Natale, G., Flottes, M.-L., Rouzeyre, B., Verbauwhede, I.: A new scan attack on RSA in presence of industrial countermeasures. In: Schindler, W., Huss, S.A. (eds.) COSADE 2012. LNCS, vol. 7275, pp. 89–104. Springer, Heidelberg (2012)
9. Nara, R., Togawa, N., Yanagisawa, M., Ohtsuki, T.: Scan-based attack against elliptic curve cryptosystems. In: 2010 15th Asia and South Pacific Design Automation Conference (ASP-DAC), pp. 407–412, January 2010
10. Da Rolt, J., Das, A., Di Natale, G., Flottes, M., Rouzeyre, B., Verbauwhede, I.: A scan-based attack on elliptic curve cryptosystems in presence of industrial design-for-testability structures. In: 2012 IEEE International Symposium on Defect and Fault Tolerance in VLSI and Nanotechnology Systems (DFT), pp. 43–48, October 2012
11. Liu, Y., Wu, K., Karri, R.: Scan-based attacks on linear feedback shift register based stream ciphers. ACM Trans. Des. Autom. Electron. Syst. **16**(2), 20:1–20:15 (2011)
12. Hely, D., Bancel, F., Flottes, M.L., Rouzeyre, B.: Test control for secure scan designs. In: Proceedings of the 10th IEEE European Symposium on Test, ETS 2005, pp. 190–195. IEEE Computer Society, Washington, DC (2005)

13. Nyberg, K.: Generalized feistel networks. In: Kim, K., Matsumoto, T. (eds.) ASI-ACRYPT 1996. LNCS, vol. 1163, pp. 91–104. Springer, Heidelberg (1996)
14. IEEE standard test access port and boundary-scan architecture. In: IEEE Std 1149.1-2001, pp. i-200 (2001)
15. Ali, S.S., Sinanoglu, O., Saeed, S.M., Karri, R.: New scan-based attack using only the test mode. In: Margala, M., da Luz Reis, R.A., Orailoglu, A., Carro, L., Silveira, L.M., Ugurdag, H.F. (eds.) VLSI-SoC, pp. 234–239. IEEE, Istanbul (2013)
16. Sengar, G., Mukhopadhayay, D., Roy Chowdhury, D.: An efficient approach to develop secure scan tree for crypto-hardware. In: International Conference on Advanced Computing and Communications, ADCOM 2007, pp. 21–26, December 2007
17. Hély, D., Flottes, M.L., Bancel, F., Rouzeyre, B., Bérard, N., Renovell, M.: Scan design and secure chip. In: IOLTS, pp. 219–226. IEEE Computer Society (2004)
18. Das, A., Ege, B., Ghosh, S., Batina, L., Verbauwhede, I.: Security analysis of industrial test compression schemes. IEEE Trans. CAD Integr. Circuits Syst. **32**(12), 1966–1977 (2013)
19. Da Rolt, J., Di Natale, G., Flottes, M.L., Rouzeyre, B.: On-chip test comparison for protecting confidential data in secure ICS. In: 2012 17th IEEE European Test Symposium (ETS), p. 1, May 2012
20. Ali, S.S., Sinanoglu, O., Saeed, S.M., Karri, R.: New scan attacks against state-of-the-art countermeasures and DFT. In: HOST, pp. 142–147. IEEE (2014)
21. Ali, S.S., Sinanoglu, O., Karri, R.: Test-mode-only scan attack using the boundary scan chain. In: Natale, G.D. (ed.) ETS, pp. 1–6. IEEE, Paderborn (2014)

# Quantitative Optimization and Early Cost Estimation of Low-Power Hierarchical-Architecture SRAMs Based on Accurate Cost Models

Yuan Ren[(⊠)] and Tobias Noll

Chair of Electrical Engineering and Computer Systems,
RWTH Aachen University, Aachen, Germany
{ren, tgn}@eecs.rwth-aachen.de

**Abstract.** Dedicated low-power SRAMs are frequently used in various system-on-chip designs and their power consumption plays an increasingly crucial role in the overall power budget. However, the broad amount of choices regarding the capacity, wordlengths and operational modes make it hard for designers to determine the optimal SRAM architecture. Additionally, many low-power techniques and circuits are frequently utilized but not supported by previously proposed cost models. In order to solve these problems, a cost-model based quantitative optimization approach is proposed. In particular, a fast and accurate power estimation model is built for aiding the low-power SRAM designs. It precisely fits the various complex SRAM circuits and architectures. The quantitative approach provides useful conclusions early in the design phase guiding further optimizations. The estimation error of the power model has been proven to be less than 10 % compared to results based on time-hungry extracted-netlist simulations in a 40-nm CMOS technology.

**Keywords:** SRAM · Power model · Quantitative parameter optimization

## 1 Introduction

SRAMs are widely used in many applications as caches etc. due to their fast access speed but also contribute significantly to area cost and power consumption. Particularly in system-on-chip design, dedicated SRAMs with optimized architecture and circuits are often applied for achieving low-power. The optimization of those dedicated SRAMs for lowest possible power at a given performance is quite challenging task because of the complexity of the design space. An attractive approach is to perform a quantitative optimization based on cost models. Such cost models not only support the optimization process but also allow for early cost estimation in the system conception phase. The focus of the study is laid on the power cost considering the increasingly significant role of power consumption of SRAMs.

From the low-power perspective, SRAMs with hierarchical architecture, as described e.g. in [1–4], are very attractive choices. A quantitative optimization approach for the hierarchical-architecture SRAMs deserves further research.

© IFIP International Federation for Information Processing 2015
A. Orailoglu et al. (Eds.): VLSI-SoC 2013, IFIP AICT 461, pp. 69–93, 2015.
DOI: 10.1007/978-3-319-23799-2_4

Figure 1 provides a block diagram of such a hierarchical-architecture SRAM of 2 K words with a 45 bit-wordlength. Apart from the timing control circuits, the memory matrix and the address decoders dominate the total power consumption. These two components exhibit a large design space regarding the underlying architecture and circuits. In the hierarchical architecture the memory matrix is typically organized in $2^m$ ($m = 3$) columns. Each column includes a local timing generator, a bit cell column and a local wordline decoder. A bit-cell column consists of $2^n$ ($n = 4$) local blocks and a local block is sub-divided into $2^u$ ($u = 4$) words vertically. Thereby, the long bitlines and wordlines are both divided into global and local lines for reducing the switched capacitances. Moreover, the use of local sense amplifiers further reduces the power consumption by decreasing the signal swing on the long interconnects. Furthermore,

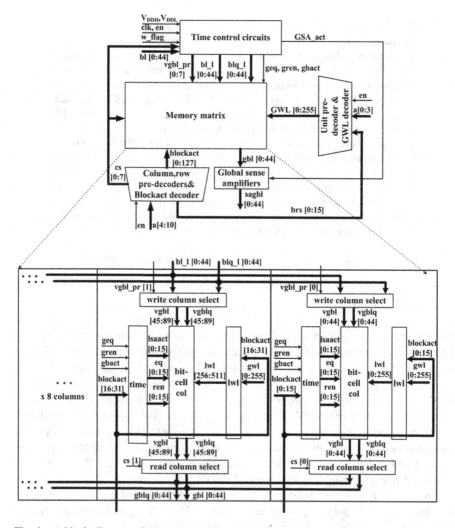

**Fig. 1.** A block diagram of a conventional on-chip SRAM with a hierarchical architecture

the bit cell column could consist of various efficient circuits, such as assist circuits [1], stable bit cell and bit-interleaved technique [2] and pre-charge schemes [3, 5]. Apparently a large design space exists for selecting hardware-efficient architectures and the underlying circuits. Especially for SRAMs with different capacities and features, the time to market constraints make design space difficult to be explored. Therefore, there is a strong demand to come up with a cost model, by which architecture parameters, local circuits and power reduction techniques are characterized and quantitatively analyzed.

Many available power cost models were investigated for hierarchical-architecture SRAMs using various low-power circuits and techniques. As it is illustrated in Table 1, the widely used CACTI tool [6] is a tool to understand large caches in the context of microprocessors. It focuses on microprocessor caches (including cache coherency techniques) and with fewer possibilities for choices of circuits and techniques, in [1–3, 5]. For on-chip SRAMs CACTI is found very inaccurate due to its incompatibility with specific circuits and techniques so that it cannot be used as an optimization or design guiding tool. The power model in [7] cannot be used for SRAMs with low-power architectures containing divided bitline and divided wordline structures. Moreover this, it cannot deal with a variety of efficient specific circuits. In [8] only the traditional subdivided bitline structure is discussed without considering other possible low-power architectures or circuits. Moreover they do not consider LSAs in their model since the LSAs significantly contribute to the leakage power. The approach in [9] requires a complex reference design of a whole SRAM whose characterization is time-consuming, which makes it not practical for designers at the early design stage. Moreover, neither LSA in a hierarchical architecture nor energy-efficient circuits for local blocks are included. The power model in [10] discussed a binary tree SRAM based on the approach in [7] which makes it similarly inappropriate. Moreover, the energy consumed by long interconnects existing in the binary tree organization is not considered in the total energy consumption in a proper way. Hence, these models cannot help designers in making quantitative decisions about architecture and circuits.

A predictive and mature design flow for on-chip SRAMs must simultaneously consider energy (E), area (A) and speed (T) properties. For this reason a cost estimation environment is under elaboration serving as an efficient design aid and a quantitative optimization tool. Figure 2 sketches the overall flowchart of this environment. The SRAM specifications are given by the capacity in number of words and wordlength. The first task is to determine the optimal architecture and most effective circuit

**Table 1.** Estimation approaches investigation

|  | [6] | [7] | [8] | [9] | [10] | This work |
|---|---|---|---|---|---|---|
| Hierachical using LSA | Y | N | N | Y | N | Y |
| Specific efficient Circuits | N | N | N | N | N | Y |
| No Reference Design Needed | Y | Y | Y | N | Y | Y |
| Validation Technology | ≥32 nm | 130 nm | 65 nm | N.A | 45 nm – 180 nm | 40 nm |

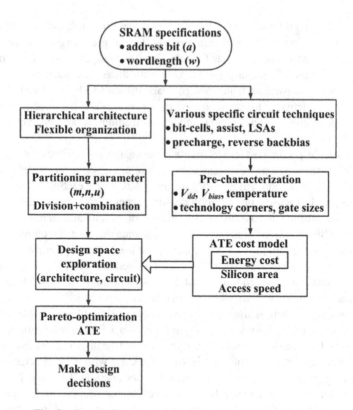

**Fig. 2.** Overall flowchart of the cost estimation environment

techniques. A hierarchical architecture is taken as the subject to be analyzed and optimized. The architectures are specified by the partitioning parameters $(m, n, u)$. Here, parameter $m$ is the column address decoder width, which denotes the number of columns $(M = 2^m)$ and $n$ is the row address decoder width, which denotes the number of rows $(N = 2^n)$ in a memory matrix. Parameter $u$ is the unit address decoder width, which denotes the number of cells $(U = 2^u)$ in a column unit. On the whole, the three parameters define the partitioning and organization of a hierarchical-architecture SRAM with a total capacity of $M*N*U$ words being equal to $2^a$ address bits with wordlength $(w)$. The decomposition and combination possibilities of the three parameters are explored for selecting the optimal architecture partitioning.

Besides the choices related to partitioning regarding the design space, there exists a wide choice of various energy-efficient circuit techniques. These circuit techniques, such as the ones related to the bit cells, assist circuits and local sense amplifiers (LSA) cause additional overhead and complexity to the overall design. The consumed energy is difficult to evaluate and estimate since it depends on the context in which these circuits are used. Their non-standard features cannot longer be characterized using the available models which only include standard features. Hence there must be a quantitative benchmarking tool to assess these circuits and techniques. Accordingly, their respective power consumption should be estimated and compared while using different

configurations so that the optimal one can be selected. A pre-characterization methodology is employed for capturing their distinct features and quantifying the analysis. With
these 2 sets of inputs, partitioning parameters and specific circuit techniques, a
design-space exploration is carried out, while building a cost (A, T, E) model for on-chip
SRAMs. This way a Pareto-optimization is carried out by trading off the three costs (A,
T, E). Finally the design decisions regarding architecture and circuits are made.

The idea of a cost-model based pre-characterization of elementary components (i.e.
logic gates and bit cells) is further explained in Fig. 3. Given specification parameters
$(a, w)$, all the possibilities of the partitioning parameter $(m, n, u)$ are generated and then
these possibilities are evaluated by the presented cost model. An ATE cost database is
built by proper circuit simulation of extracted component netlists, which depends on
the use case (e.g. $V_{dd}$, $V_{bias}$), technology corners, temperature, frequency and gate sizes.

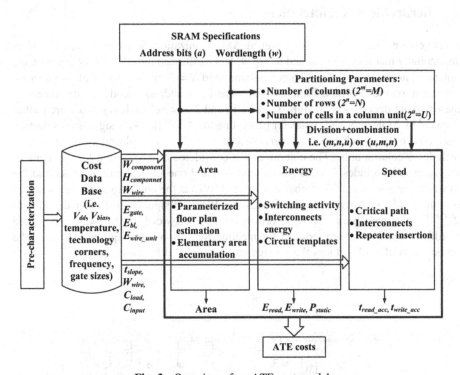

**Fig. 3.** Overview of an ATE cost model

- The area can be estimated by a parameterized floor plan estimation and an accumulation of elementary widths and height values (e.g. $W_{components}$, $H_{components}$).
- In the energy model, the elementary energy values of basic circuits (e.g. $E_{gate}$) are
  accumulated with the partitioning parameters and switching activity probabilities.
  The interconnect energy is estimated from the wire length and the energy per unit
  length ($E_{wire\_unit}$). Finally the total energy consumption is derived by an accumulation of elementary energy (e.g. $E_{bl}$) from all used circuit components.

- The speed can also be derived by using the cost data base (e.g. $t_{slope}$, $W_{wire}$, $C_{load}$, $C_{input}$) and a elementary delay accumulation along the critical path involving long resistance-capacitance interconnects.

In this contribution, we focus on the energy cost model and the relevant optimization approach. In the proposed model, only a few necessary basic circuit components (i.e. basic bit cells) need to be characterized. These circuit components could be verified by a number of Monte-Carlo simulations for ensuring robustness. Moreover, the pre-characterization including simulation time and model building only requires couple of hours and afterwards the estimation results can be acquired in a few minutes. Therefore, the total effort of the cost model is much less compared to a complete reference design.

## 2  Hierarchical Architecture

A conventional hierarchical low-power SRAM organization including address decoders and memory matrices is illustrated in Fig. 4. It is partitioned into $2^{(m+n)}$ blocks which are organized as an array of $M = 2^m$ block columns and $N = 2^n$ block rows, while $m$ and $n$ are dependent on the decompositions of column and row address decoders. The outputs of these two pre-decoders, $2^m$ column select (CS) and $2^n$ row select (RS) signals, are further decoded by NOR or NAND gates for generating the $2^{(m+n)}$ Blockact signals for selecting a specific block. Each block is composed of $U = 2^u$ words placed vertically and it includes $w$ column units. The column unit is considered as a basic unit for the memory matrix, which includes $2^u$ cells per column unit and one LSA. A unit decoder and the row decoder generate $2^{(u+n)}$ global wordlines (GWL) at the output to access the selected row in the block. Afterwards, the GWLs and Blockact signals are further decoded to $2^{(m+n+u)}$ local wordlines (LWL) to access the selected word. In this way, bitline and wordline capacitances are reduced for meeting the low-power requirement. Also, the introduction of LSA reduces the voltage swing on global bitlines.

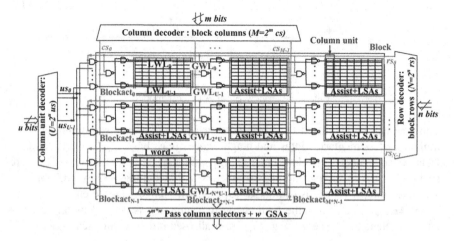

**Fig. 4.** Hierarchical-architecture SRAM organization comprising DWL structure

As discussed before, the memory matrix is organized into $M = 2^m$ block columns. In these block columns various complex but efficient circuits are utilized. In Fig. 5, a block column is shown for exemplifying these specific circuits. It is composed of a local timing-control signal generator, a LWL decoder and a bit cell column. In the local timing-control signal generator, the global timing pulse signals are combined with the Blockact signals to generate local timing pulse signals for the $N = 2^n$ blocks. Similarly in the LWL decoder, the GWL signals running through the whole memory matrix are combined with the Blockact signals to generate LWL signals for each word in the bit cell column. The bit cell column is instantiated by high-threshold voltage bit cells with reverse back-biasing long channels, equalizer pre-charge scheme, read/write assist circuits and a wide local sense amplifier [5]. A block in a bit cell column is composed of $w$ column units. Each column unit includes $U = 2^u$ 6T cells, assist circuits and a LSA.

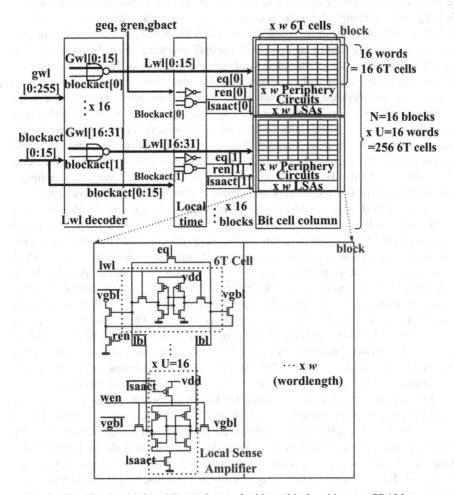

**Fig. 5.** Specific circuits found in a column of a hierarchical-architecture SRAM macro

The choice of $m$ and $w$ defines the parasitic wordline capacitances and the wordline structure. Either a non-divided wordline (non-DWL) or a DWL structure can be selected according to the capacity and wordlength. The parameter $n$ defines the bitline hierarchy and therewith affects the global and local bitline capacitances. Especially, charging and discharging the bitlines contributes significantly to the overall power consumption. The number of cells $u$ in one column unit determines to a large extent the minimum energy consumption for one operation. The $n$ and $u$ must be carefully selected for trading the least frequent use of LSAs and the minimum switching capacitances.

## 3  Partitioning Impact Analysis

SRAMs typically include two major contributors to power consumption: the address decoders and the memory matrices. In the hierarchical architecture (Fig. 4), the way of dividing and combining the address decoders determines how the memory matrix is partitioned into sub-blocks. A probabilistic estimation approach is employed for estimating the switching activity and power consumption of the address decoder especially regarding whether or not a distributed wordline structure is used. The memory matrices including complex assist and periphery circuits, which consume a large portion of power, were also modeled and characterized. Four basic circuit templates and a power estimation method are proposed to extract and describe the architecture and circuit characteristics for the hierarchical architecture. The specific circuits used within the four circuit templates can be altered without changing the estimation approach itself. Various power reduction techniques, e.g. precharge schemes in [3, 5], circuit techniques in [1, 2, 5], can be pre-characterized and benchmarked in the same configurations, which makes this model very appropriate for customized SRAM designs.

For an SRAM with $a$ address bits comprising a capacity of $2^a$ words with a wordlength $w$, a flow chart of the power estimation model is shown in Fig. 6. The two portions constituting the power model are the address decoder and the memory matrix. For the address decoder, $a$ address bits are divided into three sections $(m, n, u)$, which are decoded by the three pre-decoders including column, row and unit decoder. In the 2nd stage, a block decoder combines RS and CS signals to generate the Blockact signals. A word-row decoder uses RS and US signals for generating the GWL signals. In the 3rd step, a word decoder uses both Blockact and GWL signals to produce the LWL signals. The three decoders are all composed of NAND or NOR gates and are arranged in a matrix-like select circuit. The sum of the power consumed by the pre-decoders and the matrix-like select circuits provides an estimate of the total power estimation of the whole address decoder. For the memory matrix, the parameters $(m, n, u)$ are used for quantifying and analyzing the bitline and wordline structure. Since the parameters represent the number of the sub-modules and determine the final SRAM architecture, their respective impact is analyzed and attributed to the components of the memory matrix. The parameter $m$ determines the capacitances of the horizontal global wordlines (HGBL) and the amount of pass transistors used as column selectors. The number of the Blockact and GWL signals affects the capacitances of vertical global bitlines (VGBL) and GWLs respectively. Finally, the choice of $u$ has an impact on the power consumption from LBLs of accessed cells, assist circuits, and LSAs. Therefore,

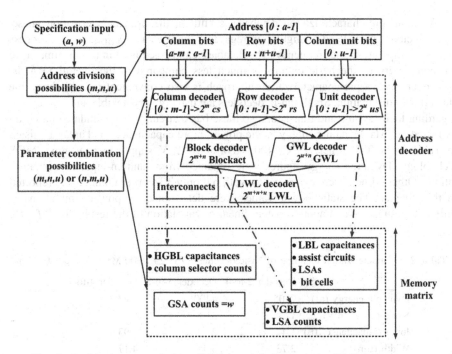

**Fig. 6.** Partitioning parameter possibilities and their impact on SRAM components

a quantitative analysis about the dependency relations is made between the combinations of ($m$, $n$, $u$) and all the power contributors. Given the specifications $a$ and $w$, all the possible partitioning parameters ($m$, $n$, $u$) are evaluated by estimating the respective power consumption. Finally, the optimal parameter selection is saved for fulfilling different ATE design requirements, such as minimum power consumption.

# 4 Power Model of Address Decoder

## 4.1 Basic Circuits of Address Decoder

As shown in Fig. 6, the address decoder includes three pre-decoders and three distributed decoders. The three pre-decoders can be decoders comprising either a large fan-in or a small fan-in, depending on their input numbers. The other three intermediate decoders are regarded to be matrix-like select circuits which are composed of logic gates distributed in a matrix. A probabilistic method is employed for modeling the underlying switching activities of these logic gates, by which the transition power consumption of the matrix-like select circuit is estimated. The large fan-in decoder is composed of a matrix-like select circuit and two small fan-in decoders. Therefore, if the energies associated with small fan-in decoders and basic gates are available, the energy of the three pre-decoders and the three distributed decoders can be derived by the probabilistic method. Also, a realistic topology estimation approach is used to estimate the wire capacitances and area of different ($m$, $n$, $u$).

A circuit pre-characterization database is built in the pre-characterization phase, which includes the related configuration regarding the use case ($V_{DDH}$, $V_{DDL}$), process corners, temperature and frequency. The database can be acquired in a short time since the complexity of the basic circuits is much less compared to the overall SRAMs. Moreover, such a pre-characterization approach is also convenient for estimating the static power dissipation. Small fan-in decoders are usually very flexible and customized regarding their layouts and transistors, so these basic circuits were simulated based on extracted-netlists. Dynamic energy, static power, input capacitances and areas are listed in Table 2 for TT corner, 25°C, 400 MHz and 0.9 V supply in a 40-nm CMOS technology. Dynamic energy figures were obtained from random-input power simulations. Other corners were evaluated as well, but only TT corner numbers are reported in this chapter. The static power values were determined by power simulations at different frequencies and approximately linear extrapolation of the results for $P(f = 0)$.

**Table 2.** Characterization database of basic decoders (TT, 25°, 400 MHz, $V_{DDH}$ = 0.9 V)

|                        | Decoder 2-to-4 | Decoder 3-to-8 | Decoder 4-to-16 |
|------------------------|----------------|----------------|-----------------|
| Dynamic energy (aJ)    | 2105           | 4400           | 8460            |
| Static power (nW)      | 12             | 31             | 56              |
| Input Capacitance (fF) | 1.44           | 2.44           | 3.93            |
| Width (µm)             | 2.73           | 3.45           | 4.17            |
| Height (µm)            | 2.02           | 3.53           | 5.63            |

## 4.2   Switching Activity

Besides the energy of the basic decoders (Table 2), the matrix-like select circuits formed by NAND or NOR gates also contribute significantly to the total power consumption. Such circuits are typically acting as distributed decoders and are located among the memory matrices. As illustrated in Fig. 7, a distributed decoder composed of NOR gates has an aspect ratio given by $R$ rows and $C$ columns. When another address is accessed, not only the corresponding gates switch but also the other gates in the row and column are charged and then discharged. As different transitions of each gate lead to different amounts of consumed energy, the corresponding energy of each NOR gate in its transition cases must be estimated separately. Additionally, for the overall matrix-like circuits composed of NOR gates four switching cases (Fig. 7) exist. For each switching case the energy and switching probability are also derived.

In Table 3, a subset of the database for the consumed energy of the basic NOR gates is shown for each possible input transition. E.g. the transition $00 \rightarrow 01$ of a two-input NOR gate is depicted by the decimal equivalents $0 \rightarrow 1$. Hence, a transition $10 \rightarrow 01$ is depicted by 21 and its switching energy is denoted by $E_{NOR}^{21}$, and so on. In particular, the static power of the four "no transition" situations (00, 11, 22, 33) is also included in Table 3, where the total energy is obtained when the frequency is set to 400 MHz. A NAND matrix-like select circuit can be pre-characterized and estimated in the same way as well.

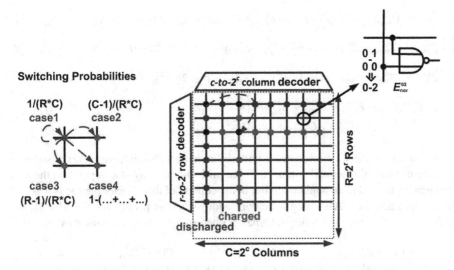

**Fig. 7.** Four switching cases and their switching probabilities in a distributed decoder

For a distributed decoder with ($R$ x $C$) NOR gates four possible switching cases exist. *Case1* means no switching of the selected column or row. *Case2* means a switching of the selected column within the same row. *Case3* means a switching within the same column. *Case4* means a switching from one gate to another gate located in a different row and a different column. In order to elaborate the switching details and its energy distribution, *Case2* is exemplified in four steps as shown in Fig. 7. Since the switching happens in the same row, it means that one cross point in the matrix is selected and another one in the same row is unselected. (a) Hence, the selected NOR gate switches from 1 to 0 and another unselected one switches from 0 to 1. (b) Horizontally in the selected row, ($C$-2) NOR gates have no switches and their inputs stay at 1. (c) Vertically, ($R$-1) NOR gates switch from 2 to 3, which means they are discharged in the relevant column. Also, ($R$-1) NOR gates switch from 3 to 2 which means they are charged in another column. (d) The remaining NOR gates do not switch and stay at 3. Using the transition energy depicted in Table 3 the respective energy of the four switching cases is derived as

**Table 3.** Energy of NOR gate for all possible input transition possibilities (TT, 25°, 400 MHz, $V_{DDH}$ = 0.9 V, $V_{DDL}$ = 0.3 V)

| Inputs transitions | 00 | 11 | 12 | 13 | 01 | 02 | 03 | 23 |
|---|---|---|---|---|---|---|---|---|
| Total energy(aJ) | 11 | 4 | 400 | 68 | 213 | 320 | 235 | 68 |
| Inputs transitions | 22 | 33 | 21 | 31 | 10 | 20 | 30 | 32 |
| Total energy(aJ) | 2 | 3 | 315 | 228 | 705 | 655 | 880 | 228 |

$$E_{DecMatrix}^{Case1} = E_{NOR}^{00} + (R-1) \cdot E_{NOR}^{22} + (C-1) \cdot E_{NOR}^{11} + (R-1) \cdot (C-1) \cdot E_{NOR}^{33} \tag{1}$$

$$E_{DecMatrix}^{Case2} = E_{NOR}^{01} + E_{NOR}^{10} + (R-1) \cdot (E_{NOR}^{23} + E_{NOR}^{32}) + (C-2) \cdot E_{NOR}^{11} + (R-1) \cdot (C-2) \cdot E_{NOR}^{33} \tag{2}$$

$$E_{DecMatrix}^{Case3} = E_{NOR}^{02} + E_{NOR}^{20} + (C-1) \cdot (E_{NOR}^{13} + E_{NOR}^{31}) + (R-2) \cdot E_{NOR}^{22} + (R-2) \cdot (C-1) \cdot E_{NOR}^{33} \tag{3}$$

$$\begin{aligned} E_{DecMatrix}^{Case4} = & E_{NOR}^{03} + E_{NOR}^{12} + E_{NOR}^{21} + (R-2) \cdot (E_{NOR}^{23} + E_{NOR}^{32}) + E_{NOR}^{30} + (C-2) \\ & \cdot (E_{NOR}^{13} + E_{NOR}^{31}) + (R-2) \cdot (C-2) \cdot E_{NOR}^{33}. \end{aligned} \tag{4}$$

In particular, the four cases occur with different probabilities, which are associated with the number of rows and columns. These probabilities may also depend on the way the memory is used in an application but in the context of this chapter the focus is set on the random accesses. Assuming a random address access pattern for the SRAM, the probabilities are derived as follows. Dynamic energy of the matrix-circuit is estimated as

$$\begin{aligned} E_{matrix}(R,C) = & E_{DecMatrix}^{Case1} \cdot (1/(R \cdot C)) + E_{DecMatrix}^{Case2} \cdot (C-1)/(R \cdot C) + E_{DecMatrix}^{Case3} \cdot (R-1)/(R \cdot C) \\ & + E_{DecMatrix}^{Case4} \cdot (1 - 1/(R \cdot C) - (R-1)/(R \cdot C) - (C-1)/(R \cdot C)). \end{aligned} \tag{5}$$

The equation was verified using several different combinations of rows and columns and shows 5 % estimation error compared to extracted-netlist simulation results.

## 4.3    Energy Cost Related to Interconnects

As technology keeps shrinking the role of interconnects becomes increasingly significant in the total power budget. Particularly interconnects incur large capacitive loads in the dense SRAM layout. As described in Fig. 1, the 1st stage pre-decoders and the 2nd stage decoders are typically placed around the memory matrix. The 3rd stage LWL decoders are distributed into the block columns. Hence, the aspect ratio of the LWL, local timing circuits and the bit-cell column must be considered together. For estimating the associated interconnect lengths, a floor plan containing the dominating memory matrix and address decoder must be determined in advance.

Since different layout floor plans result in different wire and coupling capacitances, two typical placements are selected as possible layout organizations. In the reference floor plans, a matrix circuit is always much larger than the other two sub-blocks. Therefore, a compact topology exhibiting smaller area is selected. As shown in Fig. 8, a horizontal placement leads to different interconnect lengths compared to a vertical placement. For a large fan-in decoder, two pre-decoders and a matrix-like select circuit are placed in both ways for evaluation purposes. For the given floor plans the total area, interconnect lengths and wire capacitances are estimated and compared. By assessing which placement is more compact for the overall floor plan, the two arrangements are selected.

The height and width of the two pre-decoders are denoted as $(H_{pre1}, W_{pre1})$ and $(H_{pre1}, W_{pre2})$, which are obtained from the pre-characterization given in Table 2. The height and width of basic gates $(H_{Gate}, W_{Gate})$ such as NOR or NAND gate are also available. Given the two placement possibilities, the height and width of the required

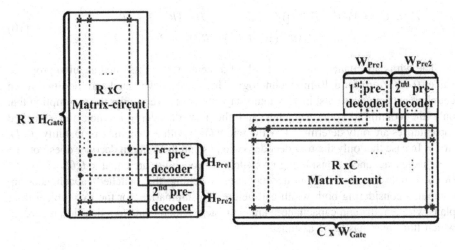

**Fig. 8.** Two empirical placement orientations for wire capacitance estimation

wiring can be derived for horizontal $(H_h, W_h)$ and vertical $(H_v, W_v)$ placements respectively.

$$H_h = H_{Gate} \cdot R, \ W_h = W_{Gate} \cdot C + W_{Pre1} + W_{Pre2} \tag{6}$$

$$H_v = H_{Gate} \cdot R + H_{Pre1} + H_{Pre2}, \ W_v = W_{Gate} \cdot C \tag{7}$$

As the wire lengths in the two sub-blocks are much shorter compared to the matrix circuits, the following criterion is used to select the more compact topology. If holds, the placement should be horizontal, otherwise a vertical placement is applied. Subsequently, the wire lengths can be estimated by computing the amount of gates and their individual sizes in the selected placement. The two floor plans can be used either for a large fan-in decoder or a memory matrix and its surrounding circuits. For a global SRAM floor plan (Fig. 1), the two pre-decoders are replaced by a LWL decoder and a local control timing generator. The matrix-like select circuits are replaced by a memory matrix column. Thereby, a floor plan of a block column is determined. The decision procedure to estimate the global wire capacitances is similar.

$$abs\left(H_{Pre1} + H_{Pre2} - H_{Gate} \cdot R\right) < abs\left(W_{Pre1} + W_{Pre2} - W_{Gate} \cdot C\right) \tag{8}$$

Considering the switching activities of the relevant wires the energies for switching the interconnects in the two possible topology scenarios are estimated as

$$\begin{aligned} E_h(R, C) = \ &Vdd^2 \cdot 0.08 \cdot [W_h \cdot (C - 1) + H_h \cdot (R - 1)]/(R \cdot C) \\ &+ Vdd^2 \cdot 0.08 \cdot (W_h + H_h) \cdot (R \cdot C - R - C - 2)/(R \cdot C) \end{aligned} \tag{9}$$

$$E_v(R,C) = Vdd^2 \cdot 0.08 \cdot [W_v \cdot (C-1) + H_v \cdot (R-1)]/(R \cdot C)$$
$$+ Vdd^2 \cdot 0.08 \cdot (W_v + H_v) \cdot (R \cdot C - R - C - 2)/(R \cdot C) \tag{10}$$

The wire capacitance per unit length of a metal wire is assumed as an appropriate value (*0.08fF/μm*) for a 40-nm technology. This value is evaluated and modified when coupling capacitances exist in very dense layouts. Moreover, under the assumption that only the column decoder switches and the row decoder does not, the switched capacitances are only determined by the width ($W_h$) with a switching probability *(C-1)/ (R·C)*. In case that only the row decoder switches and the column decoder does not, the switched capacitances considering its switching probability are equal to *0.08 ·H_h·(C-1)/ (R·C)*. If both row and column decoders are switching, the switched capacitances are computed considering both width and height. To summarize, for the two typical floor plans wire lengths and capacitances are estimated, which leads to a decision regarding which floor plan has to be assumed.

### 4.4    Verification of Address Decoder Estimation Model

For low-power SRAMs with large capacities and long word length, it is inevitable that a DWL structure is superior to non-DWL. Because in the non-DWL structure long wordlines suffer from the half-select problem and numerous bitlines are needlessly precharged. As shown in Fig. 9, in a DWL structure the block row decoder which generates 2n RS signals is used twice instead of only once in non-DWL structure. Also an extra distributed GWL decoder is used in a DWL structure which brings additional area cost. But the benefit of a DWL structure is that switching occurs within a smaller memory matrix and thereby the total energy is significantly reduced. Therefore this is a tradeoff between the power and area of the address decoder and memory matrix.

For the energy estimation of the DWL-address decoder, large fan-in decoders with $(n + u)$ inputs can be handled by a nested loop calculation using smaller fan-in decoder data from Table 2 and the relevant matrix-like selected circuits. The energies of distributed decoders in the 2$^{nd}$ and 3$^{rd}$ stage are estimated by the approach described above. The dynamic energy and static power figures are derived as

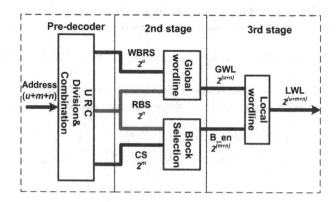

**Fig. 9.** Divided wordline (DWL) structure for address decoder

$$E_{dyc\_tot} = E_{dyc}(n) + E_{dyc}(u) + E_{matrix}(N, U) + E_{wire}(N, U) + E_{dyc}(m) + E_{matrix}(M, N)$$
$$+ E_{wire}(M, N) + E_{matrix}(N \cdot U, M) + E_{wire}(N \cdot U, M) \tag{11}$$

$$P_{sta\_tot} = P_{sta}(n) + P_{sta}(u) + P_{sta}(m) + P_{sta\_matrix}(N, U)$$
$$+ P_{static\_matrix}(M, N) + P_{sta\_matrix}(N \cdot U, M) \tag{12}$$

The dynamic energy of three pre-decoders are represented by $E_{dyc}(n)$, $E_{dyc}(u)$ and $E_{dyc}(m)$. The parameters $m$, $n$ and $u$ denote the input widths of the three decoders respectively. The energy can be acquired from Table 2 (optionally in combination with small fan-in decoders and matrix-like circuits). For the second stage, energy figures for word-row and block decoders are given by $E_{matrix}(N,U) + E_{wire}(N,U)$ and $E_{matrix}(M, N) + E_{wire}(M,N)$. $N = 2^n$ and $U = 2^u$ represent the number of rows and columns of the matrix-circuit. Note that in the 3$^{nd}$ stage a matrix ($N \cdot U$, $M$) is applied instead of a matrix ($N \cdot U$, $M \cdot N$) since every GWL signal only needs $2^m$ Blockact signals to select the word in that column, cf. in Fig. 9. For an address decoder in a non-DWL structure there is no use of GWLs. Therefore, the energies from $E_{matrix}(M, N)$ and $E_{wire}(M, N)$ are not counted into the total energy.

Figure 10 shows the simulated energy versus the estimated energy of a non-DWL-1 K address decoder and a DWL-4 K address decoder. The breakdown energies are compared accordingly. In particular, the energy associated with wiring capacitance is quite low compared to other components. This is explained by a short global interconnect length and non-significant coupling. For larger address decoders and denser layouts, the energy contribution from interconnects cannot be neglected any

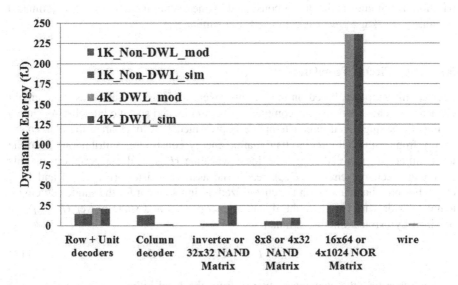

**Fig. 10.** Simulation v.s. estimation energy for a 1 K Non-DWL and a 12-to-4 K DWL decoders

more. It can be seen that the $4 \times 1024$-NOR-Matrix circuit dominates the overall power for the 4 K DWL decoder. The comparison indicates that the estimation errors of the address decoder power model are less than 10 %.

# 5 Power Model of the Memory Matrix

The contribution of the memory matrix to the total memory access energy is dominated by the cycle-based pre-charge and discharge of long bitlines. For low-power memory matrix designs, assist circuits, bit cells and pre-charge schemes span a large design space complicating the power modeling. Their complex features bring significant influences on the layout placement location and the switching capacitances. Accordingly, the total energy cannot be computed by directivity accumulating their respective individual energies. Additionally, the use of LSAs in [1] brings low-voltage swing at global bitlines and high-voltage swing at local bitlines. The complexity with multiple VDD plays at larger scale which makes it more difficult to estimate the power consumption. As before, the variable partitioning parameters ($m$, $n$, $u$ and $w$) result in different access gates and parasitic capacitances due to different wire lengths. Another challenge is that read, write and standby operations must be considered separately, including a hierarchical bitline structure and the memory cell toggling state. In order to solve these issues, four circuit templates are proposed to act as a black box for pre-characterization. In this way a database depending on the use case ($V_{DDH}$ and $V_{DDL}$), technology corners, temperature and the characteristics of gates (width) and wires is generated. Finally, the elementary energies from assist circuits, bit cells and vertical global bitlines are separated by our estimation approach. Combined with the partitioning parameters the power consumed by the overall memory matrix is estimated accurately. Leakage power is estimated in a similar way.

## 5.1 Four Circuit Templates

Four circuit templates based on the circuits given in [5] are presented as basic circuit elements for characterizing the complex assist circuits and specific bit cells. As shown in Fig. 11, a single cell circuit template is presented first to separate the elementary energy from multi cell circuits. Its dynamic energy consists of contributions from the local bitline of each cell ($E_{lbl}$), the local wordline ($E_{lwl}$) and the periphery circuits including precharge circuits ($E_{pre}$), read/write assist transistors ($E_{ren}/E_{wen}$) and LSA ($E_{lsa}$). For pre-characterization the customized design a layout for the single cell circuit template is drawn. This way the dynamic energy ($E_1$) and static power ($P_{static1}$) are obtained by extracted-netlist simulation

$$E_1 = E_{pre} + E_{ren} + E_{lwl} + E_{lsa} + E_{lbl}. \tag{13}$$

For separating the elementary energy from the local bitline of each cell ($E_{lbl}$), a column unit circuit template is drawn in Fig. 12. Its dynamic energy ($E_2$) and static power ($P_{static2}$) are also obtained from extracted-netlist simulation. In the same way its

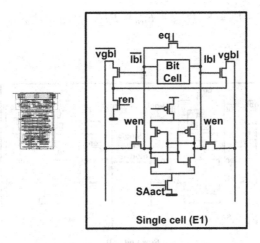

**Fig. 11.** A single cell circuit template

total energy ($E_2$) is decomposed to several elementary energies. By taking the LSA and periphery circuits apart, the energy from the 1–8 cells are linearly interpolated. Thereby, the energy consumed by local bitline of each cell ($E_{lbl}$) is derived

$$E_2 = E_{pre} + E_{ren} + E_{lwl} + E_{lsa} + 8 \cdot E_{lbl} \tag{14}$$

$$E_{lbl} = (E_2 - E_1)/7 \tag{15}$$

For further separating the elementary energy from the periphery circuits, a row unit circuit template is designed as shown in Fig. 13. In the same manner this fraction is separated by calculating $E_3$ and $E_2$.

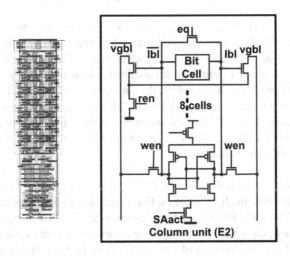

**Fig. 12.** A column unit circuit template

$$E_3 = 8 \cdot \left(E_{pre} + E_{ren} + E_{lbl}\right) + E_{lwl} + E_{lsa} \tag{16}$$

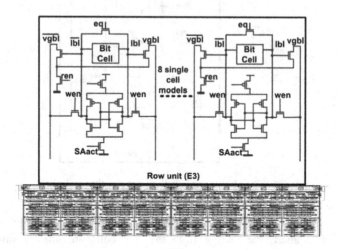

**Fig. 13.** A row unit circuit template

$$E_{pre} + E_{ren} + E_{lwl} + E_{lsa} = (E_3 - E_2)/7. \tag{17}$$

Similarly, a column circuit template is created in Fig. 14, by which the elementary energy consumed by vertical global bitlines ($E_{vgbl}$) is separated.

$$E_4 = E_{pre} + E_{ren} + E_{lwl} + E_{lsa} + 8 \cdot E_{lbl} + 7 \cdot E_{vgbl} \tag{18}$$

$$E_{vgbl} = (E_4 - E_2)/7. \tag{19}$$

Since $E_1...E_4$ and $P_{static1}...P_{static4}$ are pre-characterized by simulating the extracted-netlists of the four circuit templates, the elementary energy values $E_{lbl}$, $E_{pre+ren+lwl+lsa}$, $E_{vgbl}$ can be derived. This way the dynamic energy for read/write operations and static power of the four circuit templates are obtained. It is assumed that a toggle condition occurs for each write operation. As before, the simulation configuration is TT corner, 25° C, 400 MHz and 0.9 V supply voltage in 40 nm CMOS technology. The voltage swing of *vgbl* pair was chosen to 300 mV to guarantee robust operations. The estimation approach is the same for other technology corners but the pre-characterization must be modified based on a Monte-Carlo simulation.

**Read Operation.** As mentioned before, read and write operations are studied separately due to their different characteristics. For a read operation of a hierarchical SRAM with the use of LSAs, the bitline/wordline capacitance, the LSA along with read/write assist and precharge circuit are the main energy consuming components. The dynamic energies $E_{lbl}$ and $E_{lwl}$ are the sum of the energies due to the wiring capacitance itself

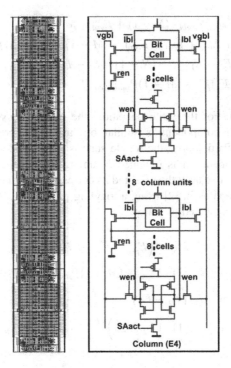

**Fig. 14.** A column circuit template

and the capacitances attached to the memory cells. In addition, the energy consumed by the static components of the unselected memory matrices is attributed to the dynamic energy, comprising a significant portion. The static power ($P_{static1} \ldots P_{static4}$) of the four circuit templates can be acquired using the same approach as before by separating the dynamic energy of each component. Particularly the pass transistors acting as column selectors are also included in the model. The static power of the global sense amplifiers (GSA) and the pass transistors are obtained by multiplying their count with the static power of two simple circuits: a GSA circuit and a pass transistor circuit. As a consequence, according to the parameters of memory matrix defined above for a hierarchical architecture, standby power of a column block can be estimated as

$$
\begin{aligned}
P_{static\_col} &= w \cdot (U \cdot N \cdot P_{lbl\_staic} + P_{gsa\_pass\_static}) + w \cdot (P_{pre\_static} + P_{ren\_static} + P_{lwl\_static} + P_{lsa\_static}) \\
&= w \cdot (U \cdot N \cdot (P_{static2} - P_{static1})/7 + P_{gsa\_pass\_static})) + w \cdot ((P_{static3} - P_{static2})/7)
\end{aligned}
\tag{20}
$$

Finally, the overall dynamic energy of reading a bit from the memory matrix is estimated. The partitioning parameters ($m$, $n$, $u$) are converted to the number ($M = 2^m$, $N = 2^n$, $U = 2^u$) of partitioned components in memory matrix. The total energy is calculated by parameterized accumulating the elementary energies ($E_{lbl}$, $E_{pre+ren+lwl+lsa}$, $E_{vgbl}$, $E_{gsa}$, $E_{pass}$). Particularly, the energy from the unselected parts in the memory matrices is calculated independently and then added to the total dynamic energy.

$$
\begin{aligned}
E_{read\_bit} &= w \cdot U \cdot E_{lbl} + E_{vgbl} \cdot (N-1) + E_{gsa} + M \cdot w \cdot E_{pass} \\
&\quad + \left( E_{pre} + E_{ren} + E_{lwl} + E_{lsa} \right) + (M-1) \cdot P_{static\_col}/f \\
&= w \cdot U \cdot (E_2 - E_1)/7 + (N-1) \cdot (E_4 - E_2)/7 + E_{gsa} + M \cdot w \cdot E_{pass} \\
&\quad + (E_3 - E_2)/7 + (M-1)P_{static\_col}/f.
\end{aligned}
\tag{21}
$$

**Write Operation.** For the write operation, the method to separate the dynamic write energy of each component is similar but using the pre-characterized write energies in Table 4. Particularly, the toggle state is not considered here because the energy of the write operation is obtained assuming a toggle event for each write. A toggle state does not occur all the time and its corresponding energy can be estimated using a similar approach as in [2] using a toggling probability. As a result, the write cycle energy can be calculated as follows.

$$
\begin{aligned}
E_{write\_bit} &= w \cdot U \cdot E'_{lbl} + \left( E'_{pre} + E'_{wen} + E'_{lwl} + E'_{lsa} \right) \\
&\quad + (N-1) \cdot E'_{vgbl} + (M-1)P_{standby\_col}/f \\
&= w \cdot U \cdot \left( E'_2 - E'_1 \right)/7 + \left( E'_3 - E'_2 \right)/7 \\
&\quad + (N-1) \cdot \left( E'_4 - E'_2 \right)/7 + (M-1) \cdot P_{standby\_col}/f.
\end{aligned}
\tag{22}
$$

**Table 4.** Energy of four circuit templates (TT, 25°, 400 MHz, $V_{DDH}$ = 0.9 V, $V_{DDL}$ = 0.3 V)

| Circuit Templates | | Cell | Column unit | Row unit | Column |
|---|---|---|---|---|---|
| Dynamic energy (pJ) | Write | 4.26 | 5.25 | 25.75 | 12.58 |
| | Read | 2.91 | 3.71 | 22.47 | 5.88 |
| Static power (nW) | | 3.23 | 24.37 | 25.88 | 195.74 |

## 5.2 Verification of Memory Matrix Model

Several memory matrices have been simulated in 40-nm CMOS technology to validate the model equations above. In Fig. 15 the dynamic power break-down of a 64-KByte memory matrix is shown. It is observed that the energy of local bitlines dominates the power consumption in a memory matrix as compared to the other circuits.

Figure 16 shows a comparison of simulation and estimation data for four memory matrices of different capacities (64, 128, 256, 1 K). Assuming a read access operation the four extracted-netlists were simulated using the same configuration. As shown in Table 5, the dynamic energies are compared to the estimated data and the differences are below 10 %. For the leakage power, the same comparisons are performed and the estimation errors are also below 10 %.

To further demonstrate the accuracy, four memory matrices with a fixed number of 64 words and with word lengths 8, 16, 32, 64 are implemented. As shown in Fig. 17 the

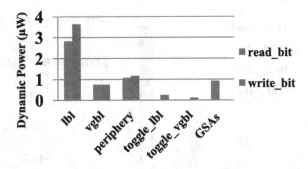

**Fig. 15.** Dynamic power component for a memory matrix (64 words 8 bit)

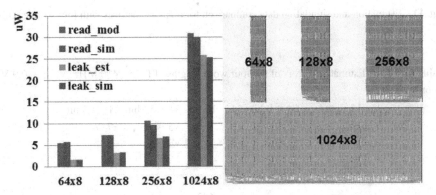

**Fig. 16.** Estimation and simulation data comparison for memory matrices with four capacities

**Table 5.** Model Estimation Errors of the four capacities (TT, 25°, 400 MHz, $V_{DDH}$ = 0.9 V, $V_{DDL}$ = 0.3 V)

| Capacity | 64 × 8 bit | 128 × 8 bit | 256 × 8 bit | 1024 × 8 bit |
|---|---|---|---|---|
| Dynamic energy | −5 % | −1 % | 9 % | 3 % |
| Static power | −4 % | −4 % | −5 % | 2 % |

estimation data are comparable to extracted-netlist simulation data. Both for dynamic energy and leakage power the estimation error remains below 10 %, as listed in Table 6.

# 6  Optimization Results

The power model created in this work takes all the dominating power contributors of on-chip SRAMs into account, which include an address decoder, memory cells and assists circuits, local and global sense amplifiers, driver circuits and interconnect capacitance. Figure 18 shows the power model applied for estimating the power

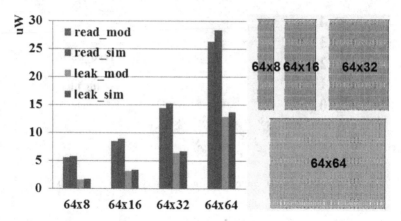

**Fig. 17.** Estimation and simulation data comparison for memory matrices with four wordlengths

**Table 6.** Model Estimation Errors of the four word lengths (TT, 25°, 400 MHz, $V_{DDH}$ = 0.9 V, $V_{DDL}$ = 0.3 V)

| Word lengths | $64 \times 8$ bit | $64 \times 16$ bit | $64 \times 32$ bit | $64 \times 64$ bit |
|---|---|---|---|---|
| Dynamic energy | −5 % | −5 % | −5 % | −7 % |
| Static power | −4 % | −4 % | −3 % | −6 % |

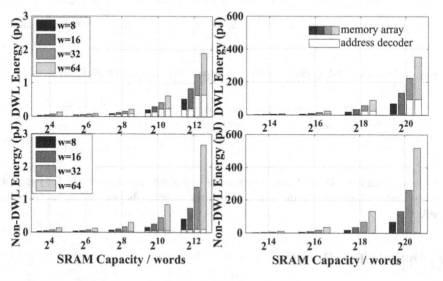

**Fig. 18.** Dynamic energy vs address bits & wordlengths for two architectures. The yellow bottom and the rest part of one bar represent the contributions of the address decoder and the memory matrix respectively (Color figure online).

consumption of SRAMs for various capacities and wordlengths. Minimum read dynamic power data is given due to more frequent read operation in caches. The model is applicable for capacities ranging from 16 to 1 M words and four wordlengths (8, 16, 32, 64). The figure illustrates how DWL and hierarchical LSA architecture affect the read power of SRAMs as function of different capacities and wordlengths. Moreover it indicates the different power contributions from address decoder and memory matrix to the dynamic read power.

In addition, the power model can be used for optimizing a specific SRAM by determining the optimal parameter combination. As discussed before, many possibilities exist for partitioning the memory matrix, the corresponding address decoder, given the three parameters partitioning parameters $(m, n, u)$, and many options for circuit implementations. Depending on the optimization criteria parameter combinations are picked from all possible implementations options. Note that the impact of process variations on leakage power is included in the power model.

A Pareto-optimization is made by considering silicon area and read power of the different partitioning parameters. Figure 19 shows how to use this approach to optimize a 1 K Byte SRAM for achieving a power and area tradeoff. In the scatter plot, there are ten architectures presenting relatively good area and power, which are picked from all the generated architectures. Four Pareto-optimal implementations are marked, in which two architectures deliver low area and the other two deliver low read power. Depending on the user's requirements a selection can be made, for instance the green point deliving a favorable area/power tradoff.

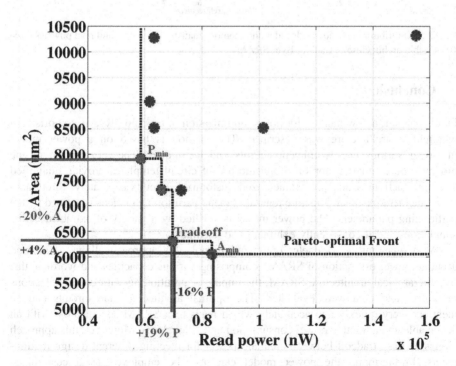

**Fig. 19.** Area cost vs read power tradeoff for a 1 K-Byte SRAM

Figure 20 shows a direct area/power break-down for the same ten possible architectures in Fig. 19. The contributions of the address decoder and memory matrix to the
overall area and read power are shown and analyzed quantitatively. Between the worst
case and best case solution a difference is observed for area and power up to 41 % and
62 % respectively.

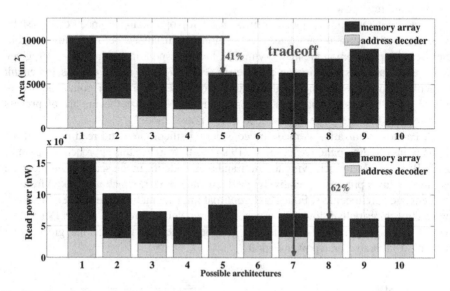

**Fig. 20.** Contribution of address decoder and memory matrix to area cost and read power for the
10 possible architectures of a 1 K Byte SRAM

# 7   Conclusion

In this chapter, a new method for power optimization of on-chip SRAMs comprising a
hierarchical architecture was described. The method is based on a power model
including various energy-efficient circuits and techniques. The introduction of the
probabilistic estimation approach and the use of circuit templates provide quantified
switching activities and pre-characterized customized circuits separately. Simultaneously the hierarchical architecture regarding many partitioning choices is defined by the
partitioning parameters. The power model is verified by a variety of extracted-netlist
simulations and it consistently exhibits good accuracy.

As a quantitative parameter optimization tool, this approach allows a fast and
accurate power estimation of SRAMs comprising various capacities and wordlengths.
In a hierarchical-architecture SRAM, the impact of partitioning with circuit selections
on power and area were evaluated. The optimal architecture and circuits can be
identified very quickly and accurately which leads to a SRAM specification with an
achievable and attractive power consumption and silicon area. Moreover, this approach
allows an easy tradeoff between area and power for meeting different design requirements. Furthermore, the power model can also be employed as a customized

benchmark for comparing various local circuits using the same architecture. Finally, this approach can easily be extended to other CMOS technologies due to its circuit templates and switching activity analysis.

# References

1. Sharma, V., et al.: A 4.4 pJ/access 80 MHz, 128 kbit variability resilient SRAM with Multi-Sized sense amplifier redundancy. IEEE J. Solid-State Circuits **46**(10), 2416–2430 (2011)
2. Clerc, S., et al.: A 65 nm SRAM achieving 250 mV retention and 350 mV, 1 MHz, 55fJ/bit access energy, with bit-interleaved radiation soft error tolerance. In: 2012 Proceedings of the ESSCIRC (ESSCIRC), pp. 313–316. IEEE (2012)
3. Rooseleer, B., Dehaene, W.: A 40 nm, 454 MHz 114 fJ/bit area-efficient SRAM memory with integrated charge pump. In: 2013 Proceedings of the ESSCIRC (ESSCIRC), pp. 201–204. IEEE (2013)
4. Ren, Y., Noll, T.G.: An accurate power estimation model for low-power hierarchical-architecture SRAMs. In: 2013 IFIP/IEEE 21st International Conference on Very Large Scale Integration (VLSI-SoC), pp. 144–149.IEEE (2013)
5. Ren, Y., et al.: Low power 6T-SRAM with tree address decoder using a new equalizer precharge scheme. In: 2012 IEEE International SOC Conference (SOCC), pp. 224–229. IEEE (2012)
6. Muralimanohar, N., et al.: CACTI 6.0: A tool to model large caches. Technical report (2009). http://www.hpl.hp.com/techreports/2009/HPL-2009-85.pdf
7. Liang, X., et al.: Architectural power models for sram and cam structures based on hybrid analytical/empirical techniques. In: IEEE/ACM International Conference on Computer-Aided Design, ICCAD 2007, pp. 824–830. IEEE (2007)
8. Do, M.Q., et al.: Leakage-Conscious Architecture-Level power estimation for partitioned and Power-Gated SRAM arrays. In: 8th International Symposium on Quality Electronic Design, ISQED 2007, pp. 185–191. IEEE, Washington, DC (2007)
9. Donkoh, E., et al.: A hybrid and adaptive model for predicting register file and SRAM power using a reference design. In: 2012 49th ACM/EDAC/IEEE Design Automation Conference (DAC), pp. 62–67. IEEE (2012)
10. Sun, L., et al.: Low power and robust binary tree SRAM design for embedded systems. In: 2013 International Symposium on Electronic System Design (ISED), pp. 87–92. IEEE (2013)

# Low-Power Low-Voltage ΔΣ Modulator Using Switched-Capacitor Passive Filters

Ali Fazli Yeknami[1(✉)] and Atila Alvandpour[2]

[1] School of Electrical Engineering and Computer Science,
Oregon State University, Corvallis, OR, USA
fazliyea@onid.oregonstate.edu
[2] Department of Electrical Engineering,
Linköping University, Linköping, Sweden
atila.alvandpour@liu.se

**Abstract.** A low-voltage low-power fourth-order active-passive ΔΣ modulator with one active stage is presented. The input-feedforward architecture is adopted, which improves the voltage swing prior to the quantizer. This enables a simpler comparator design and cascade of three passive filters. The passive integrator, as an alternate option to its power-hungry active counterpart, and the non-idealities associated with it are investigated. The active integrator used at the input stage provides most of the loop gain, which suppresses the thermal noise from the succeeding stages and minimizes the non-idealities in the comparator, such as noise and offset. The active integrator employs a two-stage amplifier with load compensation, whose DC-gain is boosted by a partially body-driven technique. The modulator, operated from a 0.7 V supply and clocked with 256 kHz sampling frequency, achieves 84 dB SNR and 80.3 dB SNDR over a 500 Hz signal bandwidth, while it dissipates only 400 nW power.

**Keywords:** Passive integrator · Delta-sigma modulator · Low-voltage · Low-power · Active-passive modulator · Feedforward architecture

## 1 Introduction

Biomedical electronics including portable medical devices, ambulatory and in-site hospital equipments and body implantable devices, in particular, have gained significant attention in healthcare. Low energy consumption is one of the major design concerns for prolongation of the battery lifetime or other limited source of energy. The analog-to-digital converters (ADCs) are the key building blocks of such devices. Delta-sigma modulator is a powerful ADC technique because of its higher accuracy in low-speed applications (e.g., medical applications).

Passive integrator, as an alternative to the power-hungry active integrator, is a significant approach in the design of low-power and low-voltage delta-sigma (ΔΣ) modulators for reducing the analog power consumption [1–6]. However, due to the lack of DC gain inside the passive filter (or integrator), the modulator is sensitive to noise coupling, thereby affecting the signal-to-noise ratio (SNR). Modulators in [1, 2] employ switched-capacitor (SC) gain-boosted passive filter to somewhat compensate for the

© IFIP International Federation for Information Processing 2015
A. Orailoglu et al. (Eds.): VLSI-SoC 2013, IFIP AICT 461, pp. 94–118, 2015.
DOI: 10.1007/978-3-319-23799-2_5

lack of gain. However, achieving very high gain requires unrealistically large capacitive area as well as high sensitivity to parasitic capacitances [3]. In [4] no DC gain is used in the second-order loop filter. Instead, a three-stage preamplifier is exploited before the comparator to compensate for the gain, which is a power consuming solution.

Due to no gain, the signal experiences a large suppression inside the passive filter, making the comparator design a challenging task. The comparator non-idealities including noise, DC offset, and hysteresis directly limit the modulator resolution [5, 6]. The third-order modulator in [5] makes use of the passive filter in the first and third stages and an active Gm-C filter in the middle stage in order to compensate for the loop gain and to mitigate the comparator's offset and noise. In addition, the Gm block is to isolate the two pole sectors from each other and to prevent inter-stage loading between them. The fourth-order active-passive modulator in [7] utilizes a low-power amplifier topology in the first integrator, which can suppress the comparator non-idealities and the thermal noise from the succeeding passive stages, resulting in significant reduction of the capacitive area.

This chapter introduces a new approach for power reduction in the ΔΣ modulators. It describes the design of the basic passive filter and the non-idealities associated with it. The traditional passive modulators using cascade-of-integrators feedback (CIFB) architecture are briefly reviewed and their advantages and disadvantages are explained in details. Then, a fourth-order feedforward active-passive modulator is presented using only one active stage, which mitigates some of the fundamental problems associated with the traditional passive ADCs.

The input feedforward architecture has an extra path from the input of the modulator to the quantizer [8–11]. This small architectural modification eliminates the signal component inside the loop filter; therefore the filter only processes the quantization noise [11]. This distinct feature of the feedforward modulator structure encourages the cascading of three power-efficient SC passive filters despite their large attenuation. Moreover, the voltage swing at the quantizer input is the sum of the input signal and the suppressed quantization noise (processed by the filter), which eases the comparator design without requiring any preamplifier circuit. Significant power reduction can thus be achieved due to (i) the reduced sampling clock frequency by employing a fourth-order active-passive loop filter; (ii) the removal of the power-consuming preamplifier prior to the comparator, unlike the traditional passive modulators with feedback architecture; (iii) the use of power-efficient passive integrators; (iv) the relaxed amplifier design requirements in the full input-feedforward modulator structure [8, 9]; (v) an accurate and low attenuation passive adder for summation of the input and feedforward paths, and (vi) last, but not least, the reduced supply voltage helped to scale down the power consumption from digital blocks.

The rest of the chapter is organized as follows. Section 2 discusses the issues associated with the design of passive modulators using feedback structure. Section 3 describes both the architecture-level and circuit-level design of the proposed fourth-order active-passive modulator, followed by the simulation results in Sect. 4. Section 5 presents the performance comparison of this modulator with respect to the previously reported passive modulators. The chapter is then summarized in Sect. 6.

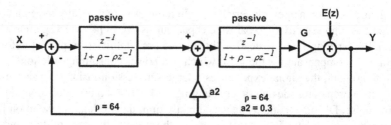

**Fig. 1.** The linearized model of the $2^{nd}$-order passive $\Delta\Sigma$ modulator using distributed feedback topology [7] (Courtesy of IEEE)

## 2 Passive Modulator Design Using CIFB Topology

In this section we take a closer look at the challenges concerning the design of passive modulators implemented by the CIFB architecture. The CIFB topology has no forward connections to the quantizer input, unlike the CIFF topology, but requires internal digital-to-analog converters (DACs) which are fed back to the input and the intermediate filters. In other words, a fourth-order CIFB modulator topology needs four feedback DAC branches to each integrator's input, while a CIFF modulator structure needs only one feedback DAC from the output to the input. Thus, the DAC circuitry is much simpler in a CIFF modulator structure.

### 2.1 System-Level Considerations

The linear model of the second-order passive $\Delta\Sigma$ modulator with two-pole lowpass filter and single-bit quantizer is shown in Fig. 1. To determine the signal and noise transfer functions (STF and NTF), a linear model is used for the quantizer. It is a gain stage, $G$, followed by additive white quantization noise. The gain factor $G$ in a conventional active modulator is estimated as unity [12] assuming the integrators swing is maintained close to the reference voltage. In a passive modulator the signal swing at the quantizer input is much weaker than the reference level, due to the successive attenuation by the passive filters [1–3], resulting in a non-unity $G$. This gain is lumped into the comparator input, according to Fig. 1, and is a function of the passive filter's pole location [3]. An estimate of this gain is given by [2, 4] in which the overall loop gain is approximated to be unity at half of the sampling clock frequency, $f_s/2$. For an overall loop filter transfer function $H_T$, the estimated $G$ can be calculated as $1/|H_T(f_s/2)|$. On the other hand, since the modulator is a nonlinear system, an accurate value of the quantizer gain can only be obtained from the nonlinear simulations [13].

For a simple passive filter shown in Fig. 2, the ideal transfer function can be given in the $z$-domain as

$$H(z) = \frac{V_{out}(z)}{V_{in}(z)} = \frac{-z^{-1}}{1 + \rho - \rho z^{-1}} \tag{1}$$

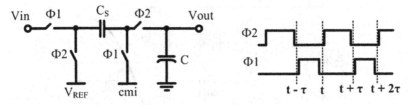

**Fig. 2.** Passive lowpass filter in a single-ended form together with two-phase non-overlapping clocks [7] (Courtesy of IEEE)

where $\rho = C/C_s$. The low-frequency gain is unity and the −3 dB cut-off frequency can be calculated from Eq. (1) as

$$f_{-3dB} = \frac{f_s}{2\pi(\rho + 1)} \tag{2}$$

where $f_s$ is the sampling clock frequency. Taking $f_s = 500$ kHz, $C_s = 2$ pF, determined from the thermal noise requirement, and $C = 128$ pF, placing the −3 dB bandwidth around 1 kHz, the NTF and STF of the second-order passive modulator shown in Fig. 1 can be approximated as:

$$NTF(z) = \frac{1}{1 + 0.3GH + GH^2} = \frac{1.36 - 2.77z + 1.41z^2}{1 - 2.38z + 1.41z^2} \tag{3}$$

$$STF(z) = \frac{GH^2}{1 + 0.3GH + GH^2} = \frac{0.02z^2}{1 - 2.38z + 1.41z^2} \tag{4}$$

Figure 3 depicts the magnitude of the NTF and STF. As expected, the passive modulator suffers from the limited in-band quantization-noise suppression due to lack of gain in the passive loop filter, resulting in low SNR. Unlike the conventional active ΔΣ ADCs which has unity-gain STF at low frequencies, some signal attenuation is obtained in the passive modulator. As clearly seen, this attenuation (or loss) is −3.5 dB at low-frequency, which can also be obtained by substituting $z = 1$ into STF Eq. (4) This is the fundamental problem of the passive filters and the major performance limiting factor in the passive modulators, which terminates to an extremely low voltage swing at the quantizer input. For the second-order passive modulator presented in [4], as an example, the integrators output swing is in the order of 10 mVrms and 100 μVrms, respectively, for a full scale (FS) input that the comparator has to detect it. A highly sensitive comparator is then required to distinguish the signal from the noise coupled inside the loop. Therefore, the comparator in this design employs a three-stage preamplifier circuit in order to compensate for the required loop gain, dissipating a large amount of analog power in this block. To the best of our knowledge, most of the existing passive ADCs have been designed based on the CIFB topology [1–4], which rely only on second-order loop filter. Cascading more than two passive filters is impractical because the very large signal attenuation inside the loop demands multi-stage power-consuming preamplifier circuit prior to the comparator.

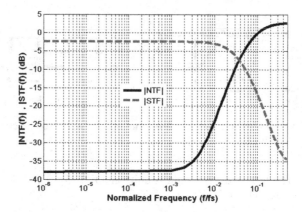

**Fig. 3.** The magnitude of NTF and STF of a $2^{nd}$-order passive modulator with $\rho = 64$ [7] (Courtesy of IEEE)

## 2.2 Low-Voltage Compatibility

One of the most significant advantages of the passive filter is that it can function at very low supply voltage as long as the gate of the switches is driven adequately. Utilizing advanced switches developed to date, the switch overdriving problem can simply be alleviated. Low-$V_{TH}$ switch [8, 14], gate-boosted [15, 16] or boot-strapped switches [17] are several examples of such modern switches. Energy harvesting and biomedical implant systems are two applications where ultra low-voltage circuit design is compulsory and highly demanding. Conventional analog circuit topologies are no longer useful in these systems. Therefore, new circuit techniques have been developed recently, which have enabled ultra low-voltage operation of the $\Delta\Sigma$ ADCs [15, 16]. Body-input operational transconductance amplifiers (OTAs) and body-input gate-clocked comparator operating at 0.5 V in [15] eliminated the constraint on the threshold voltage. Moreover, inverter-based integrators were realized by overdrive voltages near the $V_{TH}$ in the modulator presented in [16] using a switched-capacitor (SC) biasing scheme, where charge pump clock boosting scheme were utilized for sufficient switch overdrive. These combinations have made it possible to develop a $\Delta\Sigma$ modulator operated from a power supply below 0.3 V. Both modulator prototypes rely on power-hungry active integrators at which analog circuit design is a challenging task at such low supply voltages, due to the limited headroom and small available signal swing. For a given $g_m$, a body-input OTA requires several times larger bias current than a typical gate-input OTA, thereby preventing the target modulator to achieve a high power-efficiency. In addition to charge-pump clock boosting, the inverter amplifier biased near $V_{TH}$ needs special biasing and common-mode feedback (CMFB) circuitries that can operate with a 0.25 V supply voltage, imposing circuit overhead and additional power consumption.

An alternative approach for designing a low-voltage low-power $\Delta\Sigma$ modulator is the substitution of power consuming OTAs by the power-efficient passive integrators [1, 3]. Despite the lack of gain and therefore larger sensitivity to noise coupling inside the loop filter, the passive integrators suggest significant power reduction and ability to operate at low supply voltages. A 0.7 V second-order modulator was implemented in [3] using a fully passive filter and the standard feedback topology. It only consumes 430 nW power while obtaining 70 dB peak SNR. Due to very low signal swings of the passive integrators, high dynamic range signals can be applied at the modulator input. Since digital power is the dominant source of the power consumption in the aforementioned design, scaling down of the power supply could significantly contribute in the overall power reduction. A 0.5 V fully passive modulator was presented in [1] based on the design in [3] using a charge-redistributed gain-boosted passive filter in the second stage, a body-driven gain-enhanced preamplifier prior to the comparator, and a low-voltage comparator circuit. The switch overdrive problem was mitigated by low-$V_{TH}$ transistors while the non-linear sub-$V_{TH}$ leakage current of the critical switches was suppressed by an analog T-switch scheme [14]. The modulator achieves 71 dB peak signal-to-noise-and-distortion (SNDR) from a supply voltage of 0.5 V, while dissipating only 250 nW power. The attained figure of merit (FOM) is 86 fJ/convertion-step, where FOM is calculated as Power/($2^{ENOB} \times 2 \times BW$) with $ENOB$ as the effective number of bits (or resolution) and $BW$ as the input signal bandwidth.

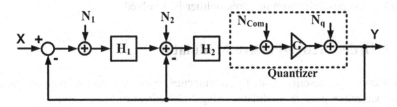

**Fig. 4.** Noise sources in a single-loop second-order passive modulator [7] (Courtesy of IEEE)

## 2.3 Performance Limiting Factors

Here the main limiting factors that avoid the passive modulators from obtaining a high resolution will be discussed. As mentioned before, the lack of gain and significant signal suppression inside the passive loop filter make the design of high-resolution comparator a critical and challenging task. To revisit other issues concerning the comparator design, the linear model of a second-order single-loop modulator, shown in Fig. 4, is considered in which all the noise sources are specified. The baseband output signal can be approximated as:

$$Y \approx X + N_1 + \frac{N_2}{H_1} + \frac{N_{Com}}{H_1 H_2} + \frac{N_q}{G H_1 H_2} \tag{5}$$

where $H_1$ and $H_2$ are the integrators transfer functions, $N_1$ and $N_2$ are their input-referred noise, respectively, while $N_{Com}$ and $N_q$ represent the comparator input referred noise and quantization noise. Since both filters have no DC gain, only quantization noise obtains some lowpass filtering, due to the loop gain $G$ provided by the quantizer. On the other hand, for a certain SNR the thermal noise ($kT/C$ noise) of the passive filters can be mitigated by scaling up the capacitors size (area penalty).

However, $N_{Com}$ is the only noise term that is not subject to any attenuation at low frequencies simply because $H_1$ and $H_2$ have no gain. $N_{Com}$ is any non-idealities of the comparator including the thermal noise, low frequency $1/f$ noise, and offset voltage. To alleviate these non-idealities the passive modulator in [2] utilizes a preamplifier whose input devices have a W/L ratio of 200 μm/1.2 μm, imposing about 0.5 pF at the comparator input. Moreover, in the passive delta-sigma ADCs due to no gain in the stages preceding the comparator, the offset of the overall ADC is defined by that of the comparator [4].

To alleviate the non-idealities of the comparator, several solutions have been tried in the past [5, 6] where at least one active stage was used to suppress the input-referred noise and the dc offset.

To summarize, due to a very small signal swing at the quantizer input of the passive ADCs using CIFB topology, the comparator design is a crucial and difficult task, limiting the design scaling to higher-order modulator. In the following section, a fourth-order modulator will be presented that employs three successive passive filters using cascade-of-integrators feedforward (CIFF) topology, resulting in voltage swing improvement at the comparator input. As a result, the comparator design becomes simpler and no power-consuming preamplifier is involved.

# 3    4-th Order Active-Passive Modulator

In this section we describe both the architecture-level and circuit-level design of a fourth-order active-passive modulator using full feedforward topology.

## 3.1    Architectural Design

Full feedforward architecture has become popular in recent years for low-power and low-voltage modulator design [8–11, 16]. We take advantage of this architecture to improve the voltage swing at the quantizer input, a drawback of the passive modulators using traditional CIFB topology. As a result, the comparator design becomes simpler and no preamplifier stage is required prior to the comparator.

**Modulator Topology.** Figure 5 shows the block diagram of the single-loop fourth-order modulator topology with single-bit quantizer. An active integrator is used in the first stage, while three SC passive filters are employed in the following stages. The passive filters were described using the transfer function given by Eq. (1). The feedforward branches are summed at the input node of the quantizer. The optimal coefficients of the designed modulator are calculated from the behavioral simulation and are summarized in Table 1. It must be pointed out that the actual coefficients $a_i$ for $i = 2, 3, 4$ is $1/(1 + \rho)$ which is included into the passive filter transfer function in Fig. 5. The NTF can be calculated as

$$NTF(z) = \frac{z^4 + 2.03z^3 - 11.76z^2 + 13.42z - 4.69}{z^4 - 7.91z^3 - 5.97z^2 - 15.19z + 4.64} \tag{6}$$

The magnitude plot of the NTF is shown in Fig. 6.

Behavioral simulation indicates that the signal amplitude at the quantizer input is 40 mV for a FS input, much lower than the reference voltage, 0.5 V in this design. Since the delta-sigma ADC is a nonlinear block, the equivalent gain of the quantizer can be directly calculated from the simulation.

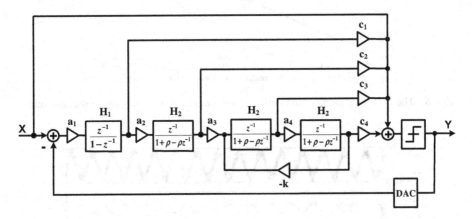

**Fig. 5.** Block diagram of the single-loop fourth-order full feedforward active-passive ΔΣ modulator with one active integrator in the first stage [7] (Courtesy of IEEE)

**Table 1.** Modulator coefficients [7] (Courtesy of IEEE)

| Filter coefficients | Feedforward coefficients | Resonator coefficient |
|---|---|---|
| $a_1 = 0.2$ | $c_1 = 2$ | |
| $a_2 = 1$ | $c_2 = 3$ | $k = 1/64$ |
| $a_3 = 1$ | $c_3 = 2$ | |
| $a_4 = 1$ | $c_4 = 5$ | |

A local resonator feedback loop with a gain coefficient of $k$ is used to move a pair of the NTF zeros to the edge of the signal band. In this way, some SNR improvement can be achieved.

**Integrators Output Swing.** A behavioral simulation with −1.94 dBFS input signal is accomplished to show the integrators output swing and the summed voltage level at the quantizer input. The reference voltage is set to 0.5 V. It is worth to be mentioned that the signal component leaks to the loop filter, due to the attenuation by the passive summation network. As can be seen from Fig. 7, the largest swing is observed at the first integrator output, however it is still within 60 % of the reference voltage. The reduced voltage swing enables the OTA, the most critical and power consuming block, to have a relaxed slew-rate requirement, hence low power consumption. The output swing at the succeeding passive integrators decreases continually. As the loop filter in a

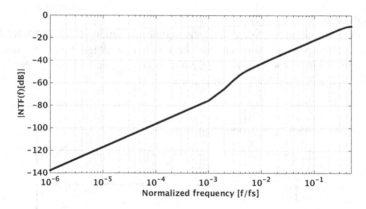

**Fig. 6.** The NTF magnitude of the designed 4th-order modulator neglecting the resonator

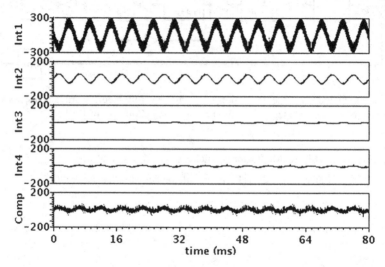

**Fig. 7.** Integrators output swing in mV using a −1.94 dBFS, 187 Hz input signal. Comp represents the comparator input signal, and *Inti* ($i$ = 1–4) represents the $i$th integrator output [7] (Courtesy of IEEE)

full feedforward topology ideally only processes the quantization noise [13], the continuous attenuation of the passive integrators does not harm the input signal. In contrast to the feedback or CIFB topology, the feedforward topology has a signal path from the modulator input to the quantizer. Therefore, the voltage level at the quantizer input is still large enough for the comparator to detect it without requiring a stringent preamplifier circuit.

More details of circuit design are explained in the following section. One thing should be noted is that, since the single-bit quantizer is used, the integrators in the full feedforward architecture still contain the attenuated signal component, particularly in the first integrator.

## 3.2    Circuit-Level Design

This section describes the overall modulator circuit and its building blocks.

**Passive Filter Design.** The passive filter used as integrator in the second to fourth stages was shown in Fig. 2. The larger ρ places the filter pole to a lower frequency, according to Eq. (2). Intuitively, the overall loop gain is distributed among the first active pole sector and the quantizer gain, while the low frequency DC gain of the passive integrators is unity.

The parameter $\rho = C/C_s$, in general, is selected so that the –3 dB cut-off frequency, calculated from Eq. (2), to be placed near the edge of signal bandwidth. The simulation demonstrates that the voltage swing at the quantizer input is almost constant for $\rho \geq 32$, as shown in Fig. 8a. On the other hand, the parameter ρ can also be determined from the SNDR simulations, which consider both the quantization noise and distortion performance. The simulation result shown in Fig. 8b illustrates an optimal ρ of 64. The sampling and integrating capacitors are therefore selected as 0.25 pF and 16 pF, respectively.

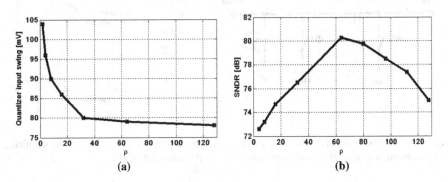

**Fig. 8.** (a) Simulated voltage swing at the quantizer input; (b) simulated SNDR across ρ. –1.94 dBFS, 187 Hz sinusoidal signal was applied in both cases [7] (Courtesy of IEEE)

In practical implementation of the passive filter (Fig. 2), the parasitic capacitors introduced by the top and bottom plates of the sampling and integrating capacitors can influence the filter transfer function, low frequency gain and pole location, given by Eqs. (1) and (2). Here we examine the effect of these parasitics on the filter's and ΔΣ modulator performance. Considering the filter of Fig. 9a for which the most significant parasitic capacitors are lumped into $C_P$, the filter transfer function given by Eq. (1) can be modified to

$$H_P(z) = \frac{-z^{-1}}{1 + \rho + \beta - \rho z^{-1}} \tag{7}$$

where $\rho = C/C_S$ and $\beta = C_P/C_S$. Compared to Eq. (1), the term $\beta = C_P/C_S$ is excessive and is created because of the parasitic capacitor at the internal node. The integrator (filter) loss and –3 dB cut-off frequency can be calculated from Eq. (7) as follows:

$$A_{0_P} = |H_p(z = 1)| = \frac{C_s}{C_s + C_p} < 1 \qquad (8)$$

$$f_{-3dB} = \frac{f_s}{2\pi} \cdot \frac{C_s + C_p}{C + C_s + C_p} \qquad (9)$$

where $A_{0_P}$ is the magnitude of $H_p(z)$ at DC. Compared to Eq. (2), the net effect of the parasitic capacitor is the higher passband attenuation (DC gain of less than unity) as given by Eq. (8) and the shift of the –3 dB cut-off frequency to a higher frequency as given by Eq. (9), which can degrade the quantization noise suppression. As an example, with $f_s = 500$ kHz, $C_S = 2$ pF, $C = 64$ pF and the estimated $C_P = 100$ fF, the

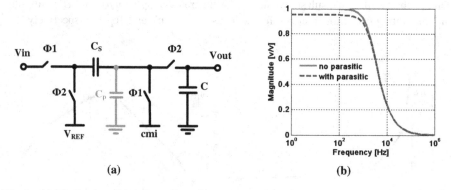

(a)                                          (b)

**Fig. 9.** (a) The basic passive filter associated with lumped parasitic capacitor; (b) the simulated transfer function with/without parasitic capacitor [3] (Courtesy of IEEE)

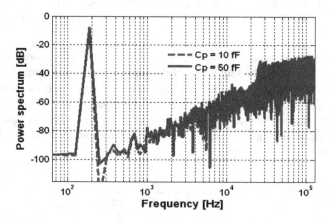

**Fig. 10.** Simulated output spectra of the fourth-order modulator with addition of 10 fF and 50 fF parasitic capacitor in the passive integrators of the second to fourth stages

filter transfer function with/without parasitic capacitor is simulated. Figure 9b indicates that in the presence of $C_P$ the gain decreases from unity to 0.95, while the pole shifts from 2.4 kHz to 2.54 kHz. The results can also be verified by inserting the parameters into Eqs. (8) and (9), showing a good agreement between the simulation results and calculations.

Furthermore, the impact of parasitic capacitors of the passive filters on the overall performance of the designed fourth-order modulator was simulated. Figure 10 shows the power spectra of the modulator with 10 fF and 50 fF parasitic capacitors inserted in the internal node of the passive integrators of the second to fourth stages.

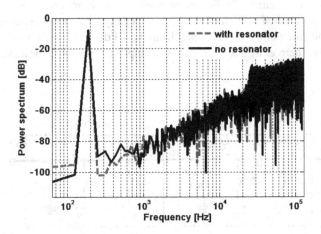

**Fig. 11.** Simulated output spectra with/without local resonator using a −1.94 dBFS, 187-Hz input signal [7] (Courtesy of IEEE)

The achieved simulated SNDR is 79.6 dB and 77.4 dB from 10 fF and 50 fF parasitic capacitors, respectively. The third and fifth harmonic distortions also grow by 3 dB when the parasitic capacitor value increases from 10 fF to 50 fF. Consequently, the implementation of the sampling and integrating capacitors of the passive filters is very important to avoid large internal parasitics.

**Inter-Stage Loading.** Another non-ideality which can influence the performance of the passive modulators is the inter-stage loading effect. To explain this, we consider the cascade of two basic passive filters, illustrated in Fig. 2, for the sake of clarity. Figure 12 shows the resulting $2^{nd}$-order passive filter and its equivalent model in the sampling phase, Φ1. Clearly seen in Fig. 12b, there is charge-sharing between integrating capacitor $C_2$ of the first stage and the sampling capacitor $C_{S3}$ of the next stage. During the sampling phase, this charge-sharing may cause a sampling error, and can reduce the integrator's accuracy. This phenomenon is also called inter-stage loading effect, i.e. the sampling capacitor of the following stage loads the previous stage. The sampled voltage corresponding to the time instance $n$ at node $x$ (Fig. 12b) can be written as

$$V_x(n) = \frac{C_2}{C_2 + C_{S3}} V_{out2}(n-1) \qquad (10)$$

One way to prevent the $2^{nd}$-order filter (Fig. 12a) from the inter-stage loading is to fully isolate the two passive stages from each other by using a buffer or an active integrator in the middle [5, 6]. However, this is a power-consuming approach, which requires a power-hungry active integrator. Another practical solution to cope with this problem is the proper capacitor sizing. By keeping $C_2 \gg C_{S3}$ the fraction $C_2/(C_2 + C_{S3})$ in (10) approaches one. For instance, in the designed modulator $C_2$ and $C_{S3}$ are 16 pF and 0.25 pF, respectively. Thus, there is only 1.5 % sampling error in the second passive filter, due to charge-sharing. To further decrease the error, relatively larger integrating capacitor $C_2$ is required, which imposes area penalty and more attenuation. On the other hand, the value of $C_2$ was obtained from the −3 dB bandwidth requirement given by (2). Clearly, there exist trade-offs among sampling error, pole location, attenuation and area.

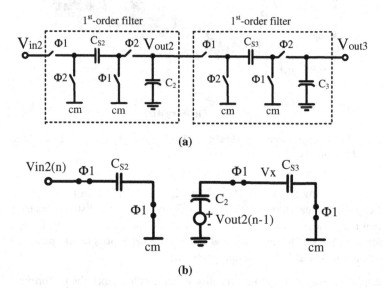

**(a)**

**(b)**

**Fig. 12.** (a) A $2^{nd}$-order passive low-pass filter built from the cascade of two basic passive filters, (b) Equivalent model in sampling phase $\Phi1$

**Local Resonator.** The purpose of the local resonator feedback loop used in the designed modulator is to move a pair of the NTF zeros to the edge of the signal band, improving the in-band noise shaping. The resonator creates a simple negative feedback loop with a gain coefficient $k$ of 1/64. The resonator is simple to be realized using SC implementation (two switches and one small capacitor). Figure 11 shows the simulated output spectra with/without local resonator. A 5 dB SNDR improvement was achieved in this way at the expense of a small area penalty.

**Partially Body-Driven Gain-Enhanced Amplifier.** Several OTA topologies were designed and carefully analyzed [18, 19] for ultra-low-power delta-sigma modulators. Among them a two-stage load-compensated amplifier was selected because of its higher power-efficiency, rail-to-rail voltage swing, and minimal load for a balanced gain-bandwidth (GBW) and phase margin. While two-stage Miller amplifier and single-stage current-mirror OTA have been commonly used for low-power and low-voltage modulators [8, 20], we exploit the two-stage load-compensated OTA topology because of its privilege in low bias current and low speed environment of the target medical application [21, 22]. Due to low bias current (in the range of 100 nA) in this design, the output resistance of the OTA is intrinsically high and the dominant pole of the output load $C_L$ is then placed at very low frequency using a minimal load capacitor value (2 pF load). Therefore, in this low clock speed application the load compensation is preferred to the Miller compensation as it prevents additional power consumption for driving the Miller capacitor.

A fully-differential partially body-driven and gain-enhanced two-stage amplifier with load-compensation was developed for the modulator's input active stage. The detailed circuit is shown in Fig. 13. To reduce the power, the input common-mode level of the OTA is set to 0.35 V (i.e., $V_{DD}/2$), which is limited by the gate-source voltage of M1a-M1b, and the drain-source voltage of M0. Low-$V_{TH}$ transistors are used to provide more headroom for the low-voltage analog design. Meanwhile, the bodies of the p-MOS transistors (i.e., M2, M3, and M6) are tied to half of the $V_{DD}$ (the common-mode level of the ΔΣ modulator) to further decrease the threshold voltage, providing even more operating headroom.

The cascode topologies such as telescopic or folded cascode do not exist in low-voltage analog design, which brings rail-to-rail voltage swing at the cost of restricted DC gain. A body-driven positive feedback is adopted at the output stage (M6a/M6b) to enhance the gain without significant power increase. The transistors M6a and M6b form a cross-coupled connection at their body terminals, which introduces negative conductance $-g_{mb6}$ at the output nodes (Vo+ and Vo−). In this way, the overall output conductance is effectively decreased, which boosts the total DC gain. The overall DC gain can be expressed as

$$A_0 = \frac{g_{m1}}{g_{ds1} + g_{ds2}} \cdot \frac{g_{m3} + g_{m6}}{g_{ds3} + g_{ds4} + g_{ds5} + g_{ds6} - g_{mb6}} \tag{11}$$

The size of M6a/M6b is chosen such that the conductance $g_{mb6}$ becomes 65 % of the term gds3 + gds4 + gds5 + gds6. With this option the amplifier is stable and gives high enough DC gain. As shown in Fig. 14, with gain-enhancement technique the typical DC gain and GBW increase from 39.6 dB and 670 kHz to 50.4 dB and 1.12 MHz, respectively. Figure 15 also shows the gain and phase plot of the OTA under process and temperature variations (−20°C to +85°C). The worst-case gain and GBW are 43 dB and 600 kHz, respectively, which are adequate for the target SNR, according to system-level simulations. Using typical simulations, the OTA achieves 50.4 dB DC gain, 60° phase margin and 1.2 MHz GBW with a 2 pF load, while dissipating 250 nW power.

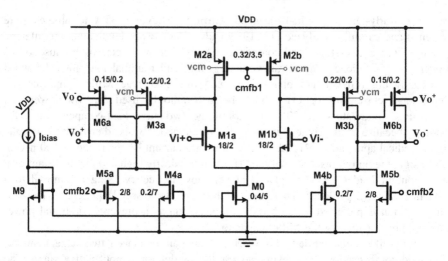

**Fig. 13.** The proposed two-stage load-compensated amplifier employing body-driven gain-enhancement technique; the bodies of p-MOS transistors are tied to the modulator common-mode voltage vcm = $V_{DD}/2$. Sizes are given in μm unit

Since for a given bias current the $g_m$ of the weak inversion transistor is almost five times larger than that of a strong inversion [23], the main transistors (M1, M3, and M6) are driven in the weak inversion region, while other transistors are biased in the moderate inversion region. This can also help to decrease the thermal noise of the mentioned transistors that is represented by $2kT\gamma/g_{m1}$.

**Passive Adder.** In the designed modulator a passive SC network is employed for the summation of the feedforward branches in order to avoid power consumption due to an active adder. However, careful design consideration is needed to prevent significant

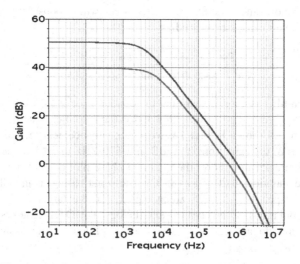

**Fig. 14.** The simulated typical DC gain with/without gain-enhancement technique

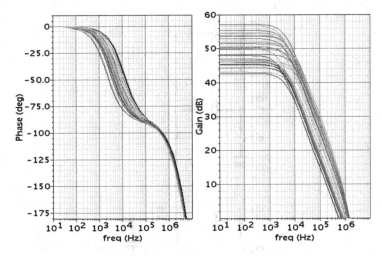

**Fig. 15.** Bode diagram of the gain and phase response across process and temperature variations

voltage attenuation prior to the quantizer. Figure 16 shows the used adder in its single-ended form. In $\Phi1$ the input and integrators output are sampled onto feedforwarded capacitors $Cf0$–$Cf4$, while in $\Phi2$ these capacitors are discharged. Using superposition principle and the voltage divider across $C_{Com}$, the output voltage $V_{out}$ can be expressed as

$$V_{Out} = \frac{Cf0}{Cf0 + C_{Com}} V_{in+} + \frac{Cf1}{Cf1 + C_{Com}} V_{o1+} + \cdots + \frac{Cf4}{Cf4 + C_{Com}} V_{o4+} \qquad (12)$$

where $V_{in+}$ is the positive input, $V_{oi+}$ ($i = 1$–$4$) is the $i$-th integrator's output, and $C_{Com}$ models the parasitic capacitor at the comparator input. An important design consideration at this point is to keep the $C_{Com}$ a low value in order to avoid voltage attenuation. In the designed comparator, the estimated input parasitic is less than 100 fF. With this value and the capacitor values listed in Table 2, the output voltage given by (12) reduces to

$$V_{Out} = 0.9V_{in+} + 0.95V_{o1+} + 0.97V_{o2+} + 0.95V_{o3+} + 0.98V_{o4+} \qquad (13)$$

In the modulator block diagram shown in Fig. 5, it is assumed that the input-feedforward coefficient (from input $x$ to quantizer input) is unity. It can be shown that the corresponding STF is one in all frequencies. In modulator realization with passive adder shown in Fig. 16, however, the input-feedforward coefficient reduces to 0.9 rather than unity. As a result, the STF can be modified to

$$STF = \frac{0.9 + H}{1 + H} \qquad (14)$$

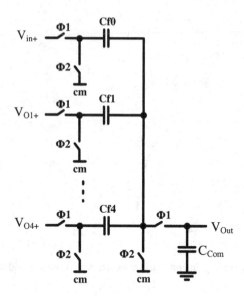

**Fig. 16.** Passive adder. Single-ended scheme is shown for the sake of simplicity. $V_{oi+}$ ($i = 1$–$4$) is the $i$-th integrator's output, and $C_{Com}$ represents the parasitic capacitor at the input of the comparator

It can be shown that the loop filter $H$ is equal to $0.4H_1 + 0.6H_1H_2 + 0.4H_1 H_2^2 + H_1 H_2^3$, where $H_1$ is the transfer function of the first active integrator, and $H_2$ is the transfer function of each passive integrator in the following stages (Fig. 5). For the sake of simplicity, the local resonator is omitted and is not considered in the function $H$. The magnitude plot of the STF is shown in Fig. 17. To summarize, the attenuation due to the passive summation is dealt with a low input parasitic capacitor in the designed comparator circuit. In turn, a power-consuming amplifier in an active adder is prevented, leading to a power-efficient modulator design.

**Single-Bit Quantizer.** The existing passive ADCs [1–5] make use of the traditional CIFB architecture, which primarily suffer from the extreme signal suppression. This makes the comparator design a challenging task. The use of preamplifier stages, as a power consuming solution, prior to the comparator circuit is essential for detecting the very weak signal. As an example, 35 % of the total power dissipation in the design presented by [1] comes from the preamplifier.

The single-bit quantizer in this design is composed of a dynamic regenerative comparator followed by a SR latch [20]. No pre-amplification stages were used, which lead to a significant power saving. The simple reason is that, compared to the traditional CIFB modulator architecture, the selected CIFF architecture relaxes the voltage swing requirement at the quantizer input. In other words, the voltage amplitude at the comparator input node of the designed feedforward modulator is the sum of the input signal, the first active integrator's output swing and the attenuated output swing from the succeeding passive integrators, which is relatively larger than that of a modulator implemented by a CIFB structure. This can be clearly seen in Fig. 7. We then utilize

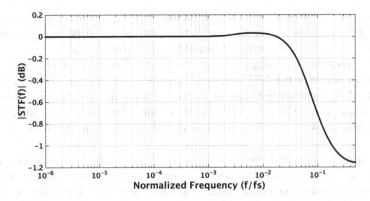

**Fig. 17.** The STF magnitude of the designed 4th-order modulator

a simple and power-efficient quantizer circuit without pre-amplifications [7]. The circuit schematic is shown in Fig. 18. When clock signal *clk* goes low, the nodes *x* and *y* are precharged to $V_{DD}$. While *clk* goes high, the precharged nodes start to discharge to ground by transistors M1a and M1b. The amount of discharge currents depend on the input signals. The cross-coupled transistors, M3a and M3b, form a positive feedback loop and amplify the difference in the inputs to a full-rail output. As the comparator is a dynamic circuit and is clocked by the non-overlapping clock phases, a slow clock causes leakage current flow through the branches. Therefore, high-$V_{TH}$ and low-power (hvtlp type) transistors of the used 65 nm CMOS technology were utilized to suppress the leakage. The total power consumption of the comparator and latch is less than 10 nW.

**Complete Modulator Circuit.** The overall modulator circuit is shown in Fig. 19. It employs a fourth-order loop filter implemented by single-loop full feedforward architecture. It has four integrators including an active one in the first stage and three

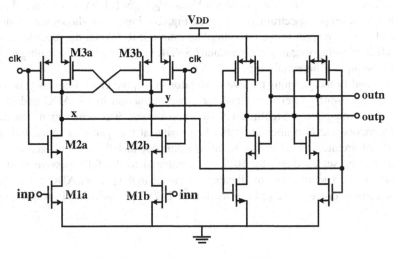

**Fig. 18.** Dynamic comparator and SR latch

passive ones in the following stages. The summation at the quantizer input is performed by using a SC network. A simple dynamic comparator is utilized as single-bit quantizer, while the power consuming preamplifier is removed in total.

A basic resonator feedback composed of two switches and a small capacitor $C_b$ is employed to optimize the NTF's zero location near the edge of signal bandwidth. A 5 dB SNR improvement can be obtained according to the simulation. The common-mode voltage is set to the middle of the power supply, i.e. 0.35 V. The reference voltage is set to 0.5 V, which is defined by $V_{REFP}$ of 0.6 V and $V_{REFN}$ of 0.1 V.

The capacitor value of the first integrator (i.e., $C_{S1}$) and the signal feedforward path (i.e., $C_{f0}$) are selected to fulfill the $kT/C$ noise requirement of the modulator with a safe margin [10]. The other modulator sampling and feedforward capacitors (i.e., $C_{Si}$ and $C_{fi}$ for $i = 2, 3, 4$) are chosen to satisfy the modulator coefficients listed in Table 1. The first integrating capacitors (i.e., $C_1$) is chosen to realize the coefficient $a_1 = 0.2$, while the rest of the integrating capacitors (i.e., $C_i$ for $i = 2, 3, 4$) are selected from the passive filter requirement, as discussed in Sect. 3.2. It is worth to be pointed out that the first active stage suppresses the thermal noise or $kT/C$ noise of the succeeding passive filters, thereby reducing the capacitor sizes drastically. Moreover, the resonator capacitor $C_b$ is 0.25 pF in order to realize the resonator gain coefficient of 1/64. The capacitor values are summarized in Table 2.

# 4  Simulation Results

The proposed modulator was designed in a 65 nm CMOS technology and was simulated using a 256 kHz sampling clock frequency. Table 3 summarizes the simulation results. The modulator achieves 84 dB and 80.3 dB peak SNR and peak SNDR, respectively, from a 0.7 V supply. A −2.85 dBFS (i.e., 0.18 V peak amplitude), 109 Hz differential input signals were applied to the modulator input, while the reference voltage was set to 0.5 V (i.e., $V_{REFP}$ of 0.6 V and $V_{REFN}$ of 0.1 V), as shown in Fig. 19. The simulated output spectrum is shown in Fig. 20. Figure 21 shows the modulator peak SNDR with respect to the oversampling ratio (OSR). When the modulator is run at 1.0 MHz sampling frequency, the attained SNDR is 86 dB while dissipating 650 nW power. The input differential range is 1 $V_{PP}$.

Compared to the previous passive modulator in [3], the clock frequency is halved by using higher-order filter, beneficial for power reduction in the ADC and the following decimating filter. Significant SNR improvement was achieved by cascading four integrators and also alleviating the low swing at the quantizer input with input feedforward architecture. It is important to point out that the total capacitor area is estimated to be scaled down by 50 %, as compared to the fully passive modulator presented in [3]. The total sum of all capacitor values in the passive ADC in [3] and the proposed fourth-order active-passive modulator is 280 pF and 138 pF, respectively.

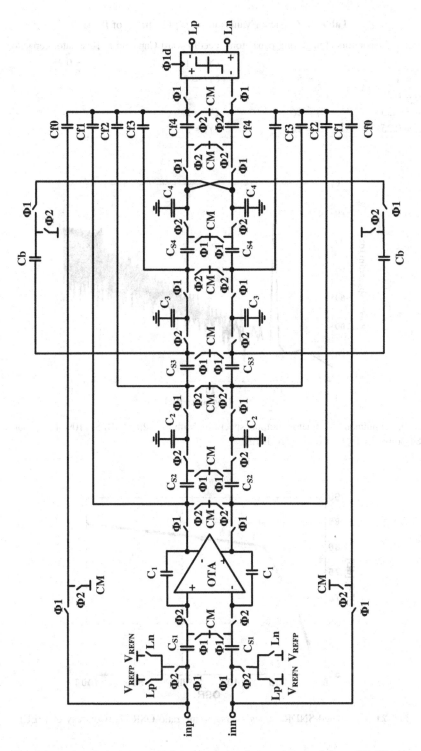

**Fig. 19.** Schematic of the proposed fourth-order active-passive modulator [7] (Courtesy of IEEE)

**Table 2.** Capacitor values in pF [7] (Courtesy of IEEE)

| Sampling capacitors | Integrating capacitors | Feedforward Capacitors | Resonator capacitor |
|---|---|---|---|
| | | $Cf_0 = 1$ | $Cb = 0.25$ |
| $C_{S1} = 1$ | $C_1 = 5$ | $Cf_1 = 2$ | |
| $C_{S2} = 0.25$ | $C_2 = 16$ | $Cf_2 = 3$ | |
| $C_{S3} = 0.25$ | $C_3 = 16$ | $Cf_3 = 2$ | |
| $C_{S4} = 0.25$ | $C_4 = 16$ | $Cf_4 = 5$ | |

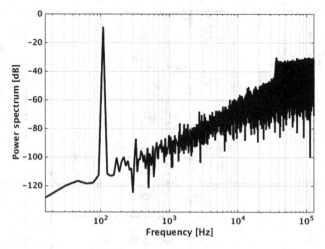

**Fig. 20.** Simulated modulator output spectrum with a –2.85 dBFS, 109 Hz input and 16384-points FFT [7] (Courtesy of IEEE)

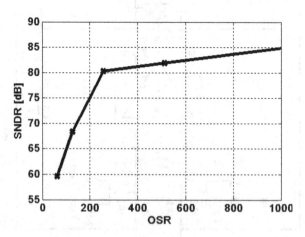

**Fig. 21.** Simulated SNDR versus oversampling ratio OSR [7] (Courtesy of IEEE)

**Table 3.** Perfprmance results [7] (Courtesy of IEEE)

| Technology | 65 nm CMOS | |
|---|---|---|
| Supply voltage | 0.7 V | |
| Clock frequency | 256 kHz | 1.024 MHz |
| Signal bandwidth | 500 Hz | |
| Input range | 1.0 V differential | |
| Peak SNR | 84 dB | 92.8 dB |
| Peak SNDR | 80.3 dB | 86 dB |
| Power | 400 nW | 650 nW |

## 5 Comparison of the Power Efficiency

The performance of the presented modulator in Sect. 3 is compared with previously reported modulators using passive filter(s) in Table 4. Two commonly used FOMs (Walden and Schreier FOMs) are defined below:

$$FOM_W = \frac{Power}{2^{(SNDR-1.76)/6.02} \times 2 \times BW} \tag{15}$$

$$FOM_S = DR_{dB} + 10\log(\frac{BW}{Power}) \tag{16}$$

The $FOM_W$ favors low-resolution ADCs, whereas the $FOM_S$ favors high-DR ADCs. The passive modulator presented in [3] with 0.43 μW power consumption and medium resolution (68 dB SNR from a 0.7 V power supply) looks attractive when using $FOM_W$ definition, as given by Eq. (15). When considering $FOM_S$, the hybrid second-order and fourth-order modulators present the FOM of 156.5 and 175, respectively, which demonstrate high power-efficiency among the modulators [2–6]. In particular, the

**Table 4.** Performance comparison with previously reported modulators using passive filter

| Reference | Type | BW [Hz] | Sampling rate [MHz] | SNDR [dB] | DR [dB] | Power [μW] | FOM$_W^a$ [pJ/step] | FOM$_S^b$ [dB] |
|---|---|---|---|---|---|---|---|---|
| [2] Chen | DT passive | 20 k | 10 | 67 | 78 | 250 | 3.41 | 157 |
| [4] Chen | DT passive | 100 k | 104 | 74.1 | 80.5 | 830 | 1.0 | 159.7 |
| [5] Yousry[e] | DT APDSM[c] | 10 M | 640 | 56 | 54 | 5500 | 0.55 | 146.6 |
| [6] Das | CT APDSM[d] | 600 k | 256 | N/A | 86 | 5400 | N/A | 166.5 |
| [3] Fazli | DT passive | 0.5 k | 0.5 | 65 | 65 | 0.43 | 0.3 | 144 |
| [3] Fazli | DT APDSM | 0.5 k | 0.25 | 70 | 70.5 | 1.27 | 0.49 | 156.5 |
| [7] Fazli[e] | DT APDSM | 0.5 k | 0.256 | 80.3 | 84 | 0.4 | 0.05 | 175 |

[a]FOM$_W$ = Power/($2^{ENOB} \times 2 \times BW$) known as the Walden FOM.
[b]FOM$_S$ = DR(dB) + 10log (BW/Power) known as the Schreier FOM.
[c]DT-APSDM = Discrete-Time Active-Passive Delta-Sigma Modulator.
[d]CT-APSDM = Continuous-Time Active-Passive Delta-Sigma Modulator.
[e]Simulation results were provided in [5, 7].

fourth-order modulator in [7] employing a feedforward architecture presents an excellent energy-efficiency when both $FOM_W$ and $FOM_S$ are applied.

# 6  Summary

The ultimate purpose of this design was to improve the ADC resolution by solving some of the fundamental problems associated with the traditional passive modulators, discussed in Sect. 2, such as extremely low voltage swing at the quantizer input and the comparator non-idealities including offset and noise. Furthermore, cascading three passive filters became possible by using feedforward modulator architecture.

Significant power reduction was obtained through (i) the reduced clock frequency by using a fourth-order and power-efficient loop filter, (ii) the removal of the power consuming preamplifier and (iii) the relaxed amplifier performance requirements in the full feedforward modulator structure.

The main advantage of the first active filter is that it can suppress the comparator nonidealities to a high extent. Additionally, due to the gain of this stage the thermal noise from the succeeding passive filters is also attenuated, resulting in significant capacitor area reduction.

Since in the feedforward architecture the loop filter mainly processes the quantization noise, the continual attenuation along with the passive integrator does not harm the signal components, another advantage of using passive stages in the feedforward structure. Therefore, three cascades of passive filters were exploited to create higher-order noise-shaping, which can decrease the OSR or sampling clock frequency leading to huge digital and analog power reduction. Furthermore, the input feedforward structure is suited well for low-power $\Delta\Sigma$ modulator design due to offering low integrators swing, which relaxes the slew rate requirement of the OTAs.

Therefore, the slew rate and GBW of the OTA in the active stage were scaled down.

The impact of parasitics of the sampling and integrating capacitors on the performance of passive filter and the overall modulator was investigated and the simulation results were included.

Compared to the second-order passive modulator implemented in 65 nm technology [3] using distributed feedback architecture, the clock frequency in the proposed modulator reduced from 500 kHz to 256 kHz, which is beneficial for both analog performance scaling down and digital power reduction. The SNDR improved from 65 dB to 80 dB (2.5-bit resolution improvement), while the attained power of 400 nW is in the same order as the previous design (i.e., 430 nw). In other words, the power-efficiency (or FOM) of the overall modulator was enhanced from 296 fJ/step to 47 fJ/step, showing the effectiveness of combined feedforward structure and cascade of passive integrators. The attained FOM of 47 fJ/step makes this design a suitable candidate for low-voltage low-power ADC designs intended for medical applications.

# References

1. Yeknami, A. F., Alvandpour, A.: A 0.5-V 250-nW 65-dB SNDR passive ΔΣ modulator for medical implant devices. In: IEEE International Symposium on Circuits and Systems (ISCAS), pp. 1–4 (2013)
2. Chen, F., Leung, B.: A 0.25-mW low-pass passive sigma-delta modulator with built-in mixer for a 10-MHz IF input. IEEE J. Solid-State Circuits 32(6), 774–782 (1997)
3. Yeknami, A.F., Qazi, F., Alvandpour, A.: Low-power DT ΔΣ modulators using SC passive filters in 65 nm CMOS. IEEE Trans. Circuits Syst. I 61(2), 358–370 (2014)
4. Chen, F., Bakkaloglu, B., Ramaswamy, S.: Design and analysis of a CMOS passive ΣΔ ADC for low power RF transceivers. Analog Integr. Circ. Sig. Process 59(2), 129–141 (2009)
5. Yousry, R., Hegazi, E., Ragai, H.F.: A third-order 9-Bit 10-MHz CMOS ΔΣ Modulator with one active stage. IEEE Trans. Circuits Syst. I 55(9), 2469–2482 (2008)
6. Das, A., Hezar, R., Byrd, R., Gomez, G.: A 4$^{th}$-order 86 dB CT ΔΣ ADC with two amplifiers in 90 nm CMOS. In: ISSCC Digest of Technical Papers, pp. 496–612 (2005)
7. Yeknami, A. F., Alvandpour, A.:. A 0.7-V 400-nW fourth-order active-passive delta-sigma modulator with one active stage. In: 21st IEEE International Conference on Very Large Scale Integration (VLSI-SoC), pp.1–6 (2013)
8. Roh, J., Byun, S., Choi, Y., Roh, H., Kim, Y.G., Kwon, J.K.: A 0.9-V 60-μW 1-bit fourth-order delta-sigma modulator with 83-dB dynamic range. IEEE J. Solid-State Circuits 43(2), 361–370 (2008)
9. Zhang, J., Lian, Y., Yao, L., Shi, B.: A 0.6-V 82-dB 28.6-μW continuous-time audio delta-sigma modulator. IEEE J. Solid-State Circuits 46(10), 2326–2335 (2011)
10. Wang, J., Matsuoka, T., Taniguchi, K.:. A 0.5 V feedforward delta-sigma modulator with inverter-based integrator. In: Proceedings of ESSCIRC, pp. 328–331 (2009)
11. Yao, L., Steyaert, M., Sansen, W: A 1-V, 1-MS/s, 88-dB sigma-delta modulator in 0.13-μm digital CMOS technology. In: Digest of Technical Papers of Symposia on VLSI Technology and Circuits, pp. 180–183 (2005)
12. Rabii, S., Wooley, B.A.: The Design of Low-Voltage, Low-Power Sigma-Delta Modulators. Kluwer Academic Publishers, Boston (2002)
13. Norsworthy, S., Schreier, R., Temes, G.C.: Delta-Sigma Data Converters: Theory, Design, and Simulation. IEEE press, New York (1997)
14. Ishida, K., Kanda, K., Tamtrakarn, A., Kawaguchi, H., Sakurai, T.: managing subthreshold leakage in charge-based analog circuits with low-$V_{TH}$ transistors by analog T-Switch (AT-Switch) and super cut-off CMOS (SCCMOS). IEEE J. Solid-State Circuits 41(4), 859–867 (2006)
15. Pun, K.P., Chatterjee, S., Kinget, P.R.: A 0.5 V 74-dB SNDR 25-kHz continuous-time delta-sigma modulator with a return-to-open DAC. IEEE J. Solid-State Circuits 42(3), 496–507 (2007)
16. Michel, F., Steyaert, M.S.J.: A 250 mV 7.5 μW SNDR SC ΔΣ modulator using near-threshold-voltage-biased inverter amplifiers in 130 nm CMOS. IEEE J. Solid-State Circuits 47(3), 2326–2335 (2012)
17. Abo, A., Gray, P.: A 1.5-V, 10-bit, 14.3-MS/s CMOS pipeline analog-to-digital converter. IEEE J. Solid-State Circuits 34(5), 599–606 (1999)
18. Yaknami, A.F., Qazi, F., Dabrowski, J.J., Alvandpour, A.: Design of OTAs for ultra-low-power sigma-delta ADCs in medical applications. In: International Conference on Signals and Electronic Systems (ICSES), pp. 229–232 (2010)

19. Yeknami, A.F., Alvandpour, A.: A 2.1 µW 80 dB SNR DT delta-sigma modulator for medical implant devices in 65 nm CMOS. Analog Integr. Circ. Sig. Process **77**(1), 69–78 (2013)

20. Yao, L., Steyaert, M., Sansen, W.: A 1-V 140-µW 88-dB audio sigma-delta modulator in 90-nm CMOS. IEEE J. Solid-State Circuits **39**(11), 1809–1818 (2004)

21. Yeknami, A.F., Alvandpour, A.: A 2.1 µW 76 dB SNDR DT delta-sigma modulator for medical implant devices. In: IEEE NORCHIP Conference, pp. 1–4 (2012)

22. Yeknami, A.F. : Low-power delta-sigma modulators for medical application. Linkoping University Electronic Press, Dissertation, p. 1563 (2014)

23. Tedja, S., der Spiegel, J.V., Williams, H.H.: Analytical and experimental studies of thermal noise in MOSFETs. IEEE Trans. Electron. Devices **41**, 2069–2075 (1994)

# Fine Grain Precision Scaling for Datapath Approximations in Digital Signal Processing Systems

Seogoo Lee[✉] and Andreas Gerstlauer

Department of Electrical and Computer Engineering,
The University of Texas at Austin, Austin, TX, USA
{sglee,gerstl}@utexas.edu

**Abstract.** Finding optimal word lengths in digital signal processing systems has been one of the primary mechanisms for reducing complexity. Recently, this topic has been explored in a broader approximate computing context, where architectures allowing for fine-grain control of hardware or software accuracy have been proposed. One of the obstacles for adoption of fine-grain scaling techniques is that they require determining the precision of all intermediate values at all possible operation points, making simulation-based optimization infeasible. In this chapter, we study efficient analytical heuristics to find optimal sets of word lengths for all variables and operations in a dataflow graph constrained by mean squared error type of metrics. We apply our method to several industrial-strength examples. Our results show a more than 5,000x improvement in optimization time compared to an efficient simulation-based word length optimization method with less than 10 % estimation error across a range of target quality metrics.

**Keywords:** Power reduction · Approximate computing · Word length optimization · Digital signal processing

## 1 Introduction

Scaling internal system precision continues to be one of the most important mechanisms to reduce implementation complexity and hence improve performance and power consumption in digital signal processing (DSP) systems. Traditionally, fixed-point word lengths of custom hardware or software implementations are set to match worst-case operating conditions determined at design time. In more aggressive recent power saving methods, a system's precision is dynamically and adaptively configured in reaction to changing operating points while maintaining a certain signal quality level [3,7,9,10]. Such dynamic precision scaling mostly targets application-specific hardware implementations [3,7,10], although software implementations also exist [9]. Precision scaling can be realized by bit-level clock gating of the least significant bits as shown in Fig. 1. The maximum number of bits for any operation of an application should be

© IFIP International Federation for Information Processing 2015
A. Orailoglu et al. (Eds.): VLSI-SoC 2013, IFIP AICT 461, pp. 119–143, 2015.
DOI: 10.1007/978-3-319-23799-2_6

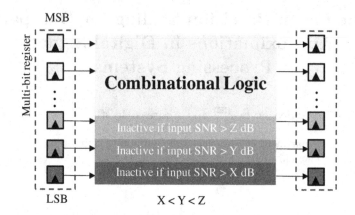

**Fig. 1.** A realization example of precision scaling

enough to support worst-case conditions, but some of the lower bits can remain inactive for different operating points. At a constant clock rate and hence performance, a power reduction comes from the reduced activity of the gated sequential and associated combinational cells.

More recently, similar scaling of precision has been considered in the broader context of approximate computing (AC) [22]. Approximate computing generally exploits tradeoffs between computational complexity and energy or performance at various levels ranging from algorithms to transistors. Recent work in this area has been focused on precision-scalable software realizations on general-purpose programmable approximate processors [19, 20]. Similar to traditional fixed-point hardware design, word length of computations in the underlying hardware is thereby flexibly controlled through source-level program annotations and instruction set extensions.

In all cases, there is a significant burden on designers or programmers to carefully control precision of individual variables and operations in order to maximize energy savings while meeting overall application-level quality goals. Given the large number of variables and operating points to optimize for, traditional simulation-based approaches are too time-consuming. This is a main reason why fine-grain precision scaling is not widely employed, where designers and programmers instead resort to conservative worst-case analysis, self-adjusting runtime schemes [3, 7], which come with additional overhead, or coarse-grain approaches that assume the same precision or a limited number of precision levels across the whole design, which leaves additional power saving opportunities through fine-tuning of each variable's word length unexploited.

By contrast, in this chapter, we investigate novel analytical techniques that resolve some of the drawbacks of previous work. Our method calculates the optimal set of word lengths at design time using statistical analysis [23]. Compared to the methods that require long simulations, our approach can dramatically reduce the design time. Moreover, fine tuning of word lengths with low overhead improves power consumption compared to coarse-grain or run-time precision determination. At the core of our precision optimization technique is an accurate and fast error estimation capability, which, when coupled with a similar power model, provides the basis for developing corresponding optimization formulations and algorithms.

The chapter is organized as follows: after a brief summary of the related work in Sect. 2 and the problem definition in Sect. 3, our error (Sect. 4) and power (Sect. 5) models at the basis of our optimization formulation are described. Results as applied to several design examples are shown in Sect. 6. Finally, Sect. 7 concludes and discusses future work.

## 2  Related Work

Fixed-point conversion and word length optimization has a long history of research dating back to [1, 4]. In a fixed-point representation, there are basically two considerations in determining a word length, the number of integer bits and the number of fractional bits. Integer bits are related to the dynamic range of a signal, where an insufficient integer bit width causes saturation errors. By contrast, fractional bits are related to the precision and introduce quantization errors.

For determining the optimal number of both integer and fractional bits, analytical or simulation-based methods have been introduced. Simulation-based methods are widely used to estimate fixed-point performance. For example, Sung et al. [11] add a signal-to-quantization noise ratio (SQNR) block to quantify the finite word-length effects when the word-length in the implementation of the system changes. In [12], various word length search methods are summarized and compared. The efficiency of simulation-based methods is analyzed to determine the number of simulations needed to reach optimum word lengths. The complexity of a full search is $O(N^s)$, where $N$ is the number possible word lengths for each decision variable, and $s$ is the number of variables. It is shown that the complexity can be dramatically reduced down to $O(s)$ by using efficient search methods that rely on sensitivity information but may run into local minima.

Among the various analytical techniques, the authors in [21] show that optimally determining the number of fractional bits in linear time invariant (LTI) systems is a NP-hard problem. In [15], the authors adopt affine arithmetic (AA) to model the min/max error propagation of quantization noise. However, static min/max approaches are not appropriate for fine-grain precision scaling. They are known to be overly conservative. Furthermore, in applications such as communication systems, additive white Gaussian noise (AWGN) sources from the outer channel environment are hard to characterize in a min/max form. The research done by Shi and Brodersen [16] analyzes quantization noise with perturbation theory instead. They measure the sensitivities of input word lengths to output noise by simulations and use this information in their constraint function. Constantinides et al. find optimal word lengths by evaluating the variance of quantization noise through the system transfer function and subsequently formulating the optimization as a mixed integer linear programming (MILP) problem [13]. Finally, in [17] a variance propagation method is applied to quantization noise analysis in a fast Fourier transform (FFT) block, whereas Menard et al. [14] propose a similar method for generalized dataflow graphs. Because their method can be used both for linear and nonlinear systems and is suitable for general DSP applications, we adopt it for statistical word length analysis and optimization in this chapter.

On the application side, the authors of [7] introduce the concept of dynamic precision scaling for power savings in wireless communication systems by forcing lower significant bits to zero if the current signal quality is better than a predetermined minimum requirement. There are two drawbacks in their work: the authors use the same word length across the whole design and their method requires dedicated training symbols to find the best word lengths at run time in a self-adjusting scheme, which introduces additional overhead that negates some of the power savings. In [3], the authors use both precision and voltage scaling to maximize power reduction. They first optimize word lengths according to the channel environment and then use these word lengths to find the optimal voltage that still satisfies a required error rate. Their method is robust to process variation, but it also incurs run time overhead. In [9, 10], word lengths are optimized at design time to avoid the run time overhead. In [9], the authors target software-defined implementations of wireless systems, and use simulations to support fine-grain optimization of all variables but only consider powers of 2 as word lengths. In [10], optimal word lengths are also determined by slow simulation, where precision is instead allowed to decrease when it can be absorbed in increasing base noise under varying bit error requirements.

Finally, in the approximate computing domain, the authors in [19] propose Java-based language extensions to support programmer annotations for specifying variables and computations that can be approximated on top of an underlying architecture that supports such approximations. The work in [20] proposes such instruction-set and micro-architecture extensions that enable operation-level precision scaling for energy savings in a computation-oriented vector processor. In all of these cases, however, source- or binary-level annotations have to be manually determined by the programmer using other optimization techniques.

## 3   Problem Formulation

Our approach applies to world length optimization of fractional bits in DSP datapaths. As such, we assume that the number of integer bits has already been determined by a range analysis. We only consider systems with fixed-point number representations. Since floating-point computations are more accurate but come with a large complexity, fixed-point computations are still preferred in many energy-constrained applications.

Applications are inherently error-tolerant DSP systems, which can have input signal noise and allow for a certain amount of additional error noise at their primary outputs. These type of systems exists, for example, in wireless communications, image/video processing and machine learning. We assume that applications are represented as dataflow graphs (DFGs) of addition and multiplication operations. Many data-dominated, regular DSP applications such as filters, transforms, or general matrix computations fall into this category. We further limit our target applications to systems that can be characterized by mean squared error (MSE) quality metrics, such as a given or desired signal-to-noise ratio (SNR) or peak SNR (PSNR) at primary inputs and outputs.

Our word length optimization procedure is shown in Fig. 2. Our optimization problem is to minimize power consumption subject to output quality constraints under given input and quantization noises. We start by building a floating-point model of our system, which is simulated to obtain a set of target output SNRs and a set of possible input SNRs, which form the operating points of an application. These are the inputs to our optimization problem. From the floating-point model, we also extract the DFG of the system. With the DFG, we build power cost and quality constraint functions, which are functions of an operating point and word lengths. Then, we solve our optimization problem in order to determine an optimal set of word lengths that minimizes power consumption while satisfying the output quality requirement of a chosen operating point. This process is repeated for all possible operating points.

Figure 3 shows the conceptual change in the output quality and power consumption that results from precision scaling. An operating point is defined by a possible input quality and a required minimum output quality. In the example of Fig. 3, we assume that a single output quality goal must be met across multiple possible input SNRs. Scaling reduces the precision to minimize power

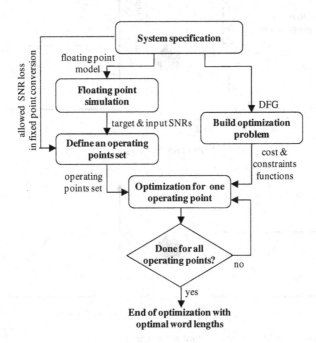

**Fig. 2.** Optimization procedure

consumption such that a constant targeted output quality is maintained for any input condition that would otherwise lead to a better-than-required quality. Note that the same concept can be applied to systems with just a single better-than-worst-case input SNR or with multiple output quality goals for different input conditions.

In general, the system can have one or more possible operating points or operating scenarios. An operating point is defined by a given input quality and a required output quality. Possible operating points of a system are combinations of a set of $N$ possible input conditions $\Phi = \{Q_{in,1}, Q_{in,2}, ..., Q_{in,N}\}$ and a set of $M$ desired output quality goals $\Psi = \{Q_{out,1}, Q_{out,2}, ..., Q_{out,M}\}$. We only scale precision when the output quality of the system under the current input condition is larger than a current output quality goal, i.e. when there is room for energy reduction by injecting additional quantization errors. For all other operating points, the application will be configured to work at full precision, i.e. in a best effort manner.

The decision variables of the optimization problem are the word lengths of the scalable fixed-point variables in the DFG of the application. Assume that the set $\mathbf{F}$ of $K$ decision variables is:

$$\mathbf{F} = \{F_1, F_2, ..., F_K\}. \tag{1}$$

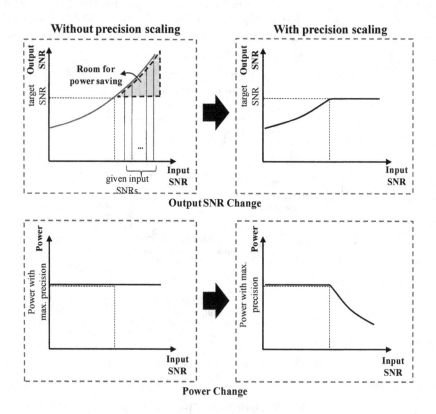

**Fig. 3.** Quality and power change by precision scaling

In our statistical analysis, we first find the maximum word length of each variable at the worst-case operating point, i.e. where the application should work at its fullest precision. The hardware needs to be designed to support these worst-case word lengths. For a software implementation on a general-purpose processor, the full precision is the maximum precision of the adders and multipliers in the processor's datapath. These word lengths define the upper bound of each decision variable as follows:

$$0 < F_i \leq \mathrm{F}_{\mathrm{MAX},i}, \tag{2}$$

where $\mathrm{F}_{\mathrm{MAX},i}$ is the maximum word length for the $i$-th decision variable $F_i$.

We solve different optimization problems for different operating points ($\mathrm{Q}_{\mathrm{in},n}$, $\mathrm{Q}_{\mathrm{out},m}$). Each optimization problem becomes:

$$\min_{\mathbf{F}} \ P(\mathbf{F}) \tag{3}$$

$$\text{subject to}$$

$$N(\mathrm{Q}_{\mathrm{in},n}, \mathbf{F}) \leq \mathrm{Q}_{\mathrm{out},m}, \tag{4}$$

$$0 \leq F_i \leq \mathrm{F}_{\mathrm{MAX},i}, \ \forall i, \tag{5}$$

where $P(\mathbf{F})$ and $N(\mathrm{Q}_{\mathrm{in},n}, \mathbf{F})$ represent power and noise models to estimate implementation cost and output quality as a function of word lengths and input conditions. Corresponding fast yet accurate analytical noise and power models are at the core of our statistical optimization and will be described in the following sections.

We introduce our models on two examples, an FFT in an orthogonal frequency division multiplexing (OFDM) wireless communication system and an inverse discrete cosine transform (IDCT) in JPEG decoder. The FFT example can operate under multiple different input conditions depending on the external channel conditions. Similarly, the IDCT example can have multiple operating points as defined by the compression rate in the encoder. The final results of applying our optimization to both examples will be given in Sect. 6.

## 4    Noise Model

The output quality is determined by the input noise and the injected noise from word length scaling, the latter being in the form of quantization noise. Our approach is heuristic because (1) we use a pseudo quantization noise (PQN) model [17] instead of exact distribution functions of noise, and (2) we consider the quantization of system coefficients, such as twiddle factors or filter coefficients as additive noise injection, which ignores associated changes of the transfer function. In contrast to other approaches [17], This allows us to consider coefficient quantization noise. The impact on the transfer function and corresponding inaccuracies in our method are, however, specific to a given application.

We assume that quantization noise sources as well as input noise sources are independent. It is well known that we can get the variance $\sigma^2$ after addition and multiplication of two independent random variables as follows:

$$\text{Addition: } \sigma^2 = \sigma_1^2 + \sigma_2^2 \qquad (6)$$

$$\text{Multiplication: } \sigma^2 = \mu_1^2\sigma_2^2 + \mu_2^2\sigma_1^2 + \sigma_1^2\sigma_2^2, \qquad (7)$$

where $\mu_i$ is the expectation and $\sigma_i^2$ is the variance of input random variable $i$. The output variances after subtraction or division are also available in a similar way.

Quantization noise is modeled as additive noise. If we add quantizers to two independent inputs of an adder, s1 and s2 with signal variances $\sigma_{s1}^2$ and $\sigma_{s2}^2$, respectively, we add noise sources $\sigma_{n1}^2$ to $\sigma_{s1}^2$ and $\sigma_{n2}^2$ to $\sigma_{s2}^2$. At the output of the addition, the noise and signal variances therefore become $\sigma_n^2 = \sigma_{n1}^2 + \sigma_{n2}^2$ and $\sigma_s^2 = \sigma_{s1}^2 + \sigma_{s2}^2$, respectively. Hence, the total variance is $\sigma^2 = \sigma_s^2 + \sigma_n^2 = \sigma_{s1}^2 + \sigma_{s2}^2 + \sigma_{n1}^2 + \sigma_{n2}^2$.

### 4.1   Noise Analysis for One Decision Variable

We use a pipelined 256-point FFT with four series-connected radix-4 stages to derive and demonstrate our noise model. The overall FFT structure and the DFG for one stage of the FFT are shown in Fig. 4. The first two additions are for the butterfly and the following multiplier and adder represent the complex twiddle multiplication. Only calculation of the real phase is shown. The same computation is performed for the imaginary phase. There can be two quantization points in each stage of the FFT that affect the number of fractional bits: quantization of the input and of the twiddle factor. For simplification, we use a single word length for those two quantization points.

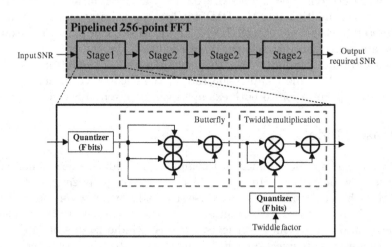

**Fig. 4.** The pipelined 256-point FFT structure and DFG for one radix-4 stage

The input to the FFT can be modeled as a sum of the error-free input with variance $\sigma_{s_{in}}^2$ and additive input noise with variance $\sigma_{n_{in}}^2$. Furthermore, the variance of quantization noise with $F$ fractional bits and uniform distribution under a round-to-nearest rounding is $\sigma^2_{n_{quan}} = \frac{1}{3}2^{-2F-2}$. The variance at the output of the butterfly is then also a sum $\sigma^2_{butterfly} = \sigma^2_{s_{butterfly}} + \sigma^2_{n_{butterfly}}$ of the error-free output variance $\sigma^2_{s_{butterfly}} = 4\sigma^2_{s_{in}}$ and the noise variance $\sigma^2_{n_{butterfly}} = 4(\sigma^2_{n_{in}} + \sigma^2_{n_{quan}}) = 4\sigma^2_{n_{in}} + \frac{1}{3}2^{-2F}$, including input quantization noise.

The butterfly output becomes the input to twiddle multiplication. The other input, the twiddle factor is a sum of the ideal, sinusoidal twiddle factor with variance $\sigma^2_{s_{twiddle}} = 1/8$ (for a 4-stage, 256-point FFT) and additive quantization noise $\sigma^2_{n_{quan}}$. We assume that all signals and variables have zero mean ($\mu = 0$) and that $\sigma^2_{s_{in}}$ is gain-controlled to 1. Therefore, the output variance after one FFT stage is

$$\sigma^2_{out} = 2(\sigma^2_{s_{butterfly}} + \sigma^2_{n_{butterfly}})(\sigma^2_{s_{twiddle}} + \sigma^2_{n_{quan}}) \tag{8}$$

$$\approx 1 + \sigma^2_{n_{in}} + (\frac{2}{3} + \frac{2}{3}\sigma^2_{n_{in}} + \frac{1}{12})2^{-2F} \tag{9}$$

$$= 1 + \sigma^2_{n_{out}} \tag{10}$$

With this, we can use the allowed performance loss in the floating- to fixed-point conversion process for our optimization. For example, if the allowed performance loss in SNR is 0.2 dB for fixed-point conversion, given an input SNR of 11.6 dB and the signal power of 1 ($\sigma^2_{n_{in}} = 0.069$), the minimum word length to get a 11.4 dB output SNR ($\sigma^2_{n_{out}} = 0.072$) becomes $F = 5$. We can find the same value through simulation. By contrast, min/max propagation using affine arithmetic [15] with a $\pm 3\sigma$ min/max of the input AWGN would result in $F = 9$. This reflects that static analysis with min/max propagation is conservative.

## 4.2   Extension to Multiple Stages

We extend the above analysis to an FFT with multiple stages and hence decision variables. The output noise from the first stage becomes the input noise to the second stage and propagates through the whole FFT. At the end of the FFT, a noise constraint function can be represented as a function of the variance of the input noise ($\sigma^2_{n_{in}}$) and a set of word lengths $F_i$ for each stage $i$. For our four-stage FFT example, the output noise variance from the first stage is a function of $\sigma^2_{n_{in}}$ and $F_1$ as shown in the previous subsection:

$$\sigma^2_{n_{out,1}} = f(\sigma^2_{n_{in}}, F_1), \tag{11}$$

where $f()$ is defined as

$$f(\sigma, F) = \sigma + (\frac{2}{3} + \frac{2}{3}\sigma + \frac{1}{12})2^{-2F}. \tag{12}$$

Similarly, the output noise variance from the $i$-th stage ($i > 1$) can be formulated as a function of $\sigma^2_{n_{out,i-1}}$ and $F_i$:

$$\sigma^2_{n_{out,i}} = f(\sigma^2_{n_{out,i-1}}, F_i). \tag{13}$$

In this formulation, we ignore that the input to the $i$-th stage is already quantized, i.e. that the re-quantization noise introduced in the $i$-th stage is in reality lower if $\sigma^2_{n_{out,i-1}}$ does not represent an ideal input signal with perfect precision. This leads to a small estimation error. We will demonstrate how successive intermediate quantization steps can be incorporated into our formulation in the next subsection.

Combining the above output noise formulations, the output noise variance from the last FFT stage is a function of $\sigma^2_{n_{in}}$ and $F_1$ through $F_4$, and the constraint function becomes:

$$N(\sigma^2_{n_{in}}, F_1), (F_2), (F_3), (F_4) = f(f(f(f(\sigma^2_{n_{in}}, F_1), F_2), F_3), F_4) \leq \sigma^2_{n_{out}}. \quad (14)$$

In other words, under different input SNRs $1/\sigma^2_{n_{in}}$, the targeted output SNR $1/\sigma^2_{n_{out}}$ should remain constant.

### 4.3   Extension to Multiple Inputs with Intermediate Quantization

Figure 5 shows the data flow graph of an IDCT, which has 64 inputs with different statistical properties for one IDCT calculation. In the IDCT case, input data values are already quantized integer values in the frequency domain with zero fractional bits. The inputs experience two multiplications with cosine values and are then summed up to generate a final output value. This process is repeated with different coefficients to generate 64 different outputs. There are four internal quantization points, where the last output quantization step simply removes all fractional bits. Accordingly, there are three decision variables, $F_1, F_2$ and $F_3$, where a fourth word length is hardcoded to $F_4 = 0$.

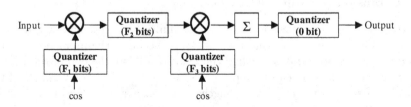

**Fig. 5.** DFG for 64-point IDCT

Different from the FFT example, we consider the effect of re-quantizing an already quantized signal down to a smaller number of bits [13]. The variance of the additional noise introduce by such a re-quantization can be modeled as the difference in quantization noise at the input and output of an internal quantizer:

$$\sigma^2 = \frac{1}{3}(2^{-2F_{OUT}-2} - 2^{-2F_{IN}-2}), \quad (15)$$

where $F_{IN}$ is the number input bits and $F_{OUT}$ is the number of fractional bits at the quantizer output. The formulation accurately considers the number of bits in an already quantized input signal, and it shows that there is no additional noise if $F_{OUT} = F_{IN}$, i.e. that $F_{OUT}$ must be the same or smaller than $F_{IN}$ to achieve an additional quantization effect. Note that quantization in the integer domain can be modeled through negative values of $F$.

We present two different formulations for IDCT noise estimation. Similar to the FFT example, we first formulate our noise model by considering all 64 input values and all cosine coefficients as realizations of one random variable each, i.e. inputs and coefficients are represented by two lumped variances. This allows us to apply the same formulation approach as in the FFT. For such a lumped model, the quantization noise variances in the first and the second coefficient quantizers are

$$\sigma_{n_{c1}}^2 = \frac{1}{3} 2^{-2F_1 - 2},$$  (16)

$$\sigma_{n_{c2}}^2 = \frac{1}{3} 2^{-2F_3 - 2}.$$  (17)

Assuming an input signal with error-free signal variance $\sigma_{s_{in}}^2$, noise variance $\sigma_{n_{in}}^2$, and integer format with zero fractional bits ($F_0 = 0$), the noise variance after the first multiplication and the following quantizer becomes:

$$\sigma_{n_{m1}}^2 \approx \sigma_{s_{in}}^2 \sigma_{n_{c1}}^2 + \sigma_{n_{in}}^2 \sigma_{s_c}^2 + \frac{1}{3}(2^{-2F_2 - 2} - 2^{-2F_1 - 2}),$$  (18)

where $\sigma_{s_c}^2$ is the error-free cosine variance. After the second multiplication and summation, the noise variance becomes:

$$\sigma_{n_{m2}}^2 = 64(\sigma_{s_{in}}^2 \sigma_{s_c}^2 \sigma_{n_{c2}}^2 + \sigma_{s_c}^2 \sigma_{n_{m1}}^2 + \sigma_{n_{c2}}^2 \sigma_{n_{m1}}^2).$$  (19)

Finally, the output quantizer rounds off all the fractional bits to make the final output values be integers. We target a PSNR metric with a fixed and known peak signal variance as quality goal. Hence, the constraint can be formulated as:

$$N(\sigma_{n_{in}}^2, F_1, F_2, F_3) = \sigma_{n_{m2}}^2 + \frac{1}{3}(2^{-2} - 2^{-2(F_2 + F_3) - 2}) \leq \sigma_{n_{out}}^2,$$  (20)

where the output noise variance is constrained to be the same or smaller than $\sigma_{n_{out}}^2$.

As a second formulation, we develop a separated model in which each of the inputs and coefficients is considered as a different random variable. Such an approach is possible for applications that operate with a fixed number of inputs in a block-wise manner, as is the case in our IDCT example. This requires more information about the functionality and the inputs of a DFG, but can achieve a more accurate noise estimation. We use different variances for each of the inputs based on expected or actual observations. Figure 6 shows the log-scaled input variance distribution for typical $8 \times 8$ IDCT frequency-domain inputs. As is well-known, we can observe that most of the input information is located at low frequencies. Especially the DC input element has a significantly higher variance than other input elements. Furthermore, the cosine values it is multiplied with

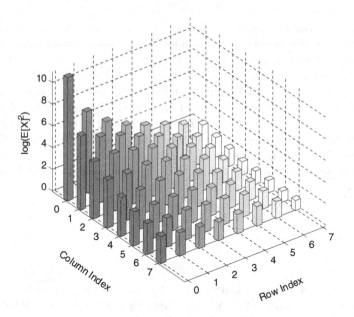

**Fig. 6.** Power distribution for $8 \times 8$ IDCT input with compression rate $= 10$

are a constant, $\frac{1}{\sqrt{2}} \cos(0)$, across all outputs being computed. This fact allows us to model the quantization noise for the DC input coefficient as a constant instead of a uniformly distributed variance, which increases estimation accuracy. All other coefficients vary per output and are thus modeled in lumped form as shown in (16) and (17).

We build a separated optimization problem treating each input element as one random variable with signal and noise variance $\sigma_{s_{\text{in}},i,j}$ and $\sigma_{n_{\text{in}},i,j}$, where $i$ and $j$ are the column and row index of the input element. Also, each of the associated cosine coefficients is treated as a random variable with pre-computed error-free signal and quantization noise variances of $\sigma_{s_{c1},i,j}$ and $\sigma_{n_{c1},i,j}$ for the first cosine coefficients, and $\sigma_{s_{c2},i,j}$ and $\sigma_{n_{c2},i,j}$ for the second ones. After the first multiplication and the following quantizer, the noise variance of the $(i,j)$ element becomes:

$$\sigma^2_{n_{\text{m1}},i,j} \approx \sigma^2_{s_{\text{in}},i,j} \sigma^2_{n_{c1},i,j} + \sigma^2_{n_{\text{in}},i,j} \sigma^2_{s_{c1},i,j} + \frac{1}{3}(2^{-2F_2-2} - 2^{-2F_1-2}). \tag{21}$$

With this, the noise variance after the second multiplication and summation becomes:

$$\sigma^2_{n_{\text{m2}}} = \sum_i \sum_j (\sigma^2_{s_{\text{in}},i,j} \sigma^2_{s_{c1},i,j} \sigma^2_{n_{c2},i,j} + \sigma^2_{s_{c2},i,j} \sigma^2_{n_{\text{m1}},i,j} + \sigma^2_{n_{c2},i,j} \sigma^2_{n_{\text{m1}},i,j}). \tag{22}$$

The final output noise variance and constraint is the same as in (20).

## 5   Power Model

The cost in our optimization problem is determined the dynamic power consumption of the system. The power consumption is the same for all input SNRs, and it only differs with the word lengths of operations in the DFG. The energy cost for an addition is thereby different from the cost for a multiplication, and both costs are affected by the active word lengths of the arithmetic computations. The total energy cost $P(\mathbf{F})$ is the sum of the energy costs $P_i$ for each operation in the dataflow graph. $P_i$ is a function of the arithmetic operation type performed to compute the $i$-th controllable variable with its active word length $F_i$:

$$P(\mathbf{F}) = \sum_i P_i(F_i). \tag{23}$$

We assume that all the bits in our design have the same transition rate of 0.5. With this assumption, dynamic power consumption is linearly proportional to the area of the circuit that is toggling. Hence, our power cost function can be represented as the number of unit hardware blocks. For combinational logic such as adders and multipliers, the cost for each stage is the same and can be represented as the number of 1-bit full adder equivalents. For sequential logic, the power consumption of a 1-bit D flip-flop (DFF) is compared to that of a 1-bit full adder in the TSMC 0.18μm target technology library used in our validations.

### 5.1   Datapath Power Analysis

For the example of one stage of the FFT, $I_a$ is the number of integer bits at the input to the FFT and $I_b$ is the number of integer bits for the twiddle factor. Then, the cost for one butterfly is

$$c' = 2 \times (I_a + F) + (I_a + 1 + F) \tag{24}$$

and the cost for one twiddle multiplication becomes

$$c'' = 2 \times (I_a + 2 + F) \times (I_b + F) + (I_a + I_b + 2 + 2F). \tag{25}$$

$I_a = 3$ including the sign bit is enough not to affect decoding performance. Also, $I_b$ is 1 since the range of twiddle factors is within $\pm 0.5$.

In each FFT stage, two intermediate values are stored: $(I_a + F)$ bits of data after input quantization and $(I_a + F + 2)$ bits of data after the butterfly. Hence, the number of DFFs used in one FFT stage becomes $(2F + 8)$. According to our synthesis results, the ratio in power consumption between a 1-bit DFF and a 1-bit full adder is 8.4, and this is used as a weight of the normalized sequential logic cost:

$$c''' = 8.4(2F + 8). \tag{26}$$

With this, the total cost of one FFT stage becomes:

$$C(F) = c' + c'' + c''' = 2F^2 + 33.4F + 32. \tag{27}$$

Note that for large FFTs, intermediate data is usually stored in SRAMs. However, since scaling is only performed for DFFs and combinational logic, the power consumption of SRAMs is not included in our analysis.

The power model for a complete 4-stage FFT is a straightforward extension of the 1-stage model. Likewise, we obtain the power model for our IDCT example in the exactly the same way as for the FFT example.

### 5.2   Overhead Analysis

If precision scaling is applied at run time to dynamically change word lengths in response to varying input conditions, an input SNR measurement block and a mapping between measured input SNRs and word lengths for all decision variables has to be added to the system. Also, if not already part of a programmable micro-architecture, combinational gates have to be added in front of the DFFs to control clock gating.

Most wireless communication systems already include SNR measurement capabilities for various uses such as channel state information feedback. In such cases, it is assumed that our approach uses the existing SNR measurement block and we do not include it in overhead analysis. Similarly, for image/video processing applications it is assumed that compression rates used in the encoder and hence SNR at the inputs of the decoder is communicated through existing out-of-band mechanisms.

By contrast, with binary on/off decisions stored in mapping tables, their size becomes $N_s \times N_d$, where $N_s$ is the number of SNR steps and $N_d$ is the number of DFFs to control. For example, $N_s = 11$ if there are 11 input SNR steps from 6 dB to 16 dB, and $N_d = 24$ for an FFT with four stages, where each stage has 6 DFFs to be controlled. The overhead in power consumption of the mapping table and additional clock gating logic is included in our power analysis shown in the results.

## 6   Results

In the following, we validate our optimization model and present optimization results demonstrating achievable gains for the FFT and IDCT examples. Since our optimization problem is neither linear nor convex, we apply adaptive simulated annealing (ASA) [18] for solving the optimization as in [15]. ASA is known to be able to adapt to changing sensitivities and has faster convergence compared to traditional simulated annealing approaches.

We perform power estimation of the generated gate-level netlists using Synopsys Design Compiler and Power Compiler with a TSMC 0.18 μm library at a 40 MHz clock. We do not specify the actual activity factors for power estimation and use the default options in the tools. We include both dynamic and leakage power consumption in all reported results. Our optimization is only targeted at dynamic power, and leakage is less than 1 μW for the more complex FFT example in 0.18 μm. For more advanced technology nodes with a larger fraction of leakage power, design techniques such as power gating can be combined with dynamic word length scaling.

## 6.1   FFT Optimization Results

We apply our approach to a 256-point FFT example in a quadrature phase-shift keying (QPSK) OFDM receiver with a cyclic prefix length of 64 assuming perfect synchronization. As shown in Fig. 7, the OFDM receiver consists of a synchronization block, a 256 point FFT, an equalizer, and a symbol de-mapper. An AWGN channel model is assumed to exist between transmitter and receiver. The FFT is used as an example to be designed in dynamically scaled fixed point form. Without loss in generality, among many implementation schemes, we assume that a pipelined radix-4 FFT is used. As presented earlier, the 256-point FFT has four radix-4 stages and each stage contains a radix-4 butterfly and a twiddle multiplication. Since we change the SNR of the system by adding quantization noise, the targeted SNR of the FFT is defined as a desired SNR at its output, which is affected both by a given input SNR and internal quantization noise sources. At design time, statistical analysis determines multiple sets of word lengths for all internal FFT variables and at all input SNRs defined through floating-point simulations. At run time, a SNR block measures the FFT's input SNR and a word length controller selects the best set of word lengths that is suitable for the current input SNR to maintain a pre-defined output SNR. We assume that perfect SNR measurement is possible. We only use fixed-point numbers with a round-to-nearest rounding method.

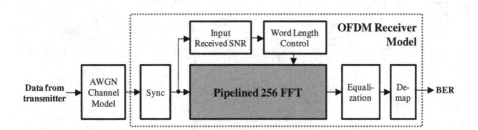

**Fig. 7.** An OFDM receiver

The final performance metric for a wireless communication system is usually the coded frame error rate (FER). In this chapter, however, we use uncoded bit error rate (BER) instead. Every FER has a corresponding BER, which is not affected by frame length and coding scheme. Our goal is to find FFT word lengths that satisfy a desired BER for any given input SNR. BER is closely related to SNR. However, BER is decision error and the relationship between SNR and BER is not linear, but a function of the noise's probability density function (PDF). It is hard to find the exact PDF of noise for a general DSP system that has quantization noises. In this chapter, we therefore assume that propagated noise at the output of an FFT stage is Gaussian distributed. From the central limit theorem, it follows that the noise at the output of a radix-4 butterfly can be approximated as Gaussian. Our simulation results also show that the output noise from twiddle multiplications, since additive, can be approximated to be Gaussian. Furthermore, the input signal is assumed to be Gaussian. This is true considering the time-domain signal of an OFDM system. Hence, although we use an SNR metric in our analysis, under the above assumptions we can estimate BER from SNR.

The method presented in this chapter, which we call dynamic scaling by variance propagation (DS-VP), is compared against four conventional methods: (1) non-scaling by full simulation (NS-FS), which only finds one set of word lengths for the worst-case operating point, (2) coarse dynamic scaling by full simulation search (CS-FS), which finds multiple sets of word lengths by full simulation, but using a single word length for all variables in a set, (3) dynamic scaling by full simulation search (DS-FS), which finds optimal sets of word lengths using full simulation, and (4) dynamic scaling by efficient simulation search (DS-ES), which finds multiple sets of word lengths using the efficient simulation approach from [12].

**Table 1.** Optimized word lengths for various target SNRs (BERs)

| Channel SNR | NS-FS $\{F_i\}$ | Power | CS-FS $\{F_i\}$ | Power [mW] | DS-FS $\{F_i\}$ | Power [mW] | DS-ES $\{F_i\}$ | Power [mW] | DS-VP $\{F_i\}$ | Power [mW] |
|---|---|---|---|---|---|---|---|---|---|---|
| **7.25dB (1%)** | | | | | | | | | | |
| <8dB | {4,4,3} | 2.52 mW | {4} | 2.53 (0.4%) | {4,4,4,3} | 2.57 (2.0%) | {4,4,4,3} | 2.57 (2.0%) | {4,4,4,3} | 2.57 (2.0%) |
| 8dB | | | {3} | 2.27 (-9.9%) | {3,3,3,2} | 2.20 (-12.7%) | {3,3,3,2} | 2.20 (-12.7%) | {3,3,3,2} | 2.20 (-12.7%) |
| 9dB | | | {3} | 2.27 (-9.9%) | {3,3,3,1} | 2.13 (-15.5%) | {3,3,3,1} | 2.13 (-15.5%) | {3,2,3,2} | 2.16 (-14.3%) |
| 10dB | | | {3} | 2.27 (-9.9%) | {3,3,2,1} | 2.05 (-18.7%) | {3,2,3,1} | 2.06 (-18.3%) | {3,2,2,1} | 1.97 (-21.8%) |
| 11dB | | | {2} | 1.94 (-23.0%) | {3,2,2,1} | 1.97 (-21.8%) | {3,2,2,1} | 1.97 (-21.8%) | {2,2,3,1} | 1.99 (-21.0%) |
| 12dB | | | {2} | 1.94 (-23.0%) | {2,2,2,1} | 1.90 (-24.6%) | {2,2,2,1} | 1.90 (-24.6%) | {2,2,2,1} | 1.90 (-24.6%) |
| **9.7dB (0.1%)** | | | | | | | | | | |
| <10dB | {4,5,4,4} | 2.63 mW | {5} | 2.94 (11.8%) | {4,5,4,4} | 2.66 (1.1%) | {4,5,4,4} | 2.66 (1.1%) | {4,5,4,4} | 2.66 (1.1%) |
| 10dB | | | {4} | 2.53 (-3.8%) | {5,5,4,3} | 2.60 (-1.1%) | {5,5,4,3} | 2.60 (-1.1%) | {4,4,4,4} | 2.57 (-2.3%) |
| 11dB | | | {3} | 2.27 (-13.7%) | {3,3,3,2} | 2.20 (-16.3%) | {3,3,3,2} | 2.20 (-16.3%) | {3,3,3,2} | 2.20 (-16.3%) |
| 12dB | | | {3} | 2.27 (-13.7%) | {3,3,3,2} | 2.20 (-16.3%) | {3,3,3,2} | 2.20 (-16.3%) | {3,3,3,1} | 2.13 (-19.0%) |
| 13dB | | | {3} | 2.27 (-13.7%) | {3,3,2,2} | 2.16 (-17.9%) | {3,3,2,2} | 2.16 (-17.9%) | {3,2,3,2} | 2.16 (-17.9%) |
| 14dB | | | {3} | 2.27 (-13.7%) | {3,3,2,2} | 2.16 (-17.9%) | {3,3,2,2} | 2.16 (-17.9%) | {3,2,2,2} | 2.06 (-21.7%) |
| **11.4dB (0.01%)** | | | | | | | | | | |
| <12dB | {5,4,5,4} | 2.75 mW | {5} | 2.94 (6.9%) | {5,4,5,4} | 2.83 (2.9%) | {5,4,5,4} | 2.83 (2.9%) | {5,4,5,4} | 2.83 (2.9%) |
| 12dB | | | {4} | 2.53 (-8.0%) | {4,5,3,3} | 2.49 (-9.5%) | {4,5,3,3} | 2.49 (-9.5%) | {4,4,4,3} | 2.57 (-6.5%) |
| 13dB | | | {3} | 2.27 (-17.5%) | {4,3,3,2} | 2.29 (-16.7%) | {4,3,3,2} | 2.29 (-16.7%) | {4,3,3,2} | 2.29 (-16.7%) |
| 14dB | | | {3} | 2.27 (-17.5%) | {3,3,3,2} | 2.20 (-20.0%) | {3,3,3,2} | 2.20 (-20.0%) | {3,3,3,2} | 2.20 (-20.0%) |
| 15dB | | | {3} | 2.27 (-17.5%) | {3,3,3,2} | 2.20 (-20.0%) | {3,3,3,2} | 2.20 (-20.0%) | {3,3,2,3} | 2.22 (-19.3%) |
| 16dB | | | {3} | 2.27 (-17.5%) | {3,3,3,2} | 2.20 (-20.0%) | {3,3,3,2} | 2.20 (-20.0%) | {3,3,2,2} | 2.16 (-21.5%) |
| Optim. time | 3.6 hours | | 6 min. | | 21.6 hours | | 1-2 min. | | 1.2-1.8 msec. | |

Table 1 shows the sets of word lengths found by the different methods across different target BERs and corresponding input SNRs. The sets of word lengths in Table 1 are the word lengths for Stage 1 to Stage 4 of the FFT, i.e. $\{F_1, F_2, F_3, F_4\}$. The table also includes estimated power consumption and optimization runtime for each approach. All experiments were performed on an Intel Core i7 workstation running at 2.7 GHz. The sets of word lengths from DS-FS are optimal and used as word length and power reference.

Our method shows a significant gain in design time compared to simulation-based methods, which makes dynamic scaling feasible even for large systems with many variables and operating points. For one operating point in our FFT example, the number of simulations using a full search is $6^4$ (4 decision variables and with a range from 1 to 6 bits each). For each simulation trial, we run 10,000 OFDM symbols corresponding to 5 million bits in order to achieve enough simulation accuracy. Each such simulation takes about 10 seconds. To find the optimal word lengths using an exhaustive search requires 3.6 h. With the preplanned simulation method from [12], the number of trials can be significantly reduced. For example, if the search starts from {2,2,2,2}, and the optimal word length set is {4,3,3,2}, optimal word lengths can be obtained with only 4 simulations. However, for dynamic scaling, a search is required for each operating point and total optimization time increases linearly with the number of operating points. Thus, even efficient simulation-based methods may still not be suitable for design-time optimization in the presence of dynamic scaling.

By contrast, our analysis method requires only about 2 ms to find a set of word lengths for one operating point, which is 5,000 times faster than the time for one simulation trial. Considering that word length optimizations can take up to 50 % of design time with conventional simulation-based approaches [12], this represents a significant improvement in productivity.

To validate the optimality and accuracy of our approach, achievable power figures using various methods are compared to those of the reference DS-FS approach. Figure 8 shows that our cost function used for optimization correlates well with the final gate-level power numbers. Nevertheless, the DS-VP method results in up to a 5 % difference in power consumption, which is a downside of achieving large gains in design time. The DS-ES method also exhibits a small 0.5 % difference in some isolated cases where it is not able to guarantee the optimal solution. We also compared fine-grain DS-based methods against dynamic scaling with coarse optimizations, i.e. using a single word length for all variables (CS-FS). Power numbers using fine-grain scaling are always the same or smaller with a reduction of up to 13.6 % even considering additional overhead for control at finer granularity.

In terms of overhead, compared to a method with no scaling (NS-FS), the extra power consumption for dynamic scaling is less than 3 % according to our synthesis results. This overhead is small compared to the average 17 % power reduction that can be achieved by dynamic scaling across varying input SNR levels. At SNR levels that are lower than the required SNR, the power numbers are larger than those for NS-FS due to the overhead of finely tuned dynamic scaling. The system, however, is not usually in such a poor environment. Hence, on average, large power savings can be expected.

Finally, Figs. 9 and 10 plot the results of performance simulations. Using DS-type methods, the system is able to maintain the targeted output BER over the full input SNR range leading to a large power reduction at higher SNR values. In Fig. 10, the BER of floating point model (FP) is also plotted as a reference. The measured BER for a targeted BER of 0.01 % ranges from 0.004 %

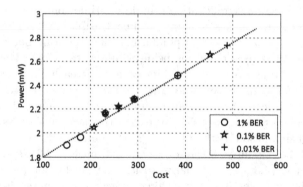

**Fig. 8.** Accuracy of cost function

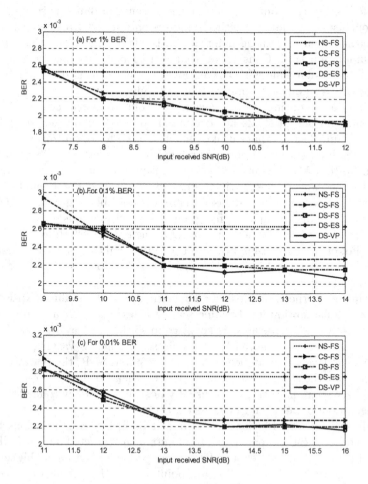

**Fig. 9.** Power comparison

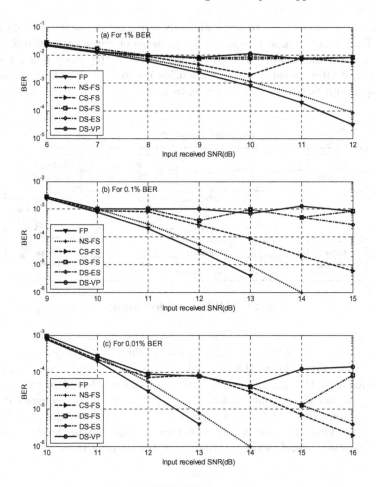

**Fig. 10.** QPSK BER comparison

to 0.014 % using our DS-VP method. Note that while in some cases the power consumption can be lower than in other DS-based methods, this comes at the cost of violating the BER constraint for those operating points. This mismatch is caused by the heuristic nature of our optimization approach.

## 6.2  IDCT Optimization Results

We further apply our approach to an IDCT block within an overall JPEG image processing chain. As shown in Fig. 11, a JPEG encoder performs color conversion, a discrete cosine transform (DCT), quantization, zigzag ordering, and finally Huffman encoding. The decoder implements a reverse processing chain, using the IDCT as its main image reconstruction block. The algorithmic quantization step in the encoder is the key for achieving lossy compression in the JPEG algorithm. It uses the fact that most of the information in a natural image exists in the low frequency region to non-uniformly quantize and scale the frequency-domain DCT components. Coupled with subsequent run-length encoding, this achieves a size reduction of the encoded bit stream at the expense of a reduced image quality after decoding. This tradeoff is controllable by the quantization and compression factor selected in the encoder.

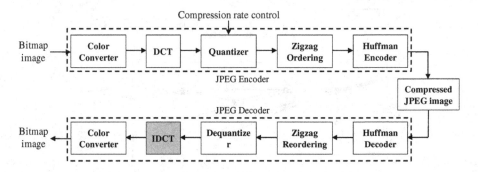

**Fig. 11.** A JPEG encoder/decoder

We apply our word length optimization to the IDCT block in the JPEG decoder, where we optimize IDCT word lengths for different operating points as determined by the algorithmic quantization factor selected in the encoder. Changing the encoder's compression rate will influence the frequency-domain noise at the input of the IDCT and hence the PSNR of the decoded image at the IDCT output. This allows us to apply different precision scaling levels depending on the compression level of the image data at the decoder input.

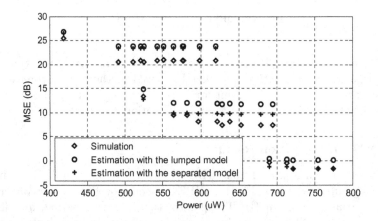

**Fig. 12.** IDCT design space of power consumption versus quality loss

We use the standard Lena image file as sample for all our experiments. Figure 12 shows the design space of power consumption and image quality loss for the IDCT. In Fig. 12, we evaluate quality by only considering image degradation due to internal IDCT quantization noise, i.e. assuming that image data at the IDCT input represents an error-free reference signal. In our estimation models, we therefore set input noise to be zero. For simulations, the output bitmap image of the fixed-point IDCT is compared against the output of a reference floating-point IDCT using real image data. Note that quality results in Fig. 12 are different from typical PSNR measurements, since errors reported here do not include losses incurred by the encoder's compression. In all cases, power results were obtained from RTL synthesis. For each of the possible word length combinations ($F_1$, $F_2$, and $F_3$ sweeped from 2 to 10 with $F_2 \leq F_1$) we plot: (1) image quality obtained from simulation, (2) quality given by our lumped estimation model, and (3) quality estimated by our separated noise model. The

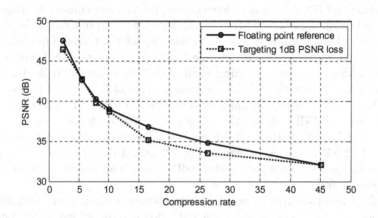

**Fig. 13.** Output image PSNR for different IDCT implementations

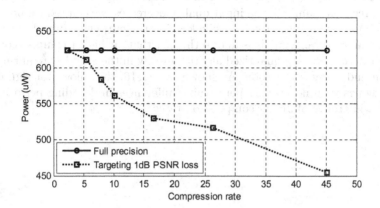

**Fig. 14.** IDCT power reduction

estimation error of the lumped model is less than 12 % compared to a simulation of the same design, with an average estimation error of 8.3 %. For the separated model, the maximum and average estimation error is 10.1 % and 5 %, respectively. These results show that the estimation accuracy can be increased with more information about the inputs to the DFG.

Figure 13 shows the final output image quality of a precision-scaled IDCT in reference to a floating-point IDCT for various operating points as defined by the encoder compression rate. Different from the FFT example that targeted a constant output SNR under varying input conditions, we optimize the IDCT to achieve a constant quality loss. We use a separated model and from simulations, we first obtain the variances of individual IDCT inputs as a function of the encoder compression rate as shown in Fig. 6. Again, our optimization problem is only concerned with quality losses incurred in the IDCT. Furthermore, it can not be assumed that compression noise is independent from frequency-domain image data. As such, we formulate a simplified model that considers encoder compression and IDCT scaling independently, i.e. we treat combined image data with compression noise as the IDCT input signal with no separate noise sources (set to zero). Then, for any compression rate, we set the targeted quality loss of the optimization problem such that the final output image PSNR will become 1 dB lower than the corresponding ideal PSNR of a simulated floating-point IDCT. For example, with a JPEG compression rate of 5, the ideal image PSNR at the IDCT output is 42.6 dB, and we optimize the IDCT to achieve an overall 41.6 dB output PSNR instead. We use our optimization framework to find the sets of optimal word lengths, and subsequently perform simulations to determine the actual PSNR losses. As shown in Fig. 13, actual PSNR losses as compared to an ideal implementation can reach 1.8 dB, which is an artifact of errors in our estimation model.

Finally, Fig. 14 shows the power reduction achieved through word length scaling. As we can observe, a higher power reduction is achieved when the compression rate is high and accordingly the input PSNR is low. The power reduction is up to 27.1 % for a compression rate of 45. This result shows another application for precision scaling: if the input quality decreases, we can reduce power by injecting more quantization noise while keeping the output quality degradation within an allowed range. This is due to the fact that, at higher compression levels, input data is already quantized algorithmically in the encoder, requiring less precision and energy to decode. As shown in Fig. 15, this allows for significant power savings with no visually perceivable differences in decoding performance across a wide range of JPEG compression rates.

(a) Floating-point IDCT, compression rate=2.3     (b) Fixed-point IDCT, compression rate=2.3

(c) Floating-point IDCT, compression rate=45     (d) Fixed-point IDCT, compression rate=45

**Fig. 15.** Floating- and fixed-point IDCT output at different compression rates

## 7   Summary and Conclusions

In this chapter, we introduced a statistical analysis method using variance propagation for word length optimization. A fine-grain optimization of precision scaling is possible and results in significant power savings. A fast yet accurate static design- or compile-time approach thereby avoids run-time overhead and the need for time-consuming exhaustive simulations. In the future, we plan to generalize our method to other types of operations and blocks in DSP systems, including optimization for other metrics, such as coded BER, and other error models, such as the ones arising from other approximation techniques. Furthermore, we plan to automate the approach, including generation of optimized hardware description language code and clock-gating logic within our flow.

**Acknowledgments.** This work has been supported by Intel and the National Science Foundation under Grant No. CCF-1018075. Any opinions, findings, and conclusions or recommendations expressed in this material are those of the author(s) and do not necessarily reflect the views of the National Science Foundation.

# References

1. Widrow, B.: Statistical analysis of amplitude-quantized sampled-data systems. Trans. Am. Inst. Electr. Eng. Part II Appl. Indus. **79**(6), 555–568 (1961)
2. Miyazaki, N., Yoshizawa, S., Miyanaga, Y.: Low-power dynamic MIMO detection for a MIMO-OFDM receiver. In: IEEE International Symposium on Intelligent Signal Processing and Communications Systems, Bangkok, pp. 1–6 (2011)
3. Nisar, M.M., Chatterjee, A.: Test enabled process tuning for adaptive baseband OFDM processor. In: 26th IEEE International Symposium on VLSI Test, San Diego, pp. 9–16 (2008)
4. Oppenheim, A.V., Weinstein, C.J.: Effects of finite register length in digital filtering and the fast fourier transform. In: IEEE Proceedings, pp. 957–976 (1972)
5. Yoshizawa, S., Miyanaga, Y.: Tunable word length architecture for low power wireless OFDM demodulator. In: IEEE International Symposium on Circuits and Systems, Island of Kos, pp. 2789–2792 (2006)
6. Shi, C., Brodersen, R.W.: A perturbation theory on statistical quantization effects in fixed-point DSP with Non-stationary inputs. In: IEEE International Symposium on Circuits and Systems, Vancouver, pp. 373–376 (2004)
7. Kim, J., Yoshizawa, S., Miyanaga, Y.: Dynamic wordlength calibration for energy reduction FFT processors in wireless LAN. In: 54th IEEE Midwest Symposium on Circuits and Systems, Seoul, pp. 1–4 (2011)
8. Nisar, M.M., Chatterjee, A.: Environment and process adaptive low power wireless baseband signal processing using dual Real-time feedback. In: 22nd IEEE International Conference on VLSI Design, New Delhi, pp. 57–62 (2009)
9. Novo, D., Bougard, B., Lambrechts, A., Van der Perre, L., Catthoor, F.: Scenario-based Fixed-point data format refinement to enable Energy-scalable software defined radios. In: Design, Automation and Test in Europe Conference and Exhibition, Munich, pp. 722–727 (2008)
10. Nguyen, H.N., Menard, D., Romuald, R., Sentieys, O.: Energy reduction in wireless system by dynamic adaptation of the Fixed-point specification. In: Conference on Design and Architectures for Signal and Image Processing, Brussels, pp. 132–139 (2008)
11. Kum, K.-I., Sung, W.: Combined Word-length optimization and High-level synthesis ofdigital signal processing systems. IEEE Trans. Comput. Aided Des. Integr. Circuits Syst. **20**(8), 921–930 (2001)
12. Han, K., Evans, B.L.: Optimum wordlength search using sensitivity information. EURASIP J. Adv. Signal Process. **2006**(1), 1–14 (2006)
13. Constantinides, G.A., Cheung, P.Y.K., Luk, W.: Wordlength optimization for linear digital signal processing. IEEE Trans. Comput. Aided Des. Integr. Circuits Syst. **22**(10), 1432–1442 (2003)

14. Menard, D., Sentieys, O.: Automatic evaluation of the accuracy of Fixed-point algorithms. In: Design, Automation and Test in Europe Conference and Exhibition, Paris, pp. 529–535 (2002)
15. Lee, D.-U., Gaffar, A.A., Cheung, R.C.C., Mencer, O., Luk, W., Constantinides, G.A.: Accuracy-guaranteed Bit-width optimization. IEEE Trans. Comput. Aided Des. Integr. Circuits Syst. **35**(10), 1990–2000 (2006)
16. Shi, C., Brodersen, R.W.: Automated Fixed-point Data-type optimization tool for signal processing and communication systems. In: 41st Design Automation Conference, San Diego, pp. 478–483 (2004)
17. Widrow, B., Kollár, I.: Quantization Noise: Roundoff Error in Digital Computation, Signal Processing, Control, and Communications. Cambridge University Press, New York (2008)
18. ASA 25.15. http://www.ingber.com//#ASA
19. Sampson, A., Dietl, W., Fortuna, E., Gnanapragasam, D., Ceze, L., Grossman, D.: EnerJ: Approximate data types for safe and general Low-power computation. In: 32nd ACM SIGPLAN Conference on Programming Language Design and Implementation, San Jose, pp. 164–174 (2013)
20. Venkataramani, S., Chippa, V.K., Chakradhar, S.T., Roy, K., Raghunathan, A.: Quality programmable vector processors for approximate computing. In: 46th Annual IEEE/ACM International Symposium on Microarchitecture, Davis, pp. 1–12 (2013)
21. Constantinides, G.A., Woeginger, G.J.: The complexity of multiple wordlength assignment. J. Appl. Math. Lett. **15**(2), 137–140 (2002)
22. Han, J., Orshansky, M.: Approximate computing: an emerging paradigm for Energy-efficient design. In: 41st IEEE European Test Symposium, Avignon, pp. 1–6 (2013)
23. Lee, S., Gerstlauer, A.: Fine grain word length optimization for dynamic precision scaling in DSP systems. In: IFIP/IEEE International Conference on Very Large Scale Integration, Istanbul, pp. 266–271 (2013)

# A Complete Real-Time Feature Extraction and Matching System Based on Semantic Kernels Binarized

Michael Schaffner[1,2]($\boxtimes$), P.A. Hager[1], L. Cavigelli[1], Z. Fang[1], P. Greisen[1], F.K. Gürkaynak[1], A. Smolic[2], H. Kaeslin[1], and L. Benini[1]

[1] ETH Zurich, Zürich, Switzerland
{schaffner,greisen,kgf,kaeslin,benini}@iis.ee.ethz.ch,
{phager,lukasc,fangz}@student.ethz.ch
[2] Disney Research Zurich, Zürich, Switzerland
smolic@disneyresearch.com

**Abstract.** Feature extraction and matching is an important step in many current image and video processing algorithms. In this work, we designed and implemented an efficient feature extraction and matching system for sparse point correspondence search in stereo video. Our system is based on the recently proposed *Semantic Kernels Binarized* (SKB) algorithm, which showed superior performance with respect to other algorithms in our evaluation. The feature extraction stage has been prototyped in 180 nm technology and the complete system with two feature extraction pipelines (left and right view) together with the matching unit have been implemented on a Stratix IV FPGA where it delivers a performance of up to 42 frames per second on 720p video. Especially due to the high throughput of up to 25 k matched descriptors per frame, our system compares favourably with recent hardware implementations of similar algorithms.

**Keywords:** Features · Matching · Binary descriptor · Semantic Kernels Binarized (SKB) · Stereo video processing · Real time · VLSI · ASIC · FPGA

## 1 Introduction

Current image and video processing pipelines commonly rely on image features in order to calculate sparse point correspondences among several images or frames. Over the past decade, numerous different algorithms and variations thereof have been devised. Earlier methods such as SIFT [14] and SURF [5] are costly to compute and the calculated descriptors consist of many floating point entries that require a significant amount of memory – which renders them less attractive for embedded devices or hardware implementations. This led to the development of more efficient *binary* descriptors such as BRIEF [8], BRISK [13], FREAK [4] and *Semantic Kernels Binarized* (SKB) [26]. These are less expensive to

© IFIP International Federation for Information Processing 2015
A. Orailoglu et al. (Eds.): VLSI-SoC 2013, IFIP AICT 461, pp. 144–167, 2015.
DOI: 10.1007/978-3-319-23799-2_7

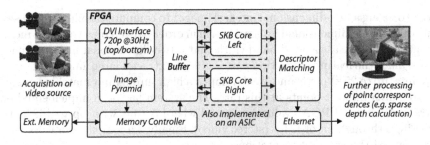

**Fig. 1.** Overview of the stereo video feature detection system with two SKB cores and one matching unit. The 'Teddy' image shown here is from the dataset provided by [20].

compute (e.g. BRIEF and SKB directly compute the binary descriptor pattern by means of intensity comparisons or thresholding), require less storage, and can be matched very efficiently using the Hamming distance.

In this work, we consider the calculation of a sparse disparity map from stereo video, as this is a crucial ingredient for certain video processing methods such as automatic stereo-to-multiview conversion [22]. Our system implements the SKB algorithm [26], as it provides competitive results in the restricted setting of stereo vision and is amenable to efficient hardware implementations. We present a hardware architecture of the whole feature extraction and matching system (a system overview is shown in Fig. 1). The feature extraction core has been implemented and fabricated in 180 nm CMOS technology, and the whole system has been implemented on a Stratix IV FPGA.

## 1.1 Related Work

There exist many FPGA and ASIC implementations of SIFT and SURF, such as [6,7,12,18,21,23]. But to our knowledge, the following two are the only other FPGA/ASIC implementations of complete feature extraction and matching systems which are based on binary descriptors. J. S. Park, et al. [16] implemented a variant of BRIEF with FAST keypoints [17] on an ASIC that has a throughput 94.3 full-HD frames per second with 512 extracted feature points per frame. J. Wang, et al. [25] propose a FPGA system which is also based on BRIEF, but with SIFT keypoints. In their implementation, they achieve a feature throughput of 60 fps for 720p video with 2k detected points. Both of these works are single view systems matching the extracted descriptors to the ones extracted from the previous frame. In contrast, our system operates on the left and right views simultaneously, and the constrained stereo camera set-up is exploited in order to match the descriptors from both views on-the-fly. Further, our system is capable of extracting and matching a much larger number of features per frame (15 k–25 k).

## 1.2 Summary of Contributions

We have developed a hardware architecture for real-time SKB feature extraction and matching from 720p stereo video for real-time stereo vision applications.

Instead of using a two-dimensional integral image[1] to compute the filter responses, we use a local one-dimensional integral image in order to overcome the large memory entries and the associated bandwidth that a two-dimensional integral image entails. Since the feature extraction part is able to extract a large amount of interest points (up to 25 k) per frame, we developed a high throughput matching engine able to match interest points at this rate. The system has been implemented on a Stratix IV based FPGA evaluation board where it runs with up to 142 MHz, delivering a throughput of 42 fps (stereo video). Finally, we compare our work with other state-of-the-art implementations.

This chapter is an extension of our conference paper [19], where we presented the feature extraction core of this system.

### 1.3    Chapter Organization

The system overview and our version of the SKB algorithm is explained in Sect. 2, and a performance simulation of the implemented configuration is shown at the end of this section. The hardware architecture is explained in Sect. 3.1, the implementation results and comparisons are given in Sects. 4 and 5 concludes the chapter.

## 2    Algorithm Details

When searching for sparse point correspondences in an image pair using features, the three main steps that have to be performed are the *interest point detection*, the *descriptor calculation* and the *descriptor matching*. In the following, we summarize these steps of our version of the SKB algorithm and point out the differences to the original [26]. A performance comparison with other descriptors is given at the end of this section.

### 2.1    Interest Point Detection

Similar to the original SKB implementation, we use a variant of the simple *Difference of Boxes* (DoB) filter to detect interest points in the image. However, our system builds upon the original DoB version of CenSurE [2] instead of the modified SUSurE DoB [9] that is used in the SKB paper. The CenSurE detector basically performs a pixel-dense scan on all scales, whereas the SUSurE detector uses a scan line sparsification to leave out pixel positions which are not likely to lead to an extremal filter response. The SUSurE detector is about 3× faster than the CenSurE in software [9], but it exhibits a data dependent, irregular flow which inhibits parallel processing of different filter scales. The DoB filter is a simplified *Laplacian of Gaussian* (LoG) filter and its response is given by the subtraction of the pixel sums within two quadratic boxes with side length $2n+1$ and $4n+1$. The advantage of this simplification is that it can be efficiently

---

[1] The 2D integral image is defined as $\mathbf{II}_{xy} = \sum_{x' \leq x} \sum_{y' \leq y} \mathbf{I}_{x'y'}$ [24].

calculated using an integral image [24], since the area of a box can be obtained by only adding/subtracting the integral image values at the box corners. The image is filtered using different sizes of this filter, thereby forming a volume of filter responses which is also denoted as *scale space*. As noted in [5,21], the largest number of interest points is found on the first few scales. Therefore, and because and in our application we do not require a large scale invariance, the scale space is limited to the first 8 scales (i.e. $n \in [1, 2, \ldots, N_{max} = 8]$).

The DoB filter responses in the scale space are checked for extremal points in a local $3 \times 3 \times 3$ neighborhood using *non-maximum suppression* (NMS), and a weak response threshold $t_{wk}$ is applied in order to filter out non-robust interest points. Since a part of the NMS neighborhood is unknown at the scale space border, maxima are not allowed to occur there. Interest points are therefore only detected on 6 out of 8 scales. Note that the integrated box areas must be properly normalized [2] such that comparisons among different scales are possible. The accuracy of the interest point coordinates could be enhanced by additional interpolation of the maxima location, but since the DoB filters are evaluated pixel-dense on each scale this is not done here. Further, no Harris corner test is performed in our implementation, since this operation is very costly and often not necessary in this application [26]. The output of the interest point detection is a set of tuples $\{(x_i, y_i, s_i)\}_{i \in \{0,1,\ldots,M\}}$, where $x_i$ and $y_i$ are the integer image coordinates and $s_i$ is the index of the scale of a particular interest point $i$.

Depending on the value of the weak response threshold $t_{wk}$, different amounts of interest points are detected. It is desirable to adjust this threshold, such that each frame of a video yields around the same number of points. Since the DoB filter responses are basically differences of image areas, their magnitudes correlate with the average gradient magnitude[2] in the image. Although this relationship may be used to set the threshold to a suitable value, we found that this does not stabilize the number of points well over a video sequence since the image content itself has a large influence on how many points are detected. A feedback loop with simple rules on how to adapt the threshold has proven to be much more effective. In our version of the DoB detector, we use the following rules

$$
t_{wk} := \begin{cases}
\text{if } I < I_{lo2} & , \max\left(t_{wk} - \Delta t_{wk2}, \ t_{wk}^{min}\right) \\
\text{else if } I < I_{lo1} & , \max\left(t_{wk} - \Delta t_{wk1}, \ t_{wk}^{min}\right) \\
\text{else if } I > I_{hi2} & , \min\left(t_{wk} + \Delta t_{wk2}, \ t_{wk}^{max}\right) \\
\text{else if } I > I_{hi1} & , \min\left(t_{wk} + \Delta t_{wk1}, \ t_{wk}^{max}\right),
\end{cases}
\tag{1}
$$

where $I_{lo2}, I_{lo1}, I_{hi1}, I_{hi2}$ are the decision boundaries, and $\Delta t_{wk1}, \Delta t_{wk2}$ are the step sizes, and $t_{wk}^{min}, t_{wk}^{max}$ are the minimal and maximal threshold values (used for saturation). Figure 2a shows the behavior of the feedback loop when applied to a test video sequence containing three scene cuts. Using 4 decision boundaries instead of only 2 allows to use larger step sizes if the number of interest points is far away from the target. Note that the step size should not be chosen too large since this may cause an oscillatory behavior. A similar functionality to control

---

[2] The average gradient magnitude is given by $m_{avg} = \frac{1}{X \cdot Y} \sum_{x=1}^{X} \sum_{y=1}^{Y} \| \nabla \mathbf{I}_{xy} \|$.

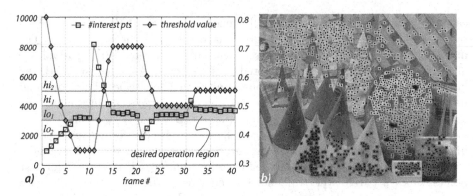

**Fig. 2.** (a) Behavior of the weak response threshold adjustment scheme in the interest point detection step (every 10 frames there is a scene change in this video sequence). The following parameter set has been used in order to stabilize the number of points between $3k$ and $4k$: $(I_{lo2}, I_{lo1}, I_{hi1}, I_{hi2}) = (2k, 3k, 4k, 5k)$, $(\Delta t_{wk1}, \Delta t_{wk2}) = (0.05, 0.1)$ and $\left(t_{wk}^{min}, t_{wk}^{max}\right) = (0.1, 1.0)$. (b) example for a sparse disparity estimation using SKB 256 bit type B descriptors (this is the left image and the estimated disparity has been color-coded). Note that there are almost no outliers even tough no post-processing step like RANSAC has been performed (Color figure online).

the population of detected interest points is provided by the *AdjusterAdapter* class in OpenCV [1].

## 2.2 SKB Descriptor Calculation

The SKB descriptor makes use of a set of sixteen $4 \times 4$ filter kernels (also called *semantic kernels*, shown in Fig. 9b) which are evaluated at 16 positions within a normalized support region around an interest point. This leads to 256 values which are binarized using a certain thresholding scheme. In [26] they propose three different binarization variants $A$, $B$ and $C$ where $A$ leads to a 256 bit descriptor and $B$ and $C$ lead to a 512 bit descriptor. Here we use the fast variant $A$ where the 256 values are binarized by comparing them against 0, i.e. only the sign bit is kept. In [26] they also define two different support regions (type $A$ and $B$) out of which we use the larger $16 \times 16$ region ($B$), as our experiments show that it performs slightly better (Fig. 3).

The $(x_i, y_i, s_i)$ tuples from the interest point detector are used to calculate the coordinates of the support region of that interest point. Bilinear interpolation is then used to resample the support region such that it fits into the normalized frame of $16 \times 16$ pixels (the normalization factors are given by the ratio of the outer DoB box size of the actual scale and the smallest scale i.e. $(4 \cdot s_i + 1)/5$). Note that we do not perform any rotational alignment as this is not necessary in the case of stereo matching. In order to facilitate the resampling step, we precompute an image pyramid by successive down sampling of the input image by a factor of two. Depending on the scale factor of an interest point $i$, the nearest pyramid level is selected as the pixel source (this concept is also known as *mipmapping* [3]). This has the advantage that aliasing artifacts are reduced in the resampled patches and that the accessed image patch is always contiguous.

## 2.3   Descriptor Matching

Generally speaking, feature matching in this context is the process of finding the optimal assignment of feature points $i \in \{1, 2, \ldots, I\}$ extracted from the left stereo image to feature points $j \in \{1, 2, \ldots, J\}$ extracted from the right stereo image. I.e. we have to solve an assignment problem of the form

$$\mathscr{S} = \arg\min_{\mathbf{S}} \sum_{i,j} (S_{ij} \cdot C_{ij}), \tag{2}$$

where $C_{ij}$ are the elements of a $I \times J$ matching cost matrix $\mathbf{C}$; and $S_{ij} \in \{0, 1\}$ are the elements of a $I \times J$ assignment matrix $\mathbf{S}$, which contains exactly $\min(I, J)$ nonzero elements, and at most one nonzero entry per row and column. As the feature descriptors are binary vectors in this case, the cost of matching a descriptor $\mathbf{d}_i$ from the left image with a descriptor $\mathbf{d}_j$ from the right image can be efficiently calculated using the *Hamming Distance* between the two vectors, i.e.,

$$C_{ij} = \sum_{k=1}^{N} (d_{ik} \;\; \text{xor} \;\; d_{jk}), \tag{3}$$

where $k$ is the bit index in the vectors. However, the assignment problem itself is computationally challenging if a globally optimal solution has to be computed. E.g., the *Hungarian Method* which is often employed to solve this kind of problems has a complexity of $\mathscr{O}(I^3)$, where $I$ is the expected number of descriptors in the left and right image. Furthermore, a direct solution of the assignment problem (2) without any further constraints may still lead to suboptimal solutions, since the geometrical relationship between the two images is completely ignored. For example the solution with the least overall cost could assign a feature point in the top right corner of the left image to a feature point in the bottom left corner of the right image, which completely violates the geometry of a rectified stereo setup. It is therefore common to constrain the search to a small window, based on the knowledge about the camera setup. In our work, we adopt a *greedy* nearest-neighbour (NN) search which is computationally efficient and – as will be seen in the performance evaluation in Sect. 2.4 – which provides sufficient accuracy. An additional *Random Sample Consensus* (RANSAC) [10] step could be performed to eliminate wrong matches, but this is currently not done in our hardware implementation. The details of the window search are given below.

**Windowed Nearest-Neighbour Search.** In this work, we match points from the left image to the right, i.e., the list of descriptors from the left image is traversed, and for each point $i$ we exhaustively search a corresponding point $j$ in a window in the right image. This window is defined by $(\Delta y, \Delta x_1, \Delta x_2)$, and the point $j$ has to fulfill the following set of constraints

$$\{|y_i - y_j| < \Delta y, \quad x_j - x_i < \Delta x_1, \quad x_i - x_j < \Delta x_2\}. \tag{4}$$

$\Delta y$ is the maximum $y$ disparity, $\Delta x_1$ is the maximum negative- and $\Delta x_2$ the maximum positive disparity. Two different $\Delta x$ values are used here, since the positive and negative disparity ranges in stereo setup are dependent on the alignment of the cameras and are often not equal. $\Delta y$ accounts for disparities in y direction that occur if the image planes of the two cameras are not completely coplanar[3]. The current descriptor $\mathbf{d}_i$ from the left image is compared to all descriptors $\mathbf{d}_j$ within the matching window (4) using the hamming distance. The point with descriptor $\mathbf{d}_j$ with the lowest hamming distance is deemed the correspondence of the point $i$ if the hamming distance lies below the matching threshold $t_{match}$ (usually $\in \{10, \ldots, 30\}$ here). Once a match has been found, the points $j$ and $i$ are removed from the descriptor lists. This method is *greedy*, but it has a complexity of only $\mathcal{O}(I \cdot C \cdot \log(J))$, where $C$ is the average number of points in the matching window (assuming that the descriptors from the right image have been sorted according to their position, and that a point lookup has complexity $\mathcal{O}(\log(J))$).

## 2.4  Descriptor Performance

**Evaluation Setup.** We developed a similar framework as K. Mikolajczyk, *et al.* [15] in order to compare the descriptor performance of different SKB variants against the implementations of SIFT [15], SURF [5] and BRIEF [8]. The difference to the framework of K. Mikolajczyk, *et al.* is that we use the Middlebury stereo test set [11], since we are interested in the performance on rectified stereo content. In the framework of K. Mikolajczyk, *et al.*, the test set comprises images with blur and JPEG distortion artifacts, different exposures, and camera rotations – which is useful to evaluate descriptors for applications where a lot of invariance is required (such as image in stitching or object recognition), but it does not model a stereo-camera setup.

The SIFT, SURF and BRIEF descriptors were all parameterized using the default configuration. The SIFT and SURF descriptors have dimensions 128 and 64, respectively, and the Euclidean distance is used to calculate their matching cost. The BRIEF descriptor has dimension 256 and the matching cost is calculated using the Hamming distance. As explained in Sect. 2.2, the SKB descriptor comes in different flavors, out of which the computationally more efficient 256 bit types $A$ and $B$ are evaluated. The fixed point model of the hardware implementation is included in the evaluation as well (type $B$). The descriptors were all evaluated on the same DoB interest points and are upright, since no orientation information is extracted in the interest point detector. The descriptor performance is assessed using *1 - precision* vs. *recall* plots. This is a parametric plot, where the matching threshold $t_{match}$ is swept from 0 to the maximum matching cost. The precision is defined as the percentage of false matches, and the recall is the ratio of the number of correct matches and the number of existing true matches. The dataset [11] provides the ground truth in the form of accurate depth maps. We use these maps in order to transform interest points from one

---

[3] This is also called *Keystone distortion*.

view to the other to check for true correspondences. In this evaluation, we always used *view1* and *view5* of the scenes. The precision-recall curves are averages over the whole test set.

**Results and Discussion.** The evaluation results are shown in Fig. 3. In Fig. 3a the Hungarian method has been used to calculate a globally optimal matching, whereas in Fig. 3b a greedy, windowed NN matching has been used. In Fig. 3c, the two different SKB types and our fixed-point implementation are compared (the curve for BRIEF is shown as a reference, here). We can observe from Fig. 3a and b that SKB outperforms all other descriptors, and has a very steep precision-recall curve, i.e., at low thresholds, many accurate point correspondences are found. This observation is in line with the claim of F. Zilly, *et al.* [26]. When comparing the results from Fig. 3a and b we can see that a globally optimal matching performs better – especially in the region with higher thresholds. There is no 'bending down' of the precision-recall curve, as can be observed in Fig. 3b. But we also note that in the low threshold region there is almost no difference. Since we intend to operate in this region, the greedy NN matching is a perfectly feasible choice. We can see in Fig. 3c that among the SKB types A and B, the latter performs slightly better, and our fixed-point implementation of SKB-B shows no performance degradation.

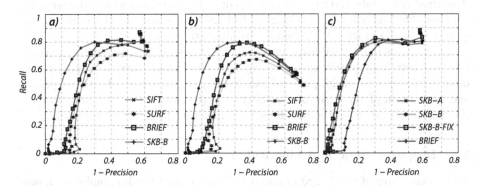

**Fig. 3.** Matching performance simulation with the stereo test set from [11]. The *recall* is the ratio of correct matches and existing correspondences between left and right image, and *1-precision* is the percentage of false matches [15]. (a) globally optimal matching, (b) greedy NN matching (left to right), (c) comparison of different SKB types and our fixed point implementation

## 3    Hardware Architecture

The complete feature extraction and matching system given in Fig. 1 was developed in several distinct stages. Initial work concentrated on designing an efficient *SKB core* in hardware. The resulting core (described in Sect. 3.2) was implemented as a custom ASIC using a relatively mature 180 nm technology from

UMC. In the later stages of the project, the development was moved to the FPGA based prototyping system Terasic DE4-530 which is based on an Altera Stratix IV FPGA (EP4SGX530KH40C2).

The presented system has been designed to be part of a much larger image processing pipeline currently in development at our institute. The overall system adds some additional constraints on the feature extraction and matching system presented here. The first constraint is the need to process stereoscopic images in a top-bottom format. In order to take advantage of existing video infrastructure, frames of a stereoscopic video that consist of a left and right image are usually encoded as a single image of an existing video format. Two widely used formats are side-by-side, which as the name implies places the two images next to each other, and top-bottom, which places one image on top of the other. The second constraint is the need for a relatively high number of interest points (and corresponding descriptors) per frame. This is because our target application multiview synthesis [22] requires many point correspondences in the order of 5 k. Since the images are processed in scan-line fashion, the system must be able to cope with clusters of interest points, which demands a throughput which is higher than the average number of points that is detected per frame. Further, not all interest points are going to lead to a match – depending on the matching threshold $t_{match}$, this number is about 60 % of the detected interest points.

One of the fundamental decisions in the entire system has been to process streaming video data and to avoid storing entire image frames within the processing core. The challenge in the design is to balance the amount of storage in the system with the practical I/O bandwidth limitations.

In the following, we will explain individual components of the feature extraction and matching system shown in Fig. 1. It consists of three main parts: The input buffering and image pyramid calculation, the detection of interest points and calculation of the descriptors, and finally the matching unit that performs the matching and sends the results out via Ethernet for further processing.

### 3.1   Image Pyramid and Line Buffer

The architecture of the image pyramid calculation and the line buffer is shown in Fig. 4a and b. The incoming 720p video is converted to gray scale and the image pyramid consisting of a 360p and 180p resolution level is calculated and stored in the off-chip RAM[4]. The image pyramid is calculated by averaging four neighboring pixels, which results in a reduction of two in both dimensions. This averaging is implemented using two adders and a delay line per reduction step. Since the two views in the input video arrive sequentially after each other in top-bottom format, only two reduction instances are required. The calculated pixel streams are then parallelized and buffered such that long bursts can be written to the off-chip memory. In our system, the external memory is a PC2-6400 DIMM, and a local memory controller interface provides a 256 bit wide access at 200 MHz

---

[4] Since we use only eight scales in our implementation, three pyramid levels are sufficient.

clock rate, resulting in a peak data rate of 1.6 GByte/s. The image pyramid calculation block itself works with the input pixel clock (72.5 MHz), and the off-chip bandwidth for 3 pyramid levels and 2 views amounts to 72.6 MByte/s at 30 fps.

The *line buffer* keeps a sliding window of each of the pyramid levels on-chip, such that the requests from the *SKB cores* can be served with low latency and without generating additional overhead to the off-chip memory. Per view, a *DoB feed* unit transfers the lowest level of the image pyramid to the *interest point detection* stage of the *SKB cores*. The corresponding sliding window of the lowest pyramid level comprises 62 rows. Of this total, 48 rows are needed to provide the 1D integral image to the *DoB feed* in column-wise chunks (see Sect. 3.2). We use the remaining 14 rows for prefetching, since the cores work on overlapping image stripes of 48 rows height, and these stripes are spaced 14 pixels apart.

Two *descriptor feed* units fetch the image patches requested by the *descriptor calculation* part of the *SKB cores* from the correct image pyramid level. Out of the eight scales that are used in the interest point detection, only the scales 2–7 can actually have interest points due to the non-maximum suppression (NMS). Since always the nearest mipmap is selected, these scales all fall onto the second and third pyramid levels. Therefore, the *descriptor feed* units only need access to these two levels. The sliding window comprises of 56 rows on the first, and 48 on the second level. This is enough to accommodate the largest descriptor that is supported (∼30 pixels), plus a margin large enough such that the requested descriptor patches do not fall outside of the sliding window[5].

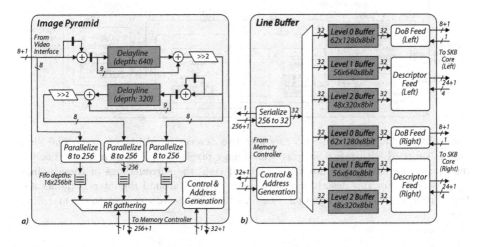

**Fig. 4.** Details of the image pyramid (a), and line buffer blocks of the feature matching system (b)

---

[5] The descriptor calculation lags behind the interest point detection and thus it can happen that requested descriptor patches lie outside of the current sliding window if there are not enough rows in the buffer.

## 3.2  SKB Core

A top-level diagram of the *SKB core* architecture is shown in Fig. 5. It is composed of two main blocks which perform the interest point detection and the descriptor calculation. The *interest point detection* unit performs a dense scan over the whole image and is constantly supplied with image data by the *DoB feed* unit of the *line buffer*. The detected interest points are temporarily stored in a FIFO before they are fetched by the *Descriptor Calculation Units (DCUs)*. Note that the interest points are distributed sparsely over the whole image. The *DCU* has been designed to handle up to 12.5 k descriptors. Depending on the desired descriptor throughput, several instances can be operated in parallel. The FIFO serves to compensate local variations in throughput. Based on the position and scale of a certain interest point, the *DCUs* request the corresponding image patch from the *descriptor feed* units in the *line buffer*. The resulting descriptors, their position, and their scale are then sent on to the *matching unit*.

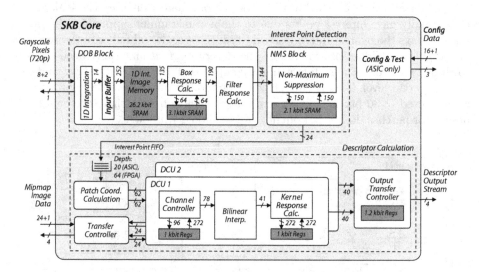

**Fig. 5.** Block diagram of the *SKB core* with two *descriptor calculation units*: The *SKB core* is supplied with raw 8 bit gray-scale image pixels. In a first step it searches for interest points within the image. In a second step, the surroundings of these points are described. For this description step, image patches around the interest points are transferred to the *SKB core* as well. The final descriptors are sent back to the *matching unit*.

**Interest Point Detection.** A total of eight DoB responses have to be evaluated for each pixel – one for each scale in the scale space. Each DoB filter response can be decomposed into a linear combination of an inner and an outer box filter response. These box filter responses are usually calculated with the aid of a 2D integral image, which allows to compute the sum over an arbitrary rectangular area by accessing only four values in the integral image [24].

The integral image requires significant amounts of memory. While a conventional 720p image using 8 bit gray values requires 7.4 Mbit, the corresponding integral image requires large 28 bit entries which results in 25.8 Mbit. When the integral image is stored off-chip, this results in a large bandwidth as eight values have to be accessed per DoB filter response. For $N_{max} = 8$ scales and an effective image size of $x_{eff} \times y_{eff} = 1248 \times 688$ pixel this results in a bandwidth of $x_{eff} \times y_{eff} \times N_{max} \times 8 \times 28$ bit/frame $\approx 1.54$ Gbit/frame. The effective image dimensions are given by $x_{eff} = x_{res} - 4 \times N_{max}$ and $y_{eff} = y_{res} - 4 \times N_{max}$, respectively.

One option to reduce this bandwidth is to transfer and locally store whole blocks of the integral image in order to leverage the spatial overlap among subsequent filters [18]. In our implementation we use only a one-dimensional local integral image. Our approach builds on the observation in [9] where they show how a box filter response can be calculated recursively, provided that a dense scan is performed on the whole image. When scanning from left to right, a box filter response can be updated by adding the new pixels the box covers on the right side, and subtracting the pixels that are no longer covered by the box on the left side (Fig. 6a).

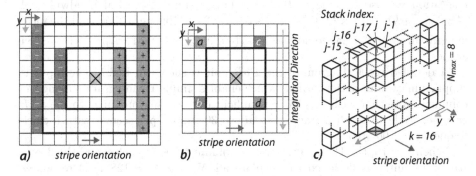

**Fig. 6.** Interest point detection details: (a) Recursive DoB filter calculation for the green pixel position. (b) 1D integral image box response update. (c) NMS evaluation: the most recently added stack has index $j$ (Color figure online).

However, the number of additions is still linearly dependent on the filter size. In our architecture, we additionally make use of the observation that the pixel groups that have to be added or subtracted are always continuous pixel columns. It is therefore possible to use a *one-dimensional integral* image which enables the calculation of 1D-sums of arbitrary length along the columns in constant time (two memory accesses and one subtraction). This allows us to update a box response by accessing only four corner values ($a$, $b$, $c$, $d$) as shown in Fig. 6:

$$B_i = B_{i-1} - (b - a) + (d - c) = B_{i-1} + (a - c) + (d - b). \tag{5}$$

The terms can be reordered such that only differences between two values in the same row need to be added. Note that the one-dimensional integral image can be easily constructed locally as the integration direction is orthogonal to the scanning direction – i.e. if the image is processed in stripes of a certain height $h$, the integration amounts to the addition of $h$ values, and is completely independent of the *width* of an image. This enables a hardware architecture that only needs to store a sliding window of the original image in a *line buffer*, and the memory bandwidth can be reduced considerably compared to a naive implementation using a two-dimensional integral image.

During processing the image is scanned on all scales in parallel, as otherwise several scanning passes through the same image would be required. The *line buffer* contains sliding windows of the input images and supplies the *DoB* block in the *SKB core* with a constant stream of raw image data. The image is processed in overlapping stripes of height $h = 4 \times N_{max} + k$, where $4 \times N_{max} = 32$ is the minimum neighborhood required for eight scales, and $k$ is the number of effectively calculated box filter responses within one column of the stripe. In order to enable non-maximum suppression in a $3 \times 3 \times 3$ neighborhood, the inner part of evaluated responses of a stripe need to be overlapped by another two pixels, i.e., subsequent stripes have a relative offset of $k - 2$ rows. A larger value of $k$ reduces the overhead due to the overlap among subsequent stripes, but it also increases the size of the local integral image buffer. In our implementation we use a value of $k = 16$. This results in a total bandwidth of $(4 \times N_{max} + k) \times x_{res} \times \left\lceil 1 + \frac{y_{eff} - k}{k - 2} \right\rceil \times 8\,\text{bit} \approx 24.1\,\text{Mbit}$ per frame, and the local integral image buffer has to hold at least $(4 \times N_{max} + k) \times (4 \times N_{max} + 1) = 1584$ entries.

A detailed block diagram of the *DoB* unit is shown in Fig. 7. The input is supplied in column-major format, which enables simple 1D integration along the columns. Note that with $k = 16$, it is sufficient to transfer one pixel to the *SKB core* per cycle to reach a frame rate above 30 frames per second with a clock frequency of 100 MHz.

When $k = 16$, the 1D-integration of a column takes 48 cycles, and the downstream circuitry is designed to calculate all $N_{max} \times k = 128$ DoB responses during this time. Some of the inner and outer boxes of the DoB-filter across different scales coincide, such that only 12 out of the total 16 boxes have to be effectively evaluated in the case of eight scales. The *1D integral image memory* is organized as a ring buffer and can hold 48 rows each with a width of 34 pixels. The rows of this memory are segmented into nine dual-port memories to ensure a collision free, parallel access for the box filter response calculation. Note that, the values are accessed in such a way that the difference of two values in one row (see previous section) can be immediately calculated at the memory output, which reduces the multiplexing overhead of the subsequent logic.

The previous box filter responses for the recursive calculation are stored in another memory block. In one computation cycle, the $k = 16$ sets of twelve box responses are sequentially loaded, updated and stored again. For faster loading and storing, as illustrated in Fig. 7, two interchangeable register banks are used: while one bank is in accumulator bank configuration, the other bank is organized as a shift register such that the intermediate values can be shifted to and from the

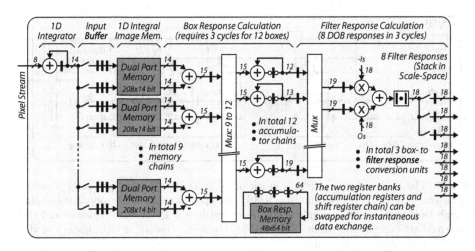

**Fig. 7.** The DoB filter block receives a dense pixel stream and calculates the DoB responses, which are output as stacks of 8 values in the scale space ($j$-th stack in Fig. 6c). The constants $I_n$ and $O_n$ are the appropriate normalization factors for the inner and outer boxes of scale $n$.

memory. In three cycles, all 12 accumulators update their box response according the method presented in (5). Finally, the weighted sums among the intermediate box responses are formed to get the DoB response. For this purpose, three units are used which are able to calculate eight DoB responses in three cycles.

The detailed block diagram of the *NMS (Non Maximum Suppression) unit* is given in Fig. 8. It receives the filter responses stack-wise from the *DoB unit* and performs NMS stack-wise on the local scale space volume. It is important to note that the $26 \times (N_{max} - 2)$ comparisons for one $3 \times 3 \times (N_{max} - 2)$ stack-neighborhood are not computed at once, but in a sequential manner as indicated in Fig. 6c: the incoming stack $j$ is compared to the upper left half of its neighborhood which has already been calculated, and the intermediate comparison results are stored. At the same time, the stack $j - 17$ is compared to the lower right half of its neighborhood, and these results are combined with the corresponding intermediate values in order to get the final result. Compared to a naive approach where the full neighborhood of a stack is stored in order to perform the NMS comparisons, this sequential approach requires to keep track of only the last $k + 1 = 17$ scale space stacks, including their intermediate comparison results. This is about $2\times$ less memory, since the intermediate results amount to only 6 bits per stack (maxima do not occur on the lowest and highest scale). After suppressing the non-maximum responses, the weak response $t_{wk}$ threshold is applied to the remaining interest point candidates. Finally, the coordinates of the points passing this test are written to the interest point FIFO. We found that a depth of 64 works well in this setting.

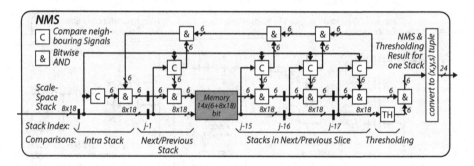

**Fig. 8.** The *NMS* block receives a stack of eight DoB responses per pixel position (*j*-th stack in Fig. 6c), performs the NMS, and applies the weak response threshold. The 8 DoB responses of a single stack are stored in 8 × 18 bit wide registers and the intermediate comparison results in 6 bit wide registers. Overall, a local history of the last 17 scale space stacks is stored.

**Interest Point Description.** In contrast to the interest point detection, the descriptor calculation operates on sparse data. It has to operate fast enough such that – on average – it is able to process all interest points in an image. Our evaluations have shown that several thousand interest points per frame are detected when setting the weak response threshold within a reasonable range of $t_{wk} \in [0.1, 1.0]$. The *interest point description* block is designed to be scalable and consists of several parallel *Descriptor Calculation Units* (DCUs) which can process up to 12.5 k descriptors per frame each. If the application requires a high throughput, this can be easily achieved by instantiating the appropriate amount of *DCUs* and adjusting the bandwidth of the image memory accordingly. The current implementation uses two *DCUs* which results in an aggregated throughput of 25 k descriptors per frame.

The *interest point description* block takes interest points from the FIFO buffer and assigns each one of them to a *DCU*, which then acquires the required data from the nearest mipmap level in the *line buffer* through the *transfer controller*. Then the received data is interpolated to a normalized 16 × 16 image patch which is convolved with several filter kernels and the responses are binarized using a threshold before the result is written to the output buffer. These steps are described in more detail below.

The interest points are read from the FIFO and the *patch coordinate calculation* block determines the parameters for the bilinear interpolator, the mipmap level and the coordinates and dimensions of the patch to be fetched from that mipmap level. The *patch coordinate calculation* unit then dispatches this information together with the interest point to an available *DCU*.

The mipmap is selected according to the scale parameter *s* of the interest points. A strategy that always selects the lower mipmap level would ensure that no information is lost, since then the image patches would always be downscaled. In our implementation, we use a different strategy that always selects the nearest mipmap (in scale). This has the benefit that the amount of data to be transferred

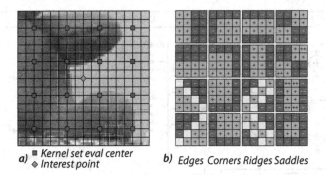

a) ■ Kernel set eval center
   ◆ Interest point

b) Edges Corners Ridges Saddles

**Fig. 9.** Descriptor details: (a) The descriptor support region is overlaid over an image patch showing the centers around which the set of semantic kernels depicted in (b) is evaluated.

to the bilinear interpolators is reduced by around a factor of two when compared to the first strategy. And although some information is lost since some patches have to be magnified, we found that the matching performance does not degrade significantly. Moreover, this strategy causes the DCUs to never access the lowest mipmap level (corresponding to the original image). This does not imply that the lowest mipmap level does not have to be stored – it is still needed by the *DoB unit* – but it does not have to be accessible by the DCUs, and the size of the sliding window buffer can be set to the minimum size dictated by the *DoB unit*.

Each *DCU* has a local pixel buffer that temporarily stores the pixel data used by the interpolator. This reduces the required throughput of the interface significantly – in some cases certain pixels are used up to nine times within a few cycles. Whenever there is enough free space in the buffer, the *DCU* requests another two lines of the mipmap image patch from the *transfer controller*. The *transfer controller* acknowledges the requests whenever it has the capacity, and passes the request on to the *line buffer* while still receiving the response to an earlier request (this overlapping of requests ensures a high utilization of the interface bandwidth). A detailed block diagram of the datapath of one *DCU* is shown in Fig. 10. First, the acquired patch from the nearest mipmap is resampled with a normalization factor in $[0.75, 1.5]$ using bilinear interpolation to complete the normalization of the support region. In a second step, the resulting row-wise stream of single pixels of the resulting $16 \times 16$ support region (Fig. 9a) is convolved with the 16 semantic filter kernels shown in Fig. 9b). Each *DCU* is able to process one interpolated pixel per cycle, which involves the evaluation of 16 kernel updates. Since the normalized image patch is processed in scan line order, it is necessary to keep track of four sets of 16 temporary kernel responses. Whenever the convolution of a set of filters is completed, it is binarized using a threshold, and the resulting part of the descriptor is written to the *output buffer*.

The raw descriptor calculation throughput of one *DCU* is one descriptor in 256 cycles which translates into around 12.5 k descriptors per frame (slightly

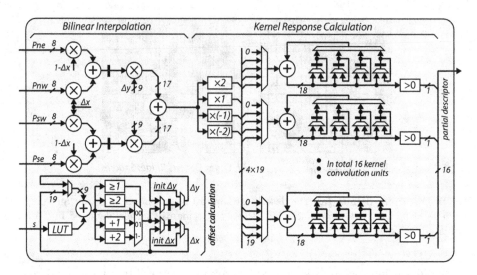

**Fig. 10.** The descriptor calculation unit (shown without the channel controller) contains a bilinear interpolator and 16 kernel response units. Note that the weights of the semantic kernels can be implemented without multipliers.

less than 13 k due to control overhead). However this assumes that image data is always present for the bilinear interpolation. This is not always the case since the size of the image patches (on the mipmap levels) that are processed vary up from $16 \times 16$ to $25 \times 25$ pixels (a factor of 2.44 in size). The effective throughput may thus be dependent on the speed of this interface. In our implementation, the interface can deliver $24 \times 100$ Mbit/s of pixel data, which depending on the patch size corresponds to between 15 k and 38 k image patches in the worst and best case including control overhead. This rate is sufficient to supply one *DCU* continuously. However, to cope with feature point clusters, it is important to have a higher throughput than what the average case suggests. This is necessary to keep the interest point FIFO size within reasonable limits. If the FIFO is too small, some of the interest points can be dropped when the density of interest points gets too large. In our design we use two *DCUs* which together are able to process at least 15 k descriptors in the I/O-limited case, and up to 25 k in the computationally limited case.

**Output Interface.** The output interface transmits each interest point together with its descriptor, i.e., the 24 bit triplet $(x, y, s)$ and the 256 bit descriptor as a data packet over a 4 bit wide bus[6] requiring 71 cycles. A *DCU* requires at least 256 cycles to calculate a descriptor. The output interface guarantees that all results can be transmitted within these 256 cycles. Each *DCU* contains an output buffer that can store two finished descriptors in order to bridge time

---

[6] This particular organization is a left-over from the initial part of the project where the *SKB core* was implemented in an external ASIC which had I/O constraints.

periods where the *output transfer controller* is busy transmitting a descriptor from a different *DCU*.

## 3.3   Descriptor Matching

In this system, we are matching interest points from the left image to the right image with a variant of the greedy, windowed nearest neighbour search explained earlier in Sect. 2.3. Since the matching process is basically an exhaustive search within the matching window, it is crucial to sort the descriptors from the right image appropriately. Otherwise the whole memory needs to be scanned for each point from the left image. In software, this is often done by using a range-tree variant (e.g. k-d tree). Here we use a different, hardware friendlier approach similar to a direct mapped cache which has a much simpler data structure management.

**Interest Point Sorting and Matching.** In the worst case our right image will contain 25 k interest points, which is very sparse and corresponds to less than 3 % of the number of pixels for a 720p image. In order to reduce both the memory and the search overhead, we have decided to use a binning method where we subdivide the entire image into uniformly sized bins. Each bin is allowed to store a small number of descriptors. In our implementation, after an exhaustive evaluation, we have decided to use a bin size of $4 \times 32$ pixels, with eight descriptor slots per bin. Assuming 25 k uniformly distributed descriptors per image, the average number of descriptors per bin is around 3.3. We use more slots per bin since sometimes clusters of interest points occur, and this may lead to a bin overflow. Our evaluations have shown that when using eight descriptor slots, the percentage of dropped descriptors is usually low and around 2 %.

In order to match a descriptor from the left image, only the bins covered by the matching window have to be accessed, as illustrated in Fig. 11. When determining the size of the matching window for the nearest neighbour search, the setup of the stereo video system has to be taken into account. The exact matching window size is dependent on the geometric setup of the two cameras. Our implementation is able to handle a maximum window size of $(\Delta y, \Delta x1, \Delta x2) = (15, 31, 255)$ which works fine for most stereo setups.

Since the calculated descriptors follow a scan-line pattern from the top-left to the bottom-right of the image[7], it is possible to use a two-dimensional cache of bins. Considering the interest point detection step-size of 14 pixels and a maximum matching window height of 30 pixels, the cache should at least span $30 + 2 \times 14 = 58$ pixels in $y$ dimension (14 pixels to write the descriptors from the current stripe, and 14 pixels for the stripe being matched). This value is rounded up to 64 rows in our implementation.

---

[7] The calculated descriptors do not necessarily follow a strict order due to the parallel *DCU*s, and since the interest point detection works column-wise in a narrow strip.

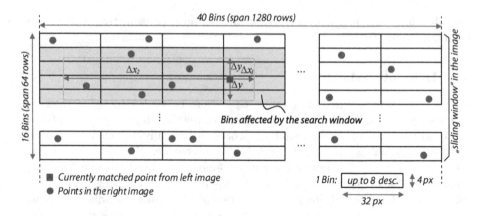

**Fig. 11.** The image is divided into bins of $4 \times 32$ pixels. Each such bin can hold a maximum of eight interest points. A sliding search window (in gray) is used to detect a match of an interest point in the left image (green) to possible candidates in the right image (red) (Color figure online).

**Matching Block Details.** A block diagram of the *feature matching unit* is shown in Fig. 12. The *feature matching* unit consists of a descriptor FIFO for the left image, a binning memory for descriptors from the right image, a valid bit memory for the bins, a *compare unit* and two control units that control the binning and matching processes.

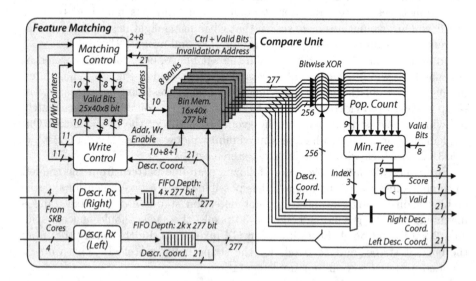

**Fig. 12.** The *feature matching unit* contains a large descriptor FIFO for the left image, a binning memory with associated valid bits for the right image, and a *compare unit* that performs 8 descriptor comparisons in parallel.

The *write control* unit contains a counter that keeps track of the sliding window position in the image. The coordinates of the incoming descriptors are checked against this position, and if the point lies within the sliding window, the *write control* unit checks the valid bits of the corresponding bin (there are eight valid bits per bin, one for each descriptor slot). If there is a free slot, the descriptor is written to that bin. Otherwise it is discarded. If the descriptor lies below the sliding window, the uppermost row of the sliding window is invalidated, moved to the bottom, and the row counter is incremented. This procedure is repeated until the descriptor coordinates lie within the sliding window.

The *matching control* unit fetches the coordinate from the left-image descriptor currently present at the output of the FIFO, and based on the sliding window parameters, it determines which bins have to be accessed. The depth of the descriptor FIFO for the left image has been set to 2 k which is the expected number of descriptors in a 64 × 1280 pixel window in the image (assuming 25 k uniformly distributed descriptors). The required throughput of the *feature matching* block in terms of comparisons per second (cps) is given by the expected number of descriptors in the left image and the expected number of descriptors in the matching window in the right image:

$$25\,\mathrm{k} \times 25\,\mathrm{k} \times \frac{30 \times (31 + 255)}{720 \times 1280} \times 30\,\mathrm{fps} = 1.74\,\mathrm{Mcps}. \qquad (6)$$

Assuming a clock frequency of 100 MHz, this corresponds to a throughput of around 1.74 comparisons per cycle. But since the descriptors can be clustered, it is necessary to provide enough throughput margin such that the *feature matching* block does not start lagging behind. In our implementation, we access one whole bin in parallel and perform 8 comparisons per cycle in order to stay on the safe side. These descriptors are sent to the *compare unit*, where the Hamming distances between the left image descriptor and all right image descriptors is calculated. Next, the index of the descriptor with the smallest Hamming distance is determined. After all bins have been loaded and compared, the coordinates of the descriptor pair with the smallest Hamming distance is output – given that the Hamming distance is below the matching threshold $t_{match}$. The valid bit corresponding to the right descriptor is then cleared.

## 4    Results

### 4.1    ASIC Implementation of the Core

As mentioned earlier, in the initial phase of the project, the *SKB core* for one view has been prototyped on an ASIC which was named SANDSTORM and which has been fabricated in 180 nm CMOS technology (a die photograph is shown in Fig. 13). Table 1 shows the key figures. At 100 MHz, one core is able to process a 720p video stream at 30 fps with 15 k–25 k descriptors per frame (depending on the distribution of the descriptor scales). As opposed to the FPGA implementation, the ASIC has a shorter interest point FIFO (20 instead of 64), does

**Fig. 13.** Microphotograph of the SANDSTORM chip

not automatically adjust the weak response threshold, and it contains an additional configuration block. This block allows to adjust parameters such as the weak response threshold, and to read out statistical information on detected and dropped interest points, as well as memory BIST results.

For comparison, Table 1 also lists the specifications of the BRIEF implementation of J. S. Park, *et al.* [16]. Note that their work has been designed for an object recognition application with different throughput requirements (1080p images, 512 descriptors per frame). Further, their implementation also contains the matching part and a large descriptor buffer (4096 entries) for testing purposes.

### 4.2  FPGA Implementation of the System

The synthesis results for an Altera Stratix IV EP4SGX530KH40C2 of our feature extraction and matching system are given in Table 2 (without memory controller, video and Ethernet interface). On this FPGA, the system runs with up to 142 MHz, delivering a throughput of 42 fps with 15 k–25 k descriptors per frame (depending on the distribution of the descriptor scales).

The results of the state-of-the art feature extraction and matching system of J. Wang, *et al.* [25] is also shown on Table 2 for comparison. Their system is based on BRIEF, and also works on 720p images. The difference is that they work on single views at 60 fps, with 2 k descriptors per frame (the descriptors are matched between subsequent frames). Their implementation uses about the same amount of DSP slices and on-chip memory bits, and uses about 2× less logic resources and around 3× less registers. But the fact that our system has a much higher descriptor extraction and matching throughput puts this into perspective.

**Table 1.** Measurement results of the SANDSTORM chip. The results from J. S. Park, *et al.* [16] are also listed as a reference.

| Physical characteristics | This work | J. S. Park, *et al.* [16] |
|---|---|---|
| Technology | UMC 180 nm (1P6M) | 130 nm (1P6M) |
| Core Voltage | 1.8 V | 1.2 V |
| Package | CQFP 120 | ? |
| # pads | 82 (I:40, O: 26, PWR: 16) | ? |
| Core Area | 3.08 mm$^2$ | 10.24 mm$^2$ |
| Complexity (with SRAM) | 254 kGE (2.4 mm$^2$) | 861 kGE |
| Logic (std. cells) | 193 kGE (1.8 mm$^2$) | 78.3 kGE |
| On-chip SRAM | 29 kbit | 1024 kbit |
| Operating Frequency | 100 MHz | 100 MHz |
| Power Dissipation | 146 mW (core), 38 mW (pads) | 182 mW |
| Performance | | |
| Functionality | IPD + FE[a] | IPD + FE + FM[a] |
| Throughput (single frames) | 30 fps (720p) | 94.3 fps (1080p) |
| Max. Desc./Frame | 15 k–25 k | 512 |

[a]The abbreviations IPD, FE and FM stand for *Interest Point Detection*, *Feature Extraction* and *Feature Matching*

**Table 2.** Key figures of the FPGA implementation of our feature extraction and matching system (without memory controller, video and Ethernet interface).

| Physical characteristics | This work | J. Wang, *et al.* [25] |
|---|---|---|
| Target FPGA | Altera Stratix IV | Xilinx Virtex 5 |
| | (EP4SGX530KH40C2) | (XC5VLX110T) |
| Maximum Clock Frequency | 142 MHz[a] | 159 MHz |
| LUTs | 33.6 k/425 k (7.9 %) | 17 k/69 k (25 %) |
| Registers | 30.7 k/425 k (7.2 %) | 11.5 k/69 k (17 %) |
| Memory bits | 4.15 Mbit/21 Mbit (19.5 %) | 4.6 Mbit/5.33 Mbit (86 %) |
| DSPs | 64/1024 (6.25 %) | 52/64 (81 %) |
| Performance | | |
| Functionality | IPD + FE + FM | IPD + FE + FM |
| Throughput (720p) | 42 fps (stereo) | 60 fps (single) |
| Desc./Frame | 15 k–25 k | 2 k |

[a]This is for the worst case corner (slow 85 C model). The pyramid calculation block runs on the pixel clock of the video interface (72.5 MHz). The synthesis results from J. Wang, *et al.* are also listed for comparison

# 5    Conclusions

First and foremost, we have shown that SKB outperforms all other evaluated descriptors on stereo content, and is thus a prime choice for efficient hardware accelerators. The presented system is able to extract and match SKB features from 720p stereo video in real-time, with 15 k–25 k descriptors per frame. We have used several innovations to allow on-the-fly computation, and have reduced the amount of intermediate data storage and necessary I/O bandwidth without compromising the detection quality. Our system was designed for an application where a large amount of matched interest points will be needed. The system still remains competitive when compared to other state-of-the-art implementations, even though it is able to extract and match nearly an order of magnitude more interest points.

# References

1. OpenCV Documentation (2014). Accessed May 2014. http://docs.opencv.org/
2. Agrawal, M., Konolige, K., Blas, M.R.: CenSurE: center surround extremas for realtime feature detection and matching. In: Forsyth, D., Torr, P., Zisserman, A. (eds.) ECCV 2008, Part IV. LNCS, vol. 5305, pp. 102–115. Springer, Heidelberg (2008)
3. Akenine-Möller, T., Haines, E., Hoffman, N.: Real-Time Rendering. AK Peters, Natick (2008)
4. Alahi, A., Ortiz, R., Vandergheynst, P.: FREAK: fast retina keypoint. In: IEEE Conference on Computer Vision and Pattern Recognition, pp. 510–517 (2012)
5. Bay, H., Tuytelaars, T., Van Gool, L.: SURF: speeded up robust features. In: Leonardis, A., Bischof, H., Pinz, A. (eds.) ECCV 2006, Part I. LNCS, vol. 3951, pp. 404–417. Springer, Heidelberg (2006)
6. Bonato, V., Marques, E., Constantinides, G.: A parallel hardware architecture for scale and rotation invariant feature detection. IEEE Trans. Circ. Syst. Video Technol. **18**(12), 1703–1712 (2008)
7. Bouris, D., Nikitakis, A., Walters, J.: Fast and efficient FPGA-based feature detection employing the SURF algorithm. In: IEEE Annual International Symposium on Field-Programmable Custom Computing Machines, pp. 3–10 (2010)
8. Calonder, M., Lepetit, V., Ozuysal, M., et al.: BRIEF: computing a local binary descriptor very fast. IEEE Trans. Pattern Anal. Mach. Intell. **34**(7), 1281–1298 (2012)
9. Ebrahimi, M., Mayol-Cuevas, W.: SUSurE: speeded up surround extrema feature detector and descriptor for realtime applications. In: "Workshop on Feature Detectors and Descriptors: The State Of The Art and Beyond" as part of IEEE Conference CVPR, June 2009
10. Hartley, R., Zisserman, A.: Multiple View Geometry, 2nd edn. Cambridge University Press (2003). ISBN-13: 978-0-521540-051-3
11. Hirschmüller, H., Scharstein, D.: Evaluation of cost functions for stereo matching. In: IEEE Conference on Computer Vision and Pattern Recognition, pp. 1–8 (2007)
12. Jeon, D., Kim, Y., Lee, I., et al.: A 470 mV 2.7 mW feature extraction-accelerator for micro-autonomous vehicle navigation in 28 nm CMOS. In: IEEE International Solid-State Circuits Conference Digest of Technical Papers, pp. 166–167 (2013)

13. Leutenegger, S., Chli, M., Siegwart, R.: BRISK: binary robust invariant scalable keypoints. In: IEEE International Conference on Computer Vision, pp. 2548–2555 (2011)
14. Lowe, D.: Distinctive image features from scale-invariant keypoints. Int. J. Comput. Vis. **60**(2), 91–110 (2004)
15. Mikolajczyk, K., Schmid, C.: A performance evaluation of local descriptors. IEEE Trans. Pattern Anal. Mach. Intell. **27**, 1615–1630 (2005)
16. Park, J.S., Kim, H.E., Kim, L.S.: A 182 mW 94.3 f/s in full HD pattern-matching based image recognition accelerator for an embedded vision system in 0.13-CMOS technology. IEEE Trans. Circ. Syst. Video Technol. **23**(5), 832–845 (2013)
17. Rosten, E., Porter, R., Drummond, T.: Faster and better: a machine learning approach to corner detection. IEEE Trans. Pattern Anal. Mach. Intell. **32**(1), 105–119 (2010)
18. Schaeferling, M., Kiefer, G.: Object recognition on a chip: a complete SURF-based system on a single FPGA. In: International Conference on Reconfigurable Computing and FPGAs, pp. 49–54 (2011)
19. Schaffner, M., Hager, P., Cavigelli, L., et al.: A real-time 720p feature extraction core based on semantic kernels binarized. In: IFIP/IEEE 21st International Conference on Very Large Scale Integration, pp. 27–32, Oct 2013
20. Scharstein, D., Szeliski, R.: High-accuracy stereo depth maps using structured light. In: IEEE Conference on Computer Vision and Pattern Recognition, vol. 1, p. I-195 (2003)
21. Sledevic, T., Serackis, A.: SURF algorithm implementation on FPGA. In: Biennial Baltic Electronics Conference, pp. 291–294 (2012)
22. Stefanoski, N., Wang, O., Lang, M., et al.: Automatic view synthesis by image-domain-warping. IEEE Trans. Image Process. **22**(9), 3329–3341 (2013)
23. Svab, J., Krajnik, T., Faigl, J., et al.: FPGA based speeded up robust features. In: IEEE International Conference on Technologies for Practical Robot Applications, pp. 35–41 (2009)
24. Viola, P., Jones, M.: Rapid object detection using a boosted cascade of simple features. In: Proceedings of the IEEE Computer Society Conference on Computer Vision and Pattern Recognition, vol. 1, pp. I-511–I-518 (2001)
25. Wang, J., Zhong, S., Yan, L., et al.: An embedded system-on-chip architecture for real-time visual detection and matching. IEEE Trans. Circ. Syst. Video Technol. **24**(3), 525–538 (2014)
26. Zilly, F., Riechert, C., Eisert, P., et al.: Semantic kernels binarized - a feature descriptor for fast and robust matching. In: Conference for Visual Media Production, pp. 39–48, Nov 2011

# An FPGA-Based Real-Time System for 3D Stereo Matching, Combining Absolute Differences and Census with Aggregation and Belief Propagation

Kyprianos Papadimitriou, Sotiris Thomas, and Apostolos Dollas[✉]

School of ECE, Technical University of Crete Akrotiri, 73100 Chania, Greece
{kpapadim,sthomas,dollas}@mhl.tuc.gr

**Abstract.** The implementation of 3D stereo matching in real time is an important problem for many vision applications and algorithms. The current work, extending previous results by the same authors, presents in detail an architecture which combines the methods of Absolute Differences, Census, and Belief Propagation in an integrated architecture suitable for implementation with Field Programmable Gate Array (FPGA) logic. Emphasis on the present work is placed on the justification of dimensioning the system, as well as detailed design and testing information for a fully placed and routed design to process 87 frames per sec (fps) in 1920 × 1200 resolution, and a fully implemented design for 400 × 320 which runs up to 1570 fps.

**Keywords:** Stereo matching · Correspondence problem · Real-time · Field programmable gate arrays · Absolute differences · Census · Belief propagation

## 1 Introduction

Stereo vision is a research area in which progress is made for some decades now, and yet emerging algorithms, technologies, and applications continue to drive research to new advancements. The purpose of stereo vision algorithms is to construct an accurate depth map out of two or more images of the same scene, taken under a slightly different angle/position. In a set of two images one image has the role of the reference image while the other is the non-reference one. The basic problem of finding pairs of pixels, one in the reference image and the other in the non-reference image that correspond to the same point in space, is known as the correspondence problem and has been studied for many decades [1]. The difference in coordinates of the corresponding pixels (or similar features in the two stereo images) is the disparity. Based on the disparity between corresponding pixels and on stereo camera parameters such as the distance between the two cameras and their focal length, one can extract the depth of the related point in space by triangulation. This problem has been widely researched by

A. Orailoglu et al. (Eds.): VLSI-SoC 2013, IFIP AICT 461, pp. 168–187, 2015.
DOI: 10.1007/978-3-319-23799-2_8

the computer vision community and appears not only in stereo vision but in other image processing topics as well such as optical flow calculation [2]. The range of applications of 3D stereo vision cannot be underestimated, with new fields of application emerging continuously, such as in recent research on shape reconstruction of space debris [3].

The class of algorithms which we study falls into the broad category of producing dense stereo maps. An extensive taxonomy of dense stereo vision algorithms is available in [4], and an online constantly renewed comparison can be found in [5], containing mainly software implementations. In general, the algorithm searches for pixel matches in an area around the reference pixel in the non-reference frame. This entails a heavy processing task as for each pixel the 2D search space should be exhaustively explored. To reduce the search space, a constraint called epipolar line can be applied. This constraint aims at reducing the 2D area search space to a 1D line by assuming that the two cameras are placed on the same horizontal axis (much like the human eyes) and that the corresponding images do not have a vertical displacement, thus the pixels which correspond to the same image location are only displaced horizontally. The epipolar line constraint is enforced through a preprocessing step called rectification, which is applied to the input pair of stereo images. In this work we concentrate on the stereo correspondence algorithm and not on the rectification step, assuming that images are rectified prior to processing. We present an FPGA-based implementation that is scalable and can be adjusted to the application at hand, offering great speed-up over a software implementation. Essentially, we extend our work published in [6], by including more results and a detailed analysis on aspects related to performance and resource utilization. We should note here that stereo matching is embarrassingly parallel and thus someone would reasonably expect getting high performance gains from a custom hardware implementation. Hence, our contributions go beyond solely achieving high performance results, and these are:

- an analysis showing how the use of aggregation alleviates the need to employ the more computationally demanding Sum of Absolute Differences (SAD) algorithm while still maintaining good results;
- an analysis on how to dimension the combination of the Absolute Diferences (AD) and the Census algorithms with aggregation in a single hardware implementation;
- the FPGA-based architecture with detailed tradeoff analysis in the use of its primitive resources (Block RAM, Flip-Flops, logic slices), which justifies the use of FPGAs in the field of stereo vision;
- a placed-and-routed design allowing real-time processing up to 87 fps for full HD 1920 × 1200 frames in a medium-size FPGA;
- a modification at the final phase of design cycle that improved by 1.6x the system performance;
- a detailed cost vs. accuracy analysis and on-FPGA RAM usage for design optimization.

The chapter is organized as follows: Sect. 2 discusses previous work, focusing mainly on hardware-related studies, and with a more up-to-date comparison of recent research results vs. those in our previous work [6]. Section 3 describes the algorithm and its individual steps. Section 4 analyses the benefits of mapping the algorithm to an FPGA with emphasis on dimensioning, and especially on the usefulness of aggregation in addition to AD and Census vs. the SAD algorithm. An in-depth discussion of our system is given in Sect. 5, including the implementation of belief propagation. Section 6 has the system performance and the usage of resources, and Sect. 7 summarizes the chapter.

## 2  Relevant Research

In recent years there is considerable work on 3D stereo vision, and in particular on hardware systems to support real-time 3D stereo vision. Most of these results are with FPGA technology, although there exist approaches with Digital Signal Processors (DSP) and Graphics Processor Units (GPU). Due to its intrinsic heavy parallelization and pipelining, it is one of the most promising candidates that can benefit from hardware implementation. However, several factors should be considered when it comes to develop such a design. The main factors are the maximum resolution supported and whether processing can be done at real-time; a rate of 30 fps is desirable for the human eye, but higher rates might be useful in industrial applications. Table 1 consolidates representative implementations in different technologies, with information on the maximum resolution and processing rate.

The work in [7] was one of the earliest ones to combine the development of cost calculation with the Laplacian of Gaussian in a DSP. More recently, several works developed different algorithms in fully functional FPGA-based systems

**Table 1.** Implementation of 3D stereo vision in different technologies

| Refernces | Resolution | Disparity | fps | Technology | Year |
|---|---|---|---|---|---|
| [7] | 160 × 120 | 32 | 30 | DSP | 1997 |
| [8] | 320 × 240 | 20 | 150 | Spartan-3 | 2007 |
| [9] | 320 × 240 | 16 | 75 | Virtex-II | 2010 |
| [10] | 320 × 240 | 16 | 574 | GPU | 2010 |
| [6] | 400 × 320 | 64 | 1570 | Virtex-5 | 2013 |
| [11] | 640 × 480 | 128 | 30 | 4 Stratix S80 | 2006 |
| [12] | 640 × 480 | 64 | 230 | Virtex-4 | 2010 |
| [13] | 640 × 480 | 54 | >30 | Spartan-6 | 2013 |
| [14] | 640 × 480 | 60 | 507.9 | Virtex-6 | 2014 |
| [14] | 1024 × 768 | 60 | 199.3 | Virtex-6 | 2014 |
| [15] | 1920 × 1080 | 300 | 30 | Spartan-6 | 2011 |
| [6] | 1920 × 1200 | 64 | 87 | Virtex-5 | 2013 |

ranging from relatively simple [8,9] to more complex ones [11,12,14,15]. The authors of [12,15] have designed full stereo vision systems incorporating the rectification preprocessing step. The work in [10] provides designs of an algorithm based on census transform in three different technologies, i.e. CPU, GPU and DSP; the maximum performance was obtained with the GPU. The authors in [16] introduced a local stereo matching scheme, making use of a guided filter for weighted cost aggregation to achieve impressive results relative to the quality of local algorithms. Their implementation on a GPU achieved real-time performance with 23 fps on average. The authors of [17] compare FPGA and GPU implementations of stereo vision to expose the trade-off between the flexibility but relatively low speed of an FPGA, and the high speed and fixed architecture of the GPU; that work highlights the relative strengths and limitations of the two systems. An interesting work reviewing algorithms suitable for low-cost FPGA implementation was published in [18], concluding that the memory footprint of the algorithm is the most important consideration given the limited on-chip memory of FPGAs; three different algorithms were demonstrated as a part of a real-time self-contained stereo vision system based on a Xilinx Spartan 6.

The supported disparity is an important parameter that scales with the image resolution. As shown in Table 1, disparity for medium resolutions should be between 64 and 128; this was the case for our functional prototype as well. Our system surpasses all previous systems in terms of performance. The system we implemented in a Xilinx Virtex-5 FPGA sustains a processing rate of 1570 fps for $400 \times 320$ frames. To the best of our knowledge this is far better than any published work. For $640 \times 533$ resolution we achieved a processing rate of 589 fps, while we support $1920 \times 1200$ resolution at a rate of 87 fps. Moreover, our analysis differs from other publications in the sense that we study the way FPGA primitive resources suit the characteristics of each stage of the stereo vision algorithm.

A more recent version of our system, aiming at a low-cost embeddable design has been published in [13]. This design is substantially smaller in FPGA resources vs. the current work, however, the design in [13] has fewer capabilities, including a 15 % loss of 3D stereo matching capability in the near depth of field, which comes from limitations in the number of pixels among which the disparities are computed (54 in [13] vs. 64 in the present work), and the number of frames per second was deliberately lowered to 30 in order to reduce power consumption; however, with a higher clock rate a higher fps rate could be achieved.

## 3   The Algorithm

A typical approach in stereo matching is to employ a local algorithm which matches corresponding pixels in the image pair. This local algorithm computes matching costs between a pixel in the reference frame and a set of pixels in the target frame and selects the match with the minimum cost. This is known as the Winner-Take-All (WTA) strategy, according to which the algorithm selects the match with the global minimum cost in the search space. Essentially, this process is equivalent to computing a 3D cost matrix (called Disparity Search Image or DSI, shown in Fig. 1) of size $W \times H \times D_{max}$, - where W the frame width, H the frame height and $D_{max}$ the size of the search space - and selecting the index of the minimum in the $D_{max}$ dimension. To improve the results, usually a cost aggregation step that acts on the DSI is interjected between the cost computing and match selecting steps. Post-processing steps can further refine the resulting disparity map.

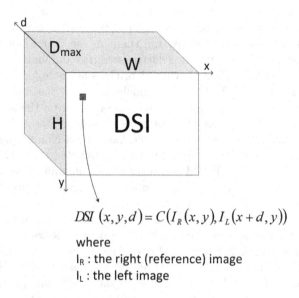

$$DSI\ (x,y,d) = C(I_R(x,y), I_L(x+d,y))$$

where
$I_R$ : the right (reference) image
$I_L$ : the left image

**Fig. 1.** Disparity Search Image (DSI) volume

Our algorithm consists of the cost computation step implemented by the Absolute Difference (AD) census combination matching cost, a simple fixed window aggregation scheme, a left/right consistency check and a scan-line belief propagation solution as a post processing step. Each step of the algorithm will be explained below, whereas the justification for the choice of this combination of algorithms will become evident from quantitative data in Sect. 4.

The AD measure is defined as the absolute difference between two pixels, $C_{AD} = |p_1 - p_2|$, while census [19] is a window based cost that assigns a bit-string to a pixel and is defined as the sum of the Hamming distance between the bit-strings of two pixels. Let $W_c$ be the size of the census window. A pixel's bit-string is of size $W_c^2 - 1$ and is constructed by assigning 1 if $p_i > p_c$ or 0 otherwise, for $p_i \in Window$, and $p_c$ the central pixel of the window. The two costs are fused by a truncated normalized sum:

$$C(p_R, p_T) = max(\frac{C_{AD}(p_R, p_T)}{C_{AD}^{Max}} + \frac{C_{Census}(p_R, p_T)}{C_{Census}^{Max}}, \lambda_{trunc}) \qquad (1)$$

where $\lambda_{trunc}$ is the truncation value given as parameter. This matching cost encompasses image local light structure (census) as well as information about the light itself (AD), and produces better results than its parts alone, as was shown in [20]. At object borders, the aggregation window necessarily includes costs belonging to two or more objects in the scene, whereas ideally we would like to aggregate only costs of one object. For this reason, truncating the costs to a maximum value helps at least limiting the effect of any outliers in each aggregation window [4].

After initializing the DSI volume with AD-Census costs, we perform a simple fixed window aggregation on the $W \times H$ slices of the DSI, illustrated in Fig. 2. This is based on the assumption that neighbouring pixels (i.e. pixels belonging in the same window) most likely share the same disparity (depth) as well. Although this does not stand for object borders and slanted surfaces, it produces good results. On the other hand, one should select carefully the size of the aggregation window $W_a$, as large windows tend to lead to an edge fattening effect in object borders while small aggregation windows lead to loss of accuracy in the inside area of an object itself, which results in a noisy output.

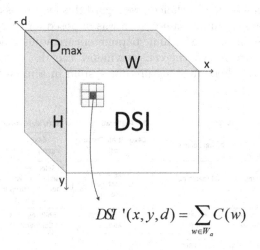

$$DSI\,'(x,y,d) = \sum_{w \in W_a} C(w)$$

**Fig. 2.** Example of $3 \times 3$ fixed window aggregation of DSI costs

Finally, we perform a left/right consistency check (LRC check) which repeats the match selection step but with the opposite frame as reference and compares the new disparity image with the original one. This process allows to detect mismatches due to occlusions (areas of the scene that appear only in one frame). Using the mismatches detected, our scan-line belief propagation solution propagates local confident matches along the scan-line, by accumulating matches that passed the LRC check in a queue (called confident queue due to that it stores only disparities that passed the LRC check), and propagating them to local matches classified as occlusions in a neighborhood queue.

## 4    Dimensioning of the FPGA Architecture

The algorithm can be mapped on an FPGA very efficiently due to its intrinsic parallelism. For instance, the census transform requires $W_c^2 - 1$ comparisons per pixel to compute the bit-string. Aggregation also requires $W_a^2$ additions per cost. For each pixel we must evaluate 64 possible matches by selecting the minimum cost. These operations can be done in parallel. The buffer architecture requires memories to be placed close to each other, as they shift data between them in a very regular way. FPGA memory primitives (BRAMs) are located in such a way they facilitate this operation. Figure 3 shows the critical components for the different steps of the algorithm. Our system shares the pixel clock of the cameras and processes the incoming pixels in a streaming fashion as long as the camera clock does not surpass the system's maximum frequency. This way we avoid building a full frame buffer; we instead keep only the part of the image that the algorithm is currently processing.

It is important to assess the need for flexibility regarding the algorithm parameters, and the gains of such a setup. First and foremost, we are seeking to build a system that is frame-agnostic. Stating differently, we aim at supporting a series of frame sizes within a range of choices; we regard this feature as obligatory. However, a limit on the maximum frame width was imposed for reasons explained in Sect. 6. In addition, all the algorithmic parameters are adjustable; the maximum disparity search range $D_{max}$, the census window size $W_c$, and the aggregation window size $W_a$. We chose to structure our system in a modular way in order

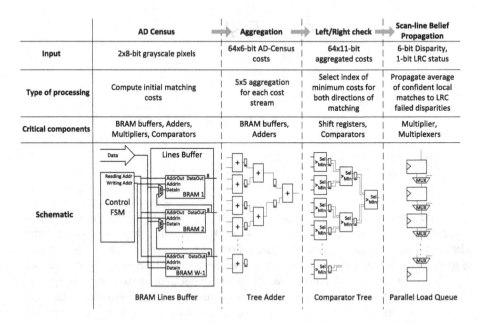

**Fig. 3.** Algorithm stages and critical components that fit well into FPGA regular structures

to easily add/remove features. Features such as scanline belief propagation and aggregation can be turned on or off selectively by the user. Figure 4 shows performance results without aggregation and with various aggregation window sizes.

In order to develop an efficient architecture it is important to understand how resources are used. In terms of sheer performance when no aggregation is used, the SAD algorithm is the best, and so it would seem that it is best to implement it in hardware. No aggregation means that the aggregation window is of size 1, when computational cost is considered, the SAD algorithm is by far more expensive than the alternatives, as it has approximately $2 \times W^2$ comparisons. It is therefore useful to consider cost vs. performance when we introduce aggregation to the system, where we notice that the system-level performance with aggregation comes close to the SAD performance, but at a lower computational cost.

The next question to answer in the development of a useful architecture is the tradeoff between the census window size vs. the aggregation window size. The effects of different census window sizes and different aggregation window sizes is illustrated in Fig. 5, which contains in a more clear form the information from Fig. 4 for the algorithms which were actually implemented in our system.

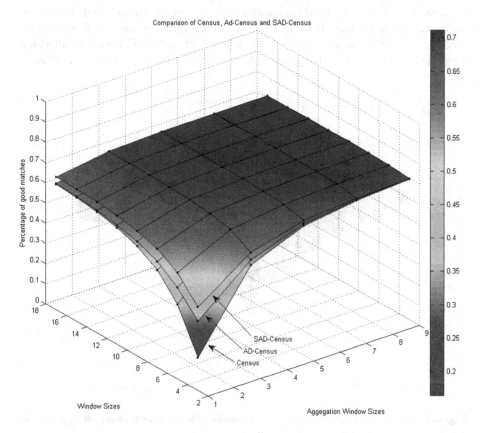

**Fig. 4.** Comparison of Census, AD and SAD performance with various aggregation window sizes

We analyzed the influence of the algorithm's parameters on the quality metric of percentage of good matches, over six (6) datasets of Middlebury's 2005 database [5]. We have settled on a $W_c = 9 \times 9$ sized census window, a $W_a = 5 \times 5$ sized aggregation window and a $D_{max} = 64$ disparity search range; these values offer a good trade-off between overall quality and computational requirements. We followed a similar procedure to determine all the other secondary parameters as well, such as the confident neighborhood queue size and the neighborhood queue size of the scan-line belief propagation module, and the LR check threshold of the LR consistency check module [10].

There are negligible gains if we choose a larger $W_c$ or $W_a$. The maximum achievable percentage of good matches was 78,36 % for AD-Census ($W_c = 7$, $W_a = 13$), therefore there is no actual benefit by choosing a large aggregation window. It is thus our choice to fix the window sizes in our implementation. Our design remains generic in any parameter aspect but it is not reconfigurable at run-time. This decision simplifies our hardware design. For purposes of evaluation and experimental verification of the design we designed our system using Xilinx FPGAs, namely, a Virtex 5 XC5VLX110T as well as a Spartan 3 1000, setting the parameters accordingly to fit the FPGA device at hand.

Last but not least, we need to consider what happens with occluded pixels from one or the other camera. It is therefore useful to allow for some resources to be used for Belief Propagation (BP), as shown in Sect. 5. Belief propagation (which uses results from the Left-Right consistency check) does not consume significant

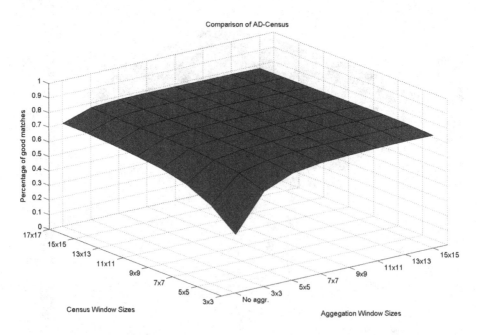

**Fig. 5.** Quality results in terms of the good matches for different census and aggregation window sizes, when using the AD-Census

resources but it solves the problem of uncertainty due to occluded pixels which would result if only one camera were used as the only reference image.

## 5   Design and Implementation

The system in Fig. 6 receives two 8-bit pixel values per clock period, each one for the corresponding image in the stereo pair. A window buffer is constructed for each data flow in two steps. Lines Buffer stores $W_c - 1$ scan-lines of the image, each in a BRAM, conceptually transforming the single pixel input of our system to a $W_c$ sized column vector. Window Buffer acts as a $W_c$ sized buffer for this vector, essentially turning it into a $W_c^2$ matrix. This matrix is subsequently fed into Census Bitstring Generator of Fig. 6, which performs $W_c^2 - 1$ comparisons per clock, producing the census bit-string. Central pixels/Bit-strings FIFO stores 64 non-reference census bit-strings and window central pixels, which along with the reference bit-string and central pixel are driven to 64 Compute Cost modules. This component performs the XOR/summing that is required to produce the Hamming distance for the census part of the cost, along with the absolute difference for the AD part and the necessary normalization and addition of the two. The maximum census cost value is 80 as there are 81 pixels in the window excluding the central pixel from calculations. Likewise, the maximum AD cost value is 255 as each pixel is 8 bits wide. As the two have different ranges, we scale the census part from the 0–80 range to a 0–255 range, by turning it into an 8-bit value. To produce the final AD-Census cost we add the two parts

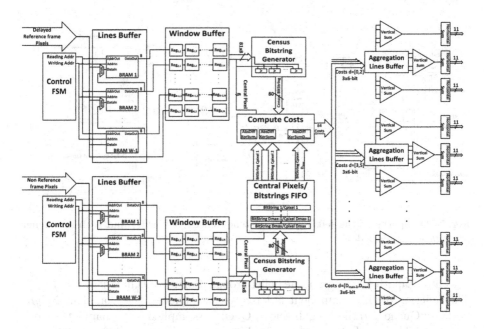

**Fig. 6.** Datapath of the cost computation (left side) and aggregation (right side)

together, resulting in a 9-bit cost to account for overflow. Truncating this cost to 6-bit produces a slight improvement in quality as discussed in Sect. 3, and also reduces buffering requirements in the aggregation step.

For the aggregation stage, 22 line buffers (Aggregation Lines Buffer in Fig. 6) are used for 64 streams of 6-bit costs, each lines buffer allocated to 3 streams. BRAM primitives are configured as multiples of 18 K independent memories, so we maximize memory utilization by packing three costs per BRAM, accepting a maximum depth of 1024 per line. Like the Lines Buffers at the input, they conceptually transform the stream of data to $W_a$ sized vertical vectors. Each vector is summed separately in the Vertical Sum components and driven to delay adders (Horizontal Sum), which output $X(t) + X(t-1) + ... + X(t-4)$. At the end of this procedure we have 64 aggregated costs.

Following the aggregation of costs, the LRC component illustrated in Fig. 7, filters out mismatches caused by occlusions; its operation is illustrated in Fig. 8. The architecture of LRC is based on the observation that by computing the right-to-left disparity at reference pixel $p(x, y)$, we have already computed the costs needed to extract the left-to-right disparity at non-reference pixel $p'(x, y)$. The LRC buffer is a delay in the form of a ladder that outputs the appropriate left-to-right costs needed to extract the non-reference disparity. The WTA modules select the match with the best (lowest) cost using comparator trees. The reference disparity is delayed in order to allow enough time for the non-reference disparities space to build up in NonReference Disparities Buffer and then it is used to index said buffer. Finally, a threshold in the absolute difference between $Disp_{RL}(x, y)$ and $Disp_{LR}(x, y)$ indicates the false matches detected.

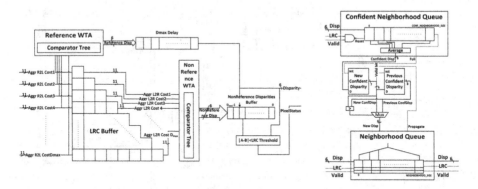

**Fig. 7.** Datapaths of the left/right consistency check (left side) and scan-line belief propagation (right side)

The datapath for the scan-line belief propagation algorithm is shown in Fig. 7. The function of this component is based on two queues: the Confident Neighborhood Queue and the Neighborhood Queue. As implied by its name, the Confident Neighborhood Queue places quality constraints on its contents, meaning

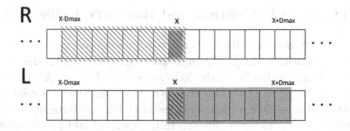

**Fig. 8.** Top row has pixels of the Right image, whereas bottom row has pixels of the Left image. The grey pixel in the center of the Right image has a search space in the Left image shown with the broad grey area. To determine the validity of $Disp_{RL}(x, y)$, we need all left-to-right disparities in the broad grey area, thus we need right-to-left costs up to $x + D_{max}$. The same stands for the diagonal shaded pixel in the center of the Left image.

that only disparities passing the LR consistency check are written in it. Furthermore, at each cycle it calculates the average of the confident disparities, as this value will ultimately be propagated to non confident ones in the neighborhood queue. This average is calculated by a constant multiplier, using fixed point arithmetic and rounding to reduce any number representation errors. On the other hand, the Neighborhood Queue simply keeps track of local disparities and their LR status. When the Propagate signal is asserted (active when a new confident disparity is calculated and stored in the New Confident Disparity register), the NewDisp is written to all records with a false LRC flag. NewDisp is selected to be Previous Confident Disparity when this value is smaller than New Confident Disparity, otherwise it is assigned New Confident Disparity, effectively propagating confident background depths.

We report, below, some noticeable points regarding system operation:

- A small frame of unknown disparities is formed around the final disparity image, where due to the image boundaries, the windows cannot be formed and thus disparities cannot be computed.
- Searching for matches near the image boundary leads to reduced or trivial disparity search spaces. In such cases our system finds the best match in the possible range. Left/Right Consistency check filters out any incorrect matches due to small search spaces.
- Belief propagation is activated on each end of line regardless of the LRC indication, in order to fill in the occluded right area of the image.
- In order for high resolutions to work acceptably, the user needs to either increase the $D_{max}$ accordingly or alternatively to reduce the inter-camera spacing. The second option is preferable as it has no computational consequences, whereas increasing $D_{max}$ has a cost on FPGA resources. Moreover, as the features of the images are now more spaced out in pixel distances, the other parameters of the system need also to be adjusted in order to maintain output quality.

# 6    Performance Evaluation and Resource Utilization

The system which was described, above, can process one pixel pair per clock period, after an initial latency. The most computationally intensive part of the main stage of the algorithm lies in the XOR/sum module of the AD census, which computes the XOR/sum of 64 80-bit strings at the same time. A similar situation stands for the WTA module, which performs 64 11-bit simultaneous comparisons. We cope with both bottlenecks through fully pipelined adder/comparator trees in order to increase the throughput. After the initial implementation, we added extra pipeline stages to further enhance performance. Below we present the differences between the initial (unoptimized) design, and the second (optimized) design. Table 2 shows the performance results of the system implemented in a Xilinx Virtex-5 FPGA. The maximum clock after place and route for the unoptimized design is 131 MHz, while for the optimized design is 201 MHz. Table 3 has the differences in resource utilization between the two designs; it demonstrates that for a speed improvement of over 50 %, the resource utilization penalty is rather small. Based on data we gathered from the tools, the critical path lies on a control signal driving the FSM of the aggregation line buffers; 16,6 % is attributed to logic while the rest 83,4 % of the delay is due to routing.

**Table 2.** Design clock and processing rates for the optimized vs. unoptimized design in Virtex XC5VLX110T FPGA for various resolutions

|  | $100 \times 83$ | $384 \times 320$ | $644 \times 533$ | $1024 \times 853$ | $1600 \times 1333$ | $1920 \times 1200$ |
|---|---|---|---|---|---|---|
| Unoptimized design (131 MHz) | 15,783 fps | 1,066 fps | 384 fps | 150 fps | 61 fps | 56 fps |
| Optimized design (201 MHz) | 24,216 fps | 1,635 fps | 589 fps | 230 fps | 94 fps | 87 fps |

**Table 3.** Resource utilization of the unoptimized vs. optimized design in Virtex XC5VLX110T FPGA for $D_{max} = 64$, $W_c = 9$, $W_a = 5$

|  | Slices (%) | LUTs (%) | Flip-Flops (%) | BRAMs (%) |
|---|---|---|---|---|
| Available | 17,280 | 69,120 | 69,120 | 148 |
| Unoptimized design (131 MHz) | 13,556 (78 %) | 37.107 (53 %) | 39,565 (57 %) | 59 (39 %) |
| Optimized design (201 MHz) | 14,239 (82 %) | 37,986 (55 %) | 41,792 (60 %) | 59 (39 %) |

We should point out here that $W_c$, $W_a$ and $D_{max}$ parameters are related with tasks carried out in parallel, thus they do not affect system performance but only resource utilization. Table 4 has the distribution of resources along with the percentage breakdown in each type of resources for the optimized design.

We conducted several experiments by varying the parameters in each stage so as to assess system performance in terms of scalability and increase in resource utilization. Tables 5, 6, 7 have the FPGA resource results for different parameter values. It is obtained that the design clock is not affected. At the same time we observe that once a parameter increases, the amount of resources needed

**Table 4.** Resource utilization of the optimized design in Virtex XC5VLX110T FPGA for $D_{max} = 64$, $W_c = 9$, $W_a = 5$

|  | LUTs (%) | Flip-Flops (%) | BRAMs (%) |
|---|---|---|---|
| Available | 69,120 | 69,120 | 148 |
| Total consumed | 37,986/69,120 (55 %) | 41,792/69,120 (60 %) | 59/148 (40 %) |
| AD census | 25,135/37,986 (66 %) | 29,167/41,792 (70 %) | 8/59 (14 %) |
| Aggregation | 6,547/37,986 (17 %) | 7,312/41,792 (17 %) | 51/59 (86 %) |
| Left/Right check | 4,638/37,986 (12 %) | 4,734/41,792 (11 %) | 0/59 (0 %) |
| Scanline belief propagation | 543/37,986 (1.5 %) | 634/41,792 (1.5 %) | 0/59 (0 %) |

for a resource category might increase drastically while another category is not affected, i.e. in Table 6 as $W_c$ increases, the amount of flip-flops and LUTs increases as opposed to the amount of BRAMs which remains unchanged.

**Table 5.** Impact of $D_{max}$ on resource utilization and performance, when $W_c = 9$ and $W_a = 5$

| $D_{max}$ | LUTs (%) | Flip-Flops (%) | BRAMs (%) | Max Clock |
|---|---|---|---|---|
| 16 | 10,284 (14 %) | 12,531 (18 %) | 30 (20 %) | 201.207 MHz |
| 32 | 19,148 (27 %) | 22,687 (32 %) | 30 (20 %) | 201.045 MHz |
| 64 | 37,986 (54 %) | 41,792 (60 %) | 59 (39 %) | 201.518 MHz |

**Table 6.** Impact of $W_c$ on resource utilization and performance, when $D_{max} = 64$ and $W_a = 5$

| $W_c$ | LUTs (%) | Flip-Flops (%) | BRAMs (%) | Max Clock |
|---|---|---|---|---|
| 5 | 21,637 (31 %) | 21,866 (31 %) | 59 (39 %) | 201.086 MHz |
| 7 | 29,813 (43 %) | 31,840 (46 %) | 59 (39 %) | 201.113 MHz |
| 9 | 37,986 (54 %) | 41,792 (60 %) | 59 (39 %) | 201.518 MHz |

Aggregation of the costs consumes most of our BRAM resources, as we have to construct $D_{max} \times W_a$ cost line buffers (a total of $D_{max} \times W_a \times FrameWidth \times CostSize$ bits must be buffered). BRAM primitives of Virtex 5 FPGAs support only certain aspect ratios. The vendor tool employs these primitives to construct bigger memories, using an allocation algorithm. Memories with different widths/depths from those ratios are mapped to the closest possible solution but may not use the resources optimally. Memories with ratios of $1 \times 16\,K$ (16,384 elements of 1-bit), $2 \times 8\,K$, $4 \times 4\,K$, $9 \times 2\,K$, $18 \times 1\,K$, $36 \times 512$ are guaranteed to utilize a single $18\,K$ primitive and thus use the resources optimally.

**Table 7.** Impact of $W_a$ on resource utilization and performance, when $D_{max} = 64$ and $W_c = 9$

| $W_a$ | LUTs (%) | Flip-Flops (%) | BRAMs (%) | Max Clock |
|---|---|---|---|---|
| 1 (off) | 28,505 (41 %) | 33,047 (47 %) | 9 (6 %) | 201.005 MHz |
| 3 | 34,618 (50 %) | 38,660 (55 %) | 31 (20 %) | 201.167 MHz |
| 5 | 37,986 (54 %) | 41,792 (60 %) | 59 (39 %) | 201.518 MHz |

In addition, very large frame sizes cause parameter bloating. In specific, images with $1800 \times 1500$ resolution require at least $D_{max} = 180$ for achieving satisfactory results in terms of quality (without altering the current camera baseline). While keeping the other parameters constant ($W_c = 9$, $W_a = 5$), such a large $D_{max}$ would require buffering $180 \times 5 \times 1800$ elements in the aggregation stage.

Due to the above we decided to put a limit on the image width. Restricting the frame width to 1024 pixels allowed us to:

- Pack at least two lines per 18K BRAM using a $18 \times 1K$ BRAM primitive configuration. For each cost line we allocate $9 \times 1024$ bits.
- Avoid excessive parameter bloating.

Using AD-Census, the costs are 9-bit long as described earlier. This benefits our design as BRAM primitives can be used optimally in a $18 \times 1\,K$ configuration. Using pure Census, cost size is reduced to 7-bits. We can maximize BRAM usage by using 9-bit costs, so we have room to increase census window size $W_c$ up to $21 \times 21$, with little additional cost to resource usage.

If the cost size is less than 9-bits or if the frame width is less than 1024 we can pack more lines. This aspect of our design is also parametric, as depending on the frame size and cost size, each BRAM can fit up to 6 lines in a $36 \times 512$ BRAM configuration.

In an effort to reduce BRAM consumption even further, we performed a cost size-accuracy tradeoff experimental analysis, depicted in Fig. 9. AD-Census was redefined as:

$$ADCensus' = min(ADCensus, SaturationValue) \qquad (2)$$

Selecting saturation values to be power of 2, can reduce cost size and thus fit more data into the BRAMs that implement the aggregation buffers. Our analysis shows that there is a slight benefit in doing so: for a saturation value of 63 (cost size reduced to 6-bits), and for the default $W_c$ and $W_a$ values of 9 and 5 respectively, we observe a 0.5 % improvement over the cost without saturation.

This is an important result because it puts our quality almost on par with a $W_c = 11$ and $W_a = 5$ parameter set. This slight improvement is attributed to the reduction of the influence of outliers within the aggregation window by truncating the cost. With 6-bit costs, we can pack 3 streams of costs per Aggregation Lines Buffer, thus reducing BRAM consumption even further. Note that all the

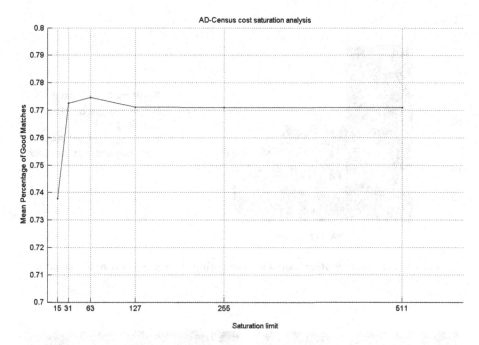

**Fig. 9.** Cost size/accuracy analysis. The peak value shifts to the right as the true maximum cost increases.

results presented so far with regard to FPGA resource utilization, correspond to designs incorporating the previous optimizations.

Figure 10 shows the effect of optimizations on BRAM utilization for $W_c = 9$, $W_a = 5$, $D_{max} = 64$ and a maximum frame width of 1024 pixels. Operating with small frame sizes allows for optimal algorithm performance.

We performed extensive verification of our designs Fig. 11 has the set of images we used to test our prototype. We entered stereo images and we compared the software and the FPGA output over the ground truth. The SW version aimed to support the validation phase; we developed it in Matlab prior to the FPGA design. In terms of the physical setup for the verification, Fig. 12 shows the methodology we followed to validate the FPGA system. The values of the pixels in the output of the FPGA processing were subtracted from the values of the pixels in the output of the SW, pixel-per-pixel so as to create an array holding their differences. We obtained that SW and HW produced similar results. The error lines are attributed to a slightly different selection policy in the WTA process of the LRC stage. In particular, when it comes to compare two equal cost values, our SW selects one cost value randomly, while our HW selects always the first one. This variation occurs early in the algorithmic flow, thus it is not only propagated but it is also amplified in the belief propagation module where local estimates of correct disparities are spread to incorrectly matched pixels along the scan-line. Finally, the errors at the borders that occur in both SW and

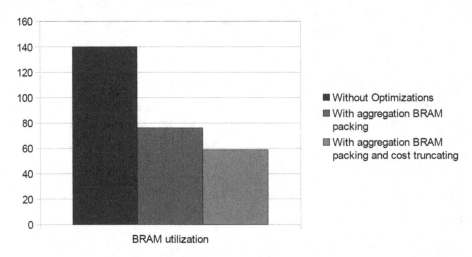

**Fig. 10.** BRAM resource utilization with the optimized aggregation buffer structure

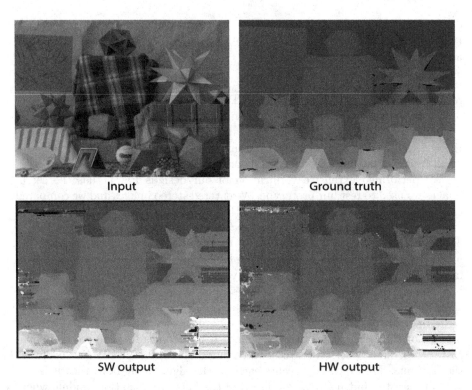

**Fig. 11.** Top row has Moebius $400 \times 320$ input dataset from Middlebury database and the ideal (ground truth) result. The bottow row has algorithm's output from SW and HW implementations.

HW outputs as compared with the ground truth, are due to the unavoidable occlusions at the image borders.

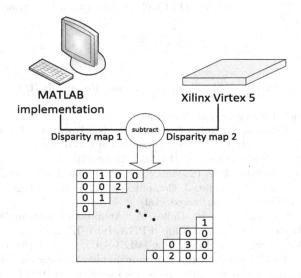

**Fig. 12.** Validation methodology

The actual prototype in the Virtex-5 FPGA can process images of up to $400 \times 320$ resolution. We put our efforts on building a high-speed stereo matching design, rather than solving the I/O issue. Instead, at off-line time we send images into internal BRAMs through a serial protocol; once the entire image is stored in the BRAMs the design starts processing it. We used hardware means for measuring the time to complete the FPGA processing, and by performing experiments on different images - mainly from Middlebury database - we achieved a processing rate of 1570 fps. To the best of our knowledge this outperforms any published FPGA-based system.

## 7 Conclusions and Future Work

In this chapter we presented the architecture and implementation of a real time stereo matching algorithm in an FPGA, which utilizes efficiently the strengths of this device. We validated the system on a prototype, and we exceeded real-time requirements by a large margin for various parameter configurations. In the future we will place our efforts to more advanced aggregation schemes as they are the key to better quality disparity maps for local methods. Another point that would benefit from further research is the scan-line belief propagation method, which we plan to augment to two dimensions and thus eliminate its streaking artifacts. Also we plan to complete the stereo vision core algorithm with rectification and full camera integration.

**Acknowledgement.** This work has been partially supported by the General Secretariat of Research and Technology (G.S.R.T), Hellas, under the project AFORMI- Allowing for Reconfigurable Hardware to Efficiently Implement Algorithms of Multidisciplinary Importance, funded in the call ARISTEIA of the framework Education and Lifelong Learning (code 2427).

# References

1. Ballard, D.H., Brown, C.M.: Computer Vision. Prentice-Hall, Englewood Cliffs (1982)
2. Marr, D.: Vision. Freeman, San Francisco (1982)
3. Di Carlo, S., Prinetto, P., Rolfo, D., Sansonne, N., Trotta, P.: A novel algorithm and hardware architecture for fast video-based shape reconstruction of space debris. EURASIP J. Adv. Sig. Process. **2014**(1), 1–19 (2014)
4. Scharstein, D., Szeliski, R.: A taxonomy and evaluation of dense two-frame stereo correspondence algorithms. Int. J. Comput. Vis. **47**(1–3), 7–42 (2002)
5. http://vision.middlebury.edu/stereo/eval/
6. Thomas, S., Papadimitriou, K., Dollas, A.: Architecture and implementation of real-time 3D stereo vision on a Xilinx FPGA. In: IFIP/IEEE International Conference on Very Large Scale Integration (VLSI-SoC), pp. 186–191, October 2013
7. Konolige, K.: Small vision systems: hardware and implementation. In: Proceedings of the International Symposium on Robotics Research, pp. 111–116 (1997)
8. Murphy, C., Lindquist, D., Rynning, A.M., Cecil, T., Leavitt, S., Chang, M.L.: Low-cost stereo vision on an FPGA. In: Proceedings of the IEEE Symposium on Field-Programmable Custom Computing Machines (FCCM), pp. 333–334, April 2007
9. Hadjitheophanous, S., Ttofis, C., Georghiades, A.S., Theocharides, T.: Towards hardware stereoscopic 3D reconstruction, a real-time FPGA computation of the disparity map. In: Proceedings of the Design, Automation and Test in Europe Conference and Exhibition (DATE), pp. 1743–1748, March 2010
10. Humenberger, M., Zinner, C., Weber, M., Kubinger, W., Vincze, M.: A fast stereo matching algorithm suitable for embedded real-time systems. Comput. Vis. Image Underst. **114**(11), 1180–1202 (2010)
11. Masrani, D.K., MacLean, W.J.: A real-time large disparity range stereo-system using FPGAs. In: Proceedings of the IEEE International Conference on Computer Vision Systems, pp. 42–51 (2006)
12. Jin, S., Cho, J.U., Pham, X.D., Lee, K.M., Park, S.-K., Munsang Kim, J.W.J.: FPGA design and implementation of a real-time stereo vision system. IEEE Trans. Circuits Syst. Video Technol. **20**(1), 15–26 (2010)
13. Rematska, G., Papadimitriou, K., Dollas, A.: A low-cost embedded real-time 3D stereo matching system for surveillance applications. In: IEEE International Symposium on Monitoring and Surveillance Research (ISMSR), in Conjunction with the IEEE International Conference on Bioinformatics and Bioengineering (BIBE), November 2013
14. Jin, M., Maruyama, T.: Fast and accurate stereo vision system on FPGA. ACM Trans. Reconfigurable Technol. Syst. (TRETS) **7**(1), 3:1–3:24 (2014)
15. http://danstrother.com/2011/01/24/fpga-stereo-vision-project/
16. Rhemann, C., Hosni, A., Bleyer, M., Rother, C., Gelautz, M.: Fast cost-volume filtering for visual correspondence and beyond. In: Proceedings of IEEE Conference on Computer Vision and Pattern Recognition (CVPR), pp. 3017–3024, June 2011

17. Kalarot, R., Morris, J.: Stereo vision algorithms for FPGAs. In: IEEE Conference on Computer Vision and Pattern Recognition Workshops (CVPRW), pp. 9–15, June 2010

18. Mattoccia, S., Stereo vision algorithms for FPGAs. In: IEEE Conference on Computer Vision and Pattern Recognition Workshops (CVPRW), pp. 636–641 (2013)

19. Zabih, R., Woodfill, J.: Non-parametric local transforms for computing visual correspondence. In: Eklundh, J.-O. (ed.) ECCV 1994. LNCS, vol. 801, pp. 151–158. Springer, Heidelberg (1994)

20. Mei, X., Sun, X., Zhou, M., Jiao, S., Wang, H., Zhang, X.: On building an accurate stereo matching system on graphics hardware. In: Proceedings of the IEEE International Conference on Computer Vision Workshops (ICCV), pp. 467–474, November 2011

# Minimizing Test Frequencies for Linear Analog Circuits: New Models and Efficient Solution Methods

Mohand Bentobache[1,2]([✉]), Ahcène Bounceur[3], Reinhardt Euler[3],
Salvador Mir[4,5]([✉]), and Yann Kieffer[6]([✉])

[1] LAMOS Laboratory, University of Bejaia, 06000 Bejaia, Algeria
mbentobache@yahoo.com
[2] LMPA Laboratory, University of Laghouat, 03000 Laghouat, Algeria
m.bentobache@lagh-univ.dz
[3] Lab-STICC Laboratory, University of Brest, 20, Avenue Victor Le Gorgeu,
29238 Brest, France
{Ahcene.Bounceur,Reinhardt.Euler}@univ-brest.fr
[4] University of Grenoble Alpes, TIMA, 38000 Grenoble, France
Salvador.Mir@imag.fr
[5] CNRS, TIMA, 38000 Grenoble, France
[6] LCIS Laboratory, University of Grenoble Alpes, 26900 Valence, France
Yann.Kieffer@esisar.grenoble-inp.fr

**Abstract.** This work presents new approaches to minimize the number of test frequencies for linear analog circuits. The cases of single and multiple fault detection regions for multiple test measures are considered. We first address the case when the injected faults have a single detection region in the frequency band. We show that the problem can be formulated as a set covering problem with a matrix having the consecutive-ones property for which the network simplex algorithm turns out to be very efficient. A second approach consists in modeling the problem by means of an interval graph, leading to its solution with a specific polynomial-time algorithm. A case-study of a biquadratic filter is presented for illustration purposes. Numerical simulations demonstrate that the two different approaches solve the optimization problem very fast. Finally, the optimization problems arising from multiple detection regions are modeled and solution approaches are discussed.

**Keywords:** Set covering problem · Consecutive-ones property · Analog circuit testing · Linear programming · Interval graphs

## 1 Introduction

Testing of analog circuits to verify their functionality is a time consuming and expensive task. In order to reduce costs, testing for the presence of faults that affect the device structure leads to more structured and cheaper test sets. Although the number of faults to be tested may indeed be very large, a reduced

© IFIP International Federation for Information Processing 2015
A. Orailoglu et al. (Eds.): VLSI-SoC 2013, IFIP AICT 461, pp. 188–207, 2015.
DOI: 10.1007/978-3-319-23799-2_9

set of tests that are simple to apply may be sufficient to achieve high fault coverage values. There is today a pressing need from the Semiconductors Industry to provide these fault coverage measures and optimized tests, especially in the context of SoC (System-on-Chip) devices that embed digital and mixed-signal blocks in a single chip.

Multi-frequency tests (i.e., multi-tone sinusoidal signals) have been classically considered for the test and diagnosis of linear analog devices such as analog filters. Since the effect of parametric and catastrophic faults varies as a function of frequency, it is possible to derive a minimal set of test frequencies either for the detection or for the diagnosis of all potential faults. To optimize the set of test frequencies, the approaches based on sensitivity analysis have typically addressed parametric faults [1,2]. However, these approaches are not accurate for very large deviations, such as those that result from catastrophic faults. On the other hand, the approaches based on fault simulation can handle catastrophic faults, but at the expense of very time consuming simulations when realistic faults at transistor-level are considered. Today, it is evident that fault simulation of analog circuits is becoming essential in order to optimize test sets relying on new techniques to accelerate fault simulation.

In this context, this work proposes a new technique for the optimization of multi-frequency tests for linear analog circuits. Fault simulation is used to obtain the frequency intervals for the detection of each fault. New efficient algorithms are then presented for the selection of the optimal set of test frequencies within these intervals for the detection of all faults. A simple case-study is used to illustrate the algorithms. Numerical simulations with randomly generated problem instances demonstrate the good time complexity of the proposed algorithms, with a large improvement over previous approaches [3]. We notice that the test optimization algorithms are general, applicable to any case-study requiring an optimization of multi-frequency tests based on fault simulation data. This technique is today feasible for analog filters, but it is also applicable to other analog devices such as analog-to-digital converters or radio-frequency front-ends requiring multi-tone tests, provided that fault simulation data are made available.

This work is organized as follows: in Sect. 2, the mathematical formulation of the Set Covering Problem (SCP) is reviewed and some definitions are given. In Sect. 3, we present the mathematical formulation of the problem of minimizing the number of frequency intervals necessary to detect the faults of an analog circuit, and we study the specific structure of the related coefficient matrix. In Sect. 4, we present two approaches for solving the problem: the Linear Programming (LP) approach and the interval graph approach, and a numerical example is given for illustration purposes. In Sect. 5, we present a mathematical formulation of the problem to minimize the number of test measures necessary for detecting the faults of an analog circuit. In Sect. 6, we present a case-study of testing a biquadratic filter. In Sect. 7, we carry out a large-scale numerical study in order to compare both approaches and to evaluate their time complexity. Finally, Sect. 8 concludes the work and provides some perspectives.

## 2    The Set Covering Problem

In this section, we present the set covering problem, we cite the existing methods for solving this problem and some of its applications. Finally, we present the corresponding mathematical model and some definitions.

### 2.1    Overview

The Set Covering Problem is one of the most important models in combinatorial optimization. Indeed, a wide range of real-world problems can be modeled as SCP, namely: railway crew scheduling, airline crew scheduling, facility location, etc. The practical importance of the SCP has motivated many researchers to develop efficient algorithms and heuristics for finding good solutions in reasonable time. We can cite: exact algorithms based on branch-and-bound or branch-and-cut [4], greedy heuristics [5], Lagrangian-based heuristics [6], genetic algorithms [7], etc. In order to test the efficiency of the proposed algorithms, there exists a library of SCP Benchmarks (Beasley's OR Library [8]).

The set covering problem is known to be NP-hard [9]. However, there exist some particular forms of the SCP which are polynomial-time solvable such as the SCP with a constraint matrix having the consecutive-ones property (i.e., the ones in each row appear consecutively). This particular case, denoted in the following by SCP-C1P, can be solved efficiently with LP algorithms.

### 2.2    Some Definitions

Let $M = \{1, \ldots, m\}$ and $N = \{1, \ldots, n\}$ be two sets of indices. Let $A = (a_{ij}, i \in M, j \in N)$ be a binary $(m \times n)$-matrix and $c = (c_j, j \in N)$ be an integer $n$-vector. The value $c_j, j \in N$, may represent the cost of column $j$. We assume without loss of generality that $c_j > 0$ for all $j \in N$. We say that a column $j \in N$ covers a row $i \in M$ if $a_{ij} = 1$. A set $S \subseteq N$ is called a cover if each row $i \in M$ is covered by at least one column $j \in S$. The problem of finding a cover $S$ of minimum cost can be formulated as an ILP (Integer Linear Programming) problem as follows:

$$\min \ z = c^T x, \tag{1a}$$

$$\text{subject to } Ax \geq \mathbf{1}_m, \ x \in \{0, 1\}^n, \tag{1b}$$

where $\mathbf{1}_m$ is the $m$-vector of ones. When $c_j = 1$, for all $j \in N$, problem (1) is called a *unicost set covering problem*.

**Definition 1** ([10]).
• *A* block *of 1's (block of 0's) in a row of a binary matrix $A$ is a maximal set of consecutive 1-entries (0-entries) in this row.*
• *A binary matrix has the* strong consecutive-ones property *(strong C1P) if in every row the 1's appear consecutively, that is, if every row contains at most one block of 1's.*
• *A binary matrix has the* consecutive-ones property *(C1P) if its columns can*

*be permuted in such a way that the resulting matrix has the strong C1P. If an ordering for the columns of a binary matrix yields the strong C1P, it is called a C1-ordering.*

- *A graph $G$ is an* interval graph *if its vertices can be mapped to intervals on the real line such that two vertices are adjacent if and only if their corresponding intervals have non empty intersection.*
- *A binary matrix is* totally unimodular *if every square submatrix has determinant 0, 1, or $-1$.*

# 3    Minimization of Test Frequencies to Detect All the Faults of an Analog Circuit

In [3], the problem of selecting a minimum number of test frequencies is formally presented and solved using boolean expressions. However, when the number of faults is large, the technique used is not efficient. In this section, we present a mathematical formulation of the general problem as a set covering problem. We show that, under some special conditions on the considered faults, the coefficient matrix of the SCP will have the C1P. Moreover, we suggest an interval graph formulation of the problem.

## 3.1    Mathematical Formulation of the Problem as an SCP-C1P

Consider a given linear analog circuit $\mathbf{C}$. Let $\mathcal{F} = \{F_1, F_2, \ldots, F_m\}$ be the set of all faults which can occur in $\mathbf{C}$. Let $T$ be a test measure which will be used in the fault detection process. In order to detect a given fault $F_i$ using the test measure $T$, test signals with maximum amplitude and at different frequencies in the interval $[f_{min}, f_{max}]$ are used as inputs of the analog circuit. The fault is detected if the test measure $T$ exceeds a fixed threshold $\tau$. Fault simulation allows then to compute, for each fault $F_i$, the frequency intervals for which the threshold is exceeded. These intervals are called the *detection regions* of fault $F_i$. Note that each fault can have one, two or more detection regions. Let $n_i$ be the number of detection regions of the fault $F_i$ and $\mathcal{R}_i = \{R_{i1}, R_{i2}, \ldots, R_{in_i}\}$ be the set of all the detection regions of the fault $F_i$. Note that these detection regions are disjoint: for each two detection regions $R_{ip}$ and $R_{iq}$, we have $R_{ip} \cap R_{iq} = \emptyset$. After that, we sort in increasing order the bounds of the different detection regions, we find the vector of frequencies:

$$f = (f_0, f_1, \ldots, f_n), \text{ with } f_0 < f_1 < f_2 < \cdots < f_{n-1} < f_n. \tag{2}$$

Then, we compute a set of $n$ frequency intervals $\mathcal{I} = \{I_1, I_2, \ldots, I_n\}$ as follows:

$$I_1 = [f_0, f_1[, \ I_2 = [f_1, f_2[, \ldots, \ I_n = [f_{n-1}, f_n[. \tag{3}$$

We denote by $A = (a_{ij}, i = 1, \ldots, m, \ j = 1, \ldots, n)$ the matrix which is defined as follows:

$$a_{ij} = \begin{cases} 1, \text{ if } \exists k \in \{1, \ldots, n_i\} : I_j \subseteq R_{ik}; \\ 0, \text{ otherwise.} \end{cases} \tag{4}$$

The problem consists in finding a minimal-cardinality set of frequency intervals $S \subseteq \mathcal{I}$ which can detect all the possible considered faults. One frequency for each selected frequency interval (typically in the middle of the interval) can be used in the optimized test set. This problem can be formulated as a unicost set covering problem: for each $S \subseteq \mathcal{I}$ and each frequency interval $I_j$, $j \in \{1, \ldots, n\}$, we define a binary variable as follows:

$$x_j^S = \begin{cases} 1, & \text{if } I_j \text{ belongs to the set } S; \\ 0, & \text{otherwise.} \end{cases} \tag{5}$$

Now, if $x = (x_j, j = 1, \ldots, n)$ is any vector of binary variables, then the mathematical model corresponding to this problem will be given by:

$$\min \ r = \mathbf{1}_n^T x, \tag{6a}$$

$$\text{s.t. } Ax \geq \mathbf{1}_m, \ x \in \{0, 1\}^n. \tag{6b}$$

**Remark 1.** The matrix $A$ cannot have more than $2 \sum_{i=1}^m n_i$ columns.

**Proposition 1.** If $n_i = 1$, for $i = 1, \ldots m$, i.e., each fault has a unique detection region, then the matrix $A$ will have the strong consecutive-ones property.

*Proof.* Let $F_i, i \in M$, be a given detected fault and $R_{i1} = [\alpha_i, \beta_i]$ be the unique detection region of fault $i$. By construction, $R_{i1}$ can be written as a union of $k$ consecutive intervals $I_{j_1}, I_{j_2}, \ldots, I_{j_k}$, where $\alpha_i$ is the lower bound of $I_{j_1}$ and $\beta_i$ is the upper bound of $I_{j_k}$. (Two intervals are consecutive if they have a common bound). Since the intervals $I_{j_r}$ correspond to the consecutive columns $a_{j_r}$ of $A$ for $r = 1, \ldots, k$, the detection regions correspond to the rows of $A$, and $I_{j_r} \subseteq R_{i1}$, i.e., $a_{ij_r} = 1$ for $r = 1, \ldots, k$.

Note, that the previous proposition is very important because it gives a simple sufficient condition for the matrix arising in our application to have the strong C1P.

In the following we consider only problems with faults having one detection region.

Following Proposition 1, ILP problem (6) is a unicost set covering problem with a coefficient matrix having the strong C1P (SCP-C1P). More precisely, it is given by:

$$\min \ z = \sum_{j=1}^n x_j, \tag{7a}$$

$$\text{s.t. } \sum_{j=lx(i)}^{rx(i)} x_j \geq 1, \ i \in M, \ x_j \in \{0, 1\}, j \in N, \tag{7b}$$

where for each row $i$, $lx(i)$ denotes the leftmost index $l$ for which $a_{il} = 1$ and $rx(i)$ the rightmost index $r$ for which $a_{ir} = 1$. To get the LP-relaxation of the above problem, we simply exchange the integrality constraints against the non-negativity constraints [11]. Thus, we get the following LP problem:

$$\min \ z = \sum_{j=1}^{n} x_j, \tag{8a}$$

$$\text{s.t.} \ \sum_{j=lx(i)}^{rx(i)} x_j \geq 1, \ i \in M, \ x_j \geq 0, j \in N. \tag{8b}$$

### 3.2  Graph Formulation of the Problem

Previously, we have formulated the problem of minimizing the number of frequency intervals to detect all the faults of an analog circuit using an ILP model. In this subsection, we suggest a new formulation based on the concept of interval graph: we denote the detection region of fault $i$ by the interval $[a_i, b_i]$ for $i \in M$. Let the interval graph $G = (F, E_F)$ be defined as follows:

$$F = \{[a_i, b_i], \ i \in M\}, E_F = \{F_i F_j : ]a_i, b_i[ \cap ]a_j, b_j[ \neq \emptyset\}. \tag{9}$$

In the next section we will suggest a polynomial algorithm using this interval graph for solving the considered problem.

## 4  Approaches for Solving the Minimization Problem of Frequency Intervals

In this section, we suggest two approaches for solving the problem of minimizing the number of frequency intervals necessary to detect all the faults of an analog circuit.

### 4.1  LP Approach

Let us recall the following results:

**Theorem 1** ([12]). *An (m × n)-matrix A with entries 0, 1 and −1 is totally unimodular if and only if each collection of columns from A can be partitioned into two column sets such that in each row the sum of the entries of the first set and the sum of the entries of the second set differ by at most 1.*

**Theorem 2** ([13]). *Let A be an m × n integral matrix. Then the polyhedron defined by $Ax \leq b$ and $x \geq 0$ is integral for every integral vector b if and only if A is totally unimodular.*

*Remark 2* ([10]). *Any matrix A having the C1P fulfills the conditions of Theorem 1 and, hence, is totally unimodular.*

Following Theorem 2 and Remark 2, any basic feasible solution of the LP problem (8) represents a cover for the SCP-C1P (7). Therefore, we can find an optimal solution using LP algorithms such as the primal or dual simplex method [14], the support method [15], the hybrid direction algorithm [19], etc. However, it is more efficient to transform the SCP-C1P into a min-cost network flow problem [10].

Let us make the Veinott-Wagner transformations [20] for the variables of problem (8): we introduce the variables $y_j$, $j = 1, \ldots, n + 1$ such that $x_j = -y_j + y_{j+1}$, $j = 1, \ldots, n$. Hence, we obtain the following equivalent LP problem:

$$\min z = -y_1 + y_{n+1}, \tag{10a}$$
$$\text{s.t.} \quad -y_{lx(i)} + y_{rx(i)+1} \geq 1, i \in M, \tag{10b}$$
$$-y_j + y_{j+1} \geq 0, \; j \in N. \tag{10c}$$

The dual of the above problem has $m + n$ variables $v_1, v_2, \ldots, v_{m+n}$ and $n + 1$ constraints and it is given by:

$$\min w = -\sum_{j=1}^{m} v_j, \tag{11a}$$
$$\text{s.t.} \quad \sum_{j=1}^{m+n} a'_{1j} v_j = -1, \tag{11b}$$
$$\sum_{j=1}^{m+n} a'_{ij} v_j = 0, \; i = 2, \ldots, n, \tag{11c}$$
$$\sum_{j=1}^{m+n} a'_{(n+1)j} v_j = 1, \; v_j \geq 0, \; j = 1, \ldots, m + n. \tag{11d}$$

where $A' = (a'_{ij}, i = 1, \ldots, n+1, j = 1, \ldots, m+n)$, and $A'$ has exactly one 1 and one $-1$ in each column. Remark that the LP problem (11) is a min-cost network flow problem. Thus, it can be solved by the network simplex algorithm. The scheme of the LP approach to solve the problem is described in the following steps:

**Step 1.** Compute the frequency intervals necessary to detect the different faults using relation (2);

**Step 2.** Compute the constraint matrix of the SCP-C1P using relation (4);

**Step 3.** Make the Veinott-Wagner transformations. Let $V$ be the constraint matrix of the LP problem (10);

**Step 4.** Compute the constraint matrix $A'$, the $(n+1)$-vector of right-hand-sides $b'$ and the cost $(m + n)$-vector $c'$ of the min-cost network flow problem (11):
$$A' = V^T, \; b' = (-1, 0, \ldots, 0, 1)^T, \; c' = \begin{pmatrix} -\mathbf{1}_m \\ \mathbf{0}_n \end{pmatrix};$$

**Step 5.** Solve the min-cost network flow problem with the network simplex algorithm.

## 4.2    Interval Graph Approach

In order to solve the problem using the interval graph $G$ defined by (9), we suggest the following algorithm:

**Algorithm 1.**
- Sort the vertices $F_i$, $i = \overline{1, m}$ by increasing order of their upper bounds $b_i$;
- Compute the frequencies $f_k$, $k = \overline{0, n}$ with (2);
- Set $S = \emptyset$, $label(i) = 0, i = \overline{1, m}$;
- For $i = 1$ to $m$
    - If $label(i) = 0$, then
        - Find the index $k$ such that $b_i = f_k$ and set
          $S = S \cup \{[f_{k-1}, f_k[\}$;
        - For $j = i + 1$ to $m$
            If $F_j$ is adjacent to $F_i$ in $G$, then set $label(j) = 1$;
            endif
            endfor
      endif
  endfor

The input of this polynomial algorithm is the interval graph $G$ and the output is a minimal-cardinality set $S$ of frequency intervals, which detects all the faults.

Note, that it is not necessary to construct the whole interval graph: we can use only its vertices, i.e., detection regions of the different faults, and replace the test "If $F_j$ is adjacent to $F_i$ in $G$" by the test "If $a_j < b_i \leq b_j$".

*Remark 3.* Contrarily to the LP approach, the interval graph approach uses the detection regions of the considered faults directly, i.e., without transforming the problem.

## 4.3    Numerical Example

*Example 1.* We consider an analog circuit with five faults. The detection regions of these faults are: $R_1 = [1, 80]$, $R_2 = [160, 1700]$, $R_3 = [1, 1400]$, $R_4 = [1400, 2000]$ and $R_5 = [1000, 1500]$. Let us compute the minimal-cardinality set of frequency intervals necessary to detect all the five faults with the two approaches.

**LP Approach:** First, we compute the different frequency intervals $I_j, j = 1, \ldots, n$: we sort the different bounds of the detection regions in increasing order, we get the vector $f = (f_i, i = 0, \ldots, 7) = (1, 80, 160, 1000, 1400, 1500, 1700, 2000)$. Thus, the different frequency intervals are computed as follows: $I_1 = [1, 80[$, $I_2 = [80, 160[$, $I_3 = [160, 1000[$, $I_4 = [1000, 1400[$, $I_5 = [1400, 1500[$, $I_6 = [1500, 1700[$ and $I_7 = [1700, 2000[$. The question is then: among all these seven intervals, which one must be included in a minimal-cardinality set? In order to answer this question, we solve the following $ILP$ problem:

$$\min z = \mathbf{1_n}^T x, \tag{12a}$$

$$\text{s.t. } Ax \geq b, \ x \in \{0,1\}^n, \tag{12b}$$

where $x^T = (x_1, x_2, x_3, x_4, x_5, x_6, x_7)$, $b^T = (1,1,1,1,1)$ and

$$A = \begin{pmatrix} 1 & 0 & 0 & 0 & 0 & 0 & 0 \\ 0 & 0 & 1 & 1 & 1 & 1 & 0 \\ 1 & 1 & 1 & 1 & 0 & 0 & 0 \\ 0 & 0 & 0 & 0 & 1 & 1 & 1 \\ 0 & 0 & 0 & 1 & 1 & 0 & 0 \end{pmatrix}. \tag{13}$$

It is easy to remark that the constraint matrix has the consecutive-ones property. Using the Veinott-Wagner transformations $(x_j = -y_j + y_{j+1}, \ j = 1, 2, \ldots, 7)$, we get the following equivalent LP problem:

$$\begin{aligned} \min z &= (c')^T y \\ \text{s.t. } Vy &\geq b', \end{aligned} \tag{14}$$

where $y \in \mathbb{R}^8$, $c' = (-1, 0, 0, 0, 0, 0, 0, 1)^T$, $b' = (1,1,1,1,1,0,0,0,0,0,0,0)^T$ and

$$V = \begin{pmatrix} -1 & 1 & 0 & 0 & 0 & 0 & 0 & 0 \\ 0 & 0 & -1 & 0 & 0 & 0 & 1 & 0 \\ -1 & 0 & 0 & 0 & 1 & 0 & 0 & 0 \\ 0 & 0 & 0 & 0 & -1 & 0 & 0 & 1 \\ 0 & 0 & 0 & -1 & 0 & 1 & 0 & 0 \\ -1 & 1 & 0 & 0 & 0 & 0 & 1 & 0 \\ 0 & -1 & 1 & 0 & 0 & 0 & 0 & 0 \\ 0 & 0 & -1 & 1 & 0 & 0 & 0 & 0 \\ 0 & 0 & 0 & -1 & 1 & 0 & 0 & 0 \\ 0 & 0 & 0 & 0 & -1 & 1 & 0 & 0 \\ 0 & 0 & 0 & 0 & 0 & -1 & 1 & 0 \\ 0 & 0 & 0 & 0 & 0 & 0 & -1 & 1 \end{pmatrix}. \tag{15}$$

The dual problem of the LP problem (14) is

$$\begin{aligned} \min w &= -(b')^T v \\ \text{s.t. } V^T v &= c', \ v \geq 0, \end{aligned} \tag{16}$$

where $v \in \mathbb{R}^{12}$. Remark that the LP problem (16) is a min-cost network flow problem. The primal and dual optimal solutions obtained by the network simplex algorithm of CPLEX are:

$$v^* = (0,0,1,1,0,0,0,0,0,0,0,0)^T, \ y^* = (0,1,1,1,1,2,2,2)^T. \tag{17}$$

Hence $x^* = (1,0,0,0,1,0,0)^T$, which means that a minimal-cardinality set of frequency intervals is $S = \{I_1, I_5\} = \{[1, 80[, \ [1400, 1500[\}$.

**Interval Graph Approach:** Let $G = (F, E_F)$ be the graph defined by (9). First, we sort the vertices of the graph $G$ in increasing order of their upper bounds, we get:

$$F_1 = [a_1, b_1[ = [1, 80[, \quad F_2 = [a_2, b_2[ = [1, 1400[, \quad F_3 = [a_3, b_3[ = [1000, 1500[,$$
$$F_4 = [a_4, b_4[ = [160, 1700[ \text{ and } F_5 = [a_5, b_5[ = [1400, 2000[.$$

The vector of frequencies computed by (2) is then

$$f = (f_0, f_1, \ldots, f_7) = (1, 80, 160, 1000, 1400, 1500, 1700, 2000).$$

The different iterations of the interval graph algorithm are as follows:

We set $S = \emptyset$ and label$(i) = 0$, $i = \overline{1, 5}$.

For $i = 1$, $b_1 = 80$, $f_k = f_1 = 80$, $S = \{[f_0, f_1[\} = \{[1, 80[\}$.     The unique adjacent vertex of $F_1$ is $F_2$ (the edge $F_1 F_2 \in E_F$ because $a_2 < b_1 < b_2$), so we set label$(2) = 1$.

For $i = 2$, we have label$(2) = 1$, so we pass to $i = 3$.

For $i = 3$, $b_3 = 1500$, $f_k = f_5$, $S = \{[f_0, f_1[, [f_4, f_5[\} = \{[1, 80[, [1400, 1500[\}$. The adjacent vertices of $F_3$ are $F_4$ and $F_5$, so label$(4) = 1$ and label$(5) = 1$.

For $i = 4$, we have label$(4) = 1$, so we pass to $i = 5$.

For $i = 5$, we have label$(5) = 1$. Since $i = m$, a minimal-cardinality set of frequency intervals is $S = \{[1, 80[, [1400, 1500[\}$.

### 4.4   Case of Multiple Detection Regions

Let us illustrate this case by the following numerical example:

*Example 2.*

| Faults | Detection regions |
|--------|-------------------|
| $F_1$ | $R_{11} = [1, 80]$ |
| $F_2$ | $R_{21} = [160, 200]$, $R_{22} = [300, 1700]$ |
| $F_3$ | $R_{31} = [1, 1400]$ |
| $F_4$ | $R_{41} = [1400, 2000]$ |
| $F_5$ | $R_{51} = [1000, 1500]$ |

The vector of frequencies computed by (2) is then

$$f = (f_0, f_1, \ldots, f_9) = (1, 80, 160, 200, 300, 1000, 1400, 1500, 1700, 2000).$$

The frequency intervals are:

$$I_1 = [1, 80[, \ I_2 = [80, 160[, \ I_3 = [160, 200[, \ I_4 = [200, 300[, \ I_5 = [300, 1000[,$$
$$I_6 = [1000, 1400[, \ I_7 = [1400, 1500[, \ I_8 = [1500, 1700[, \ I_9 = [1700, 2000[.$$

The constraint matrix of the SCP is then given by

$$A = \begin{pmatrix} 1\,0\,0\,0\,0\,0\,0\,0\,0 \\ 0\,0\,1\,0\,1\,1\,1\,1\,0 \\ 1\,1\,1\,1\,1\,1\,0\,0\,0 \\ 0\,0\,0\,0\,0\,0\,1\,1\,1 \\ 0\,0\,0\,0\,0\,1\,1\,0\,0 \end{pmatrix}. \tag{18}$$

Let us remark that this matrix loses the consecutive-ones property because the second row does not have consecutive ones. Therefore, we cannot apply the techniques suggested above to solve it. If this case occurs in practice, the branch-and-cut algorithm of CPLEX can be applied to solve the ILP problem. For this example, CPLEX gives us the optimal solution: $x^* = (1, 0, 0, 0, 0, 0, 1, 0, 0)^T$. So a minimal-cardinality set of frequency intervals is

$$S = \{I_1, I_7\} = \{[1, 80[, \ [1400, 1500[\}. \tag{19}$$

*Remark 4.* Although the constraint matrix of the previous SCP does not possess the consecutive-ones property, solving the LP relaxation gives us the optimal solution $x^* = (1, 0, 0, 0, 0, 0, 1, 0, 0)^T$. This means that for this type of problems the LP relaxation can give a good approximate solution for the optimal one (good upper bound for the optimal value). That is why we expect the branch-and-cut algorithm of CPLEX (or any other solver) to produce an optimal solution in a few iterations in case that the optimal solution of the LP-relaxation is not optimal for the SCP. Further numerical experiments have to be carried out in order to confirm this assertion.

## 5   Minimization of the Number of Test Measures Necessary for Detecting All the Faults of an Analog Circuit

Previously, we have assumed that only one test measure is used in the testing process. However, in practice, often we use several test measures. So if $k$ is the number of the used test measures, we need to solve $k$ SCPs for solving the problem of frequency interval minimization. Therefore, solving the problem of minimization of test measures beforehand can dramatically reduce the CPU time of solving the whole optimization process.

Consider a given analog circuit $\mathcal{C}$. Let $\mathcal{F} = \{F_1, F_2, \ldots, F_m\}$ be the set of all faults which can occur in $\mathcal{C}$. Let $\mathcal{T} = \{T_1, T_2, \ldots, T_k\}$ be the set of $k$ test measures to be used in the fault detection process. We denote by $H = (h_{ij}, i = 1, \ldots, m, \ j = 1, \ldots, k)$ the Fault-Test-Measure (FTM) matrix which is defined as follows:

$$h_{ij} = \begin{cases} 1, \text{ if the test measure } T_j \text{ detects the fault } F_i; \\ 0, \text{ otherwise.} \end{cases} \tag{20}$$

The problem consists in finding the minimal-cardinality set of test measures which can detect all the considered faults. This problem can also be formulated as a unicost set covering problem: for each test measure $T_j$, $j = 1, 2 \ldots, k$ and any set $S \subseteq T$, we define a binary variable as follows:

$$x_j^S = \begin{cases} 1, & \text{if the test measure } T_j \in S; \\ 0, & \text{otherwise.} \end{cases} \tag{21}$$

Hence, the mathematical model corresponding to this problem is given by:

$$\begin{aligned} & \min p = \mathbf{1}_k^T x, \\ & \text{s.t. } Hx \geq \mathbf{1}_m, \ x \in \{0,1\}^k. \end{aligned} \tag{22}$$

The optimal solution for this integer linear programming problem constitutes a desired minimal-cardinality set of test measures which detect all the faults. Note that, in general, the coefficient matrix of this problem does not have a specific structure, so the branch-and-cut algorithm of CPLEX can be used to solve this problem.

Once a minimal-cardinality set of test measures determined, we can solve the problem of frequency interval minimization for each test measure in this set.

The global optimization scheme for testing a linear analog circuit with multiple test measures is shown in Fig. 1.

# 6    Case-Study

To illustrate our approach, similar to [3], we will now present a case-study biquadratic filter as shown in Fig. 2. There are 6 test measures for this circuit that correspond to the common-mode signal at the input and at the output of each operational amplifier. For simplicity, only catastrophic (10 MOhm open and $1\,\Omega$ short) faults in the passive components are considered. Due to the differential design, only 16 different faults need to be considered.

We denote the test measures by $T_1, T_2, \ldots, T_6$ and the faults by $F_1, F_2, \ldots, F_{16}$. Figure 3 shows the frequency behavior of test measure $T_1$ for some of these faults. The detection regions of each fault $F_i$, $i = 1, 2, \ldots, 16$ using test measures $T_j$, $j = 1, 2, \ldots, 6$ are computed using the fault simulator developed in [21,22]. Note, that the simulation results obtained in [21] indicate that test measures $T_2, T_4$ and $T_6$ do not detect any fault. Hence, we only consider test measures $T_1, T_3$ and $T_5$. For simplicity also, we have only considered nominal simulations of the catastrophic faults. In practice, Monte Carlo simulations of each catastrophic fault should be considered, and worst-case detection regions be computed (that is, the intersection of the detection regions for each Monte Carlo instance).

First, we start by minimizing the number of test measures necessary for the detection of the sixteen faults. Following simulation results, test measure $T_1$ detects the faults: $F_1, F_2, \ldots, F_8$; $T_3$ detects the faults $F_9, F_{10}, F_{11}, F_{12}$ and

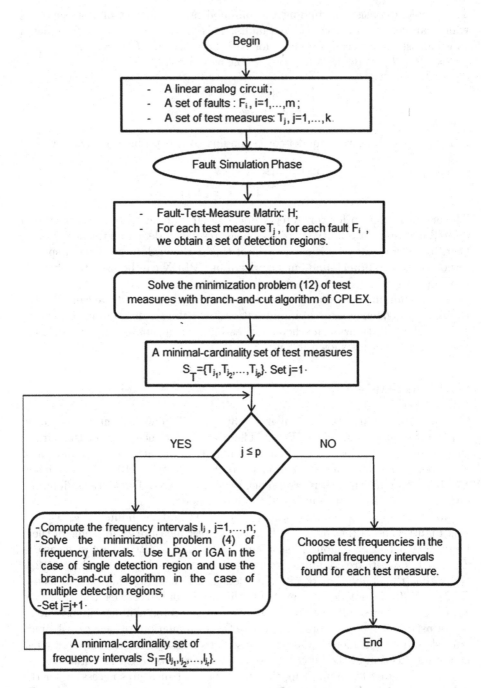

**Fig. 1.** Global optimization scheme for testing analog circuits with multiple test measures

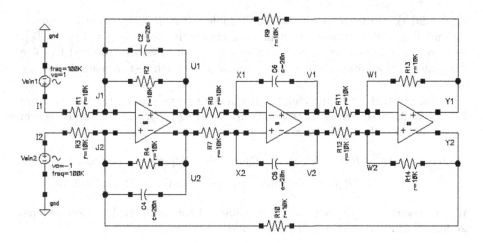

**Fig. 2.** Biquadratic filter

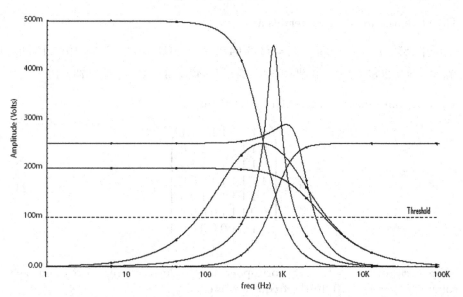

**Fig. 3.** Output signals using test measure $T_1$

$T_5$ detects the faults $F_{13}$, $F_{14}$, $F_{15}$, $F_{16}$. So the FTM matrix corresponding to the minimization problem of test measures is

$$H^T = \begin{pmatrix} 1\,1\,1\,1\,1\,1\,1\,1\,0\,0\,0\,0\,0\,0\,0\,0 \\ 0\,0\,0\,0\,0\,0\,0\,0\,1\,1\,1\,1\,0\,0\,0\,0 \\ 0\,0\,0\,0\,0\,0\,0\,0\,0\,0\,0\,0\,1\,1\,1\,1 \end{pmatrix}. \qquad (23)$$

Observe, that since test measures $T_2$, $T_4$ and $T_6$ do not detect any faults, the matrix $H$ contains only three columns which correspond to the test measures

$T_1$, $T_3$ and $T_5$. Without solving the SCP problem (22), it is clear that a minimal-cardinality set of test measures which detects all the faults is $S = \{T_1, T_3, T_5\}$. Now, that a minimal set of test measures is at hand, we can proceed to solve the problem of minimization of test frequencies for each test measure belonging to this set.

First, we start by minimizing the frequency intervals under the test measure $T_1$: the faults detected using test measure $T_1$ are $F_1, F_2, \ldots, F_8$. The detection regions of the different faults are

$$R_{11} = [1, 10^5], \ R_{21} = [85, 3732], \ R_{31} = [85, 3732], R_{41} = [1, 2685],$$

$$R_{51} = [1, 3442], \ R_{61} = [336, 1566], \ R_{71} = [1, 1014] \text{ and } R_{81} = [647, 10^5].$$

When we sort in increasing order the bounds of the different detection regions, we find the following vector of frequencies:

$$f = (f_0, f_1, \ldots, f_9) = (1, \ 85, \ 336, \ 647, \ 1014, \ 1566, \ 2685, \ 3442, \ 3732, \ 10^5).$$

Therefore, the frequency intervals are

$$I_1 = [1, 85[, \ I_2 = [85, 336[, \ I_3 = [336, 647[, \ I_4 = [647, 1014[, \ I_5 = [1014, 1566[,$$

$$I_6 = [1566, 2685[, \ I_7 = [2685, 3442[, \ I_8 = [3442, 3732[ \text{ and } I_9 = [3732, 10^5[.$$

The constraint matrix of the SCP (6) is then:

$$A = \begin{pmatrix} 1 & 1 & 1 & 1 & 1 & 1 & 1 & 1 & 1 \\ 0 & 1 & 1 & 1 & 1 & 1 & 1 & 1 & 0 \\ 0 & 1 & 1 & 1 & 1 & 1 & 1 & 1 & 0 \\ 1 & 1 & 1 & 1 & 1 & 1 & 0 & 0 & 0 \\ 1 & 1 & 1 & 1 & 1 & 1 & 1 & 0 & 0 \\ 0 & 0 & 1 & 1 & 1 & 0 & 0 & 0 & 0 \\ 1 & 1 & 1 & 1 & 0 & 0 & 0 & 0 & 0 \\ 0 & 0 & 0 & 1 & 1 & 1 & 1 & 1 & 1 \end{pmatrix}, \tag{24}$$

where each row $i$, $i = 1, \ldots, 8$, corresponds to the detection region $R_{i1}$ and each column $j$, $j = 1, \ldots, 9$, to the frequency interval $I_j$.

Since the matrix $A$ has the consecutive-ones property (each fault has a unique detection region), the optimal solution of the SCP (6) can be obtained using the network simplex algorithm. In our example, this leads to the following optimal solution: $x^* = (0, 0, 0, 1, 0, 0, 0, 0)^T$ and $r^* = 1$, i.e., a minimal-cardinality set of intervals detecting all the faults is $S = \{I_4\}$. Therefore, it is sufficient to use a single test frequency belonging to the interval $[647\,Hz, 1014\,Hz[$ to detect all the faults $F_1, F_2, \ldots, F_8$.

Similarly, when we use the test measure $T_3$, we detect the faults $F_9, F_{10}, F_{11}$ and $F_{12}$. The corresponding detection regions are

$$R_{91} = [159, 7957[, R_{10,1} = [1, 1740[, \ R_{11,1} = [1, 1739[ \text{ and } R_{12,1} = [159, 7940[.$$

The different frequency intervals are

$$I_1' = [1, 159[, \ I_2' = [159, 1739[, \ I_3' = [1739, 1740[,$$

$$I_4' = [1740, 7940[ \text{ and } I_5' = [7940, 7959[.$$

The constraint matrix of the SCP is

$$A = \begin{pmatrix} 0\ 1\ 1\ 1\ 1 \\ 1\ 1\ 1\ 0\ 0 \\ 1\ 1\ 0\ 0\ 0 \\ 0\ 1\ 1\ 1\ 0 \end{pmatrix}. \tag{25}$$

Hence, for the test measure $T_3$, the solution of the SCP (6) is obvious, that is, a single test frequency belonging to the interval $I_2' = [159\,Hz, 1739\,Hz[$ detects all the faults $F_9, F_{10}, F_{11}$ and $F_{12}$.

Finally, with test measure $T_5$, we detect the faults $F_{13}, F_{14}, F_{15}$ and $F_{16}$. The corresponding detection regions are

$$R_{13,1} = [1, 2798[, \ R_{14,1} = [1, 1413[, \ R_{15,1} = [1, 1412[ \text{ and } R_{16,1} = [1, 2794[.$$

The different frequency intervals are

$$I_1'' = [1, 1412[, \ I_2'' = [1412, 1413[, \ I_3'' = [1413, 2794[ \text{ and } I_4'' = [2794, 2798[.$$

The constraint matrix of the SCP is

$$A = \begin{pmatrix} 1\ 1\ 1\ 1 \\ 1\ 1\ 0\ 0 \\ 1\ 0\ 0\ 0 \\ 1\ 1\ 1\ 0 \end{pmatrix}. \tag{26}$$

Thus, for the test measure $T_5$, the solution is obvious again, that is, the frequency interval which detects all the faults $F_{13}, F_{14}, F_{15}$ and $F_{16}$ is $I_1'' = [1\,Hz, 1412\,Hz[$, and a single test frequency belonging to this interval is required.

## 7  Numerical Experiments

In order to compare the efficiency of the two approaches presented in Sect. 4 (LP approach and the interval graph one), we have implemented them in C++ programming language and carried out large-scale numerical experiments on a set of randomly generated test instances using an Intel(R) Core(TM)2 Duo CPU P8600 @ 2.40 GHz machine with 4 GB of RAM.

We have generated 60 problems with number of faults

$$m = 500,000; 600,000; 700,000; 800,000; 900,000; 1,000,000. \tag{27}$$

The detection region bounds are generated in the interval $[1\,Hz, 10^5\,Hz]$. For each class of test problems with $m$ faults, we generate ten problems. We have solved the different instances with the LP approach (LPA) using the network simplex method of the LP and ILP solver CPLEX [23] and the suggested interval graph algorithm (IGA). The CPU time of the two approaches IGA and LPA are reported in Table 1.

Let $[a_i, b_i]$ be the detection regions of the faults $F_i$, $i = 1, \ldots, m$. In the following, we give the implementation details for the LP approach:

**Step 1.** Compute the set of frequency intervals $\mathcal{I}$ as follows:

- sort the bounds of the detection regions in increasing order: let $f$ be the vector of these sorted bounds;
- delete duplicate elements from $f$, and let $f = (f_0, f_1, \ldots, f_n)$;
- set $\mathcal{I} = \{I_j = [f_{j-1}, f_j[, \ j = 1, \ldots, n\}$;

**Step 2.** Compute the constraint $(m \times n)$-matrix of the SCP-C1P as follows:

- set $fmax = f(n)$ and compute the vector $t$ of dimension $fmax$ as follows:
- set $t(k) = 0$, for $k = 0, \ldots, fmax$;
- set $t(f(j)) = j$, for $j = 0, \ldots, n$;
- set $lx(i) = t(a_i) + 1$ and $rx(i) = t(b_i)$ for $i = 1, \ldots, m$;

**Step 3.** Make the Veinott-Wagner transformations: compute the constraint matrix $V$ of the LP problem (10) as follows:

- for $i = 1, \ldots, m$; for $j = 1, \ldots, m + n$:

$$V_{ij} = \begin{cases} -1, & \text{if } j = lx(i); \\ 1, & \text{if } j = rx(i) + 1; \\ 0, & \text{otherwise}; \end{cases} \tag{28}$$

- for $i = m + 1, \ldots, n + 1$; for $j = 1, \ldots, m + n$:

$$V_{ij} = \begin{cases} -1, & \text{if } j = i - m; \\ 1, & \text{if } j = i - m + 1; \\ 0, & \text{otherwise}; \end{cases} \tag{29}$$

**Step 4.** Compute the constraint matrix $A'$, the $(n + 1)$-vector of right-hand-sides $b'$ and the cost $(m + n)$-vector $c'$ of the min-cost network flow problem (11): $A' = V^T$, $b' = (-1, 0, \ldots, 0, 1)^T$, $c' = \begin{pmatrix} -\mathbf{1}_m \\ \mathbf{0}_n \end{pmatrix}$;

**Step 5.** Solve the min-cost network flow problem with the network simplex algorithm.

Note, that the efficient implementation presented above computes the constraint matrices of the SCP-C1P and the min-cost network flow problem of the LP approach in small CPU times (less than 1 second on average for all the test problems). That is why we have not reported the CPU times of computing the constraint matrices of the SCP-C1P and the min-cost network flow problem in Table 1.

**Table 1.** CPU time of the different approaches

| m | OptVal | IGA | LPA | CPU Ratio |
|---|--------|-----|-----|-----------|
| 500,000 | 560.80 | 4.10 | 3.18 | 1.29 |
| 600,000 | 611.90 | 5.30 | 3.52 | 1.51 |
| 700,000 | 672.50 | 6.70 | 3.85 | 1.74 |
| 800,000 | 704.90 | 9.40 | 4.30 | 2.19 |
| 900,000 | 762.90 | 12.00 | 4.53 | 2.65 |
| 1,000,000 | 809.10 | 16.30 | 4.76 | 3.42 |
| **Mean** | | **8.97** | **4.02** | **2.13** |

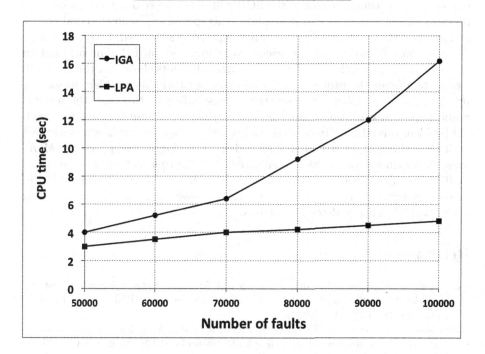

**Fig. 4.** CPU time of the two approaches: IGA and LPA

The average optimal values found by the two approaches IGA and LPA for the different test problems are shown in column OptVal. We compute the ratios of the CPU time of IGA over LPA. These ratios are shown in column CPU Ratio. Finally, the CPU time of the two approaches are plotted in Fig. 4. The LPA shows a time complexity $O(m)$, while IGA shows a time complexity $O(m^2)$, where $m$ is the number of faults.

The graphs of Fig. 4 indicate that transforming the problem into a min-cost network flow problem and solving it with the network simplex algorithm is more efficient than the interval graph algorithm. Indeed, LPA is, on average, two times faster than IGA. However, the computation time is very small even for problems with an extremely large number of faults. Therefore, the interval graph algorithm can also be used in practice by test engineers because of its simple implementation; the good CPU times (an average of 16 seconds for optimizing the test of analog circuits with 1,000,000 faults); and the fact that it solves the original problem directly.

## 8    Conclusion

In this work, we have formulated as an SCP the problem of minimizing the number of test frequencies necessary to detect a set of faults injected into an analog circuit. We have shown that when the considered faults have a unique detection region, the constraint matrix of the SCP will have the strong consecutive-ones property. After that, we have reformulated this special case using interval graphs and an algorithm working directly with this graph is suggested. In order to solve the problem efficiently, two approaches are compared: an LP approach and an interval graph approach. The obtained numerical results show that the approach which transforms the problem into a min-cost network flow problem to solve it by the network simplex algorithm is the most efficient. However, the interval graph approach can also be used by test engineers because it solves the original problem directly; its implementation is very simple and it is extremely fast with CPU times of a few tenths of seconds even for large-scale problems. Moreover, the optimization problem associated with multiple detection regions and multiple test measures is studied. Future work will focus on developing a branch-and-cut algorithm for solving efficiently the set covering problem corresponding to the case of multiple detection regions.

## References

1. Alippi, C., Catelani, M., Fort, A., Mugnaini, M.: Automated selection of test frequencies for fault diagnosis in analog electronic circuits. IEEE Trans. Instrum. Meas. **54**(3), 1033–1044 (2005)
2. Grasso, F., Luchetta, A., Manetti, S., Piccirilli, M.-C.: A method for the automatic selection of test frequencies in analog fault diagnosis. IEEE Trans. Instrum. Meas. **56**(6), 2322–2329 (2007)
3. Mir, S., Lubaszewski, M., Courtois, B.: Fault-based ATPG for linear analog circuits with minimal size multifrequency test sets. J. Electron. Test. Theory Appl. **9**, 43–57 (1996)
4. Balas, E., Carrera, M.C.: A dynamic Subgradient-based Branch-and-bound procedure for set covering. Oper. Res. **44**, 875–890 (1996)
5. Chvatal, V.: A greedy heuristic for the set-covering problem. Math. Oper. Res. **4**(3), 233–235 (1979)
6. Beasley, J.E.: A lagrangian heuristic for set covering problems. Nav. Res. Logistics **37**, 151–164 (1990)
7. Beasley, J.E., Chu, P.C.: A genetic algorithm for the set covering problem. Eur. J. Oper. Res. **94**, 392–404 (1996)
8. Beasley, J.E.: OR-library: distributing test problems by electronic mail. J. Oper. Res. Soc. **41**, 1069–1072 (1990)

9. Garey, M., Johnson, D.: Computers and Intractability: A Guide to the Theory of NP-Completeness. Freeman, San Francisco (1979)

10. Dom, M.: Recognition, Generation, and Application of Binary Matrices with the Consecutive-Ones Property. Ph.D. thesis, Institut für Informatik, Friedrich-Schiller Universität Jena, Germany (2008)

11. Matoušek, J., Gärtner, B.: Understanding and Using Linear Programming. Springer, Berlin (2007)

12. Ghouila-Houri, A.: Caractérisation des matrices totalement unimodulaires. CR Acad. Sci. Paris **254**, 1192–1194 (1962)

13. Hoffman, A.J., Kruskal, J.B.: Integral boundary points of convex polyhedra. In: Kuhn, H.W., Tucker, A.W. (eds.) Linear Inequalities and Related Systems, pp. 223–246. Princeton University Press, Princeton (1956)

14. Dantzig, G.B.: Linear Programming and Extensions. Princeton University Press, Princeton (1963)

15. Bentobache, M., Bibi, M.O.: A two-phase support method for solving linear programs: Numerical experiments. Math. Probl. Eng., **2012**, Article ID 482193, 28 (2012). doi:10.1155/2012/482193

16. Bentobache, M., Bounceur, A., Euler, R., Kieffer, Y., Mir, S.: New techniques for selecting test frequencies for linear analog circuits. In: VLSI-SoC 2013, Istanbul, Turkey, pp. 93–98, 07–09 October 2013

17. Bentobache, M., Bounceur, A., Euler, R., Kieffer, Y., Mir, S.: Efficient minimization of test frequencies for linear analog circuits. In: 18th IEEE European Test Symposium, ETS 2013, Avignon, France, p. 1, 27–30 May 2013

18. Bentobache, M., Bounceur, A., Euler, R.: Une application efficace du problème de recouvrement au test de circuits analogiques. In: ROADEF 2012, University of Angers, France, pp. 424–425, 11–13, April 2012

19. Bibi, M.O., Bentobache, M.: A hybrid direction algorithm for solving linear programs. Int. J. Comput. Math. **92**(1), 201–216 (2015)

20. Veinott, A.F., Wagner, H.M.: Optimal capacity scheduling. Oper. Res. **10**, 518–547 (1962)

21. Bounceur, A.: CAO Platform for mixed circuit testing. Ph.D. thesis, Grenoble INP (2007) (in french)

22. Bounceur, A., Mir, S., Rolíndez, L., Simeu, E.: CAT platform for analogue and mixed-signal test evaluation and optimization. In: De Micheli, G., Mir, S., Reis, R. (eds.) VLSI-SoC: Research Trends in VLSI and Systems on Chip. IFIP, vol. 249, pp. 281–300. Springer, Boston (2007)

23. CPLEX, Software available at http://www-01.ibm.com/software/integration/optimization/

# Partition-Based Faults Diagnosis of a VLIW Processor

Davide Sabena[✉], Matteo Sonza Reorda, and Luca Sterpone

Dipartimento di Automatica e Informatica, Politecnico di Torino, Turin, Italy
{davide.sabena,matteo.sonzareorda,luca.sterpone}@polito.it

**Abstract.** Reconfigurable systems are increasingly used in different domains, due to the advantages they offer in terms of flexibility: reconfigurability can also be used for managing possible faults affecting a circuit, when fault tolerance is the target. In this case the system must be able to (1) detect any possible fault, (2) identify the module (or partition) including it, and (3) take proper actions able to overcome the problem (e.g., by substituting the faulty module with a spare one). In this chapter, we address the point (2) when a Very Long Instruction Word (VLIW) processor is used by resorting to a Software-Based Self-Test (SBST) approach. SBST techniques have shown to represent an effective solution for permanent fault detection and diagnosis, both at the end of the production process, and during the operational phase. When VLIW processors are addressed, SBST techniques can effectively exploit the parallelism intrinsic in these architectures. In this chapter, we propose a new approach that starting from existing detection-oriented programs generates a diagnosis-oriented test program. Moreover, we propose (1) a detailed analysis of the generated equivalence classes and (2) a solution aimed to maximize the diagnosability of the modules composing the VLIW processor under test, thus perfectly suiting the needs of reconfigurable systems. Experimental results gathered on a case study VLIW processor show the effectiveness of the proposed approach: at the end of the presented method, the faulty module is always identified.

**Keywords:** Software-based diagnosis · Partition-based diagnosis · VLIW processor

## 1 Introduction

Reconfigurable processors [1] are increasingly used in different domains. Their key characteristic lies in the fact that they can be easily configured to match the specific requirements of the target application, e.g., in terms of performance, size, and power consumption, thus possibly making them more convenient than traditional processors. Very Long Instruction Word (VLIW) processors [2] represent a popular choice among reconfigurable processors.

When the system is used for a safety- or mission-critical application, dynamic reconfigurability may be exploited to face the effects of permanent faults: in this case the processor undergoes some test during the operational phase, aiming at detecting possible faults affecting the hardware. The test can be activated either at a specific moment in time (e.g., at power on), or periodically. As soon as a permanent fault is

© IFIP International Federation for Information Processing 2015
A. Orailoglu et al. (Eds.): VLSI-SoC 2013, IFIP AICT 461, pp. 208–226, 2015.
DOI: 10.1007/978-3-319-23799-2_10

detected, a diagnostic procedure is activated to identify the faulty partition, so that proper actions can be taken, e.g., by substituting it with a spare one, thus restoring the system integrity.

When adopting this solution, we need an effective test procedure, able to detect the highest percentage of possible faults while matching the requirements of a test performed during the operational phase (e.g., in terms of duration, size, invasiveness). Some previous works in the area [3, 4] showed that when considering VLIW processors, these goals can be achieved resorting to a functional approach, in which a suitable test program is executed and the produced results are observed (*Software-Based Self-Test* or SBST [5]). The SBST test programs can be generated starting from the processor netlist or (with some limitations) from its RT-level description [6]. Some recent work demonstrated that thanks to their regular structure, test program generation can be even automated in the case of VLIW processors [4, 7], thus overcoming the major limitation of the SBST approach, lying in the high cost for manually generating the test. On the other side, the SBST approach shows some advantages with respect to the structural approach (e.g., based on scan) when the in-field test is considered, mainly due to its easier usage and much lower area overhead.

On fault detection, the application code is typically suspended in the faulty system, thus preventing the fault to produce critical misbehaviors. Then, the system activates a diagnostic procedure, whose goal is to identify the faulty partition out of those composing the processor: in this context, each partition represents the minimal unit that can be repaired or substituted if faulty. This procedure can resort once more to SBST, i.e., to the execution of a suitable test program, whose results allow identifying the faulty partition [8].

Since the basic motivation for this work is to support the design of highly dependable systems based on dynamic reconfiguration, the goal of our diagnostic approach is to identify the faulty partition, rather than the specific fault responsible for a given misbehavior, as in other works (e.g., [9]). A similar approach was followed in [10], where the issue of self-adapting the test so that it takes into account possible units, which have been already, labeled as faulty is considered. However, no one of the previous works gives a systematic method to generate diagnosis-oriented test programs, as we do in this chapter.

This chapter proposes a method able to identify the module including the fault affecting a VLIW processor, taking into account the intrinsic features of this particular kind of processors. The proposed method is mainly composed of two parts: initially, we focus on the issue of writing an accurate diagnostic SBST test program for a generic VLIW processor. The proposed approach is based on exploiting an existing test program (targeting to fault detection, only), and on applying a set of techniques for improving it so that it can hold sufficient diagnostic properties [11] with respect to a previously defined partitioning of the processor. In the second part, the method acts on the initial partitioning, optimizing it so that the achieved diagnosability is maximized. Besides this optimization algorithm, with respect to [11] this chapter also presents a detailed analysis of the results obtained through the diagnostic test program, highlighting a number of cases in which the faults belonging to different partitions cannot be distinguished using a software-based solution (i.e., they are functionally equivalent).

The basic idea behind the first part of the method is to exploit the regularity and parallelism characterizing a VLIW processor. In particular, the technique we propose is based on splitting the original test program in small pieces (called *fragments*), and then modifying each fragment in such a way that it performs the same operation using different resources (e.g., different registers, or different ALUs). By checking which ones of the replicas of the original fragment (called *brother fragments*) generates a misbehavior, we can identify the faulty module.

In the last part of the chapter we explain how to further improve the diagnosability of a generic VLIW processor by implementing a clever partitioning. More in particular, since in the dynamic reconfigurability scenario the aim is the identification of the faulty module and not of the single possible fault, analyzing the composition of the equivalence classes generated by the diagnostic program allows to understand that (1) due to the implementation rules of the processor under test, it is not always possible to distinguish the faults in a module from those in other modules, and (2) by slightly modifying the partitioning it is possible to achieve a very high level of diagnosability.

The method we propose has been experimentally evaluated resorting to a sample VLIW processor [12]: initially, an existing test program aimed at fault detection, only, has been modified and improved, thus obtaining a diagnostic test program whose characteristics (in terms of size, duration and diagnostic capabilities) have been evaluated and compared with those of the original test program. Secondly, applying the second part of the method, the diagnosability of the considered processor has been maximized.

The chapter is organized as follows. Section 2 includes some background about the architecture of a VLIW processor. Section 3 provides an overview about diagnosis of circuits and processors and introduces some notation and vocabulary. Section 4 explains the proposed method. Experimental results on the selected case study and their analysis are presented in Sect. 5. In Sect. 6 we explain how to further improve the diagnosability of the considered VLIW processor by acting on the partitioning. Finally, conclusions and future works are described in Sect. 7.

## 2 VLIW Architecture Summary

VLIW processors are increasingly employed in systems requiring high performance combined with low power consumption. From a hardware point of view, the two most significant differences between a superscalar processor and a VLIW processor are:

- all the operations are executed by parallel independent *Computational Domains* (CDs), each one characterized by its own Functional Units;
- the scheduling adopted by the processor for instruction execution is totally static, since the compiler assigns the execution of each instruction to a determinate CD. Consequently, in a traditional VLIW processor there isn't any hardware scheduler of the operations.

As shown in Fig. 1-a, from a software point of view the VLIW assembly code is composed of a sequence of macro-instructions (also called *Bundles*): each macro-instruction is composed of a sequence of instructions. Each instruction code embeds the information items required to assign its execution to a specific Computational Domain, which is selected at the compile time.

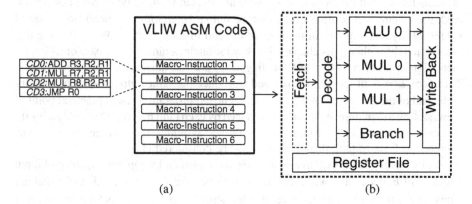

(a)                                                                      (b)

**Fig. 1.** Example of a VLIW Instruction Code format (a) and of a VLIW Architecture (b)

This scheme proved to be able, in some applications, to significantly reduce the power consumption and the silicon area if compared to traditional superscalar processors. Furthermore, the Instruction Level Parallelism (ILP) can be adequately exploited (at least in the case of data intensive applications), since a good compiler is able to detect which instructions can be executed in parallel by checking the entire program at compile time [2].

As shown in Fig. 1-b, the architecture of a generic VLIW processor is fully parametric, so that different options, such as the number and type of functional units (FUs), the number of multi-ported registers (i.e., the size of the register file), the width of the memory buses and the type of different accessible FUs can be modified depending on the application requirements. The VLIW manifest collects all the characteristics of a specific VLIW processor: it specifies the number of Computational Domains, the number and type of the Functional Units embedded into each of them, the size and access mode of the multiport Register File [4] and any other feature that must be taken in account when developing the code for the considered processor.

Considering the regularity and simplicity of the typical VLIW architecture, this kind of processors is perfectly suited for being adopted in reconfigurable systems [13], either (1) to match variable application constraints and goals, or (2) to implement highly dependable systems [14]. In the first case, the processor is implemented resorting to a programmable device, and the different components are dynamically mapped on the available resources in such a way to optimize the execution of the target application; in the second case, some spare resources are embedded in the architecture, and they are used to replace some faulty module as soon as a permanent fault is detected.

## 3  Basics on Diagnosis

Let call $F = \{f0, f1, ..., fn-1\}$ the set of $n$ faults that can affect the Unit Under Test (UUT) we are considering. Each of these faults causes the UUT to produce a given output behavior $b$ (also called *syndrome*) when a given sequence of input stimuli $I$ is applied; let denote by $b_i$ the output behavior produced by fault $f_i$, and $b_g$ the output behavior of the fault-free circuit. Clearly, $b_i = b_g$ for all undetected faults $f_i$. When SBST is considered, the assumption is often made, that the output behavior corresponds to the set of values left by the program in memory at the end of its execution. We will make this assumption throughout this chapter. The key rationale behind it is the ease of its implementation in practice, when test (or diagnosis) are run during the operational phase. Therefore, $b_i = b_j$ iff the two faults $f_i$ and $f_j$ produce the same output values in memory at the end of the execution of the test (or diagnosis) program. From a practical point of view, storing a signature of the values produced by each fault may allow to easily identify the existing faults [11]. Alternative solutions avoiding the storage even of this compressed form of fault dictionary can also be considered [15].

A given pair of faults $(f_i, f_j)$ is said to be *distinguished* by a given sequence of input stimuli $I$ iff $b_i \neq b_j$. Otherwise, they are said to be *equivalent wrt I*. All faults that are equivalent wrt to a given sequence of input stimuli $I$ are said to belong to the same *Equivalence Class wrt I*. A detected fault $f_i$ is said to be *fully diagnosed* by a sequence of input stimuli $I$ iff any couple of faults $(f_i, f_j)$ including $f_i$ is distinguished by $I$. Since two faults $f_i, f_j$ can never be distinguished if they are functionally equivalent, the number of fully diagnosed faults in a circuit is typically rather low [11].

Several possible metrics can be adopted to measure the diagnostic capabilities of a sequence of input stimuli $I$ [16].

When diagnosis is used in a reconfigurable system for identifying the partition including the fault, the precision required is lower than in other situations where diagnosis is required (e.g., for yield ramp-up): in fact, the final goal in this case is to be able to distinguish all pairs of faults belonging to different partitions, while distinguishing pairs of faults belonging to the same partitions is not of interest. Hence, for the purpose of this chapter we will exploit a metric called *Diagnostic Capability*, or *DC(I)*, which corresponds to the percentage of faults belonging to an Equivalence Class wrt I composed of faults all belonging to the same partition. In the ideal case in which DC(I) is 100 %, this would mean that I is able to always identify the partition where the fault is located. We will also exploit the notion of *Fully Diagnosed Fault with respect to Partitions (FDP)*, which is a fault belonging to an Equivalence Class composed of faults all belonging to the same partition. Clearly, DC(I) is the percentage of FDP faults with respect to the total number of faults.

## 4   Diagnostic Test Program Generation

In this section we describe a new method that allows to generate diagnostic programs for a generic VLIW processor, once its specific configuration is known.

As shown in Fig. 2, the flow aimed at the generation of the diagnostic program is composed of two main parts, denoted as *classification* and *brother fragment generation*. The result of these two steps is an accurate test program with an improved diagnostic capability.

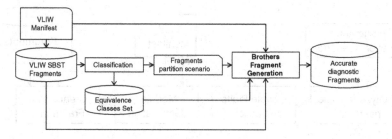

**Fig. 2.** The flow of the proposed diagnosis method

The proposed flow requires two main inputs. The former is the manifest of the VLIW processor under analysis, which contains all the features of the processor itself (which is supposed to be organized into a few partitions). The latter is a collection of small test programs aimed at fault detection, called *fragments*: each fragment performs a few test instructions (aimed at exciting a specific fault or group of faults) plus some other instructions needed to prepare the required parameters and make the results of the test instruction observable. The fragments have been generated splitting the original SBST programs [4]: the fragments should contain the lowest possible number of instructions and detect the lowest possible number of faults (while still maintaining the same total fault coverage). The set of the initial fragments is called *Initial Test Program*.

### 4.1 Classification

The classification part aims at computing the Equivalence Classes with respect to the Initial Test Program. This task can be easily performed resorting to commercial Fault Simulation tools and its final result (which requires some further custom post-processing) is the assignment of each fault either to an Equivalence Class composed of faults belonging to a single partition (in which case the fault is labeled as FDP) or to an Equivalence Class including faults belonging to different partitions.

In practice, this phase requires performing the Fault Simulation of each fragment, then processing the data base storing the syndrome of each fault, and finally computing the Equivalence Classes.

The result of this part of the method is the Fragment Partition Scenario, which consists of a database storing for each partition the list of faults belonging to it as well as their syndrome.

### 4.2 Brother Fragment Generation

The brother fragment generation part is oriented to the generation of new diagnostic fragments capable to improve the overall custom fragment diagnostic capability, thus increasing the DC(I) metric of the addressed VLIW partitions. The flow, illustrated in Fig. 3, is composed of four phases: (1) *analysis of multiple partitions*, (2) *couple faults extraction*, (3) *module identification* and (4) *creation of new fragments*. The 4 phases are repeated until a given stopping condition (e.g., based on maximum computational time, or on the achieved diagnostic capabilities) is reached.

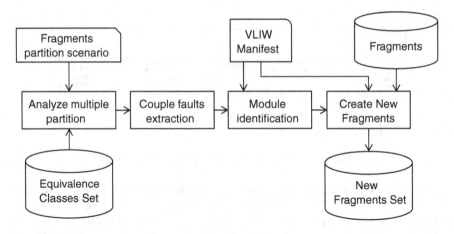

**Fig. 3.** The flow of the brother fragment generation

The "analyze multiple partition" phase elaborates the fragment partition scenario database comparing equivalence classes including faults belonging to two partitions. In details, in this step, all the equivalence classes are compared and the couple of faults equivalent and belonging to different VLIW partitions are identified.

Once the list of equivalent faults is generated, the "couple faults extraction" phase selects each couple of two fault locations, one belonging to the partition $i$ and the other belonging to $j$.

The "module identification" phase identifies the location of the two faults $i$ and $j$, analyzing the fault location hierarchy with respect to the VLIW manifest information; the result of this phase is the identification of the VLIW circuit resources involved by each fault.

Finally, the "create new fragments" phase is executed. Basically, this phase elaborates the original test fragments involved into the VLIW resource module identified by the Module identification phase and generates a new set of fragments modifying the resource used by the original test instructions. In this way, the final test program includes two or more different fragments, which are supposed to fail alternatively, depending on whether one or the other of the two partitions we want to distinguish are faulty. The pseudo-code of the Create New Fragments phase is reported in Fig. 4.

The algorithm needs the code of the original test fragment (OF), the VLIW manifest (VM) and the selected rule (R) which is provided by the module identification phase. There are two main rules that can be used for the generation of the new fragments: the first, denoted as R1, is a *register re-allocation rule* and it implies that the brother fragment will contain the same instructions of the original one, but each instruction will use different registers. In this way, by checking the results of the two fragment execution, we are able to understand if the fault is the register file (in case the two fragments results are both wrong) or one of the other VLIW module involved by the two fragments. The second rule, denoted as R2, is a *resource re-allocation rule*: simply, the new brother fragment will use a different VLIW Functional Unit to execute the test instruction of the fragment.

```
1. OF = Original Fragment;
2. VM = VLIW Manifest;
3. R  = Selected Rule;
4. FL = Faults List;
5. Analysis of the Original Fragment OF - Identification of:
   5.1. A: Test Instruction (TI);
   5.2. B: Instructions that set-up the registers used by TI;
   5.3. C: Instructions that forward  the produced results to
        observable locations;
   5.4. The registers used by A, B and C;
6. Selection of the new resources, according to:
   •  the selected rule R;
   •  the VLIW Manifest VM;
7. Brother Fragment Generation: Assigns to A, B and C the new
   resources, according to:
   •  the selected rule R;
   •  the VLIW Manifest VM;
8. FL = Fault Simulation of the Brother Fragment.
```

**Fig. 4.** The pseudo-code for the "create new fragments" phase

According to OF, VM, and R the algorithm analyzes the original test fragment considering the used test instruction (TI), the VLIW functional unit (FU), the registers used as operands (RI) and the registers used to forward the produced results to observable locations (RO). Finally, it selects a new set of resources and on the basis of the defined rules it generates a new fragment.

In Table 1, an example of original fragment and two corresponding brother fragments is shown; in this example we address a fragment in which the test instruction aims at the adder functional unit embedded in the Computational Domain 0 (referred as CD0). The first brother fragment has been generated with the rule R1 (i.e., the register re-allocation rule), in order to dismember an equivalence class containing faults embedded in the register file and in the adder functional unit of CD0. Consequently, the new brother fragment will be generated changing all the registers used to perform the test instruction and to forward the result in the data memory, without changing the functionality of the original fragment. The second brother fragment, instead, has been generated with the rule R2 (i.e., the resource re-allocation rule): practically, the test instruction of the original fragment has been moved from the computational domain 0 to the computational domain 1, leaving unaltered the other instructions composing the original fragment. In this way, if the results of the two fragments are both wrong, the fault is definitely not embedded in one of the two functional units executing the test instructions, but it belongs to another module used by the two fragments.

**Table 1.** An example of two brother fragments generated from the same original fragment.

| Original Fragment |
|---|
| ```
---< macro-Instruction 1 >---
CD0: mov $r0.1 = 11111…1
CD1: mov $r0.2 = 00000…0
---< macro-Instruction 2 >---
CD0: add $r0.3 = $r0.1, $r0.2  /*Test instr.*/
CD1: nop
---< macro-Instruction 3 >---
CD0: stw 0[$r0.63] = $r0.3
CD1: nop
------------------------------
``` |
| **1ˢᵗ Brother Fragment – Rule R1** |
| ```
---< macro-Instruction 1 >---
CD0: mov $r0.7 = 11111…1
CD1: mov $r0.8 = 00000…0
---< macro-Instruction 2 >---
CD0: add $r0.9 = $r0.7, $r0.8  /*Test instr.*/
CD1: nop
---< macro-Instruction 3 >---
CD0: stw 0[$r0.63] = $r0.9
CD1: nop
------------------------------
``` |
| **2ˢᵗ Brother Fragment – Rule R2** |
| ```
---< macro-Instruction 1 >---
CD0: mov $r0.1 = 11111…1
CD1: mov $r0.2 = 00000…0
---< macro-Instruction 2 >---
CD0: nop
CD1: add $r0.3 = $r0.1, $r0.2  /*Test instr.*/
---< macro-Instruction 3 >---
CD0: stw 0[$r0.63] = $r0.3
CD1: nop
------------------------------
``` |

## 5    Experimental Results

In this section we present the experimental results obtained using the ρ-VEX VLIW [12] processor as a case study. The ρ-VEX processor is a generic and reconfigurable VLIW processor written in VHDL language by researchers of the Delft University of Technology. The ρ-VEX processor includes most of the features of VLIW processors used by industry. For the purpose of this chapter, we considered the stuck-at fault model, although the method can be easily extended to deal with other fault models. In order to perform the stuck-at fault simulation experiments, we synthesized and implemented the ρ-VEX processor using a standard ASIC gate library. The total number of stuck-at faults in the resulting netlist is 335,336.

We divided the ρ-VEX processor in 10 partitions: the fetch unit, the decode unit, the general-purpose register file, the branch-management register file, the write-back unit, and the four Computational Domains in which the functional units are embedded. Clearly, these partitions are not uniform (in terms of number of contained resources).
```

In Sect. 6.3 we present a method able to create homogeneous partitions without changing the diagnostic results achieved by the method described in the following paragraphs.

Considering the diagnosis goal, in this Section we address only the most relevant partitions of the ρ-VEX processor, i.e., the register file and the four Computational Domains (CD0 to CD3). The number of faults enclosed in each of the four Computational Domains is not exactly the same, since some of the functional units embedded in each of them are different: for example, CD0 includes a branch unit, while CD3 embeds a memory access unit, while all the CDs include an ALU unit.

We also wrote a program (composed of about 1,200 lines of C++ code) able to compare the fault lists generated by the fault simulation step; the goal of this program is to implement the classification phase, i.e., performing the computation of the equivalence classes with respect to the adopted test programs. Our tool also identifies FDP faults, and provides information about the remaining faults.

By referring to the above 5 partitions in the ρ-VEX processor we applied the proposed method and generated the diagnostic test program. As a starting test program we use the set of fragments used for the optimized generation of an SBST program addressing the ρ-VEX processor, generated with the method proposed in [4]; this set is a selection, from an exhaustive set of possible fragments, of the fragments that allow to maximize the stuck-at fault coverage, minimizing the test size and length.

The experimental results we gathered are reported in Table 2, which includes the percentage of FDP faults with respect to the total number of faults of each partition, i.e., the Diagnostic Capability. The first column of Table 2 (denoted as Optimized SBST) is the original test set, composed of 244 fragments; its diagnostic level is rather low for all the considered partitions, since this is optimized in terms of size and length, which are often conflicting goals with respect to diagnosis. The stuck-at fault coverage reached by this test program is 98.2 % with respect to all the resources of the considered VLIW processor.

**Table 2.** Diagnostic capability

| Partition | Method | | |
|---|---|---|---|
| | Optimized SBST | Exhaustive fragments set | Proposed approach |
| Register file | 62.82 % | 84.23 % | 87.17 % |
| CD0 | 77.12 % | 77.79 % | 83.74 % |
| CD1 | 80.12 % | 81.56 % | 88.39 % |
| CD2 | 79.99 % | 80.34 % | 88.23 % |
| CD3 | 70.80 % | 72.14 % | 81.65 % |

The first step towards the improvement of the Diagnostic Capability is the use of the whole fragments set generated resorting to the method described in [4]. The results obtained with this approach are shown in the second column of Table 2 (Exhaustive Fragments Set). The improvement of the diagnosis resolution is greater when the register file is considered (the improvement for this partition is more than 21 %), while it is limited for the Computational Domains. This is mainly because the considered set of fragments is composed of 748 fragments, and 68 % of them target the test of a portion of the register file itself.

The final step of the proposed flow is the evaluation of the diagnostic capabilities of an ad-hoc fragments set, composed of the fragments of the Exhaustive Fragments Set with an additional set of fragments brothers, developed with the method proposed in Sect. 4. For the purpose of this chapter, we generated the brother fragments only for the fragments addressing the test of the ALUs (that are the most relevant components of each CD in terms of number of stuck-at faults). Moreover, we developed the brother fragments also for the memory unit (which is embedded in CD3), since this unit is used by all the fragments in order to save the results of the test instructions in the data memory; consequently, there are many equivalence classes containing a fault of this unit and an efficient diagnostic of this module is required. The resulting set of fragments is composed of 1,056 fragments, of which 308 are brother fragments. The CPU generation time for the brother fragments was approximately 21 h, of which about 85 % used for the fault simulation; the computational time has been evaluated on a workstation with an Intel Xeon Processor E5450. As shown in Table 2, the improvements due to this approach are evident if the partitions containing the ALUs (referred as CD1, CD2, CD3 and CD4) are considered: the capability to recognize if a fault is enclosed in one of these partitions is improved of about 8 % with respect to the previous approaches. The resulting diagnosability is not uniform for all the four CDs since, as explained previously, the functional units embedded into these partitions are not the same.

We also made an analysis about the Equivalence Classes wrt the last test set, focusing on those that include faults belonging to more than one partition (i.e., neglecting all FDP faults). Analyzing these equivalence classes, only, it is possible to notice that about 95 % of them are classes only including faults belonging to the same partition; moreover, if the remaining classes are considered, about 60 % of them are equivalence classes enclosing faults belonging to 2 partitions, while about 35 % are classes enclosing faults belonging to 3 different partitions, as shown in the graph of Fig. 5. The above results show that even when the diagnostic resolution of our method is not enough to identify the single partition including a fault, still it is able to identify the couple of "candidate" partitions in about 60 % of the cases.

Finally, in Table 3 some more information about the size and the execution time of the final fragments set are shown. These results confirm that optimizations, in terms of size and length, are often conflicting goals with respect to diagnosis.

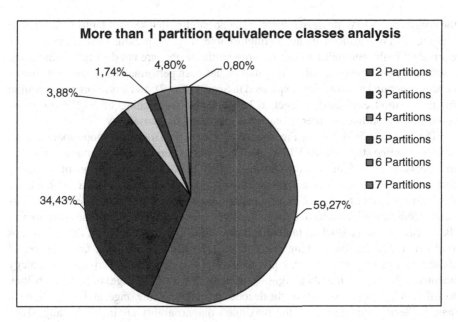

**Fig. 5.** Analysis of Equivalence Classes including faults belonging to more than one partition

**Table 3.** Size and duration of the different test sets

| Method | Size [KBs] | Execution time [Clock Cycles] |
|---|---|---|
| Optimized SBST | 1,926 | 10,601 |
| Exhaustive fragments set | 3,429 | 17,049 |
| Proposed approach | 4,899 | 24,356 |

## 6   Equivalence Classes Analysis

In this section, we present a detailed analysis aimed at (1) better understanding the achieved results, i.e., identifying the reasons that prevent the diagnostic metrics to be further increased, and (2) understanding how it is possible to reach a complete diagnosability of the partitions composing the addressed VLIW processor. Finally, we present an equivalence class-based technique aimed at improving the partitioning of the processor resources in order to achieve a scenario in which all the partitions are composed of a comparable number of logic resources, in order to make the proposed method suitable to be used in a dynamic partial reconfiguration environment [13].

### 6.1   VLIW Equivalence Classes Analysis

Using the Software-Based diagnosis method described in the previous sections, it is possible reach a high level of diagnosability. However, due to the hardware structure of the considered VLIW processor there is the possibility that several faults belonging to different VLIW partitions are not distinguishable; here, we present a list of examples of equivalent faults belonging to two or more partitions that are not distinguishable using a software-based method, only. This analysis has been performed using the equivalence classes generated with the flow explained in Sect. 4 (Fig. 2), and it is a sort of motivation for the method explained in Sect. 6.2, where the partitioning of VLIW processor resources is modified in order to reach the maximum diagnosability.

The first case is shown in Fig. 6 and represents a chain of flip-flops spanning the various pipeline stages of the VLIW processor. Let us consider, for example, a flip-flop that contains one of the bits devoted to identify the destination register of a generic instruction: clearly, this value is provided by the decode stage, and it is available in all the following pipeline stages. Each stage thus contains a flip-flop devoted to save this value. Consequently, we have a set of flip-flops connected in a chain. The behaviour of the processor when a stuck-at fault affects one of the inputs or outputs of these flip-flops is always the same, thus making impossible to identify the root cause fault. Hence, all these faults belong to the same equivalence class. Based on the partitioning strategy adopted so far (which mainly assigns to each partition a single stage) these faults belong to different VLIW partitions (i.e., the decode stage, the execute stage, and the write-back stage). Clearly, this decreases the maximum diagnosability attainable by any SBST program.

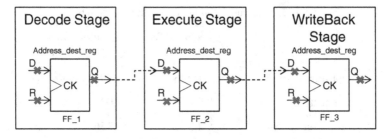

**Fig. 6.** Example of equivalent faults in different stages of the pipeline; stuck-at faults are highlighted with red x (Color figure online)

The second case is shown in Fig. 7, and it corresponds to the logic gates devoted to the decoding of a generic instruction, and to the flip-flop that contains one bit of the result of the decode operation. Also in this case, if a stuck-at fault affects one of the logic gates embedded in the decoder module or in the flip-flop that stores the result of the decoding, the resulting processor behavior is the same. Hence, it will never be possible to identify if the faulty module is the decoder belonging to the second computational domain or the flip-flop belonging to the generic decode stage module. Consequently, these faults belong to the same equivalence class but to different partitions, and contribute to decreasing the maximum achievable diagnosability.

The third case is shown in Fig. 8, and it corresponds to the register file and the generic flip-flop that contains one bit of the data retrieved from the register file itself. More in particular, both the stuck-at fault affecting the flip-flop of a register and that affecting the flip-flop containing the value of that register in another module (e.g., the generic decode

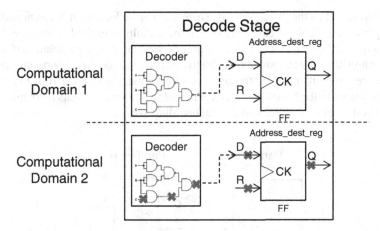

**Fig. 7.** Example of equivalent faults, considering the decoder module of the second computational domain and the decode stage containing all the instruction decode modules; stuck-at faults are highlighted with red x (Color figure online)

stage module) cause the processor to behave in the same way. Hence, by only checking the signature provided by the diagnostic program, it will never be possible to detect the faulty module; consequently, these faults belong to the same equivalence class. By only checking the signature generated by the diagnostic program explained in Sect. 4 (or by any other test program), it will never be possible to understand if the faulty module is the register file or the decode stage.

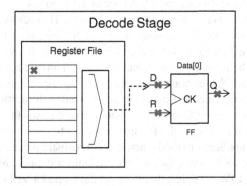

**Fig. 8.** Example of equivalent faults, considering the register file and the logic resources of the decode stage; stuck-at faults are highlighted with red x (Color figure online)

## 6.2 Maximization of the Diagnosability of the VLIW Partitions

As described in the previous sub-section, the hardware structure of the VLIW processor is organized in a way that several faults are equivalent wrt the adopted test program and not physically distinguishable using a software-based diagnosis method. In case VLIW partitions are selected on the basis of the VLIW hierarchical structure, equivalent faults may negatively affect the diagnosability, since they can be located in different partitions not uniquely identifiable in case only one of these faults is excited. Therefore, VLIW partitioning based only on hierarchical module became an ineffective solution if applied to a reconfigurable system, since it is slightly effective to identify a particular portion of the processor to be repaired through reconfiguration. As illustrated in Fig. 9, two partitions related to the VLIW hierarchical modules contain two faults belonging to the same equivalent class making impossible their diagnosability.

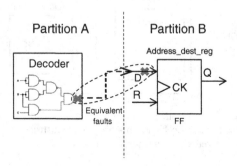

**Fig. 9.** Example of faults belonging to the same equivalent class traversing two different VLIW partitions

In order to improve the diagnosability, we defined a metric called *Equivalent Cross metric (EC metric)*, which for a given set of VLIW partitions, counts the number of equivalent fault classes crossing two or more partitions (i.e., including faults belonging to two or more partitions). In case the EC metric is nullified, the set of VLIW partitions allows a complete diagnosability of the grouped faults. This result is viable, since the EC metric supports two possible actions. The former consists in the identification of fault groups belonging to a equivalence class traversing more partitions; the latter is the possibility to move the identified equivalence class to a unique partition removing not diagnosable conditions. As an example (reported in Fig. 10), let us consider two faults belonging to a single equivalence class originally related to the partition A and partition B respectively, applying the EC metric we obtain that the two faults are in the single partition A. The minimization of the EC metric allows to obtain a DC metric equal to 100 %, however, the application of this metric is not realistic practicable just by moving equivalence fault classes between the various partitions without considering the logical composition of the VLIW modules, therefore we developed a VLIW partitioning algorithm which is able to take in account the VLIW physical implementation characteristics (e.g., the logical dimension of each VLIW partition) which is depicted in the following sub-section.

### 6.3    Improved VLIW Partitioning

The equivalence classes generated with the flow described in Sect. 4.2 can be used also to improve the VLIW partitioning, in order to obtain partitions composed of a comparable number of logic resources.

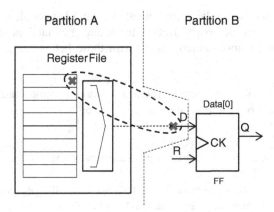

**Fig. 10.** Example of equivalent fault grouped in a unique partition in order to increase diagnosability

When a device is used in a dynamic reconfiguration environment, and a fault occurs, a diagnostic procedure is required in order to detect the faulty module; moreover, the considered system has to be divided in homogeneous partitions (i.e., having a comparable size), in order to guarantee that the reconfiguration time is always the same.

In Fig. 11 we present an algorithm that, starting from the equivalence classes set, divides a user selected partition P in several partitions, which dimension D is also selected by the user. The first step of the algorithm is aimed at the selection of the set of equivalence classes composed of faults belonging only to the addressed partition P; in this way, each addressed fault has no equivalent faults in any other partition of the considered VLIW processor. In the second step, the set of the new partitions is defined: the user selects how many partitions will contain the resources of the original one. Then, in the step 3, the resources of each equivalence class are iteratively inserted in one of the new partitions. The insertion process starts from the largest equivalence class, in order to guarantee that the equivalence classes composed of a larger number of faults are contained entirely in a single partition. At the end of the algorithm execution, we obtain a set of homogeneous partitions that contain the same resources of the original one.

Considering the diagnosability of the new partitions, the DC metric remains unchanged, since the creation of the new partitions has been done taking into account the equivalence classes: simply, the new partitions have been generated avoiding the allocation of an equivalence classes to more than one partition.

In Figs. 12 and 13 we present the results obtained applying the proposed technique to the ρ-VEX processor, where the register file module has been divided in seven different partitions, denoted as *Register_File_A*, *Register_File_B*, etc. More in particular, Fig. 12 shows the composition of the partitions, in terms of number of faults, before the application of the algorithm proposed in Fig. 11; as it is possible to notice, the number of faults belonging to the register file is high if compared with the one of the others partitions. This peculiarity is not acceptable in a dynamic reconfiguration environment, since if the diagnostic procedure detects a fault in the register file this means that a large part of the processor has to be reconfigured. Figure 13, instead, shows the results obtained after the module reorganization technique presented in this section; the obtained partitions are more homogeneous than those before the application of the proposed method.

```
1   EC_SET_P = set of equivalence classes composed of faults
    belonging to the addressed partition only;
2   NEW_P_SET = set of new partitions;
3   While EC_SET_P is not empty
    3.1. Select the largest equivalence class EC_MAX from the
         EC_SET_P;
    3.2. Find a new partition NP from the NEW_P_SET with free
         positions larger than EC_MAX.size;
    3.3. EC_MAX is assigned to NP;
    3.4. NP.FreePositions = NP.FreePositions - EC_MAX.size
    3.5. Delete EC_MAX from EC_SET_P;
```

**Fig. 11.** The pseudo-code for the redistribution of the faults belonging to a single large partition to several partitions

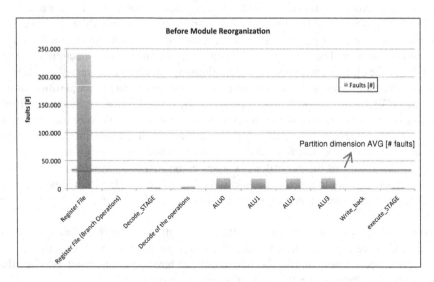

**Fig. 12.** Fault distribution in the different VLIW partitions before the module reorganization phase based on the equivalence classes

In conclusion, adopting the techniques proposed in this section and in Sect. 6.2, we obtain a complete diagnosability of the considered VLIW partitions; moreover, since the obtained partitions are quite homogeneous in terms of size, the required reconfiguration time of the partitions itself is almost the same.

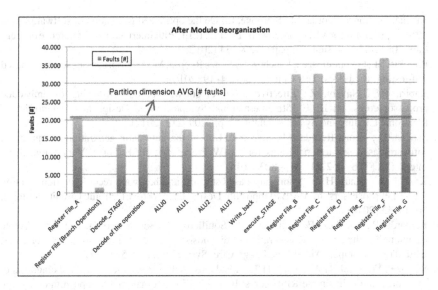

**Fig. 13.** Fault distribution in the different VLIW partitions after the module reorganization phase based on the equivalence classes

## 7    Conclusions and Future Work

In this chapter we presented a new method that starting from existing detection-oriented programs generates a diagnosis-oriented test program for a generic VLIW processor. The method exploits the parallelism (and the presence of several alternative resources) intrinsic in VLIW processors to enhance the original test program. The resulting diagnostic program is thus able in most cases to identify the faulty module and is therefore highly suitable for being used within reconfigurable systems. Moreover, we demonstrated that using the equivalence classes generated by the software-based approach, it is possible to maximize the diagnosability of the modules composing the VLIW processor under test.

As future work we plan to estimate the overall performance overhead introduced by the proposed approach and to apply the proposed method to a self-repair system based on reconfigurable device.

## References

1. Cardoso, J.M.P., Hübner, M. (eds.): Reconfigurable Computing: From FPGAs to Hardware/ Software Codesign. Springer, New York (2011)
2. Fisher, J.A., Faraboschi, P., Young, C.: Embedded Computing: a VLIW Approach to Architecture, Compilers and Tools. Morgan Kaufmann, San Francisco (2004)
3. Bolchini, C.: A software methodology for detecting hardware faults in VLIW data paths. IEEE Trans. Rel. **52**(4), 458–468 (2003)

4. Sabena, D., Sonza Reorda, M., Sterpone, L.: On the optimized generation of software-based self-test programs for VLIW processors. In: IFIP/IEEE 20th International Conference on Very Large Integration System Chip, pp. 129–134 (2012)
5. Psarakis, M., Gizopoulos, D., Sanchez, E., Sonza Reorda, M.: Microprocessor software-based self-testing. IEEE Des. Test Comput. **2**(3), 4–19 (2010)
6. Kabiri, P.S., Navabi, Z.: Effective RT-level software-based self-testing of embedded processor cores. In: IEEE 15th International Symposium on Design and Diagnostics of Electronic Circuits and Systems (DDECS), pp. 209–212 (2012)
7. Sabena, D., Sonza Reorda, M., Sterpone, L.: On the automatic generation of optimized software-based self-test programs for VLIW Processors. IEEE Trans. Very Large Scale Integr. (VLSI) Syst. **22**(4), 813–823 (2014)
8. Koal, T., Vierhaus, H.T.: A software-based self-test and hardware reconfiguration solution for VLIW processors. In: IEEE Symposium Design Diagnostic Electronic Circuits Systems, pp. 40–43 (2010)
9. Bernardi, P., Sanchez, E., Schillaci, M., Squillero, G., Sonza Reorda, M.: An effective technique for the automatic generation of diagnosis-oriented programs for processor cores. IEEE Trans. Comput.-Aided Des. Integr. Circ. Syst. **27**(3), 570–574 (2008)
10. Scholzel, M., Koal, T., Vierhaus, H.T.: An adaptive self-test routine for in-field diagnosis of permanent faults in simple RISC cores. In: IEEE 15th International Symposium on Design and Diagnostics of Electronic Circuits and Systems (DDECS), pp. 312–317 (2012)
11. Sabena, D., Sonza Reorda, M., Sterpone, L.: On the development of diagnostic test programs for VLIW processors. In: IFIP/IEEE 21th International Conference on Very Large Integration System Chip, pp. 84–89 (2013)
12. Wong, S., Van As, T., Brown, G.: ρ-VEX: a reconfigurable and extensible softcore VLIW processor. In: International Conference on ICECE Technology, pp. 369–372 (2010)
13. Sabena, D., Sterpone, L., Schölzel, M., Koal, T., Vierhaus, H.T., Wong, S., Glein, R., Rittner, F., Stender, C., Porrmann, M., Hagemeyer, J.: Reconfigurable high performance architectures: how much are they ready for safety-critical applications. In: 19th IEEE European Test Symposium (ETS), pp. 175–182, May 2014
14. Abramson, J., Diniz, P.C.: Resiliency-aware scheduling for reconfigurable VLIW processors. In: International Conference on Reconfigurable Computing and FPGAs (ReConFig), pp. 1–7 (2012)
15. Holst, S., Wunderlich, H.-J.: Adaptive debug and diagnosis without fault dictionaries. In: IEEE European Test Symposium, pp. 7–12 (2007)
16. Ryan, P.G., et al.: Fault dictionary compression and equivalence class computation for sequential circuits. IEEE International Conference on Computer-Aided Design, pp. 508–511 (1993)

# Enhanced Compressed Look-up-Table Based Real-Time Rectification Hardware

Abdulkadir Akin[✉], Luis Manuel Gaemperle, Halima Najibi, Alexandre Schmid, and Yusuf Leblebici

School of Engineering (STI), Ecole Polytechnique Fédérale de Lausanne (EPFL), Lausanne, Switzerland
{abdulkadir.akin,luis.gaemperle,halima.najibi,alexandre.schmid, yusuf.leblebici}@epfl.ch

**Abstract.** Real-time disparity estimation requires real-time rectification which involves solving the models of lens distortions, image translations and rotations. Low complexity look-up-table based rectification algorithms usually require an external memory to store large look-up-tables. In this chapter, we present an implementation of the look-up-table based approach which compresses the rectification information to fit the look-up-table into the on-chip memory of a Virtex-5 FPGA. First, a very low complexity compressed look-up-table based rectification algorithm (CLUTR) and its real-time hardware are presented. The implemented CLUTR hardware rectifies stereo images with moderate lens distortion and camera misalignment. Moreover, an enhanced version of the compressed look-up-table based rectification algorithm (E-CLUTR) and its novel real-time hardware are presented. E-CLUTR solves more extreme camera alignment and distortion issues than CLUTR while maintaining the low complexity architecture.

**Keywords:** Stereo matching · Image rectification · Compression · Real-time · Hardware implementation · FPGA

## 1 Introduction

Disparity estimation (DE) is an algorithmic step that is applied in a variety of applications such as autonomous navigation, robot and driving systems, 3D geographic information systems, object detection and tracking, medical imaging, computer games, 3D television, stereoscopic video compression, and disparity-based rendering.

The stereo matching process compares the pixels in the left and right images and provides the disparity value corresponding to each pixel. If the cameras could be aligned perfectly parallel and the lenses were perfect, without any distortion, the matching pixels would be located in the same row of the right and left images. However, providing a perfect set-up is virtually impossible. Lens distortion and camera misalignments should be modeled and removed by internal and external stereo camera calibration and image rectification processes [1].

Image rectification is one of the most essential pre-processing parts of DE. Nevertheless, many real-time stereo-matching hardware implementations [2–4] prove their

© IFIP International Federation for Information Processing 2015
A. Orailoglu et al. (Eds.): VLSI-SoC 2013, IFIP AICT 461, pp. 227–248, 2015.
DOI: 10.1007/978-3-319-23799-2_11

DE efficiency using already calibrated and rectified benchmarks of the Middlebury evaluation set [5], while some do not provide detailed information related to the rectification of the original input images [6].

In a system that processes the disparity estimation in real-time, image rectification should also be performed in real-time. The rectification hardware implementation presented in [7] solves the complex equations that model distortion, and consumes a significant amount of hardware resources.

A look-up-table based approach is a straightforward solution that consumes a low amount of hardware resources in an FPGA or ASIC [8–10]. In [8–10], the mappings between original image pixel coordinates and rectified image pixel coordinates are pre-computed and then used as look-up-tables. Due to the significant amount of generated data, these tables are stored in an external memory such as a DDR or SRAM [8, 9]. Using external storage for the image rectification process may increase the cost of the disparity estimation hardware system or impose additional external memory bandwidth limitations on the system. In [10], the look-up-tables are encoded to consume 1.3 MB data for $1280 \times 720$ size stereo images with a low-complexity compression scheme. This amount of data requires at least 295 Block RAMs (BRAM) without considering pixel buffers, thus it can only be supported by the largest Virtex-5 FPGAs or other recent high-end FPGAs.

In this chapter, we present a novel compressed look-up-table based image rectification (CLUTR) algorithm and its real-time hardware. A preliminary description of CLUTR has been presented in [11]. In this chapter, the CLUTR algorithm and its real-time hardware implementation are explained with further details. In addition, an enhanced version of the CLUTR (E-CLUTR) algorithm and its real-time hardware implementation are presented. The real-time hardware of E-CLUTR maintains the low complexity architecture of CLUTR, while it is able to rectify images under excessive mechanical misalignment of the cameras and lens distortions. Moreover, the Caltech rectification algorithm [1] which does not benefit from look-up-tables is implemented in hardware, and its hardware resource consumption results are presented to improve the hardware comparison and to evidence the efficiency of CLUTR and E-CLUTR much fairly.

This chapter is structured as follows. A typical look-up-table based rectification process is introduced in Sect. 2. The compression scheme that is used by the CLUTR algorithm is presented in Sect. 3. The proposed hardware implementation of the decompression process of CLUTR is presented in Sect. 4. The analysis of the challenges of CLUTR to rectify images under extreme conditions is presented in Sect. 5. The compression scheme of E-CLUTR is presented in Sect. 6. The hardware implementation of the decompression process of E-CLUTR is presented in Sect. 7. The implementation results of the CLUTR and E-CLUTR algorithms and their hardware resource comparisons are presented in Sect. 8. Section 9 concludes the chapter.

## 2  Typical Look-up-Table Based Solution

Look-up-table based rectification methods can be distinguished by two different image warping flows: forward mapping and inverse mapping. Forward mapping computes the rectified target pixel locations based on the given pixel locations in the original image. Inverse mapping computes the original source pixel locations based on the given pixel locations in the rectified image. The mapping requires separate tables for X and Y coordinates, and for the right and left images. Therefore, four tables are needed. The formulations for forward and inverse mappings are presented in Eqs. (1) and (2), respectively. In these equations, *ForwT* is the forward mapping table, *InvT* is the inverse mapping table, *Ori* represents the original image taken from the camera, *Rec* represents the rectified image. $Y_{Rec}$, $X_{Rec}$, $Y_{Ori}$ and $X_{Ori}$ represent the Y and X coordinates.

$$Forward: \left(Y_{Rec}, X_{Rec}\right) = \left(ForwT_y\left(Y_{Ori}, X_{Ori}\right), ForwT_x\left(Y_{Ori}, X_{Ori}\right)\right)$$
$$Rec_{(y,x)} = linear\_interpolation(nearest\ neighbours\ of\ Rec_{(y,x)})$$
(1)

$$Inverse: \left(Y_{Ori}, X_{Ori}\right) = \left(InvT_y\left(Y_{Rec}, X_{Rec}\right), InvT_x\left(Y_{Rec}, X_{Rec}\right)\right)$$
$$Rec_{(y,x)} = linear\_interpolation(nearest\ neighbours\ of\ Ori_{(Y_{Ori},X_{Ori})})$$
(2)

A typical rectification process utilizes fractional pixel precision which requires the linear interpolation of four pixels. The linear interpolation schemes for forward and inverse mappings are represented in Figs. 1 and 2, respectively. The linear interpolation process for forward mapping is more complex than the linear interpolation process of inverse mapping, since it requires additional computations and an intermediate memory consumption to find the closest target pixels in the rectified image. The look-up-table based rectification hardware architectures presented in [8–10] use inverse mapping due to its simplicity.

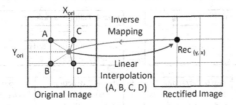

**Fig. 1.** Inverse mapping with fractional precision coordinates. Corners indicate integer pixel coordinates.

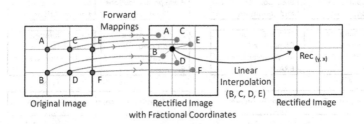

**Fig. 2.** Forward mapping with fractional precision coordinates

The size of the look-up-table depends on the size of the rectified image and the fractional precision. For example, for the rectification of $1024 \times 768$ resolution stereo images with 6 bits fractional precision, the rectification map alone requires approximately 6 MB of space in a memory. This amount of data is excessive to fit into the on-chip memory of a mid-range FPGA. Therefore, dumping look-up-tables into an external memory is preferred in the hardware implementations of [8, 9].

# 3   Proposed Compression Scheme of the CLUTR Algorithm

In contrast to the selection of the hardware implementations of [8–10], a forward mapping based rectification scheme is selected for the proposed CLUTR algorithm. In CLUTR, fractional precision is ignored. Ignoring fractional precision allows an efficient compression scheme. The negligible distortion in the rectified images originating from this simplification is analyzed in Sect. 8.

The compression scheme is presented in the flow graph in Fig. 3. The proposed compressed rectification algorithm produces four compressed tables. The compression scheme requires eight steps. The details of steps 1–2 can be found in [1]. The details of steps 3–8 are detailed in this section.

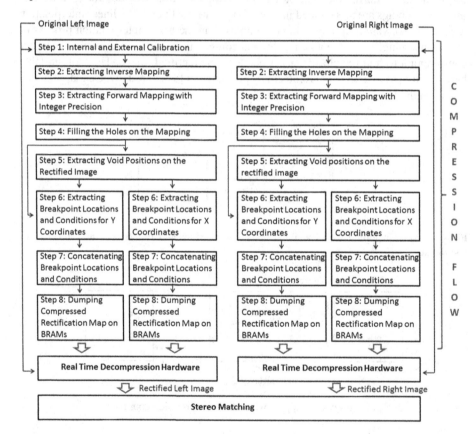

**Fig. 3.** Flow chart for the proposed compressed look-up-table based stereo image rectification process

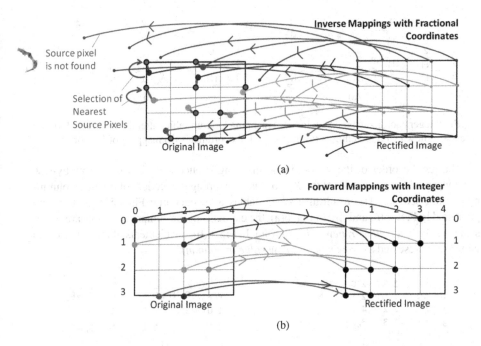

**Fig. 4.** Third step of the compression flow (a) selection of nearest source pixels from fractional inverse mapping (b) extraction of forward mapping with integer coordinates

In the third step, integer coordinate precision forward mapping is extracted from the fractional precision inverse mapping. The extraction scheme is demonstrated in Fig. 4. The example original and rectified pictures have a size of $4 \times 5$ pixels. First, inverse mapping is applied to find the fractional source pixel locations of all pixels in the rectified image. Due to the 3D rotation, some of the pixels in the rectified image cannot be related to their source pixels in the $4 \times 5$ original image, as shown in Fig. 4(a). The nearest integer coordinates of all fractional source coordinates are computed, and they are targeted onto the integer pixel coordinates in the rectified image, as presented in Fig. 4(b). Thus one-to-one mapping is provided in the third step.

The integer pixel precision forward mapping extracted for the example picture in Fig. 4 yields the look-up-tables of X and Y coordinates shown in Fig. 5. The pixels that are not targeted to any location are identified with NT. $Ori(2,2)$ and $Ori(2,3)$ are adjacent pixels, and both of them target "row no 2" of the rectified image; $Ori(2,2)$ and $Ori(3,2)$ are adjacent pixels and both target "column no 1" of the rectified image. This regular order is more apparent with higher resolution images. According to our experiments with a $1024 \times 768$ image, repetition of a single target coordinate up to 220 times is observed in the integer precision forward mapping table of X coordinates.

The method governing compressed rectification is similar to the run-length encoding technique. In the proposed coding scheme, instead of coding the run-length of the regular order, the locations where the regular order changes are encoded. These locations are called breakpoints. Moreover, the proposed scheme includes additional specific techniques to compress the integer precision forward mapping efficiently.

|   | 0 | 1 | 2 | 3 | 4 |
|---|---|---|---|---|---|
| 0 | 1 | NT | 0 | NT | NT |
| 1 | 2 | NT | 1 | NT | 1 |
| 2 | NT | NT | 2 | 2 | NT |
| 3 | NT | 3 | 3 | NT | NT |

(a)

|   | 0 | 1 | 2 | 3 | 4 |
|---|---|---|---|---|---|
| 0 | 1 | NT | 3 | NT | NT |
| 1 | 0 | NT | 2 | NT | 3 |
| 2 | NT | NT | 1 | 2 | NT |
| 3 | NT | 0 | 1 | NT | NT |

(b)

**Fig. 5.** Integer coordinate precision forward mapping look-up-tables after the third step. Regular orders are shown with red ellipses (a) mapping of Y coordinates (b) mapping of X coordinates.

The regular order of the Y coordinate mapping is encoded following a row-by-row scheme, and the regular order of the X coordinate mapping is encoded following a column-by-column scheme. The resulting look-up-tables after encoding Figs. 5(a) and (b) are presented in Figs. 6(a) and (b). In Fig. 6(a), the elements of the compressed table are represented as *(column number, new value in row)*. In Fig. 6(b), the elements of the compressed table are represented as *(row number, new value in column)*.

|   |   |   |   |   |
|---|---|---|---|---|
| 0 | 0, 1 | 1, NT | 2, 0 | 3, NT |
| 1 | 0, 2 | 1, NT | 2, 1 | 3, NT | 4, 1 |
| 2 | 0, NT | 2, 2 | 4, NT |
| 3 | 0, NT | 1, 3 | 3, NT |

(a)

| 0 | 1 | 2 | 3 | 4 |
|---|---|---|---|---|
| 0, 1 | 0, NT | 0, 3 | 0, NT | 0, NT |
| 1, 0 | 3, 0 | 1, 2 | 2, 2 | 1, 3 |
| 2, NT |  | 2, 1 | 3, NT | 2, NT |

(b)

**Fig. 6.** Coded regular orders after the third step (a) coded mapping of Y coordinates (b) coded mapping of X coordinates

The high number of NT pixels dramatically increases the number of breakpoints. This issue becomes more pronounced for high resolution images. Therefore, the fourth step of the compression algorithm fills the NT pixel locations to keep the regular order. In order to fill the NT pixel locations, the same order is repeated vertically and horizontally for Y and X locations, respectively. After the fourth step, Fig. 5 is transformed into Figs. 6 and 7 into Fig. 8.

|   | 0 | 1 | 2 | 3 | 4 |
|---|---|---|---|---|---|
| 0 | 1 | 1 | 0 | 0 | 0 |
| 1 | 2 | 2 | 1 | 1 | 1 |
| 2 | 2 | 2 | 2 | 2 | 2 |
| 3 | 3 | 3 | 3 | 3 | 3 |

(a)

|   | 0 | 1 | 2 | 3 | 4 |
|---|---|---|---|---|---|
| 0 | 1 | 0 | 3 | 2 | 3 |
| 1 | 0 | 0 | 2 | 2 | 3 |
| 2 | 0 | 0 | 1 | 2 | 3 |
| 3 | 0 | 0 | 1 | 2 | 3 |

(b)

**Fig. 7.** Look-up-tables after filling the NT pixels using the fourth step (a) mapping of Y coordinates (b) mapping of X coordinates

After the first two steps, two or more source fractional coordinates can have the same pixel coordinate in the original image as their nearest neighbor, as presented in Fig. 9(a). However, after step three and four, every integer pixel coordinate of the original image is targeted to a single coordinate in the rectified image. Consequently, some pixels in the

| 0 | 0, 1 | 2, 0 |
|---|------|------|
| 1 | 0, 2 | 2, 1 |
| 2 | 0, 2 |      |
| 3 | 0, 3 |      |

(a)

| 0 | 1 | 2 | 3 | 4 |
|------|------|------|------|------|
| 0, 1 | 0, 0 | 0, 3 | 0, 2 | 0, 3 |
| 1, 0 |      | 1, 2 |      |      |
|      |      | 2. 1 |      |      |

(b)

**Fig. 8.** Coded regular orders after filling the NT pixels using the fourth step (a) coded mapping of Y coordinates (b) coded mapping of X coordinates

rectified image may be void, as presented in Fig. 9(b). These pixels will remain as void, i.e. black pixels, in the rectified image if they are not filled. The fifth step is applied to fill these voids. As shown in Fig. 10, the pixels on the original image which target the pixel coordinates that are located on the row above these voids are marked. Marked pixels are used to fill the voids as source pixels which have double targets (DT). Thus, DT pixels are used to concurrently target two vertically neighboring pixels on the rectified image.

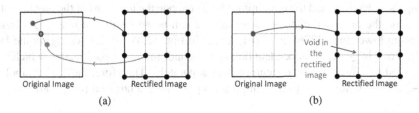

**Fig. 9.** Visualization of the reason for the voids on the rectified image (a) inverse mappings with fractional coordinates (b) forward mapping with integer coordinate

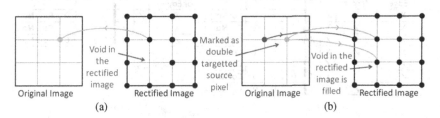

**Fig. 10.** Filling the voids in the rectified image in the fifth step (a) finding the source location of a pixel at one row above the void (b) marking the source pixel as double targeted pixel

The sixth step of the algorithm extracts the breakpoint locations and analyzes the behavior of the breakpoints. As shown in Fig. 8, the difference between the new and previous target locations equals plus or minus one, which can be encoded consuming less data than encoding the exact integer coordinates. An example of coding the behavior of the cells in Fig. 8 is presented in Fig. 11 as *(location, behavior)*. The initialization coordinates are provided in the first column of the look-up-table for Y coordinates, and in the first row of the look-up-table for X coordinates. The next breakpoint values are identified with $\pm 1$. Moreover, dummy breakpoints are inserted at the edges of the image to simplify the hardware implementation. Dummy insertions are represented by (5,0) and (4,0) in Fig. 11(a) and (b), respectively.

(a)

| 0 | 1,0 | 2,-1 | 5,0 | ← 3 brakpoints in a row |
|---|-----|------|-----|---|
| 1 | 2,0 | 2,-1 | 5,0 | |
| 2 | 2,0 | 5,0 | | 2 brakpoints in a row |
| 3 | 3,0 | 5,0 | ← | |

(b)

| | 0 | 1 | 2 | 3 | 4 |
|---|---|---|---|---|---|
| | 1,0 | 0,0 | 3,0 | 2,0 | 3,0 |
| | 1,-1 | 4,0 | 1,-1 | 4,0 | 4,0 |
| | 4,0 | | 2,-1 | | |
| | | | 4,0 | 2 brakpoints in a column | |

3 brakpoints in a column

**Fig. 11.** Coding the behavior of breakpoints at the sixth step (a) coded mapping of Y coordinates (b) coded mapping of X coordinates

In the seventh step, the locations and behaviors of the breakpoints are concatenated and stored in a data array. Every BRAM in a Virtex-5 FPGA has 1024 addresses and it can be configured to store one array composed of $1024 \times 36$ bits or two arrays composed of $1024 \times 18$ bits. The BRAMs of the FPGAs are configured to store 18-bits in each address in the proposed concatenation scheme. As shown in Fig. 12, 3-bits are used for coding the behaviors, and the remaining 15-bits encode the locations of the breakpoints. Therefore, the proposed concatenation scheme can be applied to an image that has a resolution lower than $32767 \times 32767$ pixels. In Fig. 12(a), DT and changing the last targeted row by $\pm 1$ are independent breakpoint conditions of Y coordinates, which can be applied to source pixels, concurrently or separately. Therefore, the "X" symbol in the $-1$ and $+1$ columns of Fig. 12 implies keeping the last targeted row coordinate.

(a)

| BreakPoint Conditions | | Concatenation of 18-bits | | | | | |
|---|---|---|---|---|---|---|---|
| Initialization or Edge | Double Target | -1 | +1 | 17th | 16th | 15th | 14th-0th |
| X | X | ✓ | X | 0 | 1 | 0 | Col No |
| X | X | X | ✓ | 0 | 0 | 1 | Col No |
| X | ✓ | X | X | 1 | 0 | 0 | Col No |
| X | ✓ | X | ✓ | 1 | 0 | 1 | Col No |
| X | ✓ | ✓ | X | 1 | 1 | 0 | Col No |
| ✓ | X | X | X | 0 | 0 | 0 | Col No |
| ✓ | ✓ | X | X | 1 | 0 | 0 | Col No |

(b)

| BreakPoint Conditions | Concatenation of 18-bits | | | | | |
|---|---|---|---|---|---|---|
| Initialization or Edge | -1 | +1 | 17th | 16th | 15th | 14th-0th |
| X | ✓ | X | 0 | 1 | 0 | Row No |
| X | X | ✓ | 0 | 0 | 1 | Row No |
| ✓ | X | X | 0 | 0 | 0 | Row No |

**Fig. 12.** Concatenation of the locations and behaviors at the seventh step (a) for the mapping of Y coordinates (b) for the mapping of X coordinates

The number of breakpoints in every row of the Y table and the number of breakpoints in every column of the X table depend on the distortion of the lens, the resolution of the image sensor and the mechanical misalignment. The experimental setup used in this chapter consists of $1024 \times 768$ resolution cameras. In the experiments, cameras are aligned in parallel configuration without using any sensitive mechanical placement tool. At most 21 breakpoints are observed in any given row of Y tables, and at most 17 breakpoints are observed in any given column of X tables. Data arrays of CLUTR are created for 24 possible breakpoint locations for Y tables and 20 possible breakpoint locations for X tables to support more challenging distortion conditions. Therefore, storing the X and Y tables for the right and left images requires 38 BRAMs which can even be supported by low cost FPGAs. The data arrays that are programmed into the BRAMs are converted into coefficient (COE) files using MATLAB.

In the eighth step, 38 BRAMs are instantiated as single port ROMs. The pre-computed compressed rectification maps are programmed into the BRAMs using the Xilinx ISE 12.4 and COE files.

## 4    Real-Time Decompression Hardware of CLUTR

The decompression process is simpler than the off-line compression process in terms of computational complexity. The proposed rectification module can be used as a hardware accelerator taking place between the camera interface hardware and the on-chip memory controller, as shown in Fig. 13. The rectification module is used for the left and right cameras separately. The rectification module processes source pixel values as $Ori_{(Yori, Xori)}$ and the respective source row and source column coordinates as $Y_{ori}$ and $X_{ori}$. The rectification module computes the target row and target column coordinates as $Y_{Rec}$ and $X_{Rec}$, and the 1-bit $DT$ signal to identify double targeted locations. $Ori_{(Yori, Xori)}$ is delayed for 6 clock cycles and $Rec_{(Yrec, Xrec)}$ is given as an output. Due to the pipelined structure of the hardware, inputs can be consecutively received and outputs can be consecutively provided.

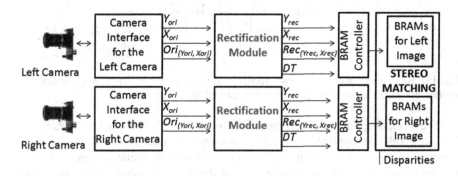

**Fig. 13.**  Example utilization of the proposed rectification hardware

The top-level block diagram of the rectification module is presented in Fig. 14. The rectification module involves $(768 \times 24 \times 18)/(1024 \times 36) = 9$ BRAMs to store the compressed table of Y coordinates and $(1024 \times 20 \times 18)/(1024 \times 36) = 10$ BRAMs to store the compressed table of X coordinates. Half of 1 additional BRAM is used to store the last break point locations and the last target X coordinates of the row which is located above the row currently being processed.

The block diagram of the decompression hardware of Y coordinates is presented in Fig. 15. The hardware resets itself every time $X_{ori}$ is equal to zero which implies that the first pixel of a new row is fetched from the camera. The target Y coordinate of the first incoming pixel in a new row is loaded from the ROM and written to the output register of $Y_{Rec}$. For every consecutive pixel, $X_{ori}$ is compared to the coordinate of the next breakpoint which is loaded from the ROM. When a breakpoint is reached, the $Y_{Rec}$ value

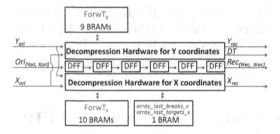

**Fig. 14.** Top-level block diagram of the proposed rectification hardware of CLUTR

is changed using a multiplexer depending on the coded behaviors of the breakpoints. Meanwhile, the hardware loads the coordinate of the next breakpoints to compare with the upcoming $X_{ori}$.

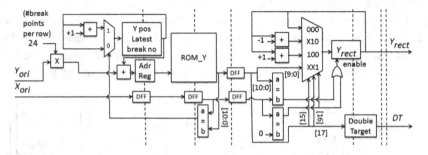

**Fig. 15.** Block diagram of the proposed rectification hardware for decompressing the table of Y coordinates. Pipeline stages are presented with dashed lines.

The block diagram of the decompression hardware of X coordinates is presented in Fig. 16. Pixels are supplied by the camera row-by-row, whereas the X coordinates are compressed column-by-column. This situation causes one important difference between the decompression hardware architectures of the X and Y tables. When the camera provides pixels of a new row, the decompression hardware needs to keep record of the previous $X_{Rec}$ coordinates and the last checked breakpoint address in the ROM for the respective column of the previous row. Two $1 \times 1024$ size data arrays are needed to store this information. These arrays are named *array_last_break_x* and *array_last_target_x* in Fig. 14. These arrays are concatenated for respective column coordinates of the original image, and stored into one half of the 1 BRAM, which is named X_last_data_BRAM in Fig. 16. The values in X_last_data_BRAM are replaced with the new ones when a breakpoint is reached for the respective $X_{Ori}$. The decompression hardware of the Y coordinates does not comprise these arrays because Y coordinates are compressed row-by-row. Therefore, the last $Y_{Rec}$ can be directly used for computing the next $Y_{Rec}$ of the next pixel in the same row of the original image. The decompression hardware of X coordinates operates in a similar fashion as the decompression hardware of Y coordinates, with the exception of keeping record of the information about the previous row.

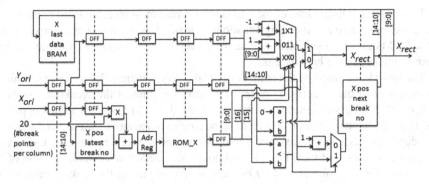

**Fig. 16.** Block diagram of the proposed rectification hardware for decompressing the table for X coordinates

The proposed rectification hardware can be used in any stereo-matching system. The stereo matching process can be started when the required amount of rows is buffered in the BRAMs of the stereo matching hardware. Processed rows in these BRAMs can be overwritten by new rows during the stereo matching process.

The hardware architectures presented in [9, 10] require large pixel buffers due to the inverse mapping scheme. The proposed decompression does not need large pixel buffers between the camera interface and the rectification modules. In contrast, the hardware requires these pixels buffers for the rectified image. However, typically DE hardware implementations already include BRAMs to buffer the pixels [2–4, 6]. Therefore, these buffers can be used for the proposed decompression hardware. Thus, using the proposed rectification hardware on a complete DE system may not need additional large pixel buffers.

## 5    Limitations of the CLUTR

In an ideal case, i.e. where the cameras are perfectly parallel and lenses do not have distortion, two breakpoints are required for every row of the look-up-table for Y coordinates and two breakpoints are required for every column of the look-up-table for X coordinates. One of these two breakpoints is needed to define the initial breakpoint location to target coordinate 0, and the other one is needed to define the final target location as the horizontal or vertical size of the image. In the classical case of a real-time working environment, the mechanical set-up of the stereo-matching system should be carefully designed to be close to an ideal case. Still the main goal of the rectification consists of solving lens distortions and sensitive mechanical misalignments.

According to tests applied to the CLUTR algorithm and hardware, the pixel location difference of two consecutive breakpoints typically reaches more than 15 pixels and the number of breakpoints is smaller than the pre-defined breakpoint capacity of the ROMs of CLUTR. Therefore, CLUTR successfully rectifies the images when the lens distortion and the mechanical misalignments are not excessive. However, unusual conditions bring limitations on the CLUTR hardware.

Two important limitations of the CLUTR hardware must be considered to maintain its suitability to rectify challenging situations. The first limitation relates to the capacity of the ROMs to store a sufficient number of breakpoints. The second limitation relates to the frequency of the breakpoints.

The limitation caused by the number of breakpoints is mainly due to the mechanical misalignment of the cameras. In order to identify the limit of the breakpoint storage capacity of ROMs, two cameras are manually rotated around 3 degrees around opposite directions of all rotational axis. This test can be considered as an excessive misalignment of a carefully designed mechanical setup of the stereo-matching system. Using the compression scheme of CLUTR, 43 breakpoints are needed in the look-up-table of X coordinates for one column, and 69 breakpoints are needed in the look-up-table of Y coordinates for one row. The pre-defined breakpoint capacity of CLUTR does not support this condition. Overcoming this first limitation is straightforward to achieve by increasing the size of ROMs to store more breakpoints.

CLUTR supports rectification if the two breakpoints of the Y coordinates have at least 4 pixel position difference. When a breakpoint location is reached, the hardware needs to read the next breakpoint from ROM. The address computation and reading the next break-point from the ROM consume 4 clock cycles. The camera continues to send pixels and the camera controller increases $X_{Ori}$ during the address computation and reading breakpoints from the ROM. Therefore, if there are multiple breakpoints in 4 consecutive pixels, CLUTR is not able to apply a breakpoint condition to those pixels. Hence, the limits of the CLUTR hardware to successfully rectify stereo images is exceeded if breakpoints are frequent, i.e. if two breakpoints of Y coordinates in a row have less than 4 pixel position difference. Since the breakpoints of X coordinates are coded column by column but the camera sends pixels row by row, the time to process consecutive breakpoints in same column and consecutive rows is sufficiently long. Therefore, frequent breakpoints in the same column of the look-up-table of X coordinates does not cause a limitation. The frequency limitation of CLUTR is visually explained in Fig. 17.

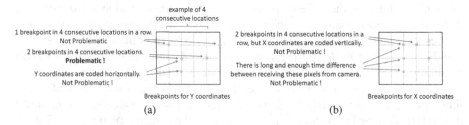

**Fig. 17.** Visualization of the breakpoint frequency capacity of the X and Y coordinate mappings (a) breakpoints for the mapping of Y coordinates (b) breakpoints for the mapping of X coordinates

The main reason for the occurrence of frequent breakpoints is the high number of adjacent void pixels, which is caused by excessive camera misalignment or lens distortion. An example of one such challenging condition is presented in Fig. 18. As shown in Fig. 18(b), 4 out of 5 consecutive pixels are marked as breakpoints. 3 out of these 4 breakpoints are DT breakpoints which are coded in the look-up-table of Y coordinates,

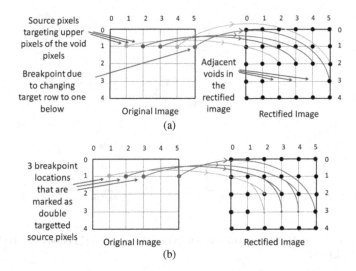

**Fig. 18.** Visualization of the reason for the frequent breakpoints (a) finding the source locations of three pixels that are targeting one row above of the three consecutive voids (b) four breakpoints in consecutive five locations

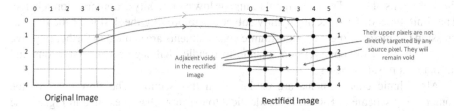

**Fig. 19.** Visualization of the reason for the voids which can not be filled by CLUTR

and the other one is located at $Ori(1,5)$ which requires changing the target row number from 2 to 3. This challenging example case exceeds the limits of CLUTR, since CLUTR is not able to apply a breakpoint condition if there are multiple breakpoints in 4 consecutive pixels.

Adjacent void pixels may occur not only horizontally but also vertically. Vertically adjacent void pixels may cause void pixels, which cannot be filled by the DT feature of CLUTR. As visualized in Fig. 19, DT pixels can fill the voids located one row below the targeted pixel on the rectified image. If there are two voids which are vertically adjacent, the void below can not be filled by CLUTR since the pixel above is not targeted directly by any source pixel.

Another limitation of CLUTR is related to the usage of ROMs for the hardware implementation which increases the off-line processing duration. Using ROMs is suitable to demonstrate the efficiency of compressed look-up-table based rectification. However, after each adjustment of the camera settings and alignments, creating new compressed tables of the hardware requires re-synthesis and place & route of the implementation. Thus it takes a long time to initialize CLUTR hardware.

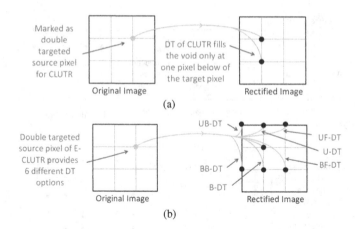

**Fig. 20.** Filling the voids on the rectified image in the fifth step (a) DT option of CLUTR (b) DT options of E-CLUTR

## 6    The Compression Scheme of the E-CLUTR Algorithm

The E-CLUTR algorithm and its hardware implementation are designed to overcome the limitations of CLUTR while maintaining the low complexity decompression scheme. The limitations of CLUTR are mainly solved by improving the design of the decompression hardware. Moreover, algorithmic enhancements are applied to further improve the efficiency of the compression scheme to handle challenging lens distortions and mechanical misalignments.

Algorithmic enhancements are explained in this section. The flow chart of the compression scheme of E-CLUTR is identical to the flow chart presented in Fig. 3. The steps 5, 6 and 7 that are shown in Fig. 3 are enhanced in E-CLUTR. The algorithmic enhancement for the compression scheme is proposed to reduce the frequency of DT breakpoints. In order to decrease the amount of consecutive breakpoints in a row, the condition type of breakpoints for filling the voids are improved. As explained in Sect. 4 in step 5, DT breakpoints are used to fill the voids that are located one pixel below the targeted pixel. To avoid any confusion, the DT condition of CLUTR is renamed as below-DT (B-DT) in E-CLUTR. In addition to B-DT, below-backward-DT (BB-DT), below-forward-DT (BF-DT), upper-DT (U-DT), upper-backward-DT (UB-DT) and upper-forward-DT (UF-DT) breakpoint conditions are defined in E-CLUTR. Using extra DT conditions, the source pixel can be targeted not only to one pixel below the target, but additional options are provided to fill any of 6 possible neighbors of the targeted pixel of the rectified image. These additional options are visualized in Fig. 20.

As presented in Fig. 21, the frequency of breakpoints in the same row is reduced compared to Fig. 18, by using BF-DT, BB-DT and U-DT breakpoint conditions. As presented in Fig. 19, vertically adjacent void pixels are problematic for CLUTR. However, these voids can be filled by multiple DT options of E-CLUTR as presented in Fig. 22.

In step 6, the breakpoints are coded considering the new DT breakpoint conditions. In the challenging example, there should be support of 2 consecutive breakpoints at least

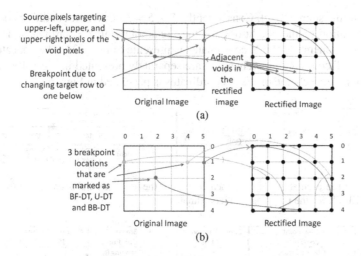

**Fig. 21.** Reducing the frequency of breakpoints using multiple DT options of E-CLUTR (a) finding alternative source locations for void pixels of rectified image (b) reduced frequency of breakpoints for the same row of the look-up-table of Y coordinates

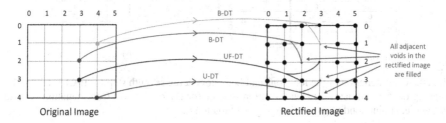

**Fig. 22.** Vertically adjacent void pixels can be filled by E-CLUTR using multiple DT options.

in 3 consecutive pixel coordinates, as presented for the breakpoints at *Ori(1,4)* and *Ori(1,5)*. Therefore, the algorithmic enhancement requires the support of at least 2 breakpoints for 3 consecutive locations as an additional constraint. The hardware based enhancement to provide this support is explained in Sect. 7.

At the edges of the rectified image, black pixels occur. These stem from the 3-D rotation of the original image and the mapping of the rectified image to the original resolution. Consequently, the effective resolution slightly decreases in the rectified image [1]. Due to this fact, changing row and column coordinates stay in the range of $\pm 1$. However, this range may not be guaranteed for all possible extreme conditions. Thus, a generic solution should cover all possible extreme situations. In order to cover the cases that create a situation beyond the challenging camera misalignment tests, $\pm 2$ row and $\pm 2$ column coordinate change options are included as a breakpoint condition in step 6 of E-CLUTR.

The concatenation scheme presented in Fig. 12 of CLUTR is modified for E-CLUTR as presented in Figs. 23, 24 and 25 using improved breakpoint conditions. The breakpoint conditions for DT conditions and row changing can be applied concurrently or separately to the source pixel. Consequently, $7 \times 5 = 35$ different conditions occur for the concatenation of the conditions for the breakpoints of Y coordinates. The brief concatenation scheme of the Y coordinates is presented in Fig. 23. The concatenation scheme for DT codes and row changing are separately presented in Fig. 24(a) and (b). The concatenation scheme of the X coordinates is presented in Fig. 25.

| Initialization or Edge | BreakPoint Conditions | | | | Concatenation of 18-bits | | | | | | |
|---|---|---|---|---|---|---|---|---|---|---|---|
| | Double Target | | Changing Row | | 17th | 16th | 15th | 14th | 13th | 12th | 11th-0th |
| | Up/Below | Forward/Backward | -/+ | 1/2 | | | | | | | |
| | | | | | DT Conditions | | | Conditions for Changing Last Targeted Row | | | Col No |

**Fig. 23.** Brief representation for the concatenation of the locations and behaviors at the seventh step of E-CLUTR for the mapping of Y coordinates

| BreakPoint Conditions | | Concatenation of 18-bits | | |
|---|---|---|---|---|
| Double Target | | 17th | 16th | 15th |
| Up/ Below | Forward/ Backward | | | |
| U | F | 0 | 0 | 1 |
| U | Non | 0 | 1 | 0 |
| U | B | 0 | 1 | 1 |
| B | F | 1 | 0 | 0 |
| B | Non | 1 | 0 | 1 |
| B | B | 1 | 1 | 0 |
| Non | Non | 0 | 0 | 0 |

(a)

| BreakPoint Conditions | | Concatenation of 18-bits | | |
|---|---|---|---|---|
| Changing Row | | 14th | 13th | 12th |
| -/+ | 1/2 | | | |
| + | 1 | 1 | 0 | 0 |
| + | 2 | 1 | 0 | 1 |
| - | 1 | 1 | 1 | 0 |
| - | 2 | 1 | 1 | 1 |
| Non | Non | 0 | 0 | 0 |

(b)

**Fig. 24.** Concatenation of the locations and behaviors at the seventh step for E-CLUTR for the mapping of Y coordinates (a) Concatenation scheme for DT options (b) Concatenation scheme for the breakpoint conditions for changing last targeted row

| BreakPoint Conditions | | | Concatenation of 18-bits | | |
|---|---|---|---|---|---|
| Initialization or Edge | Changing Column | | 17th | 16th | 15th-0th |
| | +/- | 1/2 | | | |
| X | + | 1 | 0 | 0 | Row No |
| X | + | 2 | 0 | 1 | Row No |
| X | - | 1 | 1 | 0 | Row No |
| X | - | 2 | 1 | 1 | Row No |
| ✓ | X | X | 0 | 0 | Row No |

**Fig. 25.** Concatenation of the locations and behaviors at the seventh step of E-CLUTR for the mapping of X coordinates

# 7  Real-Time Decompression Hardware of E-CLUTR

The top-level block diagram of the E-CLUTR module is presented in Fig. 26. Data arrays of E-CLUTR are created for 80 possible breakpoint locations for Y tables and 50 possible breakpoint locations for X tables to support very challenging distortion conditions. The rectification module involves $(768 \times 80 \times 18)/(1024 \times 36) = 30$ BRAMs to store the compressed table of Y coordinates and $(1024 \times 50 \times 18)/(1024 \times 36) = 25$ BRAMs to store the compressed table of X coordinates. As presented in Fig. 26, the ROMs are converted to RAM to ease the initialization of the look-up-tables of E-CLUTR after changing the camera settings. The decompression hardware for the X coordinates is presented in Fig. 27. The decompression hardware for Y coordinates is presented in Fig. 28.

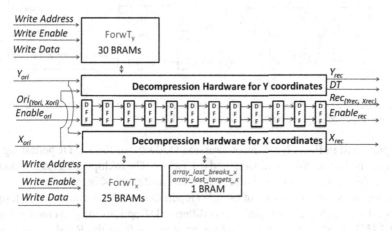

**Fig. 26.** Top-level block diagram of the proposed rectification hardware of E-CLUTR

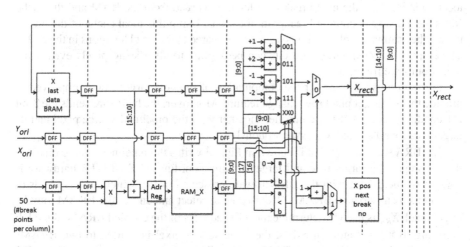

**Fig. 27.** Block diagram of the proposed rectification hardware for decompressing the table of X coordinates

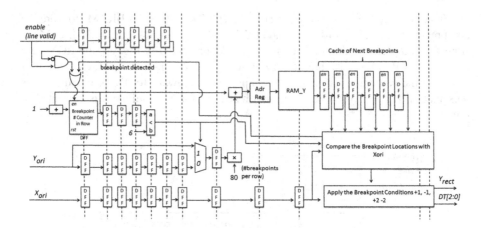

**Fig. 28.** Block diagram of the proposed rectification hardware for decompressing the table of Y coordinates. Pipeline stages are presented with dashed lines.

As presented in Fig. 27, the decompression hardware of E-CLUTR pertaining to X coordinates is similar to the hardware used in CLUTR. The multiplexing stage is adapted to provide the ±2 target pixel column change feature for the X breakpoints.

The decompression hardware of E-CLUTR pertaining to Y coordinates is redesigned to support frequent breakpoints and the six different DT options. As presented in Fig. 28, the E-CLUTR hardware reads the first six breakpoints from the RAM as soon as the camera starts to send a new row. The first breakpoint is used to initialize the target row and the next five breakpoints are buffered in a local cache. Whenever a new breakpoint location is reached, the next breakpoint location is read from the RAM and the cache shifts the existing upcoming breakpoint locations. Using this local cache of the breakpoints, the original pixel coordinates can be compared to the pixel locations in the cache. Therefore, the breakpoint conditions can be applied to all passing pixels even if the breakpoints are frequent.

The multiplexing stage for the computation of the next target row is improved to provide the ±2 target pixel row change feature. Moreover, the hardware sends the 3-bit DT condition to the BRAM controller together with the pipelined source pixel and its target locations $Y_{Rec,}$ and $X_{Rec}$, synchronously.

The BRAM controller that is shown in Fig. 13 writes the pipelined source pixels to the decompressed target row and target column coordinates. E-CLUTR hardware is verified by merging it with the DE hardware presented in [4], which buffers pixels of rows in its own, separate BRAMs. $Y_{Rec}$ is used to select and enable the BRAM to write target pixel. $X_{Rec}$ is used to determine the write address of the enabled BRAM of the DE hardware. If a DT condition exists, the same source pixel is written to two BRAMs concurrently by enabling two BRAMs that buffer two consecutive rows. If the DT condition is pointing into forward or backward positions, the address port of the BRAM that is targeted by the DT condition receives the computed target BRAM address ±1.

## 8   Implementation Results

The proposed rectification hardware architectures of CLUTR and E-CLUTR are implemented using Verilog HDL, and verified using Modelsim 10.1d. The Verilog RTL models are mapped to a Virtex-5 XCUVP-110T FPGA comprising 69 k Look-Up-Tables (LUT), 69 k DFFs and 148 BRAMs. One rectification module of CLUTR consumes 0.32 % of the LUTs, 0.28 % of the DFF resources and 14 % of the BRAM resources of the Virtex-5 FPGA. One rectification module of E-CLUTR consumes 0.63 % of the LUTs, 0.51 % of the DFF resources and 38 % of the BRAM resources of the Virtex-5 FPGA. The proposed E-CLUTR hardware operates at 212 MHz after place & route. Therefore, it can process up to 269 fps at a $1024 \times 768$ XGA video resolution. In addition, the proposed rectification hardware of CLUTR and E-CLUTR are merged with the DE hardware presented in [4]. The merged DE systems are also verified using Modelsim 10.1d.

The proposed rectification hardware of CLUTR and E-CLUTR do not need the support of external memory if the cameras are synchronized. The cameras can be perfectly synchronized by driving the cameras with same clock source and using one common I2C module for the initialization the cameras [12].

The proposed compression and decompression algorithms are evaluated using the pictures taken by the stereo camera system presented in [4]. If the cameras are not extremely misaligned, CLUTR and E-CLUTR provide identical visual and numerical results. The $1024 \times 768$ size original left and right pictures that are shown in Fig. 29 are taken under a camera misalignment condition that exceed the limits of CLUTR implementation. The example pictures and the test results of CLUTR for typical camera misalignment are presented in [11]. The original images in Fig. 29 are rectified using the Caltech rectification algorithm [1] and the proposed E-CLUTR algorithm. The rectification results of the E-CLUTR is presented in Fig. 30. The extreme rotation of the rectified image can be visually observed in Fig. 30. The breakpoint locations for the X and Y coordinates of the left image are presented in Fig. 31.

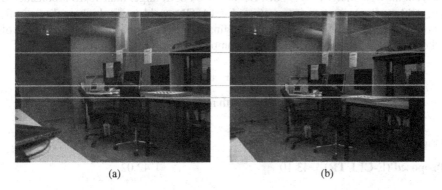

(a)                                                          (b)

**Fig. 29.** Original images have distortions as observed on the lines (a) left image (b) right image.

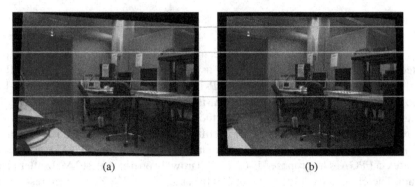

**Fig. 30.** E-CLUTR corrects distortions as observed on the lines (a) left image (b) right image.

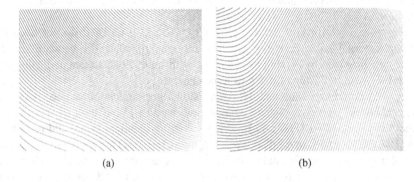

**Fig. 31.** Breakpoint locations of the left image (a) breakpoints of the targeted Y coordinates; coded row-by-row. (b) breakpoints of the targeted X coordinates; coded column-by-column

The PSNR between the rectification results of E-CLUTR and Caltech rectification algorithm are evaluated in Table 1. The PSNR of the left image is 43.10 dB, and the PSNR of the right image is 42.02 dB. Generally, a PSNR larger than 30 dB is considered acceptable to the human eye. Therefore, E-CLUTR provides very high quality rectification results. The PSNR between the original images and the rectification results of Caltech are also provided in Table 1 for comparison.

**Table 1.** PSNR (*dB*) with the rectified images produced by [1]

|  | Comparison with rectified left image [1] | Comparison with rectified right image [1] |
|---|---|---|
| Original image | 17.99 | 19.34 |
| **Proposed (E-CLUTR)** | 43.10 | 42.02 |

The hardware implementation of the E-CLUTR is compared with the stereo image rectification hardware implementations in Table 2. The hardware architecture of [7] requires a significant amount of hardware resources to support complex operations for solving the lens distortion models. Hardware architectures of look-up-table based implementations [8, 9] require an external memory. Combining the E-CLUTR with BRAM controller consumes less LUT and DFF resources than [7–9] and it does not require an external memory. The DFF and LUT consumption of [10] is not available (NA). Nevertheless, the capacity of E-CLUTR to fit the look-up-tables into the on-chip memory of the Virtex-5 FPGA is approximately two times more efficient than [10], as a benefit of its efficient compression scheme. Moreover, high precision hardware of the Caltech rectification algorithm is implemented, and its hardware consumption results are presented in Table 2 for comparison. Hardware implementations of CLUTR and E-CLUTR require much less hardware resource than the hardware implementation of Caltech rectification while providing almost same rectification results.

**Table 2.** Hardware resource comparison of the rectification hardware implementations

|  | Device | Resolution | LUT | DFF | On-chip memory (KB) | External memory |
|---|---|---|---|---|---|---|
| [7] | Virtex-4 | 752 × 480 | 3418 | 5932 | 0 | ✔ |
| [8] | Virtex-E | 640 × 512 | 2459 | 2075 | 99 | ✔ |
| [9] | Spartan-2 | 640 × 480 | ≈2396 | ≈2396 | 16 | ✔ |
| [10] | Virtex-5 | 1280 × 720 | NA | NA | 1300 | ✗ |
| Caltech hardware | Virtex-5 | 1024 × 768 | 24384 | 25346 | 0 | ✔ |
| **CLUTR** | Virtex-5 | 1024 × 768 | 227 | 197 | 90 | ✗ |
| **2 × (CLUTR + BRAM Contr.)** | Virtex-5 | 1024 × 768 | 784 | 427 | 176 | ✗ |
| **E-CLUTR** | Virtex-5 | 1024 × 768 | 434 | 350 | 252 | ✗ |
| **2 × (E-CLUTR + BRAM Contr.)** | Virtex-5 | 1024 × 768 | 2278 | 956 | 500 | ✗ |

The hardware resource consumption of E-CLUTR is higher than CLUTR hardware. However, if the cameras are extremely misaligned, the limitations of CLUTR can be exceeded. In these extreme conditions, E-CLUTR still supports rectification. Whereas, using CLUTR hardware can be more profitable if the stereo cameras are carefully aligned.

# 9    Conclusion

In this chapter, two novel compressed look-up-table based image rectification algorithms and their hardware implementations are presented. The proposed CLUTR and E-CLUTR algorithms are based on off-line compression of the rectification information to fit the tables into the on-chip memory of a Virtex-5 FPGA. The presented decompression hardware implementations of CLUTR and E-CLUTR consume negligible amounts of hardware resources, and they do not require any external memory to store the look-up-tables. The proposed hardware implementations are advantageous if using external memory is considered as an additional cost, or if the disparity estimation system has external memory bandwidth limitations. The proposed rectification hardware implementations would be even more profitable if they are adapted for high resolution multiple camera disparity estimation systems.

# References

1. Bouguet,    J.Y.:    Camera    Calibration    Toolbox    for    Matlab    (2010).    http://www.vision.caltech.edu/bouguetj/calib_doc/index.html
2. Chang, N.Y.C., Tsai, T.H., Hsu, B.H., Chen, Y.C., Chang, T.S.: Algorithm and architecture of disparity estimation with mini-census adaptive support weight. IEEE Trans. Circ. Syst. Video Technol. **20**(6), 792–805 (2010)
3. Georgoulas, C., Andreadis, I.: A real-time occlusion aware hardware structure for disparity map computation. In: Foggia, P., Sansone, C., Vento, M. (eds.) ICIAP 2009. LNCS, vol. 5716, pp. 721–730. Springer, Heidelberg (2009)
4. Akin, A., Baz, I., Atakan, B., Boybat, I., Schmid, A., Leblebici, Y.: A hardware-oriented dynamically adaptive disparity estimation algorithm and its real-time hardware. In: Proceedings of the 23rd ACM International Conference on Great Lakes Symposium on VLSI, pp. 155–160. ACM, Paris (2013)
5. Scharstein, D., Szeliski, R.: A taxonomy and evaluation of dense two-frame stereo correspondence algorithms. Int. J. Comput. Vis. **47**(1–3), 7–42 (2002)
6. Greisen, P., Heinzle, S., Gross, M., Burg, A.P.: An FPGA-based processing pipeline for high-definition stereo video. EURASIP J. Image Video Process. **1**, 18–25 (2011)
7. Son, H.-S., Bae, K.-r., Ok, S.-H., Lee, Y.-H., Moon, B.: A rectification hardware architecture for an adaptive multiple-baseline stereo vision system. In: Kim, T.-h., Adeli, H., Fang, W.-c., Vasilakos, T., Stoica, A., Patrikakis, C.Z., Zhao, G., Villalba, J.G., Xiao, Y. (eds.) FGCN 2011, Part I. CCIS, vol. 265, pp. 147–155. Springer, Heidelberg (2011)
8. Vancea, C., Nedevschi, S.: LUT-based image rectification module implemented in FPGA. In: IEEE International Conference on Intelligent Computer Communication and Processing, pp. 147–154 (2007)
9. Gribbon, K., Johnston, C., Bailey, D.: A Real-time FPGA implementation of a barrel distortion correction algorithm with bilinear interpolation. In: Proceedings of the Image and Vision Computing, New Zealand, pp. 408–413 (2003)
10. Park, D. H., Ko, H. S., Kim, J. G., Cho, J. D.: Real time rectification using differentially encoded lookup table. In: Proceedings of the International Conference on UIMC (2011)
11. Akin, A., Baz, I., Gaemperle, L.M., Schmid, A., Leblebici, Y.: Compressed look-up-table based real-time rectification hardware. In: Proceedings of the IFIP/IEEE 21st International Conference on Very Large Scale Integration, Turkey, pp. 272–277 (2013)
12. Akin, A., Cogal, O., Seyid, K., Afshari, H., Schmid, A., Leblebici, Y.: Hemispherical multiple camera system for high resolution omni-directional light field imaging. IEEE J. JETCAS **3**, 137–144 (2013)

# A Flexible ASIC for Time-Domain Decision-Directed Channel Estimation in MIMO-OFDM Systems

Andreas Minwegen[✉], Dominik Auras, and Gerd Ascheid

Institute for Communication Technologies and Embedded Systems,
RWTH Aachen University, 52056 Aachen, Germany
{minwegen,auras,ascheid}@ice.rwth-aachen.de

**Abstract.** Channel estimation is a crucial task for the overall communication performance of a wireless receiver. Compared to traditional approaches the estimation of the wireless channel can be improved by using iterative estimation with feedback from other receiver components, however the VLSI implementation of such iterative channel estimation in multiple-input multiple-output (MIMO) orthogonal frequency division multiplexing (OFDM) systems is challenging due to the high computational complexity. In this chapter we introduce the first ASIC for Decision-Directed MIMO-OFDM channel estimation which tracks channel variations using feedback from a decoder and supports M-QAM. Furthermore, timing and power dissipation trade-offs are analyzed.

**Keywords:** MIMO-OFDM · VLSI · ASIC · Channel estimation · Expectation maximization · SAGE

## 1 Introduction

Orthogonal frequency division multiplexing (OFDM) and spatial multiplexing over multiple-input multiple-output (MIMO) transmissions schemes are adopted by several recent wireless communication standards such as 3GPP Long Term Evolution (LTE) or IEEE 802.11n and beyond. Due to the concept of coherent detection in MIMO-OFDM receivers the channel estimation (CE) is a crucial and computational intensive part of the overall system and has a significant impact an the communication performance in terms of frame error rate and thus influence directly the maximal achievable throughput. Traditionally, pilot-aided channel estimation (PACE) is applied where the channel is estimated at predefined pilot positions. The complete channel over all subcarriers is obtained via interpolation. Iterative channel estimation can be used to improve the estimates which delivers promising SNR gains [1]. In the case of iterative channel estimation algorithms, a priori knowledge from the detector or the decoder is used to improve the channel estimates iteratively.

However, the gain in terms of algorithmic performance is payed for in terms of high latencies since each block that participates in the iterations has to complete its processing before the next one can start using the improved input.

© IFIP International Federation for Information Processing 2015
A. Orailoglu et al. (Eds.): VLSI-SoC 2013, IFIP AICT 461, pp. 249–265, 2015.
DOI: 10.1007/978-3-319-23799-2_12

An alternative that does not increase the latency but still provides significant benefits is the channel tracking approach. This approach [2,3] provides channel estimation updates for time instance $n + U_x$ based on the detector or decoder decisions for time instance $n$, as shown in Fig. 1.

Especially, fast fading channels are interesting scenarios for such a solution. An algorithmic investigation for a communication system similar to LTE is performed in [4] using the simplified frequency domain (FD) SAGE (space-alternating generalized expectation-maximization) algorithm, which calculates updates of the channel impulse response (CIR) estimates for M-QAM constellations. The authors of [3] present a modification that provides a gain of 2 dB for 64-QAM. This modification requires a non trivial matrix inversion. Fortunately, this matrix inversion can be avoided by iteratively processing each tap of the CIR in the time domain, as proposed by the time-domain (TD) SAGE algorithm presented in [5].

Furthermore, the authors of [6] present an analysis of the TD-SAGE algorithm in the context of LTE-Advanced. The results show that it has the potential to double the system throughput at high user mobility due to a better channel estimate and therefore, a lower frame error rate. Apart from that the authors present simulation results about the impact on the system performance of usage of variable number of feedback symbols from the decoder to the channel estimation block. These results show interesting trade-offs between the computational complexity and the algorithmic performance for the TD-SAGE algorithm. Therefore, the number of feedback symbols seems to be interesting parameter for a trade-off analysis between energy dissipation and algorithmic performance of a dedicated VLSI architecture.

*Contributions:* This chapter introduces an extension of the first ASIC implementation of the TD-SAGE algorithm which is presented in [7]. The TD-SAGE algorithm is transformed to a novel variant, further reducing the computational complexity, to what is termed the tap alternating (TA) SAGE. Apart from that this work discusses two options to further reduce the computational complexity with the penalty of a loss in algorithmic performance. Either reducing the number of feedback symbols as discussed in [6] or reducing the frequency of updating the channel estimate. A suitable VLSI architecture is presented and area, timing and power numbers are provided. The support for a variable number of feedback symbols introduces a modification to the state machine that has an impact on the critical path. Therefore the implementation results for a architectures with and without variable feedback support are presented. This work evaluates the hardware costs of channel tracking in a MIMO-OFDM system.

*Outline of the Chapter:* The remainder of the chapter is organized as follows. In Sect. 2 the system setup is introduced. Section 3 presents the implemented, modified algorithm followed by Sect. 5 deriving the ASIC architecture and details about the processing units and the memory are given. Finally Sect. 6 discusses post-layout implementation results.

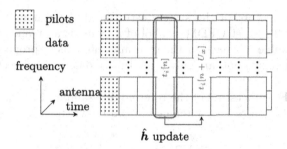

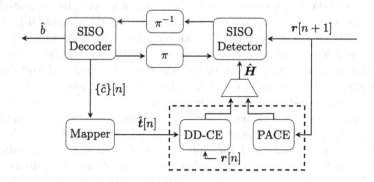

**Fig. 1.** The frame structure of the system

## 2   System Model

The system considered in this chapter is a MIMO-OFDM system using $N_T = 2$ transmit antennas and $N_R = 2$ receive antennas, with $N_K = 512$ sub-carriers and a cyclic prefix length of $N_L = 32$. First, information bits $\{b\}$ are encoded using a convolutional encoder with the generator polynomial $[133_o 171_o]$. These code bits $\{c\}$ are interleaved by a random interleaver, mapped to complex symbols using a 4-, 16- or 64-QAM modulation and then multiplexed over $N_T$ spatial streams, each corresponding to a transmit antenna. Each symbol stream is expressed as a vector $\boldsymbol{t}_i[n] = [t_i[n,0], \ldots, t_i[n, N_K - 1]]^T \in \mathbb{C}^{N_K \times 1}$, where $t_i[n, k]$ is the complex symbol at time $n$ on sub-carrier $k$ transmitted over the $i$th antenna. Each of the spatial FD streams is processed by an OFDM modulator which outputs the final TD vector $\boldsymbol{s}_i$ transmitted by the $i$th transmit antenna.

**Fig. 2.** Receiver model

The channel model used in this chapter is a frequency-selective Rayleigh fading channel with a power delay profile according to the typical urban COST259 model. It is time variant with the correlation according to Jake's model with a normalized Doppler frequency of $f_d = 1.4468 \cdot 10^{-5}$, a sub-carrier spacing of 15 kHz, a user velocity $v = 50$ km/h and a carrier frequency $f_c = 2.4$ GHz.

The frame structure of the system setup used throughout this chapter is shown in Fig. 1. The first OFDM symbol of a frame is a preamble following an orthogonal preamble scheme over the transmit antennas as proposed in [8]. The subsequent OFDM symbols are only consisting of data symbol vectors across all sub-carriers.

After the DFT processing of the received TD samples the $N_K \times 1$ vector $\boldsymbol{r}_j$ is obtained at the $j$th receive antenna and can be written as:

$$\boldsymbol{r}_j[n] = \sum_{i=0}^{N_T-1} \boldsymbol{H}_{i,j}[n]\boldsymbol{t}_i[n] + \boldsymbol{w}_j[n] \tag{1}$$

with $\boldsymbol{H}_{i,j}[n] = [H_{i,j}[n,0], \ldots, H_{i,j}[n, N_K - 1]]^T \in \mathbb{C}^{N_K \times 1}$ being the channel frequency response between the $i$th transmit antenna and the $j$th receive antenna. $\boldsymbol{w}_j[n]$ is additive white complex Gaussian noise. For the sake of a shorter notation the time index $n$ will be omitted in the remainder of the chapter.

The receiver model considered throughout this chapter is depicted in Fig. 2. Each received data symbol vector is iteratively processed by a soft-in soft-out (SISO) detector and a SISO decoder. A data symbol vector is defined as the vector over all receive antennas at the $k$th sub-carrier. Detection is performed by a max-log MAP SISO sphere detector (SD) with QR decomposition [9], while the channel decoder is a BCJR decoder providing soft information of the coded bits $\{c\}$. For the simulation results each processing block is executed twice, corresponding to one complete iteration between the detector and the decoder is performed.

The channel estimation provides the required estimate of the channel frequency response to the detector. As depicted in Fig. 2 the CE is split into two parts. First, the PACE processing block calculates an initial CIR estimate based on the preamble. This initial estimate is used to decode the second OFDM symbol of the frame. Second, the DD-CE block uses the decoder decisions of time $n$ in order to provide an updated estimate at time $n + U_x$ for the detection of the next OFDM symbol. Thus, the third OFDM symbol is detected and decoded based on the updated channel estimate. The update frequency ($U_x$) can vary depending on the considered Doppler frequency.

There is an option to adjust the computational complexity of calculation of an update of the CIR. It was presented in [6]. The idea is to reduce the feedback from the decoder and therefore reduce the number of computations. Either the full feedback is used, meaning that all modulation symbols of the previous OFDM symbol are used to calculate the CIR estimate or only every second, third and so on symbol is used in the calculation.

## 3    The TA-SAGE Algorithm

The $\boldsymbol{H}_{i,j}$ from (1) can be expressed as the DFT of the CIR: $\boldsymbol{H}_{i,j} = \mathrm{DFT}(\boldsymbol{h}_{i,j})$, where $\boldsymbol{h}_{i,j}$ is the CIR between the $i$th transmit antenna and the $j$th receive antenna. Only the calculation of the CIR estimate $\hat{\boldsymbol{h}}_{i,j} = (\hat{h}_{i,j}[0], \ldots, \hat{h}_{i,j}[N_L - 1])^T$ will be investigated in the remainder of this chapter.

The description of the TD-SAGE algorithm in [5] is modified in this chapter to remove redundant calculations for an efficient VLSI implementation.

First, a permutation matrix $\boldsymbol{P}^l$ is defined such that $\boldsymbol{P}^l\hat{\boldsymbol{t}}_i$ cyclically shifts the vector $\hat{\boldsymbol{t}}_i$ by $l$ elements with $\hat{\boldsymbol{t}}_i$ containing the $N_K$ complex remapped decoder hard decisions in the frequency domain for the $i$th antenna. Second, the TD vectors $\hat{\boldsymbol{s}}_i$ and $\boldsymbol{z}_{i,l}$ are defined as follows:

$$\hat{\boldsymbol{s}}_i = \boldsymbol{F}_{N_K}^H \hat{\boldsymbol{t}}_i \qquad \in \mathbb{C}^{N_K} \qquad (2)$$

$$\boldsymbol{z}_{i,l} = \boldsymbol{P}^l \hat{\boldsymbol{s}}_i \qquad \in \mathbb{C}^{N_K} \qquad (3)$$

where $\boldsymbol{F}_{N_K}$ is the $N_K$ dimensional DFT matrix, $\boldsymbol{s}_j$ is the vector with the time-domain samples of the decisions from the decoder that were sent via the $i$th transmit antenna. $\boldsymbol{z}_{i,l}$ is the by $l$ elements cyclically-shifted time-domain vector. With these definitions the signal model from (1) can be reformulated in the time domain to

$$\boldsymbol{y}_j = \boldsymbol{F}_{N_K}^H \boldsymbol{r}_j = \sum_{i=0}^{N_T-1} \sum_{l=0}^{N_L-1} h_{j,i,l} \boldsymbol{z}_{i,l} + \tilde{\boldsymbol{w}}_j \qquad (4)$$

where $\tilde{\boldsymbol{w}}_j$ is the transformed noise. The estimate of $h_{j,i,l}$ at SAGE iteration $m$ is denoted as $\hat{h}_{j,i,l}^{(m)}$. A SAGE iteration is defined as the calculation of an update for one single tap of the CIR. Therefore, the SAGE iteration range is $m = 1, \ldots, N_L N_T N_i$, where $N_i$ specifies how often the algorithm iterates over the complete CIR. The initial estimate provided by the PACE is $\hat{h}_{j,i,l}^{(0)}$.

The iterations are done for each receive antenna independently. The whole processing of the algorithm is done on the TD samples and can be split into four steps that have to be executed for each receive antenna. For these steps a new variable is introduced. The residual $\epsilon_j^{(m)}$ is the vector of the values that are remaining after subtracting the reconstruction of the observation given the current CIR estimate from the real observation $\boldsymbol{y}_j$, which is basically the current estimation error. Then, the steps of the modified SAGE algorithm are the following:

**Step 1:** Initialize the residual and calculate the norm for each transmit antenna vector:

$$\epsilon_j^{(0)} = \boldsymbol{y}_j - \sum_{i=0}^{N_T-1} \sum_{m=0}^{N_L-1} \hat{h}_{j,n,m}^{(0)} \boldsymbol{z}_{n,m} \qquad (5)$$

$$||\hat{\boldsymbol{s}}_i||^2 = \sum_{k=0}^{N_K-1} \left( \mathrm{Re}\{\hat{s}_i[k]\}^2 + \mathrm{Im}\{\hat{s}_i[k]\}^2 \right) \qquad (6)$$

**Step 2:** Select the current tap by

$$l = (m-1) \quad \mathrm{mod} \ N_L \qquad (7)$$

$$i = \left( \left\lfloor \frac{m-1}{N_L} \right\rfloor \quad \mathrm{mod} \ N_T \right). \qquad (8)$$

**Step 3:** Calculate a new $\delta$ based on the decoder decisions and the previous $\epsilon$.

$$\delta^{(m)} = \frac{z_{i,l}^H \epsilon^{(m-1)}}{||\hat{s}_i||^2} \qquad (9)$$

**Step 4:** Update the selected tap and the residual by

$$\hat{h}_{j,i,l}^{(m)} = \hat{h}_{j,i,l}^{(m-1)} + \delta^{(m)} \qquad (10)$$

$$\epsilon_j^{(m)} = \epsilon_j^{(m-1)} - \delta^{(m)} z_{i,l}. \qquad (11)$$

Step 2 to 4 are repeated $N_i$ times for every tap of the estimated CIR.

A variable feedback from the decoder was evaluated in [6]. There the authors explained that they use for a reduced feedback either every second, fourth symbol and so on. In the time domain this means that only the first $N_{K_F} = N_K/F_b$ time-domain samples are used to calculate an update of the CIR estimate. The variable $F_b$ is defined to be a power of two, where $F_b$ greater 8 is not considered. This can be directly realized using the formulars (5)–(10) with the first elements of the vectors $z$, $s_i$ and $\epsilon_j$ respectively.

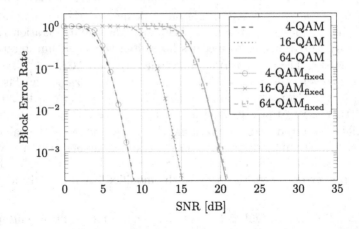

**Fig. 3.** Block error rate for the TA-SAGE with 4-,16- and 64-QAM. Using all available time-domain samples ($N_K$)

## 4    Algorithm Evaluation

Figure 3 shows the block error rate (BLER) for the investigated modulation schemes 4-,16- and 64-QAM using a floating-point implementation. A block is defined as one code word which is spread over one OFDM symbol. The simulations for 4-, 16- and 64-QAM were performed with $N_i = 3$ iterations. The number of estimated taps is $N_L = 32$ which equals the length of the cyclic prefix. This is a worst case assumption for the presented OFDM system which is used throughout this work. Besides the floating-point simulations the results for a fixed-point implementation are shown in Fig. 3. The degradation due to the fixed-point arithmetic is negligible.

For the following evaluation the modulation 4-QAM was chosen exemplary and the number of internal iteration is $N_i = 1$. In Fig. 1 the update frequency is given by $U_x$. In the following two different options to reduce the computational complexity by a factor of four are evaluated for two different exemplary operation points. The plot depicted in Fig. 4 shows the algorithmic performance for 4-QAM and a mobile device speed of $v = 50$ km/h and an $U_x = 1$ and $U_x = 4$. The loss in algorithmic performance is about 1 dB at a BLER of 1 %. Additionally the BLER for a reduced feedback from the decoder is plotted. There $F_b$ equals 4 which means that every 4th symbol from decoder is used to calculate the update of the CIR estimate. In this case leads to the same computational complexity than using the full feedback but updating the CIR estimate only every 4th OFDM symbol. From an algorithmic perspective it can be concluded from Fig. 4 that for the given mobile speed and the same computational complexity it is a better choice to update the CIR estimate every 4th OFDM symbol using the full decoder feedback.

Figure 5 shows a BLER plot with the same parameters of $U_x$ and $F_b$ but evaluated at a mobile device speed of $v = 100$ km/h. The loss in terms of algorithmic performance is in this case for an $U_x = 4$ about 7 dB at a BLER of 10 % using the full decoder feedback, compared to updating the CIR estimate every OFDM symbol. Apart from that it also shows a clear error floor at a BLER of $3 \cdot 10^{-2}$. The second option using only one 4th of the decoder feedback for the calculations shows at $v = 100$ km/h a loss of 2 dB at a BLER of 10 %. The plot depicted in Fig. 5 also shows that at the given speed it is better to use a fourth of the decoder feedback every OFDM symbol instead, when the computational complexity should be kept constant.

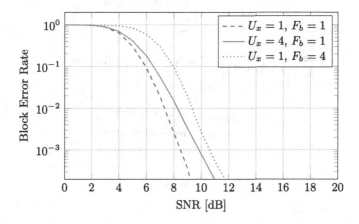

**Fig. 4.** Block error rate for the TA-SAGE with 4-QAM at a speed of $v = 50$ km/h

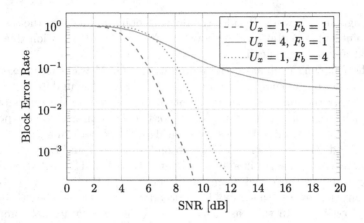

**Fig. 5.** Block error rate for the TA-SAGE with 4-QAM at a speed of $v = 100\,\mathrm{km/h}$

## 5  TA-SAGE VLSI Architecture

The architecture is split into three processing units and three different memories. The processing units are the residual update (RU) unit, the scalar product (SP) unit and the tap unit. The memories are the residual memory, the TX memory which stores the re-modulated symbol decisions from the decoder and the tap memory used to store all taps of the channel impulse response $\boldsymbol{h}$. Figure 6 shows these blocks and depicts the memory accesses from each block.

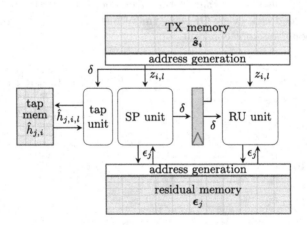

**Fig. 6.** High level architecture

### 5.1  Processing Schedule

The processing is split into four different phases: load, pre-computation, iteration and write-back. The load and the write-back phases do not include any computation but are necessary to load the input data in the memories and write back the results. These phases are considered for completeness of the hardware complexity analysis. In the load phase the received data $y_j$, the current CIR estimate $\hat{h}$ and the decoder feedback $\hat{s}_i$ are loaded into the memories depicted in Fig. 6.

The first processing phase (pre-computation) corresponds to step 1 of the algorithm description. First, the scalar $||\hat{s}_i||^2$ is calculated for all transmit antennas in the SP unit. Second, the residual vector $\epsilon_j^{(0)}$ for all receive antennas is calculated in the SP and RU unit. Both units are running concurrently, processing different receive antennas. In parallel to the $\epsilon_j^{(0)}$ calculation the reciprocal of $||\hat{s}_i||^2$ is pre-computed for all transmit antennas, since it does not change over the internal iterations.

The second processing phase is the iteration phase, which corresponds to steps 2, 3 and 4 of the algorithm. Step 2 is reflected in the dedicated address generation of each memory. Step 3 is executed by the SP unit calculating the inner product of (9) and the multiplication with the scaling factor $\frac{1}{||\hat{s}_i||^2}$. The last steps of the algorithm are (11), executed on the RU unit and (10) calculated by the tap unit. To achieve full utilization of the processing units and account for the data dependencies between (9) and (11) the SP and RU unit are separated by a pipeline register and execute the calculations concurrently for different receive antennas. This is possible since there is no data dependency between different receive antennas, which is a property of the SAGE algorithm.

In the write-back phase the new calculated estimate of the CIR is written from the tap memory to the output ports.

## 5.2    Processing Units

The processing units are the parts of the architecture that are executing the calculations of (5) to (11). Apart from the algorithmic parameters defined in the previous sections, the main architectural design parameter is the data path parallelism $w$.

**SP Unit.** Section 5.1 discussed that the SP unit is used in two phases and calculates (5), (6) and (9). It can be seen from (5) that all complex multiplications can be executed in parallel. Therefore, it is possible to have a data path parallelism up to $N_K$. In (6) and (9) it is necessary to accumulate the result of the concurrent calculations. This is implemented via an adder tree. Due to the high data path parallelism (up to $w = 32$) the maximum achievable frequency is determined by these adder trees. This leads to the design decision to have a dedicated pipeline stage as shown in Fig. 7 (third pipeline stage). The separation into the first and second pipeline stage is done to avoid two real multipliers in chain. This unit includes $6 \cdot w$ multipliers and $3 \cdot \log(w) + 7 \cdot w$ adders. The multipliers in the first pipeline stage are active in the pre-computation phase and the iteration phase. The dotted part in Fig. 7 is only active during the pre-computation phase, where first $||\hat{s}_i||^2$ is computed and written into a register file

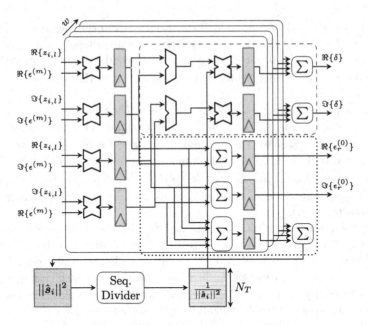

**Fig. 7.** SP Unit

and then the initial residual vector $\epsilon_j^{(0)}$ is computed while the sequential divider concurrently outputs all $\frac{1}{\|\hat{s}_i\|^2}$. The dashed part is active in the iteration phase calculating $\delta^{(m)}$.

**RU Unit.** The RU unit also computes (5). Thus, the structure of this unit differs only slightly from the SP unit. The calculation of (11) allows for parallel complex multiplications up to $N_K$. The separation into three pipeline stages for this unit is done to achieve a balanced design. The output registers are added to ensure the same latency for the RU and SP unit, which eases the scheduling of the memory accesses. The complexity in terms of multipliers and adders of the RU unit is $4 \cdot w$ multipliers and $4 \cdot w$ adders.

**Tap Update Unit.** This unit updates the current tap (10). Due to the low requirements in terms of throughput and the low complexity (2 adders) of this unit compared to the RU and SP units it is no longer discussed separately.

### 5.3 Memory Architecture

As shown in Fig. 6 the design has three different memories. Each of these memories has a dedicated controller that includes an address generation unit and multiplexers to realize the different data access schemes. The first memory is the tap memory, which stores the $N_R N_T N_L$ taps of the CIR. This memory has

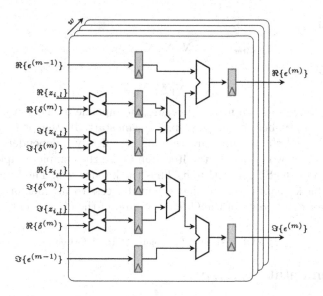

**Fig. 8.** RU Unit

the most relaxed constraints in the architecture. During the initialization phase it is read in every cycle from the RU and the SP unit with a linear addressing scheme. In the iteration phase the tap memory is read and written once per tap update, i.e. every $\frac{N_K}{w}$ cycles. Therefore, one read/write port is sufficient (Fig. 8).

The TX memory stores the $N_T N_K$ TD samples of the complex symbols of the remapped decisions from the decoder. The circular shift in (3) is realized as part of the address calculations. This memory is read by the RU and SP unit during the pre-computation phase and the iteration phase every cycle in parallel and written in the load phase. Each access reads/writes $w$ elements in parallel. Therefore, two read/write ports with a word width of $w$ elements are implemented.

The third memory is the residual memory. It stores the $N_R N_K$ $\epsilon$-values and needs to be read by the SP unit (9) and read and written by the RU unit (11) independently and concurrently with a word width of $w$ elements. Furthermore, during the pre-computation phase the SP and RU units read and write independently the residual memory (5). Thus, the residual memory has two read and two write ports with a data width matching the data parallelism $w$.

With $w$ and the algorithmic parameters $N_T$, $N_R$, $N_L$, $N_K$ and $N_i$, the cycle count of each phase can be calculated using the following equations.

**Load phase:**

$$c_{\text{load}} = N_T N_R N_L \tag{12}$$

**Pre-computation phase:**

$$c_{\text{precomp}} = N_T N_K (1 + N_L)/w + 2 \tag{13}$$

**Iteration phase:**

$$c_{\text{iter}} = \frac{N_K}{w} N_T N_R N_L N_i + 3 + 2 \tag{14}$$

**Write-Back phase:**

$$c_{\text{wb}} = N_T N_R N_L + 2 \tag{15}$$

The additive constants are needed because the pipeline of the processing units needs to be empty before the next phase can start. In the pre-computation phase the RU and the SP unit are running completely independently, leading to an overhead of two cycles. In the iteration phase the complete pipeline is the concatenation of the SP and RU unit. Thus the latency is 5. The latency of two in the write-back phase is due to the pipelined access to the memory. The total cycle count for one update of the CIR is the sum of the cycle counts of the four phases.

$$c_{\text{total}} = c_{\text{load}} + c_{\text{precomp}} + c_{\text{iter}} + c_{\text{wb}}. \tag{16}$$

## 6   Implementation Results

The architecture was synthesized using a 90 nm, 1.0 V standard-performance standard cell library with Synopsys Design Compiler 2010.12-SP2 and layouted with Cadence SoC Encounter 9.1. In the following first the implementation results for the full feedback architecture are presented assuming $N_i = 3$, $N_T = 2$, $N_R = 2$, $N_L = 32$ and $N_K = 512$. Second the results after extending the architecture to support the flexible decoder feedback is presented.

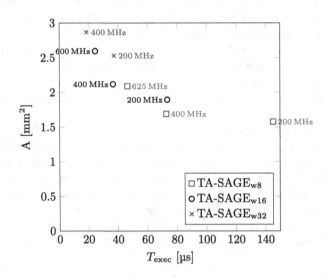

**Fig. 9.** Area-time trade-offs for different degrees of parallelism $w$ and different synthesis/layout constraints. The algorithmic parameters are $N_i = 3$, $N_T = 2$, $N_R = 2$, $N_L = 32$ and $N_K = 512$.

## 6.1   Full Feedback Architecture

Three different configurations of the architecture were implemented. A configuration is defined by its data path parallelism $w = \{8, 16, 32\}$. Each configuration was synthesized and layouted for its maximum achievable frequency and additionally for 400 MHz and 200 MHz. There are only two different design points for $w = 32$ since the maximum achievable frequency is 400 MHz.

The area-time trade-off diagram for the architecture variants is shown in Fig. 9. In this diagram $T_{\text{exec}}$ is defined as the time that the specific architecture requires to calculate a complete update of the CIR.

The best $AT_{\text{exec}} = 53.55 \, \text{mm}^2\mu\text{s}$ product is the configuration with $w = 32$ and a synthesis and layout constraint of 400 MHz. However, the following discussion will focus on the configurations with an execution time around 70 μs. The configuration with data path parallelism $w = 8$ @ 400 MHz has the $AT_{\text{exec}} = 122.81 \, \text{mm}^2\mu\text{s}$ product. Doubling the parallelism $w = 16$ and halving the frequency ($AT_{\text{exec}} = 138.9 \, \text{mm}^2\mu\text{s}$), leads to the same execution time and only a slight increase in terms of area. This stems from the fact that this architecture is memory dominated while an increase in the data path parallelism does not influence the memory as much as the data path (Table 1).

The memories in the presented architecture are implemented using standard cell based memories (SCM) [10]. In this work flip-flop SCMs are used. The TX memory needs to be split into $w$ banks each providing one word to allow for non-aligned vector accesses. This would lead to 32 macro cells for the maximum configuration, rendering floor-planning difficult. Therefore, the SCMs were utilized in this architecture.

Besides area and timing analysis, post-layout simulations were performed to obtain power estimates for the different configurations. The post-layout simulations with timing annotations were executed for independent test vectors for each configuration in order to obtain statistic toggling information. Synopsys Power Compiler uses the post-layout netlist and the annotated toggling information to calculate the average power estimates.

The results of the power analysis are shown in Fig. 10. The execution time $T_{\text{exec}}$ is the same as in the $AT$ plot depicted in Fig. 9. The power-based analysis leads to different conclusions than the $AT$-based analysis. The energy for a certain configuration to compute one CIR estimate is the $PT_{\text{exec}}$ product. Comparing the configuration $w = 8$ @ 400 MHz with $w = 16$ @ 200 MHz in terms of smallest $AT$ product leads to choose the configuration $w = 8$ @ 400 MHz. The same comparison achieving the lowest energy dissipation leads to the choice of the configuration $w = 16$ @ 200 MHz. The main reason that a doubled data path parallelism and a halved clock frequency leads to a better design decision in terms of energy dissipation is the fact that this architecture is memory dominated. This means that halving the frequency saves more energy in the memories than it is added by doubling the data path parallelism, because the memory including the memory controller is not affected as much as the processing units by an increase of the data path.

**Table 1.** Area breakdown for the TA-SAGE $w = 16$ @ 200 MHz and $w = 8$ @ 400 MHz

|  | area $w = 16$ [μm$^2$] | area $w = 8$ [μm$^2$] |
| --- | --- | --- |
| Tap mem | 74284.8 (3.98%) | 76822.6 (4.6%) |
| TX mem | 515499.5 (27.62%) | 518432.5 (31.08%) |
| Resid mem | 747217.1 (40.03%) | 767431.7 (46.01%) |
| RU unit | 154939.6 (8.3%) | 90029.9 (5.4%) |
| SP unit | 374723.8 (20.07%) | 215378.1 (12.91%) |

The area requirements of the two aforementioned design points are split into the different parts of the architecture in Table 1. As expected the tap memory is the smallest one since it only has to store $N_L N_T N_R$ elements. From this breakdown the aforementioned memory domination of this architecture is obvious. This is also supported by the layout for the configuration with $w = 8$ @ 400 MHz in Fig. 11. The layout shows that the SCM based memory approach makes it possible that the memory is placed where needed. In Sect. 5.3 the discussion of the residual memory revealed that the SP and the RU unit are either writing it in parallel with $w$ parallel accesses in the initialization phase or reading and writing it during the iteration phase. It can be seen that due to this constraints the RU unit is surrounded by the residual memory and the SP unit is placed close to it.

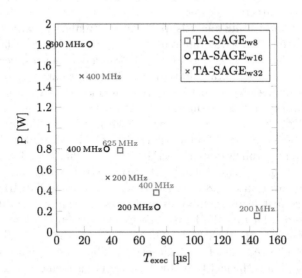

**Fig. 10.** Power-time trade-offs for different configurations of the TA-SAGE and different synthesis/layout constraints. The algorithmic parameters are $N_i = 3$, $N_T = 2$, $N_R = 2$, $N_L = 32$ and $N_K = 512$.

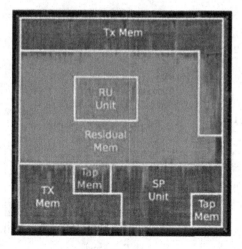

**Fig. 11.** Layout of the TA-SAGE ASIC for a parallelism degree of $w = 8$.

## 6.2  Flexible Feedback Architecture

The extension of the architecture to support the flexible feedback involved adjustments in the state machine and therefore in the schedule. Figure 12 compares the implementation results for the full and the flexible feedback architectures.

It can be seen that for 400 MHz the area increase becomes visible in the diagram. This comes from the fact, that the modifications have an influence on the critical path and therefore to achieve the given timing constraint more area has to be invested. The average increase in area is up to 10 %.

**Table 2.** Power comparision of the full and flexible feedback architecture with different frequencies and a $w = 8$

| Frequency | TA-SAGE | TA-SAGE$_{\text{flex}}$ |
|-----------|---------|------------|
| 100 MHz   | 77.63 mW | 82.84 mW |
| 200 MHz   | 152 mW   | 162.24 mW |
| 400 MHz   | 374 mW   | 400.1 mW |

The same can be observed for the power dissipation depicted in Table 2. The procentual increase in the power is the same as the area increase for this architecture configuration. Therefore, the additional power only comes from the fact that the extension for the flexible feedback support has an influence on the critical path.

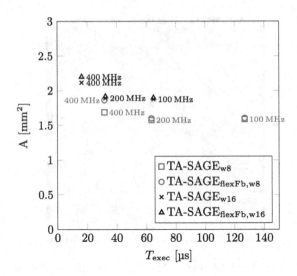

**Fig. 12.** Area-time trade-offs for different degrees of parallelism $w$ and different synthesis/layout constraints. The algorithmic parameters are $N_i = 1$, $N_T = 2$, $N_R = 2$, $N_L = 32$ and $N_K = 512$.

## 7    Conclusion

In this chapter we present to the best of our knowledge the first ASIC implementation of a decision directed channel estimation for MIMO-OFDM for M-QAM. The architecture is described and formulas for the calculation of the run-time of the algorithm depending on its parameters on the architecture are presented. The implementation is characterized in terms of area-time trade-offs and power dissipation.

It was shown, that the additional hardware costs of a channel tracking algorithm like the TA-SAGE are high compared to traditional PACE as presented in [11] but it is possible and therefore worth further investigations.

Future work will include the influence of using latched based SCMs as presented in [10] and the evaluation of mixing macro cell memories (e.g. for the residual and the tap memory) with the SCMs approach for the TX memory. Furthermore, this architecture will be compared with simplified algorithms as for example in [12].

**Acknowledgments.** This work has been supported by the UMIC Research Centre, RWTH Aachen University. The authors would like to thank Ernst Martin Witte, David Kammler, Martin Senst, Filippo Borlenghi and Uwe Deidersen for the valuable discussions and their feedback.

# References

1. Gao, J., Liu, H.: Low-complexity MAP channel estimation for mobile MIMO-OFDM systems. IEEE Trans. Wireless Commun. **7**(3), 774–780 (2008)
2. Li, Y., Seshadri, N., Ariyavisitakul, S.: Channel estimation for OFDM systems with transmitter diversity in mobile wireless channels. IEEE J. Sel. Areas Commun. **17**, 461–471 (1999)
3. Ylioinas, J., Juntti, M.: Iterative joint detection, decoding, and channel estimation in turbo-coded MIMO-OFDM. IEEE Trans. Veh. Technol. **58**, 1784–1796 (2009)
4. Xie, Y., Georghiades, C.: Two EM-type channel estimation algorithms for OFDM with transmitter diversity. IEEE Trans. Commun. **51**, 106–115 (2003)
5. Ylioinas, J., Raghavendra, M., Juntti, M.: Avoiding matrix inversion in DD SAGE channel estimation in MIMO-OFDM with M-QAM. In: 2009 IEEE 70th Vehicular Technology Conference Fall (VTC 2009-Fall), pp. 1–5, September 2009
6. Ketonen, J., Juntti, M., Ylioinas, J.: Decision directed channel estimation for improving performance in LTE-A. In: 2010 Conference Record of the Forty Fourth Asilomar Conference on Signals, Systems and Computers (ASILOMAR), pp. 1503–1507, November 2010
7. Minwegen, A., Auras, D., Ascheid, G.: A multimode decision-directed channel estimation ASIC for MIMO-OFDM. In: 2012 IEEE/IFIP 20th International Conference on VLSI and System-on-Chip (VLSI-SoC), pp. 65–70, IEEE (2012)
8. Li, Y.: Simplified channel estimation for OFDM systems with multiple transmit antennas. IEEE Trans. Wireless Commun. **1**, 67–75 (2002)
9. Studer, C., Bölcskei, H.: Soft-input soft-output sphere decoding. In: IEEE International Symposium on Information Theory, 2008, ISIT 2008, pp. 2007–2011, July 2008
10. Meinerzhagen, P., Roth, C., Burg, A.: Towards generic low-power area-efficient standard cell based memory architectures. In: 2010 53rd IEEE International Midwest Symposium on Circuits and Systems (MWSCAS), pp. 129–132, August 2010
11. Simko, M., Wu, D., Mehlfuehrer, C., Eilert, J., Liu, D.: Implementation aspects of channel estimation for 3GPP LTE terminals. In: 11th European Wireless Conference 2011 - Sustainable Wireless Technologies (European Wireless), pp. 1–5, April 2011
12. Qiao, X., Zhao, H., Han, Z., Sun, Y.: Decision-directed channel estimation for MIMO-OFDM systems. In: 5th International Conference on Wireless Communications, Networking and Mobile Computing, 2009, WiCom 2009, Beijing, pp. 1–4 (2009)

# Author Index

Akin, Abdulkadir   227
Ali, Sk Subidh   48
Alvandpour, Atila   94
Ascheid, Gerd   249
Auras, Dominik   249

Benini, L.   144
Bentobache, Mohand   188
Bounceur, Ahcène   188

Cavigelli, L.   144
Conos, Nathaniel A.   23

Dollas, Apostolos   168

Euler, Reinhardt   188

Fang, Z.   144
Fujita, Masahiro   1

Gaemperle, Luis Manuel   227
Gerstlauer, Andreas   119
Greisen, P.   144
Gürkaynak, F.K.   144

Hager, P.A.   144

Kaeslin, H.   144
Karri, Ramesh   48
Kieffer, Yann   188

Leblebici, Yusuf   227
Lee, Seogoo   119

Matsumoto, Takeshi   1
Meguerdichian, Saro   23
Minwegen, Andreas   249
Mir, Salvador   188

Najibi, Halima   227
Noll, Tobias   69

Oshima, Kosuke   1

Papadimitriou, Kyprianos   168
Potkonjak, Miodrag   23

Ren, Yuan   69
Reorda, Matteo Sonza   208

Sabena, Davide   208
Saeed, Samah Mohamed   48
Schaffner, Michael   144
Schmid, Alexandre   227
Sinanoglu, Ozgur   48
Smolic, A.   144
Sterpone, Luca   208

Thomas, Sotiris   168

Yeknami, Ali Fazli   94

Printed in the United States
By Bookmasters